D1831965

HISTORY OF KAS'MIRA (KASHMIR)

Aryans, Naga's, Evolution, Rulers, Religious Beliefs/ Worship and Goddesses of Kas'mira (Kashmir)

Foreword by

Lt Gen (Retd) S K Sinha PVSM

Brigadier (Retd) Rattan Kaul

GYAN

©Author

All rights reserved. No part of this work may be reproduced, stored, adapted, or transmitted in any form or by any means, electronic, mechanical, photocopying, micro-filming, recording or otherwise, or translated in any language, without the prior written permission of the copyright owner and the publisher. The book is sold subject to the condition that it shall not, by way of trade or otherwise, be lent, resold, hired out, or otherwise circulated without the prior publisher's written consent in any form of binding or cover other than that in which it is published.

The views and opinions expressed in this book are author(s) own and the facts reported by them have been verified to the extent possible, and the publishers are not in any way liable for the same.

ISBN: 978-81-212-1210-6

Price: ₹ 1050

Reprinted 2016

Published by

Gyan Publishing House
5, Ansari Road, Daryaganj,
New Delhi - 110002
Phones : 011-47034999, 9811692060

E-mail: books@gyanbooks.com
website: gyanbooks.com

Laser Typesetting: Rajender Vashist, Delhi
Printed at: G. Print Process, Delhi

Cataloging in Publication Data--DK
Courtesy: D.K. Agencies (P) Ltd. <docinfo@dkagencies.com>

Kaul, Rattan.

History of Kas'mira (Kashmir) : Aryans, Naga's, evolution, rulers, religious beliefs/worship and goddesses of Kas'mira (Kashmir) / Rattan Kaul ; edited by Leena Gaur, Aparna Kaul.

p. cm.
Includes index.
ISBN

1. Jammu and Kashmir (India)--History. 2. Jammu and Kashmir (India)--Kings and rulers. I. Gaur, Leena. II. Kaul, Aparna. III. Title.

DDC 954.6 23

To
Five Great Inspirers of my Life.
My Ancestor–
Pandit Bhawani Kaul
My Father–
Pandit Lamboodher Kaul
My Grandchildren–
Praharshita Gaur, Nirrit (Nirbhay)
and
Atharv Kaul (Trishay- Babba)

Contents

Lt. Gen. (Retd.) S.K. Sinha, PVSM
Ex-Vice Chief of Army Staff
Former Ambassador to Nepal
Former Governor of Assam and Jammu & Kashmir

Foreword

I am happy to write a foreword to this book on the history of Kashmir which also includes a dissertation on religious beliefs, legends and philosophy of Shaivism. The author has carried out extensive research for over ten years with great dedication to write this book. He has collected some very rare pictures, which have been printed in this book providing much information. This book is of immense value for the wealth of information it contains and his analysis of the same.

Brigadier Rattan Kaul is from the same regiment as me. He is a generation younger and I have known him as one of the finest officers of our Regiment, The 5th Gorkha Rifles (FF). I did not know of his deep interest in religious matters till he met me in Kashmir when I was Governor of Jammu and Kashmir. He told me of the history and sanctity of Bhadrakali Temple located in a remote jungle of North Kashmir. The area was frequented by the terrorists. That temple was in a state of decay and needed to be preserved. I sanctioned some funds for its renovation.

I have been a student of history and have been deeply interested in Kashmir. My association with Kashmir started from Day One on 27 October 1947, when the Indian Army went to the rescue of the people of Kashmir who had suffered a brutal and barbaric invasion launched by Pakistan. Having served several tenures in Kashmir during my army career and thereafter as Governor, I have deep attachment to Jammu and Kashmir and for its people.

Kashmir has been a jewel in the crown of India and a place of unparalleled scenic beauty. Kalidas our famous ancient poet wrote, **"The place is more beautiful than Heaven and is the benefactor of supreme bliss and happiness. It seems to me that I am taking a bath in the lake of nectar here,"** Emperor Jehangir stated *Agar Firdaus Bar Rue Zameen Ast, Hamin Ast, Hamin Ast, Hamin Ast* (If Paradise is on earth, it is here, it is here, it is here). I find it significant that unlike other people living in the Himalayas, the people of Kashmir have very Aryan features and fair complexion. People of Ladakh have Mongolian features while the Indian people living in other parts of the

Himalayas have Aryan features but not as pronounced as in the Valley. This only proves Aryans settled in the Valley from the earliest times and perhaps due to the region's geographical isolation retained their ethnic identity more than in other parts of our country.

This book is in two parts, covering the history of Kashmir Valley from the earliest times to the present in the first part and then in the second part of the book examines the philosophy and religious beliefs of the people. I shall first touch on the historical aspects, from what I call prehistoric period, not mythical period as Western historians write. Rajatarangini by Kalhan, written in the eleventh century is the only historical book written by an Indian covering the ancient period which is available to us. Our ancestors of the ancient period were great scholars in philosophy, science, mathematics, astronomy, literature, medicine and so on. However, unlike the Greeks of that era, history as a subject appears to have not been of interest to them. Courtiers sang and composed poems in praise of their rulers but that was not history. For the medieval period we rely on foreign sources and chroniclers of Delhi Sultans and Mughal Emperors. Sir Jadunath Sarkar, the doyen of Indian historians, wrote that the vanquished do not write history and as such do not appear before the bar of history. Writing of history is more the pastime of the victorious. That explains why we do not have the Indian version of the medieval period. Notwithstanding all this, Brigadier Kaul has done commendable research and written an erudite version of the 5000 years of our history. He has mentioned a little known fact that Lord Krishna passed away at the age of 125 years in 3102 B.C. At least I was not aware of this. However, there are some controversial issues that he has stated. The city of Srinagar was not founded by Ashoka the Great although during his rule the city was founded and Kashmir became a part of his Empire. Buddhist monks spread Buddhism in the Valley. The Fourth Buddhist Council was held at Kundal Vanvihar (Jullundur). The other version is that on the refusal of the ruler of Magadh (Bihar) to send Ashvaghosh, the great Buddhist philosopher to Kanishka who invaded Magadh. He came from his capital at Peshawar with his army and forcibly took away Ashvaghosh. This is the only time in history when a ruler invaded another ruler's kingdom not to acquire territory nor for the hand of a fair maiden, but to forcibly take away a philosopher. Ashvaghosh was given a place of honour in Kanishka's court. He organized the Fourth Buddhist Council at Harvan in Kashmir. Another point made in this book is that Shankaracharya the great Hindu saint from Kerala in the South never came to Kashmir. The common version is that Shankaracharya came to Shardapeeth known as a great centre of Sanskrit learning. There is a temple on the hill dominating the Dal lake in Srinagar. For centuries it has been called the Shankaracharya hill. Yet another contentious issue is that Shardapeeth was not only a temple and not a University, where scholars from different parts of the country and even abroad came for learning. These are controversial issues which need further research to come to firm conclusion. Perhaps future research may establish more conclusive results.

It is interesting that there is a Kashmiri interpretation of three of the major religions of the world. Hinduism in Kashmir is based on monotheistic Shiva philosophy in which Shiva is the ultimate supreme being and not a part of triumvirate of Brahma, Vishnu and Mahesh (Shiva). Sufi Islam is also different in Kashmir from Sufism elsewhere in its reverence for graves of Sufi patrons. The emphasis on looking after Ziarats (graves of saints) with illumination and songs is peculiar to Kashmir. Another interesting feature is that the Sufi Saints in Kashmir were all vegetarians. Similarly Buddhism of Hinayana and not Mahayana variety has flourished in Kashmir. Whereas, the emphasis in Hinayana Buddhism is to obtain the salvation of one's soul through pious deeds. The Mahayana Sect emphasises the need for working for salvation of the society. This book has provided a very good survey of various aspects of Hindu beliefs. It has been stated that the present Amarnath shrine came into existence only after the Eleventh century and had not been identified earlier. For this the author has relied on Rajatarangini written by Kalhan in the 11th Century. We have no other book of history written by an Indian during the ancient and for that matter medieval periods of our history. Kalhan has made no mention of Amarnath shrine in his book. That may lend credence to the fact that Amarnath shrine is of a later origin. Yet this Rajtarangini being the only indigenous historical record of that period cannot be accepted as gospel unless corroborated by other sources.

As Governor of Jammu and Kashmir I had started an Institute of Kashmir Studies as an autonomous unit of Kashmir University to study various aspects of Kashmiri culture, religious philosophy, art, history and so on. I appointed Dr Khwaja, a Muslim eminent scholar of Sanskrit and Shaivist philosophy as the Director of the Institute. Brigadier Kaul can be an ideal member of the faculty, advisor or Director of that Institute. His book would be of great importance for study by scholars at that Institute of learning and for anyone interested in the subject.

I strongly recommend this book for scholars in the history, culture and religious philosophies of different religions that have flourished and amicably co-existed in Kashmir in the past which has been so vitiated lately by fundamentalists and terrorism unleashed by Jehadi fanatics.

Lt. Gen. (Retd.) S.K. Sinha PVSM
Former Governor of Assam and of J&K

Preface

Sanskrit poet Kalidasa writes about Kas'mira (Kashmir) thus "**The place is more beautiful than the heaven and is the benefactor of supreme bliss and happiness. It seems to me that I am taking a bath in the lake of nectar here.**" I am lucky to have been born in the Valley of *Rishi's* and *Muni's*; a place full of supreme bliss and happiness and more so where I attained adolescence. Those were the years of bliss; a life in a joint family, a peep into the daily wheel of life and above all what Kas'mira (Kashmir) stood for. I always was keen to find roots of Aryan Saraswats and my family, which led me to a broader spectrum of 'History of Kas'mira'. However, the call of adventure took me physically away for duty to the Nation for next thirty three years; Army and my Gorkha troops. Though this duty reigned supreme in my life, yet there was continuous interaction with my land of birth.

I was fortunate to inherit an intellectual ancestry, both from paternal as well as maternal side. This kept the fire to know more about the valley, people, heritage, origins, etc. burning. Whenever I found time, there was plentiful of inclination, I read lot of books, manuscripts, scriptures and of course I was blessed with discourses from my Grandmother, who would narrate a lot about the life of our ancestors and the valley.

After retirement I had two passions; Kas'mira (Kashmir) and my Gorkha Troops. For the last ten years I have tried my best to strike a balance between the two and know more and more about Kas'mira (Kashmir); Origins of Aryans, Origins of Saraswat Brahmins of Kashmir, our ancestors, our religion, Gods and Goddesses, mode and type of worship, our rulers and lot more. I have read lot of scriptures, books, articles, holy Veda's, Nilamat Puranam, religious books on Shaivism in Bharatvarasha as well as Kas'mira, Chronicles (Rajatarangini's, *Baharistan-i-Shahi* (Chronicle in Persian) etc.), Epics etc. I also had the privilege of reading translations of some of the rare manuscripts pertaining to our way of life in earlier times. It was my earnest desire to write on all facets of Kas'mira, not in parts, as a composite complete book, which would encompass our origins, history, way of life, triumph and travails and religion, in association with Gods and Goddesses of Kas'mira. It also intended to cover the times under various religions and ruler eras.

Today our Gen X has been denied knowledge about our past, our heritage and all that our elders wanted us to know. This is a ten year research and writing effort to fulfil this need. It would fill the need of a ready reference of Aryan Saraswats. We are proud of our heritage but it is important for us to know more about it. Today's Gen X is hungry for the information of our past and browse internet to know more. I am sanguine that this book will meet their need.

I am grateful to Lieutenant General (Retired) S K Sinha, PVSM, Formerly Vice Chief of the Army Staff, Indian Ambassador to Nepal, Governor of Assam and Governor Jammu and Kashmir, for his words of wisdom and it has been my proud privilege to be guided by him during my service in the Army. These words coming from a noted soldier and great scholar means a lot to me. He is no stranger to Kas'mira (Kashmir) and during his five years as Governor of Jammu and Kashmir, he has done a lot for the state, which the whole country is very well aware of. It has been my proud privilege to be an officer belonging to 5th Gorkha Rifles (Frontier Force), of which he has been a senior decorated officer and Colonel of the Regiment. I look up to him for guidance in future as well.

My grateful thanks to various sources, known or unknown, for the rare photographs appearing in this book. My special thanks to the source for providing me rare photographs of Sharda Temple in POK (Pakistan Occupied Kashmir) and surroundings in 2004, for the first time in India. My special thanks to Mr Rohit Kaul, my son, for some of the recent photographs of heritage places in Kashmir

Over the last two years Ms Leena Gaur and Ms Aparna Kaul have taken pains to correct and edit the book. My sincere thanks to them for their effort.

The book owes its conceptualisation to extreme patience of my wife, Pushpa Kaul, and advice from my intellectual daughters. Of course best is reserved for my Grandsons Nirrit and Atharv, who from the age of three, have been asking me lot of questions about Kas'mira and ancestors, so much so they have styled and prophesised themselves as the incarnation of my ancestors. So much power to our Kas'mira!!!

Noida **Brigadier (Retired) Rattan Kaul**

Acknowledgements

For more than three decades I have been keenly studying various books, papers, ancient history of Bahratvarasha, religious scriptures, manuscripts pertaining to Aryans, their way of life, migration of Aryans to various parts of India including Kas'mira (Kashmir), their settlements and way of life, amalgamation with local inhabitants, development of their religious beliefs, customs, lore's, religious scriptures, worship etc. My visits to various renowned libraries, Institutions, places of worship and study of rituals, in particular pertaining to Aryan Saraswats of Kas'mira (Kashmir), now addressed as Kashmiri Pandits, gave me insight to the way of their life through five millenniums. It is during the last decade these thoughts have taken a shape in the form of this book.

I am grateful to Ms Leena Gaur and Ms Aparna Kaul to have taken the editing effort of the book over the last two years.

It is difficult to list various sources for such an extensive study, however, I gratefully acknowledge that I had the privilege of going through many historical accounts, scriptures, books etc., which were helpful to draw my conclusions for this book, which wonderfully recounts the triumphs and travails of Aryan Saraswat Brahmins of Kas'mira (Kashmir) (Kashmiri Pandit) and Kashmir Valley. I list some of these sources as under:

1. Rajatarangini (1148-50 AD) Codex Archetypus by *Rajanaka Ratanakantha* (1648-9 AD or 1685-86 AD) translated by Sir Auriel Stein (1900 AD).
2. Extracts of Rajatarangini Series by Jonaraja, Shrivara, Praja Bhatta and Suka.
3. Rajat of Jonaraja J.C. Dutt Delhi, 1986.
4. Shrivara - *Zaina Rajtarangini.*
5. *Baharistan-i- Shahi* (Persian)-A History of Kashmiri Muslim Kings and translations thereof.
6. All the four Veda's; Rig, Atharv, Sam and Yajur. Translations, explanations, commentary and analysis by various saints and scholars.

7. Nilamat Puranam of Kas'mira (500 BC). Translations, commentary and explanatory notes.
8. Brahma Purana-Extracts.
9. Bharatvarasha Epic *Ramayana*. Translations, commentary and explanatory notes.
10. *Mahabharata* Epic. Translations, commentary and explanatory notes.
11. Al–Beruni's Travelogue (*India*). Translations, commentary and explanatory notes.
12. Dr Buheler (*Report on Kashmir*). Translations, commentary and explanatory notes.
13. Major General Alexander Cunningham (*Ancient Geography of Kashmir, Coins of Ancient India, Coins of Medieval India, Temples of India and Kashmir*).
14. Life and Travelogues of Hieun Tsang to Bharatvarasha and Kashmir. Translations, commentary and explanatory notes.
15. Walter R Lawrence - *The Valley of Kashmir.*
16. Commentary and translated extracts of Sage Maya's *Surya Siddhanta, Arryabhattiya* of Arya Bhatta and *Brhatsmihta* by Varaha Mihir.
17. Chronology of Ancient India-Explanatory notes and commentary.
18. Chinese Travellers/Pilgrims Notes (Fahian, Ou Kong). Translations, commentary and explanatory notes.
19. Translated extracts/comments on *Suvarata's poem*, Ksemendra's *Nrpavali*, Helaraja's *Parthivavali* (9th/10th Century), Ksemendra's *Lokapr* and *Tirthas* by Pandit Sahib Ram.
20. Mahabharata Chronology and Dating of Mahabharata War (Dr Patnaik, Dr Kak and Dr Bala Krishna NASA).
21. Times of Gautam Buddha, Mahavira and Adi Shankara (BC). Commentary and explanatory notes.
22. Times and events of Kings; Ashoka and Kushan King Kanishka and successors. Commentary and explanatory notes.
23. Connected papers with Bharata War, Commentary and explanatory notes.
24. Indian Calendars and papers on ancient astronomy.
25. Biographical accounts of Kalhan, Abhinav Gupta and Bilhana.
26. Histories of Shankaracharaya's, Mutts and Acharayas (Analysis, History, Sharda Peeth, List of Acharayas and works of Acharayas)
27. Commentary and explanatory notes. on various scriptures by Adi-Shankara.
28. Scholarly known or attributed works of Madhavacharya.

29. Kashmiri Shaivism. Translations, commentary and explanatory notes. (Prof Kokiloo, Dr Kaw, Dr Subash Kak, JN Kaul 'Kamal', Justice Katju, Dinanath Shastri, Prof KN Dhar).
30. History of Kas'mira and aspects connected with Kas'mira (JL Kilam, Prof L N Dhar, PNK Bamzai, Pt Anand Kaul Bamzai, Dr Aima, Dr Kaushalya Wali, A D Majboor, Ram Krishna Kaul, Ramesh Kaul, J N Ganahar M L Pushkar, J K Jalali and (Prof C L Sapru).
31. Lal Ded – *Lal Ded* by Prof Jialal Kaul, Lala Vakh's and comments on Lal Ded, Her Times and Events.
32. Aryans; History, Origin, Settlements, Archaeological finds. Translations, commentary and explanatory notes.
33. Archaeological Surveys of Kas'mira.
34. Translations of *Shah Nama, Aine–Akbari.* Translations, commentary and explanatory notes.
35. Monuments of Kashmir by R C Kak.
36. R.K. Parimu, (Dr)-Muslim Rule in Kashmir.
37. Excavation and assessment reports of Archaeological Survey of India pertaining to Harappan Civilisation.
38. Neolithic and Megalithic sites in *Bharatvarsha;* Burzhom, Gufkral and Gurhom Sangri (All in Kas'mira).
39. Geographical survey reports of *Bharatvarsha* and Kas'mira.
40. Evolution of Himalayas.
41. *Saundarya Lahiri* by Adi Shankara and *Panchastavi.* Translations, commentary and explanatory notes.
42. History of Saraswat Brahmins. Commentary and explanatory notes.
43. Life and works of Rupabhavani, Arnimal, Narain Kaul. Commentary and explanatory notes.
44. Ancient Kashmir; Literature, Culture and Life. Translations, commentary and explanatory notes.
45. Languages and *Lipi's* of *Bharatvarasha.*
46. *Early History and Culture of Kashmir-* Dr Sunil Chandra Ray.
47. *Panini's Ashtadhyayi* (Ganapatha).
48. Kashir Dictionary. Vol. IV-Published hy Jammu & Kashmir Academy of Art, Culture and Languages.
49. Kashmir under the Sultans-Hasan, M., (Calcutta, 1959).
50. Muslim Rule in Kashmir, A D 1554–1586 - Wani, Nizam-ud-Din (1987).
51. *The Earliest Settlers of Kashmir*–R N Kaw.

1

Aryans-Immigration to Kas'mira to Saraswat Brahmins

> To thee, O Savitar, the Lord of precious things, who helpest us continually, for our share we come-Wealth, highly lauded ere reproach hath fallen on it, which is laid, Free from all hatred, in thy hands Through thy protection may we come to even the height of affluence Which Bhaga hath dealt out to us.
>
> Ne'er have those birds that fly through air attained to thy high dominion or thy might or spirit;
>
> Nor these the waters that flow on for ever, nor hills, abaters of the wind's wild fury.
>
> *Rig Veda Book–1-24- 3, 4, 5, 6*

(In this Book Kashmir in general has been referred to as Kas'mira, the ancient name given to the Valley in the oldest Scripture Nilamat Puranam (5th Century BC/4th Century AD)).

Libraries and Ancient Literature

Curiosity For The Past: These are not the triumphs and travails of Aryan Saraswat Brahmins of Bharatvarasha or Aryan Saraswat Brahmins of Kas'mira (Kashmir), commonly referred to as *Bhatta* or now *Kashmiri* Pandit, but transition of Aryan Saraswat community as a whole, through millenniums of religious philosophies, search of identity, *Gotra* orientation, honorific's; *Bhatta* and *Pandit* and selective surnames. This medium intends to emphasize on Aryan roots, genesis of specific names and surnames, honorific's, with details, to give insight of that era, before these pass into oblivion. Sri Maharaja Ranbir Singh Library at Jammu, Sri Maharaja Pratap Singh Museum at *Lal Mandi* and Research and Translation Department of Jammu & Kashmir State, established during the reign of Maharaja Ranbir Singh, hold ancient artefacts, sculptures, paintings manuscripts in Sanskrit, Sharda, Persian, Kashmiri and Urdu pertaining to transition and history of Bharatvarasha in general and Kas'mira in particular. In manuscript and history sections there are birch leaf manuscripts, hand wrought paper miniature paintings, papier-mâché artefacts, silk scrolls and volumes of manuscripts in different languages. Similar artefacts were held in the hands of many scholars, who passed them on from one generation to another. Many of these artefacts, manuscripts, scrolls were collected under the directions of Maharaja Ranbir Singh under the custody of Research and Translation Department of the State. These have been preserved and are held by Maharaja Ranbir Singh Library and Raghunath Temple Library. These artefacts have works of many scholars of the Aryan Saraswat community (Kashmir Pandit's) of recent centuries; Narain Kaul, Anand Ram Pahalwan, Tota Kaul Kardar (Father of Historian Anand Kaul and Grand Father of Historian and writer P N Kaul (Bamzai), Govind Koul, Pandit Sahib Ram, Pandit Sahaz Bhat, Bhawani Das Kachru, Bhawani Kaul, Professor Nityanand Shastri, Mukund Ram Shastri and many others. Many priceless manuscripts of Nilamat Puranam, Rajatarngini of Kalhan or its subsequent chronology from Jonaraja onwards, accounts of various Kings of Kas'mira, manuscripts, Coins and artefacts were surreptitiously taken away by so called scholars, shipped abroad and are in the possession of various museums world over. Some of these artefacts were held within the valley but for many reasons the possesors neither knew their value nor their contents. Even these have been misplaced, burned, sold for pittance or have been acquired, surreptitiously though, by private collectors. It is learnt that huge number of such priceless manuscripts, which were in the possession of Research and Translation Derpartment have been transferred to Kashmir University and lie unattended, unaccounted and with reports of pilferage.

The contribution by various scholars of Kas'mira's, during first millennium AD, mainly pertained to the sphere of religious philosophy and few chronicles. It was somewhat subdued during the initial and middle of second millennium AD. During the last few centuries the magnitiude of contributions by Aryan Saraswat Brahmin scholars was enormous, but these scholars remained near anonymous, unsung and were hardly mentioned or given credit for their scholarly work. In the exhibits, in above museums, there were few markers attributed to such scholars, but many remained as works of unknown scholars. Admittedly old scriptures had been destroyed during Muslim rule during second millennium AD, but during Dogra rule, many scriptures were retrieved or recovered, preserved, copies and translations made and were transferred to Raghunath Mandir Library and Sri Maharaja Ranbir Singh Library at Jammu. Passage of time had taken toll on ancient scriptures, held in the custody of scholars and what had been preserved by generations and was lost during various exoduses the Kas'mira Brahmin had to undertake.

Accounts and facts of ancient times, in this book, have been derived from manuscripts, scholarly works of ancient saint's, archealogical discoveries, scriptures and what has come down the centuries in the form of prominent Veda*'s* (Rig, Yajur, Sam and Atharv), *Shruti* (voice heard), *Smriti* (remembered) and translations of many scholarly works. These are not restricted to the artefacts of Kas'mira only but also those that are available in Bharatvarasha. The blank period during Muslim Rule has been filled with details from Persian Chronicles, written during the Muslim period and excerpts quoted at appropriate places. Brahmin scholars and chroniclers of that time, for obvious reasons of threat and lack of patronage, used guarded language to describe the events of that time. The description in Persian chronicles, while glorifying Muslim rule, gives events in their own words and is closer to reality; for they were part of and patronised by the system. Kas'mira, name given to the Valley in Nilamat Puranam, oldest religious scripture of Kashmir, which is also closer to pronunciation of *Kasheer* (For Kashmir), has been used for reference to Kashmir Valley and *Kashmiri* to the denizens.

Original Place of Aryans

There are two thoughts as to the origin and place of Aryans. One is that they were original inhabitants of Bharatvarasha (India, also called Hindustan) which as a whole was country of Aryans. It is scientifically known that the human race started from African Sub-Continent and over the millenniums expanded within the continent and then migrated in all directions to other continents including Europe, Central Asia and Indian Sub-Continent; Central Asian migration was deemed as the first one. A modification of this theory is that African continent was the first one for development of humans, which also took place on its own in other sub continents, in a phased manner, including Central Asia. Once this Central Asian Group developed, over the millenniums, overflow of some of this population from Eastern belt of Central Asia took place eastwards towards China. Bulk of this population settled in climatically mild areas of Central Asia and that is where they lived for a millennium. This is the population which developed over centuries, if not millenniums, into the famous race termed as Aryans. As is with any race, expanding in numbers, many groups from this civilisation moved Southwards but remained within the geographical limits of Central Asia for centuries. Subsequently, centuries later, smaller groups moved Westwards to what is now as the European continent. They had carefully and intelligently selected natural barriers as their limits of expansion, Hindukush range being one of them in the quest for Southward expansion. While this development was taking place in parts of Central Asia, each geographical area of settlement, helped in the development of the humans differently in terms of their physical features, way of life and other characteristics. Over centuries Eastern Central Asian settlements developed what is called Mongoloid features, which are predominantly the features of Eastern Central Asian Countries and further North and East (Mongolia, China). The initial human civilisation which developed in the Indian Sub Continent and even other continents, developed differently in terms of physical features and way of life. Even within the Indian Sub Continent they developed differently due to climatic and terrain conditions of different geographical pockets like South, West, Northwestern region, Northern region, Eastern plains etc. There is no doubt that population of these pockets developed independently from each other and over centuries established their own civilisation like Dravidians in the South and what is called Mohenjodaro/Harappa Civilisation in Northwestern region. While the former civilisation developed mostly in South India, the latter developed further towards Northern region and even Eastwards. Some of these groups, small in number though, developed their own small civilisation, primitive in comparison to other groups, elsewhere in Indian Sub Continent like Nagas, as they were called, in hilly and mountainous areas of Northern India. In the Eastern parts of the continent the civilisation which developed was the overflow of the groups moving from Eastern Part of Central Asia towards East and finally curving Westwards, avoiding Himalayas, till they were stopped by natural barriers like major rivers. These developed into present day civilisation of the East and Hilly Areas, with distinct features, different from those of Southern peninsula or present day Northern Region.

The other assertion is that Aryans moved into Bharatvarasha from Central Asian region. Many reasons have been attributed to their immigration; drought, increasing population, nomadic nature, need for better pastures, persecution of particular groups, catastrophes in their region etc. No single reason has been identified as the main reason for migration but it is evident that they moved slowly, in reasonably large groups, due to multiple reasons and this migration took place in different directions. Most adventurous ones moved Southwards through present day Afghanistan and Western tribal belt of Pakistan adjoining present day Iran, but remained initially West of great River Sindhu and then wheeled inwards towards the banks of Saraswati River. Their initial move of smaller groups out of Central Asia to *Sindhustan* (Bharatvarasha) is placed around 2000 BC ± and substantial numbers around 1800 ±. Some historians are of the view that this move took place; in large groups between 3700 ± 800 years and 1800 BC. May be smaller groups migrated during this initial period and settled down deeper in Bharatvarasha, isolated though from the major groups which migrated later and settled down along the Saraswati River Basin. Some of the archaeological finds in the recent past, found mostly along the Western portion of Bharatvarasha and even Pakistan may be pertaining to these smaller groups. But it must be understood that though they came from the same stock as latter immigrants. They did not and are not considered part of the main Aryan civilisation.

Appellation, pronounced *Sindhustan*, has been found in the manuscripts dating back to the period of Cyrus The Great (Of Persia - 6 Century BC); word possibly in use even at the time of immigration of Aryans, to describe the people living beyond River Indus (Sindhu), which was Eastern Boundary of then Persia. Persians/Central Asians had phonetic problem of pronouncing alphabet 'S' and pronounced it as 'H'. *Sindhustan* was pronounced as *Hindhustan*, inhabitants as Sindhu's (Pronounced *Hindhu's*), Country (*Stan*) of Sindhu's as *Hindhustan*. There is no doubt that Aryans came to Bharatvarasha from Central Asia and their entry was opposed by then inhabitants of Bharatvarasha. They had to mix, cajole, conquer, and even force their settlement at places. 'Conquered' by Aryans, word used also meant various methods other than use of force; minds, hearts etc. The lot of hubble propounding various theories over their origin, 'Aryan invasion' or 'Aryan Invaders' is unwarranted. Admittedly there may have been push overs, some settling alongside the original inhabitants and in cases of opposition use of 'force of numbers'. Use of force amongst themselves to gain territorial rights over a settlement is also distinctly possible.

Route of Immigration, Religious Development and Evolution of Vedas

Aryans moved slowly, many groups settled enroute while large groups, moved Southwards as the time passed. This move was not a burst but gradual, as this civilisation established sizeable immigrant pockets right upto river Saraswati. River Saraswati originally flowed through what is now known as present Rajasthan and portion identified as modern river *Syr-Darya* in Thar Desert of Pakistan, joining Aral Sea (North Part of Arabian Sea). It is believed and partly proved from excavations and artefacts around these excavated parts, that River Saraswati did exist and was not a mythical river and 'changed its course at least four times' before it finally dried up or disappeared. Aryans settlements, initially mostly along river River Saraswati banks (*Avesta* named it *Harahwati;* pronunciation of alphabet 'S' here also is 'H'); were regarded as most central group of Aryans. Settlements developed along River Saraswati and over centuries a new civilisation named Aryan settlements came up. It is over many more centuries that they developed a religion and a new word came into usage along these Ashrams/settlements of Saraswati River; Arya or Aryan.

Development of terminology 'Aryan' came over a period, based on the defining of certain values of an ideal immigrant of Saraswati River Civilisation. Some of these settlements were established adjacent to already existing settlements of original inhabitants of Bharatvarasha, called *Dasayu's* by these Aryans. Some of these settlements even capped over the old settlements, after they had either been vacated or abandoned by original inhabitants. There are finds which also point out to joint settlements of original inhabitants and Aryans, though restricted in number. As the River Saraswati flow started dwindling, immigrant groups moved further East. It is believed that when the first drought took place along Saraswati River, the immigrants sustained on fish of the river for considerable time, legend says twelve years, which over centuries was carried as part of food of Aryans. It is not that Aryan settlements, after firming in, were along River Saraswati only. As per common belief River Saraswati dried up in stages and by around 1200 BC it finally dried up, though not confirmed scientifically, and became a mythical river. A significant group of Aryans, closer to Northern Belt/Indus (Sindhu), had started moving Eastwards as well as Northwards, when a significant change of course of River Saraswati took place around 1600 ± BC. Centuries later they had expanded and extended up to Indus (Sindhu) and *Hindukush* in the Northwest, to the region of the seven rivers, '*Sapta Sindhu*', with its centre in the Saraswati valley and covering a great part of North and Northwest India, ranging from Indus (Sindhu) to Ganga and Sarayu (Central Uttar Pradesh). In the early centuries of later Vedic Period, also called Brahmanic Period, Aryans migrated across the Doab, a large plain that separates the Yamuna River from the Ganges. "Favour ye this my lord, O Ganga, Yamuna, O Satudri (Satluj), Parusni and Saraswati: With Asikni, Vitasta (Jhelum, Wyeth), O Marudvrdha, O Arjikiya with Susoma hear my call (Rig Veda 10: 75-5)."

This Vedic Hymn in praise of many rivers of North India, Doab Plains (Satudri (Satluj) and Vipas (Beas) and Yamuna-Ganga Basin clearly indicates that Aryans were familiar with these rivers of interior Bharatvarasha, which could have been possible only if they had intimately been connected with these rivers; like settlements along these rivers.

Since mid 19th century it has been claimed that substantial groups of Aryans migrated into India, around 1800 ± BC, possibly replacing declining Harappan civilization. The Rig Veda describes warfare and struggle for control of territory, but whether this resulted from migration or not is not clear. However, the archaeological and historical record can be interpreted to indicate a gradual migration around the end of the 2nd millennium BC of Indo-Aryan speakers to the East from the vicinity of Central Asia. It is also possible to argue that the Indo-Aryan speaking cultures had much older roots in the area. In any case, modern India is divided into two main language families, one Indo-European, its speaker's possibly linguistic descendants of migratory Aryans, and the other Dravidian, its speaker's possibly linguistic descendants of the Harappans.

Veda*'s* were composed in Saraswati River Ashrams. Over the centuries, additions and deletions were made continuously and passed on through generations by Saints and Aryan bards/priests called *Arthvan*, singing hymns of these Vedas. Rig Veda, most sacred of our religious scriptures is considered very old. The dating of start of composition of this Veda varies from around fourth millennium BC (4000 BC; 3700 BC (±) 800 years to around 1800 BC (±). Other prominent Vedas are Yajur, Sam and Atharv, preserved through centuries as *Shruti* (voice heard) and *Smriti* (remembered) and finally compiled by *Brahma Rishi.* Again dating varies from pre *Mahabarata* (3200 BC) to around 1000 BC. Vedas contain Aryan beliefs and daily life and are collection of poems and sacred hymns. This is why the period, roughly around 1600 BC, is called the Vedic Period, after the Vedas. Study of Rig Veda text suggests that the Sages, *Vedics, Rishis* lived on the banks of 'Saraswati; The Great Goddess Stream', which saw transition of Aryans to *Brahmanism* in Bharatvarasha, getting them the honorific '*Aryan Saraswat Brahmins*'.

There are many other scriptures also termed Vedas, with specific name in Bharatvarasha and Kas'mira, but all of these are of later vintages. These are generally modification of the original Vedas with certain customs, hymns, rituals pertaining to respective geographical parts of the area. Though Vedas were compiled earlier, they were written in sequential form much later, once *lipi* had been developed in the area. Rig Veda was first written in Khartoshi, also called Kharshoti, around 500 BC. Till then Vedas were passed on by the word of mouth as *Shruti* and *Smriti.* Khartoshi (Kharshoti) was prevalent script in the Northern parts of Bharatvarasha, written from right to left and is attributed to Aryans. *Brahmi* came thereafter followed by *Pali* and *Gupta Lipi*, while Devnagri script was evolved in 6th Century AD. Khartoshi (Kharshoti) script was also the prevalent script in Kas'mira from around 500 BC to 300 AD and certain writings on stones in Khartoshi (Kharshoti) have been excavated at Harvan.

Arya: To those not familiar with *Vedic* culture, the word '*Arya*' is no more than a hieroglyph, which attracts or repels according to their temperament. To some, the word has been converted to purely racial terms, an unknown ethnological quantity on which different speculations fix different values. To others, the word represents a difference of culture, because the *Vedic Rishis* had accepted a particular type of self-culture; of inward and outward practice, of ideality and of aspiration. Their gods were the supraphysical powers, who assisted the mortal in his struggle towards the nature of the godhead. All the highest aspirations of the early human race, its noblest religious temper, and its most idealistic velleity of thought are summed up in this single vocable. In later times, the word Arya expressed a particular ethical and social ideal, an ideal of well-governed life, candour, courtesy, nobility, straight dealing, courage, gentleness, purity, humanity, compassion, protection of the weak, liberality, observance of social duty, eagerness of knowledge, respect for the wise and learned and the social accomplishments. It was the combined ideal of *Brahmin* and the *Kshatriya.* Everything that departed from this ideal, everything that tended towards the ignoble, mean, obscure, rude, cruel or false, was termed un-Aryan or *Anarya* (colloquial *Anari*). There is no word in human speech that has a nobler history. In the early days of comparative philology, when the scholars sought in the history of words for the prehistoric history of peoples, it was supposed that the word Arya came from the root '*ar*', to plough, and that the *Vedic* Aryans were so called, when they separated from their kin, who despised the pursuits of agriculture and remained shephards and hunters. This speculation has little or nothing to support but we may accept the derivation as whoever cultivates field that the God has made, does not leave it barren or allow it to run to seed, but labours to exact from it its yield; an Aryan. (*Arya*: *Its Significance*).

If Arya was purely a racial term, a more probable derivation would be '*ar*', also meaning strength or valour, from '*ar*' to fight, like the name of Greek war-god Ares, brave or warlike, perhaps even arête signifying, like the Latin virtus, physical strength and courage and then moral force and elevation. Whoever makes that choice, seeks to climb level of the divine, fear nothing, not deterred by defeat etc. He is Aryan, the divine fighter, victor and noble man in fundamental sense. Aryan is he who strives and overcomes all outside and within him that stands opposed to the human advance. For him self-conquest is first, he does not consent like ordinary men and overcomes life and its energies while refusing to be dominated by hunger, cravings or enslaved by passions. He overcomes mind and its habits, does not live in ignorance, with prejudices, customary ideas, opinions, but knows how to seek and chooses to be flexible, firm and with strong will. Everything he seeks is truth, right and freedom with self-perfection as the aim of this self-conquest. Therefore, what he conquers he does not destroy and attains something higher. When it is attained, he applies it in work, love, joy and knowledge. Aryan is a worker and warrior, puts in labour of mind and body, to seek the ultimate sacred goal. He overcomes difficulty, fatigue and fights for the coming of these positives within himself and in the world. In the *Mahabharata* and *Ramayana*, right behaviour and moral conduct of the Aryan is explained in great detail. It is here the word Arya has been given another meaning; 'nobility in its purest form'. Lastly but not the least, the word Arya is linked to the word 'Ereta' or righteousness in Avestan, '*Rita*' in Vedic Sanskrit. This means law of righteousness and Aryan was one who followed the law. '*Ritu*' in Sanskrit meant the cycle of seasons, which was an integral part of that moral, physical and spiritual law of God. A '*Rishi*' was one who explained the law, in Avestan the word '*Ratu*' was a spiritual teacher of righteousness. As such, being an Aryan, meant following the path of righteousness as well as being a proud member of the Aryan people.

A Painting of Vedic God (Medieval Period).

Aryan Saraswat Brahmin Honorific

In ancient times Aryan bards sang hymns extolling their adventures and were called *Arthvan*; meaning a person of essence, who with passage of time became their priests mentioned in *Brahma Purana* as such. The definition of Brahmin in *Brahma Purana* refers to 'those who wrote, read and spoke *Vedic*' (*Vedic* was spoken by Aryans and *Brahmi* was the script (*Lipi*)). A *Shloka* in *Brahma Purana* defines a Brahmin (translated) thus;

> "The wise man overcomes anger through mind control, lust through the renunciations of desire... Through conduct he should protect mind and speech. ...Through constant vigilance he should shed fear and through the service of the wise, he should overcome pride – *Brahma Purana* 235. 40 – 42."

The honorific 'Aryan Saraswat Brahmins of Kas'mira' has been specifically used for Kashmiris, as only 'Aryan' word encompasses broader spectrum of people (Aryans) of Bharatvarasha and not Kas'mira alone. Aryan word, a derivative of word *Aryenem* in Central Asian Scripture *Avestan,* was applied as a title to themselves by our ancestors and referred to as a race; in distinction from the people they (Aryans) had 'conquered'. '*Arya*' is also title used for people 'cultivated in mind and character', whose way of life aims at 'elevating the individual soul through a disciplined life to Godhood (*Mukhti*)'. Philosophically it is a term of ethical, intellectual and spiritual excellence, applied to those who had completely mastered *Aryasatyani* (Holy Truths) and who tread *Aryamarga* (Path to *Moksha* or

Nirvana). *Aryavarta*; abode of noble or excellent ones or the sacred land of the Aryans, referred later as Bharatvarasha, was the ancient name for the geographical area South of Indus (Sindhu), extending from Northern to Central Bharatvarasha (India) including geographical limits of Kas'mira, East to Western Sea and bounded on the North and South by the *Himalayas-Hindukush-Sindhu* and *Vindhya* mountains respectively. The Bharatvarasha or *Bharat Khand* form of invocation to Gods and address has been scripted in the beginning of many rituals in religious scriptures of Brahmins of Bharatvarasha. The original word *Aryavarta*, the sacred land of '*Aryans*', also seems to have origin from words *Aryenem Vaego,* mentioned in Central Asian Scripture *Avestan. Vaego* means *Beeja* (Seed) thus meaning '*Seed of Aryans*'.

Caste System Among Aryans

Varna (Caste/class) system was prevalent amongst Aryans also and is nothing new. In mythological literature there is mention of struggle between two *Varna's*; Brahmins are said to have been led by Lord Parasuram, and the Kshatriyas by Kartaviraarjuna. Aryan bards, singing hymns, became priests called *Arthavan;* their warriors called *Ratheshwar* (Charioteer-transited to *Kshatriya*), their workers and herders of their cattle *Vastrayosh* (Transited to *Vaishya*) and their camp followers and slaves called *Hatoksha*, became *Shudra* later. It is incorrect to imply that it did not have any sociological implications for Bharatvarasha and Kas'mira Brahmins. The routes for class/caste were laid by Aryans on the banks of Saraswati River. It is that only Brahmin class got frequently mentioned but the class of followers, foot soldiers etc. existed, though considered shade lower than Brahmins. These Brahmins were generally referred to as Saraswat Brahmins. In the initial stages of immigration the move was led by a combined group of Aryans, but within the group there were different shades of workmen undertaking different tasks. It was not that only *Ratheswars* (*Kshatriya*) led the group advance. When they moved in different directions from Saraswati River area, in groups, these were not isolated groups of a particular *Varna,* but a composite group. Slowly the groups became *Arthavan* predominant, who centuries later, as a religion developed, took the honorific Brahmin. As the time elapsed and Aryans moved in deeper, towards the interior areas, the *Varna* line became thin. In fact all the *Varna* members were as active as the other, in the somewhat new philosophy of the religion called Aryavarata or the rituals they had imbibed over the peiod. Even within the *Arthavan Varna* some went deeper into Vedic religion, while others joined in day to day chorus. The former became the priests within the *Arthavan* community. Many of the former, who took deeper interest in the Vedic religion, were called *Rishis*.

The lines within *Varnas* further became thin as Aryans moved into inner areas of Bharatvarasha and all were followers of Vedic religion. As is common. graduation to upper class during such movements did take place and the numbers of the lower *Varnas* dwindled to bare essential. This happenend more in the case of *Ratheswars*, whose requirement over the peace interludes decreased. In Kas'mira Aryans came with all the *Varnas* intact. Once they mingled with the local inhabitants, the Nagas, the lower *Varnas* mixed with the *Vastrayosh* and *Ratheswars*. This continued till about 500 BC, when there is evidence of *Ratheswars* also mixing with higher *Varna*. During the first millennium AD many upper strata of the *Artharvans* took deeper interest in the religious philosophy, while others of their group undertook day to day work, many of which fell in the realm of other *Varnas*. It is these who, in the later part of the first millennium AD, evolved different type of religious philosophy. During the second millennium AD, with different type of conditions and conversions, the lower classes, fragile as they were, converted into Islam and the later centuries found these very convertees continued to do the job of the erstwhile *Hatokshas* (Slaves).

Aryan Immigration in Kas'mira

Aryan Entry into Kas'mira: It has always been asserted that Aryans moved into Kas'mira after they had settled down along Saraswati River and other nearby places, fully established with the excavations along the Doab and then closer to Kas'mira. There is a recent school of thought that Aryans came directly to Kas'mira from the Northern mountain's of Kas'mira. Yet another thought is that Aryans were original inhabitants of Kas'mira and evolution of Kashmiri Aryan race took place in Kas'mira itself, like human race in the other parts of the world. There is no historical, archealogical, scriptural proof that Aryans directly moved to *Saras* valley (Kas'mira-*Saras*-Inland Sea; Kas'mira was then called *Saras*, inhabited by Naga's (Aborigines/ Tribals) with capital at *Nilakunda* (Verinag) from Central Asia, while moving towards Saraswati River, as their route to Sindhustan (Bharatvarasha) from Central Asia was far away from *Saras* (Kas'mira).The mountains to the North of Kashmir, including Nanga Parvat Range and Pamirs are treacherous and in those times difficult to negotiate and maintain themselves over the centuries. Even now the areas are very sparcely populated with hard life. As has been mentioned, the areas North of these mountains is part of Eastern Central Asia and the migration of Central Asian people of this geographical area took place towards East and North, where the area was comparatively negotiable and sustenance possible. Rig Veda talks of Saraswati River as the focal point of Aryan civilisation and then in other verses moves Eastwards towards Doab and even talks of Kas'mira's sacred river Vitasta (Jhelum) and is not other way around.

Analysis of Nilamat Puranam, oldest scripture of Aryan Saraswat Brahmins of Kas'mira, indicates conclusively that Nagas were the original inhabitants of Kas'mira. Further it would be evident that Aryans (*Manus*) initially came to Kas'mira in smaller groups and could not stand the harsh weather and moved back when winter set in. This clearly indicates their migration through South of Kas'mira for centuries, till they decided to stay in the valley throughout the year. This has been well chronicled with the incident of an old Aryan Brahmin having been left behind and finally getting permission for Aryans to stay in Kas'mira throughout the year. From scriptures, Rajatarangini of Kalhan, South Kas'mira is mentioned as the hub of both Naga as well as Aryan settlements and it stands to reason that the route to Kas'mira was from the direction of South. For millenniums it has been proved that route to Kas'mira was through Rajapuri (Rajauri) or Panchal also called Lohara (Poonch). Legends and scientific evidence asserts that *Saras* (Kas'mira) drained its waters though *Varahakshetra* (Varahamulla, Baramulla) also proves inaccessibility of Kas'mira from North. Nilamat Puranam mentions *Daitaya's, Pis'acas* as the people of these Northern areas, so different from Nagas and Aryans. Based on some recent excavations, skeletons have been found dating nearly 4000 years old and deemed to be that of Aryans and assumed that Aryans were the original inhabitants and evolution of humans in situ. However, artefacts found in the area pertain to primitive people, possibly of Neolithic period (of the later or more advanced Stone Age; that of Nagas) dating around 2600 ± 200 BC. A genetic survey, all over the world, has established similarity of Aryan race descendants along erstwhile Saraswati River Valley, Doab and Kas'mira. The genetic survey has also found that the race of Northern areas; even now called Dards (Drava in old chronicles), are from a different race. Any move in of Aryans directly from Central Asia to Kas'mira, through the Northern route, would have these settlements also as their descendants, which is not so. Thus, the entry of Aryans into Kas'mira can roughly be placed immediately after Saraswati changed course and its water flow dwindled (1800 BC) and their entry into Kas'mira around 1600 ± 200 BC. In archealogical terms this period is termed as Megalithic period.

Prefix address of 'Aryan' for Kashmiris (people of Kas'mira) is well chronicled, including in Rajatarangini by Kalhan, who calls it as the Land of Aryan (Verse 341 Book I). Western and Indian scholars also assert that Kashmiris, without any doubt, belong to the Aryan race; 'It is certain that it (Kas'mira) was a *colony* of Aryan immigrants from Central Asia. Their features and fair complexion speaks of their inner Aryan race'.

With the selective use 'Aryan immigrants from Central Asia' it is meant that Aryans came through Central Asia to plains of Bharatvarasha and then into Kas'mira. Another Anglo Ornithologist, Thompson, is of the view that Aryans; 'A longheaded race of tall stature with narrow noses and fair complexion and their purest representatives are found today mainly in Kas'mira'.

Many Kashmiris assume *Saptrishi Samvat* approximately as authentic era of their entry to Kas'mira (It is 5088 *Saptrishi Samvat* in 2012). This is debatable as *Saptrishi Samvat* is common in Bharatvarasha also, where it was evolved by astronomer Arya Bhatta in 5th Century BC (More of this era later in Chapter 6 and 10 of the book). The legend of Aryan immigration to

Kas'mira is backed by Nilamat Puranam, an ancient scripture. As the time passed, as per the legend, many smaller groups entered the valley of *Saras* and some smaller groups came out of *Saras* and settled in Northwestern Bharatvarasha.

Gotra Genesis and Orientation-Aryans and Kas'mira

With the passage of time, Brahminical religion and *Gotra* orientation took roots as part of religious rituals amongst Aryan Saraswat Brahmins including those in Kas'mira. Many of us do not know mythology behind *Gotra* and possibly only know our *Gotra* and that *Gotra* of *Dattatreya Kaul's* starts from Sage Dattatreya (Also known as Lord *Dattatreya*). Reference to *Gotra* in Vedic literature is very infrequent. Rig Veda refers to it only at a few places; at four places it has been referred mostly in prayers to Lord *Indra*, as a 'mountain and a cloud'. There is considerable difference of opinion regarding real connotation of the word '*Gotra*' in Vedas. Many consider use of word *Gotra* in Vedas meaning 'Cowshed', while others connect it with a 'Group'. It is obvious that the connotation to a 'group' came about with the Brahaminical religion taking firmer roots. The earliest reference to its usage, referring to a 'group' or '*Gotra*' is found in *Chhandogyan Upanishad*, where an *Acharaya* (Scholar) asks the *Gotra* of one Safya Kama. However, as time passed, institution of *Gotras* was fully established by the time of Buddha; as Buddhist literature makes frequent references to *Gotras*. The sages, who founded the initial Brahaminical Gotras are seven *Sapth Rishis* and are; *Bhrigu, Angiras, Marichi, Atri, Paulaha, Pulastya* and *Vasistha*. *Rishi Paulaha* brought forth demons (*Rakshas*); sixth *Pulastya* devils (*Pisachas*); while seventh *Vasistha*, died and appeared again as a descendant of *Marichi*. Two *Gotra Rishis, Bhrigu* and *Angiras,* could not properly represent as founders of families and other three; *Jamadagni, Gautama* and *Bhardvaja* took their place.

Seven *Rishis* heading *Brahaminical Gotras* as enumerated in *Satpatha Brahmana* are; *Gautama, Bhardvaja, Jamadagni, Atri, Vasistha, Kashyapa* and *Visvamitra*. It is interesting to note that *Kashyapa*, chronicled as father of Nila, the King of *Saras* (Kas'mira) and *Visvamitra* are included in this list; slightly different from the original list. Descendants of *Kashyapa Gotra* apart from being found in Kas'mira are also found in Northern and erstwhile Northwestern belt of Bharatvarasha. This leads credence to the theory that smaller groups of Aryans, after settling down in Kas'mira moved out of Kas'mira and settled in Northern and Northwestern region of erstwhile Bharatvarasha. To this list of seven *Gotra* heads, *Agastya* has been added as eighth *Gotra* head and many *Brahaminical Gotras* of Bharatvarasha are also traced to them. These founders belonged to the era of Saraswati Bank Ashrams; not at the same time. Their descendants proliferated and with geographical changes of Saraswati River and migrated to various parts of Bharatvarasha; from Nepal to Western Ghats and Central to Northern Bharatvarasha. Five descendants of these eight *Gotra* Head ancestors were treated as of *Rishi* order and designated as *Gotra* heads; *Dattatreya* (Son of *Atri*), *Paladeva, Aupamanyava, Maudgalya* and *Dhaumyayana*. Mostly descendants of these five *Gotra* Heads and original founder *Bhardvaja* moved to Northern region of Bharatvarasha including Kas'mira. However, a sprinkling of those who had *Gotra* name of the original heads like *Gautama, Vasistha,* and *Atri* also immigrated to Northern region including Kas'mira. Tenth *Gotra Kashyapa* is common in the plains of Bharatvarasha and the valley of *Saras* (Kas'mira). Thus, technically descendants of ten Aryan *Gotra* founders moved into Kas'mira; *Dattatreya* (Son of *Atri*), *Paladeva, Aupamanyava, Maudgalya, Dhaumyayana, Bhardvaja, Gautama, Vasistha, Atri* and *Kashyapa* and not six. This also indicates immigration to Kas'mira in groups, possibly at different times, as members of a group would have been located together. These *Gotras* are also found in many parts of Bharatvarasha (Western Ghats and Konkan) though Brahmins settled in Western Ghats adhere to restricted usage of *Gotra*.

Gotra considered sacred, however, did not tag itself with a name of a person or family nor found usage as surname; but got mentioned for religious ceremonies. In Kas'mira, *Gotra* got mentioned only for religious ceremonies; marriages, etc and not as prefix or suffix to a name, as it was sacrosanct to avoid its common daily usage. Like there was no name like Sada Kaul *Dattatreya* or *Dattatreya* Sada Kaul; he was Sada Kaula Bhatta or simply Sada Kaul in medieval times. Same Sada Kaul for religious ceremonies, however, was 'Sada Kaul Bhatta *Dattatreya Gotra* Kas'mira *Vasse*' (Meaning Sada Kaul Brahmin of *Dattatreya Gotra* of Kas'mira); which he had to utter himself.

Proliferation of Gotra's in Kas'mira

Amazing that if only descendants of ten *Gotras* entered Kas'mira, approximately 200 *Gotras* and Sub *Gotra*s have been found listed in Kas'mira. The list in Bharatvarasha is much more. This proliferation dates back to early part of medieval period or earlier, as no *Rishi* heading a *Gotra* is chronicled to have existed during first millennium AD. A scrutiny of *Gotra* list gives you equally contradicting indications. The basic parameter was that *Gotra* remained unchanged and a girl and her progeny adopted her husband's *Gotra* as her new *Gotra*. Certain aberrations and adaptations have taken place as under:

- *Gotra* of five out of original eight (*Satpatha Brahmana)* were also adopted (*Gautama, Bhardvaja, Vasistha, Kashyapa and Atri*); rather than restricting these to only five of their descendants. Thus, descendants of following *Gotra* heads/founders in Bharatvarasha moved into Kas'mira; *Dattatreya* (Son of *Atri*), *Paladeva, Aupamanyava, Maudgalya, Dhaumyayana, Bhardvaja, Gautama, Vasistha, Atri* and *Kashyapa*) taking *Gotra* numbers to ten.
- New independent *Gotra* heads like *Shandliya, Kaushika* came up; antiquity and vintage of these *Gotras* cannot be ascertained. These

Gotras are predominant even today amongst the Brahmins of Bharatvarasha and is indication that these *Gotra's* manifested in Bharatvarasha also after the initial groups of Aryans moved to Kas'mira and smaller groups of their descendants moved in to Kas'mira much later as part of later immigration.

- Permutation combination of *Gotras,* which do not belong to *Rishi* order, came about by prefixing *Dar, Deva, Mitra, Swamin, Dat, and Raj* etc. Genesis of these remains unknown.
- Another set of *Gotras* appeared with descendants of the original *Gotras* starting their own appellation and combinations; like *Kaushika Atreya, Deva Bhardvaja Kaushika* etc.
- Matriarchal system has not been in vogue in Kas'mira, which could have possibly thrown up two *Gotras* in the same family; that of son and daughter-in-law. However, when the boy shifted as *Ghar Jamai* and like an adopted son; could be that their progeny opted for combination of two *Gotras*. A close study of *Gotras* in Kas'mira will indicate *Dar* and *Deva* prefixes do not indicate a separate *Gotra* but a respectful appellation of original *Gotra.* This is common amongst the *Gotras* of Bharatvarasha also.
- Kas'mira Brahmins perform their religious ceremonies and rites according to Vedas of *Laugakshi Rishi* and Nilamat Puranam, which gave birth to many more *Gotras* with prefix, suffix or combination with *Laugakshi Rishi* finding his way in the list of *Gotra* founders of Kas'mira. This is particular for Kas'miris only and also indicates assimilation of the original inhabitants of *Saras* (Kas'mira) in the main religious stream of then prevalent religion of Kas'mira. Nilamat Puranam (Dr. Buhler was responsible for delving the Puranam in English) is as sacred as Vedas to Kashmiris. Rituals etc are admix of Naga and Aryan customs and rites, which gives indication of mixture of Naga and Aryan blood in Kas'mira, restricted though, by way of marriages and progeny bringing another line of descendants. Recent selective genetic research all over erstwhile Bharatvarasha has shown that Aryans, when they came to Bharatvarasha, comprised more of men than women. Over a period of time they had to marry the local breed of women and thus their numbers proliferated. A mix of genes in such a case is inevitable. Similar would have been the case of cross mixing with Nagas in Kas'mira.

Earliest Settlers and Dating of Settlements

Earliest Settlers: As in other parts of the world, even in Bharatvarasha, appearance of man has been mystery, solved somewhat by recent assertions, claims and archaeological finds that Africa was the first place where *homo-sapiens* (Mankind) appeared. The timings and places of fully developed and grown humans still is controversial and debatable. In Kas'mira too it remained so. Many theories abounded; Kas'mira is the original place of Aryans,

Neolithic mankind in Kas'mira were Nagas, the people who developed from Palaeolithic (earlier or of crude Stone Age) to Neolithic and then to Megalithic man. The earliest and available scripture of Kas'mira Nilamat Puranam (4th - 6th Century AD) calls Nagas as the original inhabitants of Kas'mira and Aryans as immigrants. It is in 1935 some light could be thrown on the earliest settlers of Kas'mira. De Terra and Paterson carried out first exploration in Kas'mira and made first discovery of Burzahom settlement, hardly few kilometres from Dal Lake (ancient name Dalla), on the outskirts of Srinagar. Limited excavation by the duo yielded some black polished ware with incised designs, some bones and stone tools. These remains were attributed to 'either a late or an early phase of the Indus Culture of Bharatvarasha'. However, in subsequent decades many more similar sites were discovered (1969-70 team of Prof. Sankalia) including one pertaining to Palaeolithic age (earlier or of Rude Stone Age). These finds basically related to four distinct eras or periods. The earliest and the **first** were dwellings below ground level of earliest settlers (Neolithic) to fight the severe winters of Kas'mira. These dug outs with long stone Celts, crude hand made earthen pots, types of which even now continue to be used in the villages of Kas'mira, were found. There was no evidence pertaining to disposal of dead and absence of burials, indicating absence of rituals or large community living. Disposal of bodies in the nearby water bodies could not be ruled out. **Next stage** was the finding of number of structures of mud or mud bricks, some timber structures and floors made of rammed soil, suggesting some form of community living with peculiar burials within the settlement. The oval pits for burial were dug into the house floors or in the compounds with lime plastering pasting on bones. This period also pertains to advanced Neolithic period. The Neolithic culture of Kashmir Valley has its own distinctive traits, not shared by its counterparts from elsewhere in Bharatvarasha. Wide range of bone and stone tools, dwelling pits, perforated knife or blades, burials of animals with human skeletons and purposeful burial of only animals, mark it as something unique. Dwelling pits, application of red ochre on the dead, burials of animals with their masters, perforated knives of stone or harvesters and the characteristic bone tools has some similarity with Neolithic humans of hilly/mountainous areas of Bharatvarasha, North China, Southern portions of Central Asia, Afghanistan and Iran. It is difficult to specify a singular place of linkage. The **third** period excavations were massive commemorative stones and pertain to Megalithic culture, associated with arrival of Aryans in the valley. The **last** period is the early historical period, wherein mud brick structures and pottery made from red ware have been found. These are approximately of last few centuries of BC era, earlier than the Buddhist site of Harvan, which are ascribable to 3rd - 4th AD. The carbon dating of Neolithic era artefacts date between 2375 -1530 BC, while the last stage, apparently after Megalithic period, dates back to 120-110 BC. From the evidence found from such excavated settlements, it is difficult to specify governance system, nor any ritual, termed closed to a religion, can be fixed.

However, the findings indicate the following evidence together with reference in chronicles/scriptures :

- Neolithic humans in Kas'mira are not abrupt sightings of humans from within, as being propounded by some scholars, but from other areas.
- Some of these sites of later Neolithic period turned into minor concentrations of humans. These by all accounts are Nagas of more advanced Stone Age.
- From various artefacts, excavations, archaeological surveys, it has been found that *Manus* (Aryans) were of Advanced stage of lithic (stone) (Megalithic) period.
- Neolithic immigration in some parts of the valley and around it are *Dasayu* aborigines/tribals; *Dasayu* term used by Aryans in Rig Veda for indigenous people of Bharatvarasha. The period of Aryan immigration fits into the Megalithic period (1600 ± 200 BC) (*Manus* (Aryans) in Kas'mira), which in terms of scientific proof seems to find firm ground with the findings of artefacts of Megalithic people capping over the settlements and artefacts of Neolithic people.
- Neolithic men in the valley were primitive, as evidenced by survey and research, folklore or mention of these in scriptures as Nagas fits in well to this description.
- Recovered artefacts indicate side by side settlements of Nagas and *Manus* (Aryans). This also fits with the beliefs that due to their co-existence, *Manus* (Aryans) adopted many of the rituals and customs of Nagas and the latter picked up Aryans way of living, rituals and customs thus evolving a peculiar branch of Brahmanism. The terms used for the people who settled in Kas'mira are Nagas, *Daitayas, Pis'acas* and *Manus* (Aryans), appearing in that order. *Daitayas* and *Pis'acas*, however, developed away from Naga and Aryan settlements.

Dating of Early Human Settlements in Kas'mira

By all accounts earliest settlements of Kas'mira are Nagas of more advanced Stone Age, while *Manus* (Aryans) were Advanced stage of lithic (stone) period (Megalithic). In Aryan scriptures original inhabitants of Bharatvarasha are called *Krishna Yonis Dasayus; Krishna Yoni* referring to dark skinned inhabitants. In Bharatvarasha excavations at Harappa and many other places have thrown up civilization at their height between 2600-2500 BC, which collapsed around 2000-1800 BC. The height of the civilization also coincides with the Neolithic man in Kas'mira. This evolution of Neolithic man (Nagas) in Kas'mira, is also attributed to sudden outburst and indicates that Neolithic culture was evolved in the valley around 2600 ± 200 BC. Even Nilamat Puranam indicates the origin of the Nagas as the tribes of Northern India and that Naga Kings were from the stock of original inhabitants of Bharatvarasha and Kas'mira. Even the Naga Kings can be identified as; Gonandas or Janmejaya, a descendant of *Pandavas*. It is apparent that in

Kas'mira descendants of Nagas ruled Ka'smira as Kings in later centuries also. Verses 915 – 983 of Nilamat Puranam give the names of various Naga Kings, with prominence to Nila and Vasuki. The name of Naga Kings and Nagas to be worshipped (Kings) are fairly large and indicates that the Naga settlements were widely dispersed hamlets and their head was treated as a King. The density of these hamlets all across the valley, except in the West, seems to be fairly more. There is evidence of continued isolated Naga settlements in Kas'mira as late as 6th Century AD. As per research of later dynasties in AD era, there are clear indications of Naga Kings having ruled Kas'mira.

Saraswat Bhattas of Kas'mira and Surnames

Saraswat Bhattas: Kashmiri Brahmins from time immemorial are addressed as Bhattas. Genesis as to when generic address word Bhatta manifested for Aryan Saraswat Brahmins of Kas'mira, is not clear nor does any ancient scripture throw any specific light on it, but definitely is derivative of Brahmin, which got modified to Bhatta; referring to a religious individual; Brahmin. Bhatta honorific as form of address in the plains of Bharatvarasha and Nepal finds mention from BC era and even now is used as surname. The first time Bhatta has been chronicled was Arya Bhatta, an ancient Brahmin writer on Algebra and Astronomy, born in Kusuma-Pura (Modern Patna) in 5th Century BC (His most famous astrological work is the *Arya-Siddhanta.*). *Brahma Purana,* which quantifies attributes of a Brahmin, dates around 1000 BC and Bhatta appellation could have come about around this time or even earlier. With the advent of *Sufi* cult in Bharatvarasha, during 2nd Millennium, counterparts of *Sufis* from *Brahaminical* order were called Bhats (Guru Nanak had *Sufis* and *Bhats* as disciples). Bhat (Bhatt) surnames, phonetically though pronounced differently in different regions, are found in Uttaranchal, Northern Belt, Central and Western parts of the country and is surname of sizeable Brahmins in Konkan, Maharashtra and Gujarat; where they had migrated in sizeable strength. Bhattas who migrated to Gauda (Bengal) were called *Acharayas* (Scholars) and thus *Bhattacharayas*. In Nepal they became priests, ardent worshippers of *Bhadrakali* and spread *Kali* worship; mostly around *Pashupatinath* Temple. In Uttaranchal they became *Purohit* (Priestly) class, adopted surname *Purohit*, many changed profession but retained Bhatt surname. In Northern plains, few became Bhattas, many Bhatts; in both cases of *Purohit* (Priestly) class. In Central and Western parts, strict requirements of a Bhatta (*Purohit*) could not be sustained and to indicate their Brahmin roots they opted for surname only. Thus, Bhatta and *Purohit* are surnames of the same category. Bhatta has shortened version, Bhat (Bhatt); referring to same class of people.

Surname Bhat (Bhatt) in Kas'mira can also be traced to short form of Bhatta. In Kas'mira, Bhatta honorific has been associated with many personalities, scholars of 9th and 10th Century's, scriptures and specific in many cases in 14th Century and later. Kings, Ministers and scholars from outside Kas'mira used 'Bhatta' to refer to indigenous religious scholars, philosophers from 4th Century onwards. It is improbable that Aryan Saraswats carried this honorific when they entered Kas'mira. This honorific may have trickled to Kas'mira, about 2600 years back, 600 BC, after *Brahma Purana* had manifested 3000 years (1000 BC) back in Bharatvarasha. First chronicled form of address of 'Bhatta' in Kas'mira exists in the name of a Kashmiri Buddhist missionary, Shama Bhatta (5th Century AD), who went to China and Tibet to preach Buddhism. In 10th Century, a 8th Century scholar named Vakhpatiraja of Lalitaditya's period (697 to 733 AD - Kalhan's Rajatarangini Verse 144 Book IV)), chronicled as Vakhpati Bhatta, gets mentioned in many accounts concerning a debate with Adi Shankara (8/9th Century). During the same period we have Udhata Bhatta (774-813 AD), teacher of the theory of the three *Vrittis,* who also worked on Vedas and developed *Rasa* aesthetics by adding ninth *rasa* with '*calm*' as its basic emotion. We have this form of address for Shaiva Philosophers: Bhatta Kallata, Bhatta Pradyumana; Shakta worshippers: Rama Kantha Bhatta and Mahadev Bhatta of 9th and 10th Century's respectively; Bhatta Tota (10th Century), the learned scholar who taught Dramaturgy to Abhinav Gupta (933-1015 AD) and Bikhshana Bhatta (14th Century). By 11th and 12th Century, *Malechas, Turshkas* address was also used for reference to other lower strata denizens of Kas'mira.

Bhatta form of address as prefix continued, but there are indications that scholars, for ease of differentiation from common people, were referred by this 'Prefix honorific' like Bhatta Kallata, Bhatta Tota, etc. The 'honorific' was generic, referring to a community, carried when they migrated, used again on return and became synchronous with their caste. Noted scholar Dr Subash Kak in *Kashmiri Hindus and the Caste System* writes about Bhatta form of address;

> "Kashmiri Hindus call themselves *Batta*, from the Sanskrit *bhartri* meaning master. Such an appellation may be a reflection of the community's self-image that emphasizes success and excellence and it need not have any sociological implications. Two subgroups, that were sometimes considered to be separate, are *Buher*, and *Purib*: *Buher* (from the Kashmiri word for grocer) and *Purib* (for Easterner)."

The second part of the above statement itself is somewhat contradictory. *Varna* (Caste/class) system was prevalent amongst Aryans including Kashmiris and is nothing new. It is incorrect to imply that it did not have any sociological implications for Kashmiri Brahmins. It is that only Brahmin class got frequently mentioned but the class of followers, foot soldiers etc existed, though considered shade lower than Brahmins. Another scholar Pandit Ram Krishen Kaul avers:

> 'Pandit's of Kashmir, popularly known as 'Bhatta' all belong to *Brahmana* '*Varana*' (Caste/class). Bhatta is the *Prakrit* form of the Sanskrit *Bhartri* which means 'scholar', 'doctor' or the same as Pandit'.

Though the meaning of *Bhartri*, qualitative application is well fitting to Bhattas of Kas'mira, it was not self-image but the identity of the religion Kashmiris practiced which brought the usage of this word. During ancient and medieval period usage of Bhatta was not confined to Kas'mira only but in Bharatvarasha also. *Vedic,* the ancient language of Bharatvarasha, is the origin of *Brahman Purana* from which word Brahmin and thereafter Bhatta is derived. Word *bhartri,* in 'Classical' Sanskrit, sought to be source of word Bhatta, is of later vintage than *Vedic* ('Classical' Sanskrit, like Latin in the West, was a language of courtly poetry and drama and as learned language for religious texts only). Recent decipherment of Indus (*Sindhu*) Valley seals have somewhat changed the picture and perspective of ancient languages of Bharatvarasha including that of *Vedic*, *Sanskrit,* 'Classical' *Sanskrit* and *Brahmi. Brahmi* alphabet is the ancestor of all of the 200 or so modern Indian alphabets but is of later vintage than ancient *Khartoshi Lipi*. The earliest known inscriptions in *Brahmi* alphabet are those of the Emperor Ashoka (270-232 BC). The inscriptions on the seals found have been seen to be akin to *Vedic* language; though yet to be confirmed. But this does not affect the assertion made of the meaning and application of word *Bhatta* or *Bhartris*.

However, this *Vakh* of Lal Ded (*Lalleshwari* for Brahmins, *Lalla Arifa* for Muslims), where word Hyound (Hindu) instead of Bhatta has been reportedly used to refer to Aryan Saraswat Brahmins of Kas'mira and creates doubt that Bhatta was not the operative form of address during 13th/14th Century AD or even earlier.

"Shiv chuy thali thali rozaan, Mav zaan Hyound ta Musalman, Trukhay chukh ta pananuy paan parzaan Ada chay Saahibas zanni zaan."

Meaning that; 'Shiva abides in all that is, everywhere; Then do not discriminate between a Hindu or a Musalman. If thou are wise, know thyself; That is true knowledge of the Lord'.

Hyound (Hindu) appellation unknown at that time, (13th/14th Century), to Kas'mira has been used. These words of Lal Ded's wisdom were reportedly uttered somewhere between 1330 to 89 AD (Born 1320? – Died 89), when from all accounts word 'Hindu' was alien to Kas'mira; either it was Brahmin or Bhatta. Mention of Lal Ded for the first time, in any chronicle, is made in 1654 AD in *Asrarul - Abrar* (The Secret of Pious) by Baba Dawud Mushkati; nearly 300 years later. She gets mentioned again, in 1746 AD, in another chronicle, *Waqiate Kashmir* (Times of Kashmir); nearly 100 years later. Both these chronicles do not reproduce this *Vakh* in their contents, only she is mentioned in some detail. While word Musalman had found its moorings in Bharatvarasha right from 12th Century, with major invasions by Muslims, word *Hindu* referred to class ridden society of transited Hindu religion but not in Kas'mira, where other appellations, Bhattas, *Turshkas, Malechas* etc were prevalent. *Hyound*, a *Kashmiri* derivative of Hindu is imported, as invasion and spread of Islam progressed in Kas'mira and inhabitants of Bharatvarasha called them Hindus in later centuries of second millennium. The word Hindu (*Hyound*) and differentiation would have possibly come to Kas'mira after it had firmed in Bharatvarasha, around 1654 AD, when Lal Ded is mentioned for the first time; but definitely by 1746 AD, when she is mentioned again in *Waqiate Kashmir*. Could it be that effective portion of this *Vakh* was actually structured like *'Mav zaan Bhatta ta Musalman'?* This suggested *Vakh* has rhythm and rhyme or is it that *Vakhs*, and other *Vakhs* too, were modified with later prevalent appellations like Hindu, when recorded / written later or are actually of some other scholar of later vintage. Both are possible; for there is no evidence of word Hindu being referred as generic term for Brahmins or Bhattas of Kas'mira during Lal Ded's time. This is also confirmed by her another *Lalla Vakh*, where she uses the word Bhatta and not *Hyound*; "*Abhyaa'sy savikaa'sy layi vo'thuu, Gaganas svagun myuul samitsratta, Shunya gol Anaamay motuu, Yuhoy vopadiish chuy **Bhatta**.*" Translated: "By oft-repeated practice, the wide expanse of manifested universe is lifted to absorption; And the saguna world, of forms and qualities, merges in the vastness of the void with a splash of water on water falling; Then the ethereal void dissolves, and the Ineffable Supreme alone remains. This, O Bhatta, is the Truth to gain." Even a decade back, or may be even today, the two communities in the valley are called as *'Bhatta Ta Musalman'* and not *'Hyound Ta Musalman'*. In Kas'mira word *Hyuond* was used, even in recent times, for people coming from plains of Bharatvarasha. Even in Bharatvarasha the word was used loosely and it is only 190 years ago Raja Ram Mohan Roy coined the word Hindu, to describe the huge variety of faiths and sects with similar but not identical philosophies, myths and rituals.

This was not the first time use of Bhatta word has been chronicled to have been used. These words (*"Na Bhatto Aham"*) of distress were also uttered during the reign of Ram Dev (1252-73 AD), when some Bhattas (Brahmins) having been insulted by him, conspired to install somebody from amongst *Khashas* (People living closer to *Chandrabagha* River (Chenab)) on the throne. Their conspiracy did not remain a secret and an orgy of destruction and plunder was let loose by Rama Dev. Some were killed and others suppressed with atrocious mercilessness and to save themselves the cry was raised everywhere *'Na Bhatto Aham'*. This is the first recorded onslaught in history against the Brahmins of Kas'mira by their own Brahmin ruler. To add to this analysis there are three words of distress expression much chronicled, uttered in Sanskrit, during end of 15th Century forcible coversions to Islam at the threat of sword; *"Na Bhatto Aham"* (In Sanskrit, in a tone of distress, cried in pain and agony, meaning 'I am not a *Bhatta*'). These words gives sufficient indications that operative word and appellation was Bhatta and not Hindu (Hyound) during 15th Century.

Surnames

In due course, in addition to Bhatta appellation, surnames started trickling. Chronicles touching Kas'mira surnames are silent on aspects of origin and approximate dates/era when specific surnames started being used. Chronicles referring to surnames of some scholars from 6th to 13th Century AD refer to two types.

First, those who migrated to Kas'mira from 1st Century AD onwards and carried their surnames like; Buddhist Scholar Ava Gosha (Kanishka's time (25-60 AD). History mentions that Ava Gosha was a famous Buddhist Scholar from Patliputra. Then Atri Gupta (7th Century) who came from Ujjain during Lalitaditya's reign (697-733 AD), to his descendant Abhinav Gupta (933-1015 AD) and many others including Madhavacharya (1199-1276 AD) from South India (Also referred as Vidhyaranya and an ardent devotee of Adi Shankara (8/9th Century AD).

Second, indigenous (Kashmiris); like Bhatta Kallata (Pupil of Vasu Gupta; during reign of Avanti Varman (855-83 AD)), Bhatta Pradyumana, Bhatta Mahadev (9th-11th Century), all referred as Bhatta's without any other specific surname. From this it is clear that there were no surnames, other than 'Bhatta', till about 12th Century.

Late Pandit Anand Kaul (1870-1941 AD) in his book *'The Kashmiri Pandit'* writes: 'According to some authorities there were only three principal divisions viz., Bhat, Pandit and Razdan, from which are derived the distinctive appellations of Koul (Kaul), Sopori, Pandit and Raina. From these three families, as each took to a particular occupation or by adoption or intermarriage with other *Gotras*, other *Gotras* came into existence'.

It is essential to analyse above assertion by Pandit Anand Kaul, noted Kashmiri scholar of his time.

Kaula or Kaul from Shakta Worship: From available scriptures, Kaul surname is related to Shaivite beliefs, which peaked around 10th Century. Once Shaivism took roots, *Shakta* and *Kali* worship (more so in her form of *Bhadrakali*), started upwards during the time of Abhinav Gupta, an ardent *Shakta* worshipper and *Kali Bakhta*. The followers of *Shakta* worship, being Shaivites to the core, were called as *Kaulas*.

Sir John Woodroffe, pen name Arthur Avalon, an authority on *Shakta* (*Tantric*) worship says; "Moreover, though this does not seem to be recognised, it is never-the-less the fact that these *Kauli* (*Tantric*) rites are philosophically based on monistic doctrine. Now, it is this *Kaula* doctrine and practice, limited probably, as being a secret doctrine, at all time to comparatively few, which has come to be known as the *Tantra*."

9th to 12th Century is considered most blessed from religious point of view not only for Kas'mira but also for Brahmanical order of Bharatvarasha, when new appellation of Shaivism and Shakta worship found roots, followers and worshippers. Since majority of then Aryan Saraswat Brahmins of Kas'mira had Shaivism and *Shakta* worship as their belief, when it peaked around 11th Century AD; *Kaulas* formed bigger chunk of the population, more so after feat by Abhinav Gupta, which can be termed as the beginning of *Kauli* rites: *Aghoreshwara* (Enlightenment). Abhinav Gupta was instrumental in creating a tradition, remembered in Kas'mira to this day. He entered a cave while reciting the *Bhairavastava* along with 1200 disciples never to be seen again. This cave, which received the mortal frame of Abhinav Gupta, is situated at *Birwa* village, some five miles from Magam on the slopes of Pir Panchal range closer to Tosa Maidan. This feat, not commended initially, laid foundation of *Shakta* worship though it had just started spreading. The legend of his entering the cave, never to return has been immortalised in a folk verse in Kashmiri: "Bahshat Chaat Heth Su Bal Bramchari... Sari Heth Khot Shivlokas... Yete Khot Deh Heth... Kus Deh Dari... Abhinav Gupta Acharaya Zan." Translated: 'With his 1200 disciples this *Brahmchari* went to *Shivlok* with all of them in mortal form, who dares such a miracle. Remember only *Acharaya* Abhinav Gupta could do it.' This feat, followed by more scholarly works, religious scriptures by other scholars, Shaivism and *Shakta* worship peaked to give foundation to the appellation cum surname, Kaula; around 12th Century.

Shaivite Roots For Surnames

The other origin of Kaula surname is also being associated, erroneously though, with word *Mahakaal* (*Mahakoul* for Shiva. Shiva in Shiv Temple at Ujjain is referred as *Mahakaal*), word probably imported during time of Lalitaditya and Shaivite scholars Atri Gupta and Vasugupta, who belonged to this region. If Mahakoul appellation is the source of surname Kaul, then all the Brahmins around Ujjain would have been called Kouls or Kaulas! Pandit Ram Krishen Kaul in '*Sociology of names and Nicknames of India*' with special reference to Kas'mira mentions that:

> "The use of surnames in ancient Kashmir is negligible, Present Kashmiri surnames have more or less evolved during the Muslim and Sikh rule. It is stated that almost all the Kashmiri Pandit's were Kouls and they were later on subdivided according to different nicknames and with the passage of time, these nicknames became permanent surnames. There seems to be some truth in this statement primarily because all the Kashmiri Pandit's are Shaivites and *Mahakoul* is one of the names of Lord Shiva, and secondly because the number of nicknames even now attached with the surname Koul is largest of all. Moreover, in recent years the use of nicknames is being progressively discarded and the surname Koul is being adopted more than any other surname by almost all such people."

The first part of the statement is well carried, as the appellation then in use was Bhatta; a general honorific. However, the connectivity of *Mahakaal* to the surname Kaul gives way to more convincing Shri Kul form of Shakta worship. Another writer Dr Subash Kak in 'Kashmiri HIndus and the Caste System' writes:

"The dominant philosophical and religious system current in Kashmir is that of Shaivism. According to the texts of the Shaivites all those who accept the *Kula* (Shaivite) *dharma* become Kauls, irrespective of their background."

Here '*Kaula*' with '*Kula*' (Shaivite) *dharma* has been loosely associated and not associated with Shri Kul form of Shakta worship.

Surname Kaul: As time passed *Shakta* worship took firmer 'terrafirma', a new class of *Kaula Bhatta's* from other than *Dattatreya Gotra* came up; some kept this surname but majority had to shed it as invocation of *Gotra* during religious ceremonies gave up the game. *Dattatreyas* introduced a modified appellation; *Dattatreya Kaula Bhattas* to ensure 'other *Gotra*' *Kaula Bhattas* remain at a lower *Gotra* lineage pedestal than their own. This tinge of 'lineage vanity' still exists amongst *Dattatreyas,* who would make it a point to mention and flout *Dattatreya Gotra* etc in their *Kulawalis* (Family Tree) till today. With time other surnames in the form of nicknames within Dattatreya Kaula Bhattas came about, in most cases because of vocation; some a century or so old. Few surnames which came about this way; Bamzai (After Afghan tribe as they dealt in trade with the tribals. P N Kaul Bamzai son of Anand Kaul, Writer. His father was Tota Kaul Kardar), Kak (Headman - There are many *Gotras* for Kaks), Muhtasib (Ram Nath Kaul Muhtasib; writer of 19th Century), Pahalwan (Wrestler - Anand Ram Pahalwan, carried forward history written by Narain Kaul), Sahib (Learned Man-Sahib Kaul; writer) etc. Many Kauls associate origin of the Kauls and surname to particular places in Bharatvarasha like Kolhapur or to the temple city of Lord *Dattatreya* at Phandarpur (Both Maharashtra). Location of a particular temple always does not indicate the place of origin. One thing is certain that all Dattatreya Kaulas are pure Aryans.

Till about 14th Century we do not find association of Bhat, Pandit, Sopori Pandit, Razdan and Raina with any surname of Kashmiris. Even shortened version Bhat, for Bhatta, did not find full usage till other appellations came about in Kas'mira, as Bhatta continued to be generic form of address while Pandit appellation for Kas'mira*'s* is only few centuries old. Sopori Pandit; literally meaning 'Pandit's from Sopore', is a transitory name of 9th Century Suyapur (Sopore) town, founded by Suya, at the point where river Vitasta (Wyeth – Jhelum) leaves *Mahapadamsar* (Wular Lake) basin. Suya, a great engineer during Utpal Dynasty (9th Century), cleared obstructions in Vitasta (*Wyeth* – Jhelum) from *Mahapadamsar* basin to Varhamulla (Baramulla).

There is mention in Jonaraja Rajatarangini of the existence of a temple in *Mahapadamsar* and its bronze images recovered during the reign of Zain-ul-Abidin's period in detail. It has not been possible to trace the final disposal of these idols but these could possibly have been installed in nearby town of Suyapur (Sopore). Legend in Sopore says that the Shiva temple constructed on the banks of *Wyeth* (Jhelum) dates back to time when idols were found from *Mahapadamsar* (Wular Lake). The area of this *Mandir*, called *Shivpur* by many residents of this area, gave surname of *Shivpuri* to the denizens of the area. It is a fallacy that *Sihvpuris* came from *Shivpuri* (Near Gwalior - Madhya Bharat). Many residents of Sopore, identifying themselves as residents of this apple town, adopted transited name *Sopori* as surname and it was not the original surname or appellation. Even then name, as recorded in many chronicles, was Suyapur.

During 17th and early 18th Century names of many places in Kas'mira were changed during the process of Islamisation of Kas'mira and when pronounciation based on Kashmiri Language were adopted; *Suyapur* to Sopore (Pronounced in Kas'mira as *Sopur*), *Varhamullah* to Baramulla, pronounced in Kas'mira as *Varamull*, *Padampore* to Pampore/Pompur. Even Anantnag was named as Islamabad and it is only during Dogra rule that the name of Anantnag was restored in official papers. This is the time Shankaracharya Hill was called *Takht-e-Suleman* etc. *Baharistan -i- Shahi* (Persian) which enjoys the status of being the first fully detailed history of Kas'mira in Persian, written in 1614 AD, however, mentions name Sopur (Sopore), which is indicative of changes in name of place around 17th Century. *Baharistan-i-Shahi* seldom uses place names connected with Brahmins or Gods by their original name, being purely a Muslim history. (Three other historical works in Persian were written before *Baharistan-i-Shahi* and these were those of *Mulla Naderi, Qazi Ibrahim* and *Mulla Hasan Qari* but are lost and merely find mention in some old Persian chronicles and works). In fact *Sopori Pandit* and *Sopori Bhatta* address is 'sarcastic' mention of social behaviour than surname; for *Sopori Mazrath* (Hospitality) or *Sopori Bhatta Mazrath* refers to lip service hospitality. *Mazrath,* a mixed word from Persian, also indicates its later vintage.

Secondly; Pandit appellation as 'Suffix' came about in the plains of Bharatvarasha after 15th Century and as 'Prefix' in 18th Century. The origin of Pandit appellation is in the plains of Bharatvarasha and there is no evidence of it being of indigenous origin or used in Kas'mira before ex-migrant Kashmiris imported this as honorific. Similarly Pandit or Pandita appellation is generally restricted to unattached, isolated areas and selective villages and towns. Some names in later chronicles of 15th Century and later, even of recent vintage, have used Pandit appellation as suffix for some of our scholars of 15th Century, especially those during Zain-ul-Abidin's time; like Soma Pandit (Dramatist, musician and who was in charge of the Translation Department. Not to be mistaken with Soma Chandra *alias* Musa Raina, a convertee from Brahminism to Islam) who held distinguished position in the royal court of Zain-ul-Abidin (Soma Pandit authored '*Jaina Charitra*', which gives account of the Zain-ul-Abidin's reign). Since Pandit appellation had manifested in Bharatvarasha, it appears that Soma Pandit, was possibly one of the returnees to the valley with this suffix, for he was well versed in Persian, Tibetan and Sanskrit. He translated many Persian books into Sanskrit and for the first time *Mahabharata* and Rajatarangini were translated into Persian under his supervision. Pandita form of prefix address is not borne by authentically recorded chronicles of that era.

Pandit or Pandita addenda apparently have been added for names in later chronicles, which did not have any suffix or prefix when lineage and surnames were flouted. Even today one finds members of the same family having different surname; one Raina another Pandit. In later centuries some learned Brahmins in the valley had also got this addendum, in fact many addressed their family *Gurujis* as *Pandit Jee*. This is what Jia Lal Kilam, noted scholar writes in 'A History of Kashmiri Pandit's':

> "Thus the Kashmiri Pandit took his birth in his modern shape, though till then the name Kashmiri Pandit was not coined to describe this community which was described as Bhatta. Even now a Kashmiri Pandit at home describes himself as a Bhatta and it is by this name that he is described by others in Kashmir."

Thirdly; *Razdan* coined during Zain-ul-Abidin's time meant 'Royal Palace'. Actually he had constructed a palace called *Zoon Dub,* but was referred to as *Razdan* (*Raz* or *Razah* – King; *Dan* – Hearth (*Dan –Dhan*). and *Dhan* is Sanskrit word. Later *Razdan* was also referred to 'Keeper of Royal Secrets', which is more of an occupational nickname (*Reche*) for services rendered to ruling class during Muslim rule and not an ancient appellation. First time any surname other than Bhatta (Kaula; Kaul), gets mentioned is in the chronicles of Sultan Zain-ul-Abidin (1420 -74 AD). Even during this time Bhat, short for Bhatta, also was not commonly used. Shriya Bhatta (Not Shri Bhat) is the name mentioned in Jonaraja's updated Rajatarangini, when Jonaraja was alive and witness to Shriya Bhatta's feat of curing Zain-ul-Abidin. Another name Tejeh Bhat, foster-brother of Koteh Ren, also finds mention during Rinchen's time (1324- 26 AD). Shrivara's Rajatarangini (Covering 1459-1486 AD), mentions surname Bhatta (Simha, Ruppa, Karupar) who held most of the ministries during reign of Sultan Zain-ul-Abidin and Kaula (Kaul) in his chronicle. Even Praja Bhatta (Updated Rajatarangini 1486 – 1513 AD) was known as Bhatta. (Rajatarangini by Praja Bhatta has been lost for ever, though its existence finds mention in various chronicles. Some excerpts from this chronicle have been quoted in few 17th Century chronicles). It appears that Bhatta honorific address continued even in 17th Century, where we have famous Shaiva philosopher of the period; Bal Bhatta quoted in many chronicles. Kaul's were specifically mentioned during Zain-ul-Abidin's reign:

> "Madho Kaul, in charge of Northern province, Ganesh Kaul in charge of the Southern both were responsible to an inter-provincial head known as *Sadar Qanungo* by name Gopala Kaul. Under their supervision huge irrigation schemes were undertaken.

Lal Kuhl, Shah Kuhl exists even up to this day."

Though Bhatta honorific in Kas'mira, dating at least to 9th Century, is ante surname Kaul, but Kaul surname chronicled during Zain-ul-Abidin's time indicates that Kaul surname already existed, few centuries earlier.We also find Bhatta and Kaul surnames associated with some noted personalities of Kas'mira, other than those who were associated with administration during this period. One such was Keshava Bhatta, a scholar, poet and logician who went to Calcutta, where he had a discussion with Lord Gauranga (Chaitanya; Also called Chaitanya Mahaprabhu), subsequently became his devoted follower and later established his headquarters at Vrindavan (Mathura) to spread teachings of Chaitanya Mahaprabhu. Similarly Purshotam Kaul was head of an institution, where training in all branches of Sanskrit learning was imparted to students free of cost.

Fourthly; during the later part of first millennium AD, a custom prevailed in Kas'mira. Title Rajanaka, which later transited to *Renu* (Kalhan's Rajatarangini Verse 489 Book IV), was granted and appended to names of few as a mark of respect and distinction. Families subsequently carried title '*Renu*', when other surnames started sprouting. In 1325 AD, *Renu* was the appellation Rinchen bestowed to Ravan Chand, after marrying his sister Koteh Ren. Raina (Master and Possessor) is later appellation of *Renu*; names like Shringhar Raina (Malik Shankar Raina-Commander of Fateh Shah's army (1517 AD)), Sehej Raina (Nephew of Koteh Ren). Musa Raina (Converted *Kashmiri* notable, Soma Chandra before conversion) was bestowed with title of Malik, granted a *Jagir* bestowment with title *Renu*., which subsequently became Raina, after he became Chief Vazir of the Sikandar, the *But Shikan* (Idol Breaker). 'Malik' was an honorific granted to many Muslims and one odd Brahmin amongst high-ranking officials of Muslim reign, for their services especially for fighting opponents of the regime with valour; like Malik Sehej and Malik Avtar (Nephew of Koteh Ren). This appellation of Malik was subsequently carried as surname by both communities from around 14th Century.

Changes in Surnames Mid 14th Century Onwards: Advent of Islam came to Kas'mira during mid 14th Century and in its wake brought various types of clans (Persian, Afghan, Iraqi and even few Arabs), who used clan names, origins or religious beliefs, order, followings for their own form of address or identification and as surname; like *Naqashbandi's* (Named after the cult order), *Shahmiri* (Descendants of Shah Mir), *Hamdani* (Descendants of Mir Ali Hamdani (Shah-e-Hamdan)), Bamzai (Afghani clan) etc. The process of using surname amongst Muslims peaked during end 15th Century, when nearly 90 per cent of the converts had surname depending on their following of Muslim religious order, sect beliefs and vocation. Most of the neo-Muslims (Converted Bhattas), who did not have any addendum surnames simply opted for shortened version of Bhat (Bhatta). Selective methodology of identification by Muslims affected the broad spectrum of form of address of Kashmiris and slowly surnames based on vocation, residence, physical features, etc. started creeping. Most of the time it was the form of address used by his fellow religionists or ex-coreligionists (Converters), respectful or even in disdain, which stuck. Those who had maintained their reputation and respect continued to be addressed as Bhatta, Bhat or Kaula Bhatta (Kaul). This does not mean that Bhatta honorific continued for long or Kaul surname came around during Zain-ul-Abidin's reign only. By early 16th Century both appellations were common and few other surnames, mostly by converting *Khitahbs* (Honour Titles) into surnames, had surfaced amongst Aryan Saraswat Brahmins of Kas'mira.

Other Surnames: Most of the surnames other than, Bhatta, Bhat, Raina, Razdan, Renu, came about based on vocation, appearance, location or place of stay or village, even funny *Reche* (Nickname). It is difficult to establish genesis or the origin of other surnames. However, it is possible to find the origin of Dhar surname, due to the fact that clan of Dhars are next to Bhatta or Bhat, Kaul's in number. The genesis in outline is that Dhar was the honorific given to a village head, strongman or a warlord of smaller *jagir/* estate; called *Dara* pronounced as *Dhara*. This honorific was prevalent during 12th Century (Jai Simha-1128-55 AD) and continued to be used till about 14th Century. With the advent of Islam many such *Daras* converted and to differentiate themselves from Brahmin *Daras*, these convertees to Islam modified it to Dar, while Brahmins persisted with Dhar. First time Dhar (Dar) surnames are mentioned in any chronicle are Malik Bahram Dar and another Saif Dar; both during the time of Musa Raina (16th Century). A Kas'miri scholar has propounded that Dhars (Not Dars) were those who migrated to Gauda (Bengal) and retained their Dhar surname, once they returned to the valley. This assertion has no basis or proof. Dhars (Dars) are not only found in Bengal but also in Gujarat, Konkan, many places in Maharashtra and all are not Brahmins. It is essential to understand that writing or mentioning these surnames in then prevalent script Sharda or *Upbrahmbasha* or spoken language introduced subtle discrepancy in pronunciation, more so if it was uttered in Sanskrit, which got distorted while speaking in Kashmiri. The other reason is as mentioned above i.e differentiating between two community surnames (Brahmins as Dhars and Muslims as Dar). Thus, between 12th and 13th Century transition of few surnames in the shape of Honorofic's had come about in Kas'mira; from Bhatta to selective *Gotras*; general class as Kaulas. Ideally it was time for religion to take deep roots, refinement and transition of surnames but turmoil due to conversions in 14th Century put this on the back burner.

2

Kas'mira in Nilamat Puranam

May benediction of the Gods approach us, holy, to aid us with all rapid succours. Therewith may we be happily befriended, and pass triumphant over all our troubles.

Rig Veda 10- 31-1

(This chapter of heritage history of Kas'mira, *sanskars* of Kaulas *Aghoreshwara's* –Enlightened), Many words like Kas'mira (Kashmir), Kas'yapa (Kashyapa Rishi) etc. have been spelled as they were in our scriptures)

Kas'mira in Nilamat Puranam

The Vale of Gods – Kas'mira: Sanskrit poet Kalidasa writes about Kas'mira thus; (Translated) "The place is more beautiful than the heaven and is the benefactor of supreme bliss and happiness. It seems to me that I am taking a bath in the lake of nectar here." Kalhan pays tribute to Kas'mira in Rajatarangini (Verse 36 Book I), written by the chronicler between 1148-50 AD) (Translated); "There even to this day drops of sandal ointment offered by the Gods are to be seen at *Nandikshetra*, the residence of Shiva." He associates *Nandikshetra*, area of snow-clad mountains of Dras, Mahadev, Baltal and Amarkanth as abode of Shiva in Kas'mira. He further describes Kas'mira as (Translated); **"It is a country where the sun shines mildly, being the place created by Kas'yapa (Kashyapa Rishi), for his glory – big and lofty houses, learning, Saffron, icy cool water and grapes rare in Heaven are plentiful here – Kailash (Here he refers to Shiva's abode in *Nandikshetra*) is the best place in the three worlds (Tri-lok), Himalayas the best place in Kailash, and Kas'mira the best place in Himalayas."** Ancient Greeks called Kashmir '**Kasperia**' and the Chinese pilgrim Huan-Tsang, who visited the valley around 631 AD, called it "**KaShi-Mi-Lo**." Sir Walter Lawrence writes; "The valley is an emerald set in pearls; a land of lakes, clear streams, green turf, magnificent trees and mighty mountains where the air is cool, and the water sweet ...." Sir Francis Young Husband, adventurer, who blazed trail across Himalayas writes about a temple in Kashmir: "...... built on the most sublime site occupied by any building in the world-finer than the site of Parthenon, or of the Taj Mahal, or of Saint Peters or of the Escurial.....perfectly open, and even plain, gently sloping away from a background of a snowy mountains looking directly out.....the snowy ranges which bound it-so situated in fact as to be encircled, yet not overwhelmed by snowy mountains-stand the ruins of a temple second only to the Egyptians in massiveness and strength, and to the Greeks in elegance and grace..... No one without an eye for natural beauty would have chosen that special site for the construction of a temple ..." Possibly his reference here is to the great Sun Temple of Martand.

Nilamat Puranam: Our sacred religious scripture, Nilamat Puranam, is one of the famous Puranas that deals with the Valley of Kas'mira in respect of its creation, original inhabitants; Nagas, *Daitayas, Pis'acas* and *Manus* (Aryans; Aryan Saraswat Brahmins), style of living of Nagas and Aryans, religion, customs, festivals and topography. It peeps into the ancient history of Kas'mira, delves into many other aspects of the valley; its importance, customs of our ancestors, evolution of Kas'mira, its sacred rivers and lots more. In all there are 1453 verses. With passage of time some verses and parts thereof are missing. From its very composition it does not appear to be a work of a *Rishi* nor completed in one long sitting. Nilamat Puranam is named after the King Nila, Nagas of the Nagar dynasty that ruled Kashmir, however, at the end of the Puranam it reads (Translated); "This is Vitasta *Mahatmaya*. This treatise named the Nilamata is complete." The numerous *Mahatmyas* of Kas'mira are interesting sources of early historical geography; describe topography of the valley, the ancient nomenclature and various other facets of Kas'mira. Among the 51 *Mahatmyas*, traced during 19th Century, the Vitasta *Mahatmaya* (Nilamat Puranam) is the longest one; divided into 35 *Patalas* (Chapters). While many of these *Mahatmyas* are reasonably old or copied from originals, dating few centuries old, many have been compiled/composed during the 18th Century. *Mahatmyas* generally set forth the different legends connected with various places of pilgrimage, the merit to be appeared by their visits and the rites to be performed in each of the sites. They contain many early materials and local traditions and are thus valuable for a systematic study of Kas'mira.

Nilamat Puranam describes sixty-five rituals and festivals, which were celebrated, with great devotion, faith, pomp and show in Kas'mira by Kashmiri Brahmins (Aryans). Some of the rituals and festivals find mention in other Puranas. Some of these are celebrated, even today, in Kas'mira only; like *Kaw Poonim* and *Yaksha Mavas (Kechi Mavas)*. There is a general impression, even amongst Kashmiri Scholars that the Puranam talks of rituals and festivals of Naga's, subsequently adopted by Aryan Saraswat Brahmins of Kas'mira, which is not so. Many of the rituals, festivals and days mentioned in the Nilamat Puranam are common with those being followed by Aryans in Bharatvarasha, or emanating from Vedas. Thus Nilamat Puranam contains a mix of rituals those of Nagas, ones brought by Aryans and some followed by *Dasayu's* (Original inhabitants of Bharatvarasha, as they are referred in Vedas) before Aryans came to Bharatvarasha.

There is also an impression that Nilamat Puranam is completely Naga centric; not so. Admittedly there are certain places, rivers and few Naga Kings who are mentioned and are to be venerated. But Nilamat is full of mention of various Gods and Goddesses, who manifested specifically in Bharatvarasha like Durga, Bhadrakali, Shiva, etc. This is an indicator that Nilamat, while keeping the Naga's in view, has specific rituals connected with the God's and Goddesses of Bharatvarasha as well as Aryans. A specific mention of equating Naga King Nila with Indira, clearly connects it to Veda Gods and Goddesses, wherein Indira holds the prime position of God of Gods. Vedas talk about rivers, which have been imported in the Nilamat, like Ganga, Yamuna etc. Similarly *Gotra* heads like Vasishta, Pulastya, Agasta etc. have been mentioned, who have been associated with the *Gotras* of the Aryans, when they settled along the Saraswati Bank Ashrams. Places like Mathura, Prayaga etc. are also mentioned, which strengthens the argument of Nilamat having Naga, Aryan and *Dasayu's* connection. There is erroneous impression that Nilamat lays down details of rituals connected with day to day life or important events. Kas'mira's Aryan Saraswat Brahmins follow the rituals, etc. as laid down in *Laugakshi Rishi* Veda. For instance *Laugakshi Rishi's* Veda lays down 24 rituals pertaining to birth of a boy; from birth to adulthood, out of which 8 rituals are still carried out by Kashmiri Brahmins. In case of girls there are 8 rituals connected with birth to adulthood and mostly are adhered to even to this day. Use of Brahmincal calendar (Bright Moon and Dark Moon fortnight) in the Puranam, which was started in Bharatvarasha, indicates this umbilical cord to *Vedic* period and *Vedic* Aryans.

Kalhan, the great chronicler, has taken help from Nilamat Puranam for his Rajatarangini, text of which was unearthed in 1890 AD in the hand writing of Rajanaka Ratanakantha (16th Century). Kalhan traced four Kings/rulers or guardians of minor Kings of Kas'mira from Nilamat: Gonanda I, Damodar, Queen Yasomati and her son Gonanda II. He has quoted Nilamat Puranam in his memorable Rajatarangini in these words (Translated): 'That land is Protected by Nila, the lord of all the Nagas, whose regal parasol is formed by the circular pond (of the Nilakunda) with the Vitastas newly rising stream as its stick' (The circular pond of Nilakunda (Verinag) was turned into a octagonal one during the reign of Jehangir (1605-1627 AD)).

Author of Nilamat Puranam is not known nor mentioned anywhere in Nilamat or any other scripture or chronicle. It is only from conjectures, analysis of Nilamat Puranam's contents, language, environment, detailed description of customs and religious factors included in the scripture that this epical work can be attributed to an Aryan Saraswat Brahmin of Kas'mira. Similarly the period when this was composed has brought differing views on its antiquity, ranging from 500 BC to 4-6th Century AD. One can, however, be sure that the language employed originally has remained somewhat intact, during the course of centuries, till the time the composition has been actually recorded in black and white. The narration is of high scholarly content and grammatically correct in nature.

Pre BC Authorship: Gautam Buddha (May 623-547 BC) is mentioned as incarnation of Vishnu in the Puranam, even though the verse is in 'future tense' (Verses 709-715). Verses 709-710 state thus (Translated); 'O Brahman, the God Vishnu, the lord of the world, shall be (born as) the preceptor of the world, Buddha by name, at the time when the *Pusya* (*Nakshatra*) is joined with the moon, in the month of *Vaisaksha* (Baïsakh), in twenty eighth Kali Age'. Verses 710b-12 also mentions Buddha (Translated); 'Listen from as to how his worship should be performed in the bright-half, from that period onwards, in future. The image of Buddha should be bathed (with water rendered holy) with all medicinal herbs, all jewels and all scents, in accordance with the sayings of the *Sakyas* (Buddhist Monks/Scholars). The 'dwellings of the *Sakyas* (*Viharas*) should be whitewashed with care'. Based on these verses antiquity of the scripture is taken as pre BC effort, which is not so. The contents of the verses quoted above are so phrased that it talks of an era in future tense, much earlier than the actual birth of Buddha and words 'shall be born' have been used. There were no *Sakya's* or *Vihara*'s or use of these nomenclatures before birth of Buddha. They came up after he had renounced the worldly ties and taken to meditation. *Sakyas* (Buddhist Monks) and *Viharas* (Buddhist Places of Worship and Stay) increased in numbers, in Bharatvarasha, much after Buddha and even after King Ashoka (273-232 BC). *Sakyas* initially came to the valley in trickle, their numbers increasing at the fag end of BC era and Kanishka's time (AD). Similarly, dwellings of *Sakyas*, *Viharas,* came up in good numbers from 1st Century AD onwards for a century or so. The verses talk of white washing of 'dwellings of *Sakyas*, *Viharas,* therefore indicator of an AD effort. Had it been BC effort Nilamat would have mentioned Adi-Shankara (of 5th Century BC), who for Brahmins was on equal footing with that of Buddha. It also does not speak about Kas'mira King Gopaditya (417-357 BC), who established *Gopadiri Agrahara* (Shankaracharaya) or King Kanishka (100 AD), Kas'mira ruler who gave impetus to Buddhism in the valley. The verse also talks of 28th Kali Age (*Yug*). The calendar talked about in Kashmir was Saptrishi and

Kali Yug is 25 years before Sapatrishi. This date connotes 3rd year of Sapatrishi Samvat which is more than 2400 years before the actual birth of Buddha. The fact remains that even the author of Nilamat Puranam could not have forecast the birth of Lord Buddha.

Now about the script used in the scripture. The existence of Kharosthi script (Khartoshi- written from right to left) numerals on Motif Tiles found at Harvan Excavations depict inscriptions in Kharosthi (Khartoshi). These afford reliable clue to the date of the tiles and the script in vogue during that time i.e. Kharosthi (Khartoshi) script. The inscriptions of the Kharosthi (Khartoshi) script, found at Harvan, being in fully developed form, indicate that the script must have been in vogue for considerable period in Kas'mira from earlier period, which ceased to be in vogue by about 5th Century AD in Northwestern India including Kas'mira, where it had flourished. Though it is difficult to assess this period, taking it that the script was 'born' somewhere in 9th Century BC, safely its usage in Kas'mira can be 9th Century BC to around 300 AD. With the contents and scripts found, it is evident that the Puranam was not written in Khartoshi (Kharosthi). Other subtle indicators are that pre BC era had lot of stress on eating of wild game, which is not mentioned in Nilamat Puranam, a practice which declined closer to AD era, as cultivation of rice and barley picked up, which find mention in the scripture.

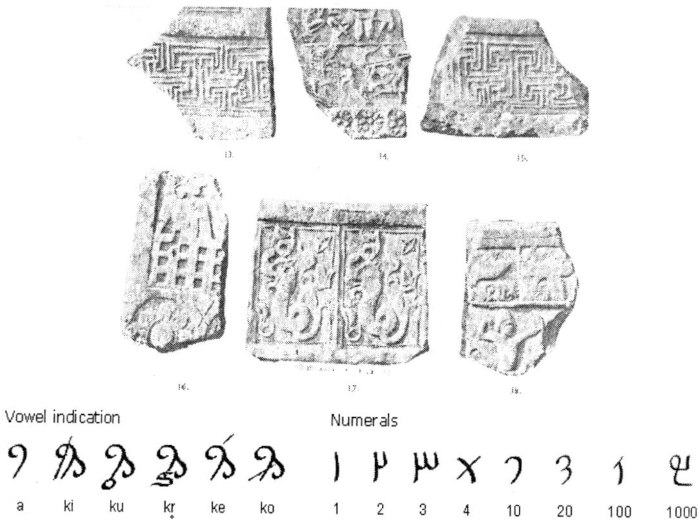

Harvan Motif Tiles Showing Kharshoti (Khartoshi) Writings.

AD Effort: Analysis of the contents, grammar used in this scripture and the language clearly indicates it having been written in highly grammatical Sanskrit and thus an AD effort. Buddhism started in Kas'mira from the time of Ashoka, who extended full control over Kas'mira, which continued till end of 100 AD with Kushan dynasty; Kanishka, Huska, Juska, Abhimanyu, Vibhisana I, Indrajit, Ravana, Vibhisana II. Buddhism continued further for a while till about 300 BC and thereafter Buddhism was on a downslide till about 515 AD, when Mihir Kula (515-550 AD), a Hun General, ascended the throne. Mihir Kula finds mention in the history of Kas'mira for his cruelty, when he killed hundreds of elephants in the forests east of Tral and more or less elephants became extinct in Kas'mira during this period. A flicker of renaissance of Brahmanism started around this time when Pravarsena II (6th Century AD) ruled the valley and this period can be taken as the era of full revival of Brahminism in Kas'mira. Pravarsena II installed *Sri Chakra* at Chakrashwar, established present city of Srinagar naming it Pravarpura, built first *Nav Setu* (Bridge) near *Maisuma* over Vitasta and gave impetus to Brahminism. However, *Sri Chakra* (*Chakrashwar*) installed by Pravarsena II is not mentioned anywhere in Nilamat Puranam as *Sharika* or *Sri Chakra* but mentions *Puja* of *Durga*. King Gopaditya (Early 7th Century), sixth in line after Mihir Kula, expelled Brahmins. The reason was that during Mihir Kula's reign many shameless practices were ascribed to them and had gone wayward. King Gopaditya invited Brahmins from outside to Kas'mira with earnest desire to give impetus to Brahminism and bring back Brahminic religious fervour in purified form. This was also the time when Buddhism had decayed. Thousands of monasteries were burnt and thousands of villages that supported those monasteries were given over to the Brahmins. It is during this period that Brahmins (Aryans) and Nagas joined together to kill Buddhists in larger numbers. This indicates continued dwellings of Nagas till about 7th Century. Brahmins having succeeded in establishing their supremacy, though gradually, set themselves in right earnest in strengthening themselves and their position. Many superstitious observances and practices were invented and scripture writing became important to revive the religion. Re-conversions from Buddhism to Brahminism were order of the day. Scholarly works of Brahminism picked up good points of Buddhism and incorporated in their rituals and scriptures. Brahminism in Kas'mira began its growth and this period saw many Kas'miri scholars (Buddhists as well as Brahmins) like Kumarjiva (Later part of Chin Dynasty 384- 417 AD), Shakyashi Badhri (405 AD), Ratna Veera, Shama Bhatta on the scene. Most importantly, Chandracharaya, a Sanskrit Grammarian, had come on the scene to give impetus to Sanskrit, which started developing after Khartoshi (Kharoshti) was passing into oblivion.

The time was ripe; Buddha and Buddhism had spread and decayed but Buddha's stature remained not only in Bharatvarasha but Kas'mira also. Brahminism started to spread again in Kas'mira. Sanskrit for writing scriptures had spread and the rulers were either Brahmins or inclined favourably towards Brahmins. During 627 – 761 AD Karkota Dynasty (Founder Durlabha Vardhana) re-established roots of Brahminism and most importantly brought Vaishnavite Philosophy to Kas'mira, which flourished further during the rule of Lalitaditya Muktapira (697-733 AD - Karkota Dynasty). This Vaishnavite philosophy is evident from the contents of the Puranam. It is evident that verses connected with Buddha in Nilamat Puranam have been included to fall in line with the accepted Vaishnavite belief in the incarnation (*Avatra-ship*) of Buddha in the rest of India in 5th Century AD. This is also confirmed by King Lalitaditya Muktapira's reign (697-733 AD), wherein being a King of Vaishnavite Philosophy tolerated Buddhism and never allowed remaining *Sakyas* and *Viharas* to be converted. The aim of the above narration including chronology of Kings is to place the environment, language and era which was fit for the conceptualisation of Nilamat Puranam.

The contents of the scripture has very brief mention of Buddhist or vegetarian habits in rituals, which indicates of waning and not ascending Buddhist philosophy; an AD era event. At places drinking on some of the festivals is mentioned, this can safely and surely indicate era of its writing to just before Gopaditya's/Pravarsena's time, as Brahmins had adopted shameless methods, which even forced Gopaditya to expel them and bring in Brahmins from outside. *Bhadrakali Puja* started in Bharatvarasha somewhere at the end of 3rd Century AD, though Goddess Bhadrakali had manifested earlier but rituals connected with her *Puja* had taken a back seat during the spread of Buddhism for obvious reasons of Buddhist's reluctance to adhere or talk of such rituals connected with Bhadrakali; animal sacrifice. There is specific mention of *Bhadrakali Puja* in Nilamat Puranam (Verse 674) (Translated); 'On that very 9th (Caitra; Chaitra), the purified man, observing fast, should worship Bhadrakali with plenty of flowers, incense and grains)'. Verse 675 (Translated); 'Bhadrakali who rules over the gods, should be worshipped on all the 9 days, (but) he who worships her on that (9th), obtains success in his undertakings)', which would have been included when *Bhadrakali Puja* had gained ground; somewhere in 4th and 5th Century AD. However, the effect of Buddhist philosophy of no animal sacrifices or meat is evident from these verses, which can be attributed to era closer to waning of Buddhist era rather than pre BC era, when sacrifices were order of the day. This was so not only in Kas'mira but whole of Bharatvarasha also. There is also mention of visit to courtesans by sporting men on certain days/functions. From various chronicles, such system is an AD era ritual, more so when Brahmins, even Kings, had adopted wayward methods of this nature, which were prominent just before Pravarsena II and Gopaditya's (early 7th Century) time. There is also no mention of another Adi Shankara (May/Jun 788 – May/Jun 820 AD) or his Shaivite rituals, philosophy in the scripture, which precludes it to be 9th Century effort Nilamat Puranam does not give us clear-cut monism; it has just paved the way for the Monistic Shaiva Philosophy of Kas'mira, thus confirming its writing during the later Vaishnavite period (5th Century), when this philosophy had just started taking rounds. Thus, lower limit of the date of writing of the Puranam may be Sixth Century BC and the upper one about the Fourth/Fifth Century AD, as Buddha, who finds mention for being worshipped as incarnation of Vishnu began from about Fourth/ Fifth Century AD. The textual study of the work shows that some alterations and additions may have been made in it, after the ninth or tenth century AD, in order to incorporate few rituals of the monistic Shaivite Philosophy of Kas'mira. Had Nilamat Puranam been composed during or after the ninth century AD there would have been more mention of monistic Shaivite Philosophy and rituals connected with it. In fact, there is lot of mention of Lord Shiva and his consort but few rituals connected with *Shiv-Parvati Pujan.*

The absence of the term '*Avatara*' and the use of the term '*Pradurbhava*' for incarnation of gods, non-mention of Kalki, Krishna's consort Radha, mention of sacred leaf of Tulsi, of Buddha as an incarnation of Vishnu in a spirit of catholicity and incorporation of its various verses into the Brahma Purana long before the time of Laxman Dev (1279-1293 AD) further indicate its date as above. It is possible that a Buddhist Scholar converted to Brahminism in 4th or 5th Century is the author of Nilamat Puranam, who wanted to remain anonymous due to his earlier religious inclinations. This is somewhat confirmed by other indicators and subtle contents; importance of Purnima's, admix of Brahmincal, Naga and Buddhist rituals. Dr Buhler, a German Scholar who travelled in Bharatvarasha and Kas'mira during mid 19th Century, gets the credit of saving its manuscript, states on page 41 of his Report, 'Its great value lies therein that it is a real mine of information regarding the sacred places of Kashmir and their legends which are required to explain the Rajatarangini and that it shows how Kalhan has used his sources'. The Nilamat Puranam was first published in 1924 with the joint effort of Professor R L Konjilal and Professor Jagdhar Zadoo. Some of the particular contents of Nilamat that may interest any present day reader are:

- A circular pattern drawn on the ground on which a 'Kas'mira' bridegroom has to stand (*Yuog*) before leaving his house or on entering the house of the bride for his marriage and finally on return stand with his bride is a direct descendant of *'Bhumisudha'* mentioned in the Puranam.
- Of the items of dress, mention may be made of *'Pravarana'*, which seems to be the same as *'Pravara'* mentioned in the *Mahabharata* as a cloth offering protection against cold. Kas'mira '*Pheran*' is most probably derived from '*Pravarana*' as mentioned in Puranam.

Kas'mira: The narration in Nilamat Puranam starts with the importance of Kas'mira during *Mahabharata* war, in the form of conversation between

King Janamejaya and Vyasa's pupil Vaisampayana. Sage Vyasa who wrote *Mahabharata*, is considered a *Rishi* and his pupil Vaisampayana answers King Janamejaya's questions in the Puranam. Puranas are written in the descriptive form, wherein two persons converse in question and answer style, as is in the case of Nilamat Puranam. The King (Janamejaya), a later descendant of Pandavas, asks Vaisampayana as to why king of Kas'mira did not participate in *Mahabharata* War since Kas'mira occupied an important place in the world at that time and why support of King of Kas'mira was not sought either by Pandu or Dhrtarashtra, while kings of various other countries, great heroes, came to the great *Bharata* war (*Mahabharata*) of his forefathers? Two words *Bharata* and *Kas'mira* figure in the narration of Nilamat Puranam right from the beginning. The reply is that the king of Kas'mira, accompanied by his army, did attend the *Suyamvara* to fight Madhava, son of Vasudeva. A fight between him and Vasudeva took place and consequently he was 'thrown down' (Killed) by Vasudeva in the combat. Out of respect for Kas'mira, coronation of his pregnant queen Yasomati was done by Vasudeva, so that posthumous child rules Kas'mira. The queen gave birth to a male child who was named Gonanda (Mostly mentioned as Gonanda II). This era, mentioned in Nilamat nearly coincides with Mahabharata war and Kalhan too begins his accounts in Rajatarangini around this event and writes about installation of Queen Yasomati on the throne of Kas'mira, as the guardian of her son King Gonanda II, by Lord Krishna.

The importance of Kas'mira requiring Vasudeva himself to coronate a woman is best narrated in Nilamat Puranam saying (Translated) "O best amongst the kings, the goddess Uma is the same as Kas'mira. What was formerly, an enjoyable, heart-enrapturing lake for six Manvantaras (Each Manvantara is said to comprise 122,688,000 years) since the beginning of the *Kalpa* (Universe), became a beautiful territory in this Manvantara." As per scriptures it was only in the later part of last (Seventh *Manavantara*) that the mountains near *Varahkshetra* (Varhamulla, Baramulla; literally means pig's snout); was broken open by the plough of Ananta (Naga King) to let out the water and valley reclaimed. He (Vaisampayana) then praises the beauty of Kas'mira (Translated); "O protector of men! all sacred places, which are on the earth, are there. Thronged with the hermitages of the sages, it is pleasant in heat and cold and is auspicious..... Not dependent on rains, enjoyable, holy, beneficial for living beings, endowed with the qualities (of producing) all grains....." Addressing King Janamejaya, he talks about the lakes and rivers of Kas'mira (Translated); "The holy region of Kas'mira is possessed of all the sacred places. There are sacred lakes of the Nagas and the holy mountains; there are holy rivers and also the holy lakes; there are highly sacred temples and also the hermitages attached to them. In the centre flows, making as it were the parting of the hair, the Vitasta - the highest goddess visibly born of the Himalaya." The name of Kas'mira does not occur in the Vedic literature. In Rig Veda, there is a hymn, which mentions the name of Vitasta (Wyeth (Also Vyath), Jhelum). Among the epics, we find the name of Kas'mira in the *Ramayana* and the *Mahabharata*. The *Mahabharata* refers in several passages to Kas'mira and their king, but in a way, which merely indicates that the valley was situated in the hilly regions to the north of Bharatvarasha.

Kas'mira Name, Sacred Rivers Sindhu, Vitasta (Wyeth, Jhelum)

Kas'mira Name: We all know that Kashmir is named after Kas'yapa, but not the genesis of Kas'mira name, which is amply enumerated in Nilamat Puranam (Verses 223- 227), wherein Vishnu tells Naga King Nila about the code of conduct of those who will live alongside Nagas in Kas'mira (Translated); "The men will worship the Nagas in whose territory they shall dwell...... Those men in this country, who will follow the good customs laid down by you, will be endowed with animals and grains." **"Prajapati is called Ka, and Kas'yapa is also Prajapati. Built by him this country will be called Kas'mira. Because water called Ka was taken out by Balarama (the plough-wielder) from this country, so this will be called Kas'mira in this world."** It is not Kas'yapa *Sar*, corrupted to Kashmir, as we believe, but phonetics of Kas'mira then to Kashmira and we have the present name Kashmir instead of Kas'mira, its original name. *Satisar* is associated with Goddess Sati (Uma, Parvati) and is not the correct name, as per the scriptures, of Kas'mira.

The sacredness of Kas'mira would be incomplete without the mention of three main water bodies of the valley, which gives significant sacredness to Kas'mira; **Sindhu (Sindh), Vitasta (Wyeth (Also Vyath, Jhelum) and Wular (Mahapadamsar).** All of these sacred water bodies finally become part of one water body; Vitasta (here the main river Sindhu (Indus) is not referred to). **Sindhu (Indus)** and **Vitasta** have been held sacred from the time Aryans settled along Saraswati Bank Ashrams and find mention in our ancient religious scriptures. Great River Sindhu (Indus), venerated from ancient times, has been a prominent river acting as boundary between Central Asia and then Bharatvarasha. Aryans, while immigrating to Bharatvarasha, had crossed this great river, which is considered the base for Indus valley civilisation. Both these rivers (Sindhu (Indus) and Vitasta (Jhelum)) get mentioned in Rig Veda. Sindhu (Indus), mythical river Saraswati and River Sarayu also get special mention, many times, in Rig Veda, thus (Translated); "Let the great Streams come hither with their mighty help; Sindhu, Saraswati, and Sarayu with waves. Ye Goddess Floods, ye Mothers, animating all, promise us water rich in fatness and in balm (Rig Veda 10:64:9)." Sindhu river is also called "heavens bearer, Sindhu (Rig Veda 10:65:13)." Similarly Vitasta's mention in Rig Veda along sacred rivers Ganga and Yamuna, gives it special sanctity amongst the rivers of entire Bharatvarasha.

Sindhu River(s): Rig Veda is resplendent with the praise of Sindhu (Indus); its flow as recorded in Rig Veda gives its own story (Translated); "Sindhu (Indus) in might surpasses all the streams that flow. Varuna cut the channels for thy forward course, O Sindhu, when thou rannest on to win the race. Thou speedest o'er precipitous ridges of the earth, when thou are Lord and Leader of these moving floods...Sindhu, unto thee the roaring rivers run. Ou leadest as a warrior king thine army's wings what time thou comest in the van of these swift streams (Rig Veda 10:75:1-4)." In Nilamat Puranam Sindhu gets mentioned thus; "*Ganga Sindhu tu vijneya* Vitasta *Yamuna tatha.*" In Kas'mira we have different rivers named Sindhu or Sindhu Ganga. In *Harmukhganga Mahatmaya*, the stream flowing towards Narannag, (Called Nund Kol), which joins Lower Sindh near Kangan, is referred as Sindhu Ganga. In *Nandikshetra Mahatmaya* Lower Sindh, emanating from Baltal area is referred as Sindhu Ganga. *Harmukhganga* and *Nandikshetra Mahatmaya's,* scriptures pertain to Gangabal and *Nandikshetra tiratha's* respectively. Present day Kishanganga River, now flowing through Pakistan Occupied Kashmir (POK) and in front of our sacred Sharda Temple, is also referred as *Maha* Sindhu in Sharda *Mahatmaya.*

Sindhu (Indus) mentioned in Vedas emanates from Tibet, crosses Ladakh Range, flows through Sakardu and Chilas (South of Gilgit) and passes through Pakistan. Its journey is tortuous, through high snow clad mountains, gorges till it meanders through plains of West Punjab (Pakistan); exactly as per the description in Rig Veda, quoted above. However, in Kas'mira any mention of Sindhu had to be with reference to any important landmark close to the valley and was Gangabal (*Harmukh*). Since Sindhu, in Kas'mira scriptures was referred as closely associated with *Nandikshetra* in the North, the first such river in the region in that direction got referred to as Sindhu (Also called as Sindh; Lower Sindh). Thus in Kas'mira there are three rivers with the name of Sindh apart from main Sindhu (Indus) River: Sindhu Ganga merging with Sindhu Ganga of *Nandikshetra*, Maha Sindhu of Sharda and Lower Sindh.

Vitasta: Similarly river Vitasta was also in the *mantras* of the Aryans and its degree of sacredness gets equated with Ganga and Yamuna in Rig Veda thus (Translated); "Favour ye this my lord, O Ganga, Yamuna, O Sutudri, Parusni and Sarasvati: With Asikni, Vitasta, O Marudvrdha, O Arjikiya with Susoma hear my call (Rig Veda 10: 75-5)." Scriptures enumerate that after Kas'yapa saw Kas'mira populated he (Translated from Nilamat Puranam) "worshipped the god S'ankara and induced the goddess Uma to purify this country by the gift of water. She - the in destroying one - is renowned as the river Vitasta." Once goddesses went to see Kas'yapa, he induced them to be rivers by saying; "The beautiful country named Kas'mira has been created by me. O possessed of pure smiles, cherish that (country) by gift of water." Kas'yapa thus got Goddesses to take the form of rivers of the vale; Goddess Lakshmi as Vis'oka; Goddess Aditi, the mother of God, as Trikoti; Goddess Saci, wife of Indra, as Harsapatha etc. Most of the Rivers whose evolution is mentioned in Nilamat Puranam cannot be identified, as over the period their names have either changed or have become extinct, though few retain their Nilamat Puranam names like; Vaitarni, Harshapatha, Vishoka (Now called Vishow), Gotami, Mahuri, Sind (Sindhu- Lower Sindh), Madhumati (Called Bandapore Nala, though Madhumati name in later chronicles is ascribed in Sharda *Mahatmaya* to a river, in Kishanganga Valley, which joins Kishanganga River at Shardi (Sharda Temple)). Madhumati River quoted in Nilamat Puranam is near Bandapore and is tributary to Wular Lake (Mahapadamsar).

The legend for Kas'yapa inducing Goddess Sati (Uma, Parvati) to be river Vitasta in Kas'mira is equally interesting. He, Kas'yapa, worshiped S'ankara (Shiva) for inducing Sati as the river, which S'ankara agreed and said to Goddess Sati; "Do as has been said by Kas'yapa." As per the advice of S'ankara Sati took the form saying (Translated); "O father of the world, I shall assume the form of a river in the Nether World. Make a stroke with your spear near the abode of Nila (Nila Kund – Verinag), where, O lord, while breaking the mountain, was (placed) the point of the plough. By that stroke of the spear I shall come out of the Nether World and shall follow the way made with the plough up to the place where there is the great river Sindhu (Indus)." S'ankara himself named her as Vitasta, because he had excavated with the spear a ditch measuring one *Vitasti*, through which the river had come out. Goddess Yamuna gave her own identity and purity in the name of Vitasta. Goddess Ganga, for her great respect and devotion for Kas'yapa, augmented Vitasta with her own part in the form of Sindhu (Sindh, Lower Sindh). Thus, in Kas'mira Sindhu (Sindh, Lower Sindh), as per the scriptures, is the form of Ganga and the Vitasta as Yamuna. The place of their confluence, Shadipur (Prayaga) is regarded as equal to Prayaga (Allahabad). Nilamat Puranam gives lucid reasoning for the Vitasta to continue its name after absorbing Sindhu at Prayaga and said to Ganga (Translated): "O possessed of beautiful colour, at Prayaga (Allahabad)- as thereafter river is called Ganga- my name is appropriated by you and in Kas'mira your name has been appropriated by me (River after Shadipur Prayaga is called Vitasta) (Verse 308)." Thus receiving good rivers in this way, the goddess Yamuna (Vitasta) became united with the Ganga (Lower Sindh - Sindhu). As per Nilamat water of Vitasta mixed with that of Sindhu is like milk mixed with nectar, beauty associated with elegance and knowledge associated with good nature. One wonders as to why Vitasta becomes more turbulent, after its calm journey beyond Varahkshetra (Varhamulla, Baramulla). Nilamat gives answer; route to be followed for Vitasta was to be treaded by a plough under the supervision of Kas'yapa, which many times he entreated her to follow. This repeated persuasion to follow the ploughed route irritated the Goddess, when she reached beyond *Varahkshetra* (Varhamulla, Baramulla), thereafter became swift with rage with accompanied murky colour. This is best narrated by the following verse of Nilamat Puranam (Translated); "Kas'yapa spoke to her: "O beautiful one, you must necessarily go by the way made with the plough, otherwise the whole country will be turned into a lake. Persuaded again and again by Kas'yapa, that excellent river went in anger through the way made with plough. So, though clear, she is seen as a dirty one at that place (Verse 311-13)." Thus Vitasta and Sindhu (Lower Sindh, Sindh) took their places in the Land of Nila; Kas'mira. Vitasta's sacredness is best narrated by the following verse attributed to Kas'yapa (Translated); "Assuming the form of a river called Vitasta, O goddess, the daughter of the mountain, you are not a river but an ascetic lady, wife of Sarva, even higher than Sarva (Verse 314 Nilamat Puranam)."

The reference to main Sindhu River comes up again in Nilamat Puranam, as Ganga in the form of Sindhu (Sindh, Lower Sindh) had merged with Vitasta and Vitasta had appropriated her name at Prayaga (Shadipur). Sindhu (Sindh, Lower Sindh) would like to regain her name when Vitasta completes her journey through Kas'mira. This conversation between Ganga (Sindhu) and Yamuna (Vitasta) rivers is best narrated in Verses 309-310 of Nilamat Puranam (Translated); "Then the Ganga said to her, "O beautiful one, I must again appropriate your name when I am designated as Sindhu (Indus)." This geographically happens at the confluence of the two rivers; where Jhelum (Vitasta) joins Indus (Sindhu), in Pakistan. The journey of Vitasta thus ends and she gets merged with great river Sindhu (Indus) and combined name after this confluence is Sindhu (Indus). One is surprised that two millenniums ago our ancestors knew the route of the rivers beyond Kas'mira and this information found its way into the naming and renaming of these rivers in various scriptures. One thing is noteworthy; irrespective of the number of Sindhus in Kas'mira, all merge with Vitasta.

Vitasta Through Millenniums: River Vitasta has been called variously; as 'Vitasta' in the Vedas, 'Hydaspes' of Aryans and Central Asian's and 'Bidaspes' of Ptolemy (Approx 87-150 AD). Sharf-ud-din, historian of Taimur (1336-1405 AD), calls it 'Dendan' or 'Gamad', Mughal emperor Jehangir (1605-27 AD), in his memoirs, called it 'Bebat'. The river is also known as 'Wyeth (Also Vyath)'. When the Muslim invaders conquered and settled in Kas'mira, they built their palaces on the banks, on the sides of the canals excavated from Vitasta. Among these *Maar* Canal (*Nala Maar*), constructed during the reign of Zain-ul-Abidin (1420-70 AD), is still remembered. This canal, which was also used as an inland-waterway till fifties, has been filled couple of decades ago. The calm flow of Vitasta, however, had not brought peace to the heart of Zain-ul-Abidin father, Sultan Sikandar (1389-1413 AD), better known as Sikandar *Butshikan*, who ravaged and razed to the ground magnificent monasteries and stone temples along the banks of the river. But Vitasta did pacify and lend peace of mind to Zain-ul-Abidin.

When Akbar (1556-1605 AD) visited Kas'mira for the first time, his procession was taken out along the river Vitasta. Records Shuka, a contemporary historian, (Updated Rajatarangini from 1514 to 1586 AD) about Akbar's River procession (Translated): "Now Jalaludina (Akbar) came to see the kingdom of Kas'mira, decked with saffron, walnut, fruits and flowers. The wives of the citizens hastened to have a glimpse of the King. One woman pointed out the King to her dear female friend who was quite eager to see him; another exclaimed with a flutter that she had seen the leader of the army; another woman with threats to her child covered her bosom and went. After the people of Kas'mira had seen the King, a continuous festivity was held in every house." During his stay, Akbar participated in the festivals of Brahman community and on 13th of *Bhadoon* (Vikrami Samvat), also known as Vitasta *Triyodashi* (*Truvah*); celebrated as birthday of Vitasta (Jhelum-*Wyeth (Also Vyeth)*), ordered illuminations all over the city and participated in the festivities.

Jehangir, who called Vitasta (Jhelum) 'Bebat', was very fond of this river. He, in his memoirs, has written (Translated); "Source of the river is at Verinag in 'Kashmir' and the story goes that a very large snake haunted the spot. A snake was guarding the source of river." The waters, he wrote, were so clear that if a small poppy seed was dropped in it, it would be visible. So much so he called this spot "heaven on earth." In 1612 AD, he (Jehangir) enclosed the gushing waters of the blue-water spring in an octagonal basin at Nila Kund (Verinag), which was circular one equated with circular parasol of King Nila. In the Moghul building spanning the spring he had the famous picture gallery of Moghul potentates, princes and allies. Tearfully, Jehangir left Verinag and Kas'mira, when he had paid his fourth and last visit in 1627 AD and died on his way over the steep rugged Himalayas with the wish that he wanted 'Nothing but Kashmir' on his lips.

Shah Jehan (1627-1658 AD) completed the work of his father at Verinag, by building aqueducts. He, however, loved Dal Lake (Ancient Name Dalla) more than he loved Vitasta. During later Sikh regime, which was heralded in 1819 AD, Sikh Subedar Colonel Mehan Singh, a popular governor, increased frequency of river processions along the river; a sight to see.

Royal Procession-River Vitasta–1868 AD.

Dogra rulers, whose sway began in 1846 AD, carried on the tradition of these processions. Maharaja Pratap Singh (1885-1925 AD) organised these processions, for and from Varhamulla (Baramulla). He would cruise up in a royal boat that had a becoming retinue. Maharaja Hari Singh (1925-1949 AD), continued this practice for many years. Pandit Jawaharlal Nehru, President Rajendra Prasad, Sadar-e-Riyasat (Head of the State, as Governor of Kashmir was called) Dr Karan Singh, Prime Ministers of Kashmir, Russian leaders Khrushchev and Bulganin were taken out in spectacular river processions along Vitasta, which had become must for visits of dignitaries and especial days of the State.

Jhelum: The River Vitasta is generally now known as Jhelum, after a place called Jhelum, now in Pakistan. The River flows through this town, which came into prominence during Jehangir's time, when he was held prisoner at this place by one of his Governor, Mahabat Khan. Miru Pandit, whose ancestors had migrated from Kas'mira to Bharatvarasha during first exodus, was in command of Nur Jehan's bodyguards and showed his military skill by being part of the group, which freed Jehangir. The name Vitasta can be traced through ancient Veda era, medieval times and even upto Mughal Kings. The name Jhelum got tagged somewhere during the middle of Mughal reign and took roots during Afghan Rule, as the area of Jhelum was part of the Mughal Empire. Since Jehangir called it Bebat, in his memoirs, it is unlikely that the name changed during his reign. It is possible that infrequent use of Jhelum name may have started during the reign of Jehangir, as while in captivity he had seen this river from close quarters at Jhelum, where he was held as captive at a place on the banks of Vitasta (Jhelum). Its usage got more common during Shah Jehan's reign (1627-58 AD) and thereafter. However during the Muslim reign Vitasta was called *'Nahr-i-Shahr'* (Canal of the City), but its original name Vitasta, generally also called Wyeth remained together with other name Jhelum.

Name Wyeth (Also Vyath): The actual source of the river Vitasta is a small village Vitastatra later called Vithavatro and now called Vithavutur, situated about one mile (1.6 Kilometres) to the Northwest of Verinag Spring. A large spring which drains into a pond close to the village is traditionally considered the main source of Vitasta. This place apparently gave the name of Wyeth (Also Vyath, a corrupted name of Vithavatro) to the river. In the *Vitasta Mahatmaya* the place is named *Vitastavartika.* The name Wyeth (Also Vyath) can also be ascribed to Kashmiri language, roughly meaning 'Large (broad) Hearted'. Kashmiri language slowly emerged from *Upbrahmbhasha* at the end of 11th Century; however, this name, Wyeth, can be ascribed to later period during Muslim rule, when Kashmiri also incorporated certain amount of Persian language.

Of deep blue colour, river Vitasta (Jhelum- Wyeth (Also Vyath)) joins the Mahapadamsar (Wular Lake). Before joining Mahapadamsar (Wular Lake), the river takes many turns and change of course keeps its pace in check. It is also believed that from the patterns the river forms, a certain type of embroidery for shawls and carpets, which is typical of Kas'mira design, was born; full of loops and curves. Flowing a total course of 450 miles (720 Kilometres), out of which 84 miles (133 Kilometres) are within the valley of Kas'mira. During the journey of Vitasta many more rivers; Vishoka, Rambh Ara, Romish, Dud Ganga, Lidder (Passing through Pahalgam), Aral, Stunt Kol (Pronounced as Chunth Kol), Aran, Pohru and many others, constitute its other tributaries in Kas'mira. To admire best the sinuous serpentine beauty of the Jhelum, one gets its magnificent view from Shankaracharya Hill. "A hundred miles of snow-clad mountain peak / On either side uprear their heads to heaven. And, flecked with light and shade and yellow foam, Broad-bosomed Jhelum wends his stately way" (C.R. Tolle Machesmall).

The Legends of Mahapadamsar (Wular Lake)

Mahapadamsar (Wular Lake): As Vitasta meanders from its abode of Nila Kund (Verinag), many rivers, mostly sacred, join it. The waters of lakes like Dal (Dalla), Manasbal, Anchar and many more water bodies also join it enroute. Sacred Madhumati River, a sacred river in the valley near Bandapur (Bandipur)(now called Bandapur Nala (Bod Kol)) joins at the Northeastern edge of Mahapadamsar (Wular Lake). In Nilamat Puranam, Madhumati River is mentioned as tributary of Vitasta and not of Mahapadamsar. Vitasta enters Mahapadamsar (Wular Lake) from the direction of Southeast and finally continues its onward journey in the direction of Southwest, flowing through the legendary towns of Suyapur (Sopur, Sopore) and *Varahkshetra* (Varhamulla, Baramulla). There are many Kings and legends that get associated with Mahapadamsar, starting from Nilamat Puranam. The legend enumerated in the Nilamat unfolds with a conversation between King Gonanda II and sage Brhadasva (Also Badaravasa), who narrates the name of Nagas, who had their abode in Kas'mira. It is a treat to read these names, as many of them find use even today, as modern first names.

Area of Mahapadamsar was the abode of one Naga King Sadangula and not a lake and was lying vacant. He (Sadangula) had been banished to the mountains of Drava (Present day Dardistan) by King Nila for his unlimited lustre and carried away women: and is best narrated from this conversation between King Nila and Mahapadma (Translated); "O best among the Nagas, having banished him from here, I allotted to him a place on Usiraka – the best of the mountains - in Drava (Dardistan). Through a device I appointed him there as a guardian of the territory and won over the people of Kas'mira through affection. Sadangula - the lord of the Nagas - has been settled by me on an even road. Honoured by the people, he lives there happily. At my request, Hari (Shiva) himself has given him protection there (Nilamat Puranam Verses 1001-4)." To trace origin of Drava (Dardistan) country; one of the groups of Saraswat Aryans strayed further North of the valley and settled there. They had identical beliefs, rituals as that of the group who came directly to valley. However, they developed differently from the main Aryan stock and were treated with disdain for their arrogant, aggressive and troublesome behaviour. The country(s) was called Darda or Drava and people as *Dards*. The area is now in Pakistan Occupied Kashmir (POK) and is called *Dardistan*.

Mahapadma had come to King Nila to seek a new place of habitation in Kas'mira for him and his large family of dependants and dependants of his dependants. Son of Vinita (Formerly a bird-Garuda) having come to know Mahapadma was living in Kas'mira, used to attack and eat up hundred of his sons and their families. King Nila spoke thus to the Naga Mahapadma (Translated); "O best among the Bhujagas (King of Serpents), all the Nagas have made their abodes here. There is no place (left) where you may dwell, O best among the Naga-chiefs. O Naga, the lord of undying ones, I do not see even a little space, which has not been thus fully occupied by the Nagas. Moreover, you are surrounded by a big family. But at this time, the beautiful territory of Sadangula is vacant. Here I give you, as your habitation, the beautiful city named Candrapura, of the king Visvagasva, in the beautiful territory, which belonged to Sadangula. Turn that into a lake." The area of

Mahapadamsar (Wular Lake) was named Candrapura, ruled by King Visvagasva. Kalhan also mentions a large city (*Candrapura*) submerged under the Wular (Mahapadamsar). King Nila also tells Mahapadma that Sage Durvasa, disguised as a mad man, had not got proper reception when he visited the habitation of Sadangula and had cursed; "It shall turn into a lake." As per King Nila he was the only one who knew of this curse, as Durvasa had told him about this curse, as a favour. He (Nila) advises Mahapadma not to delay but with an instruction (Translated); "O Naga, make your abode there. Do not delay. But (you should) importune the king Visvagasva - the protector of the earth. You should make request to that king, in disguise if due to greed, he would not give when requested to give, in disguise, he as a king, would be disgraced for not doing that which he must do." It is interesting to note that Sage Durvasa, eccentric, figures in this legend in a similar form as he appears in great epic Kalidasa's *Shakuntalam*, where he curses Shakuntala. Shakuntala, deep in thought of her husband Dushyant, forgets to greet Sage Durvasa, who curses her that "The man in whose thoughts she was, will forget her."

Mahapadma assumed the form of an old Brahmin and went to the city Candrapura. He looked at the compassionate king Visvagasva and made request to him as "*Lord Vishnu had made to Bali.*" Mahapadma said to the King (Translated): "O compassionate king, give me that much dwelling place at Candrapura, which may be sufficient for my big family." King Visvagasva promised him place in Candrapura, asking Mahapadma to occupy that much space, which may be enough for Mahapadma and his family. Having accepted the gift Mahapadma turns to his own form and spoke to the king amidst his ministers (Translated); "Go away from this city, along with your collection of money and other things, accompanied by your cavalry, elephants and chariots and surrounded by your own men. O Lord of men, the city is sufficient for me along with my family. It will turn into an extensive lake, very soon." The king went away along with his citizens, horses, elephants and host of ministers, and constructed another beautiful town at a distance of two Yojanas to the West of his own city naming it Visvagasvapura. Though this city cannot be fully identified, however, Sopur (Sopore- Suyapur) is roughly at that distance in the West of the lake. In all probability Visvagasvapura may be ancient name which was named later as Suyapur; renamed Sopur (Sopore) later.

The legend says Mahapadma flooded the city and lived there with his enlarged family. The lake was called Mahapadamsar and its dimensions and characteristics as given in Nilamat Puranam are (Translated): "One Yojana long and one Yojana wide, is highly beautiful and pleasing to the hearts of the good. Due to the influence of Mahapadma, (that lake is) devoid of wicked crocodiles." The dimensions given are much lesser than it's existing one, indicating many more changes. One thing is certain; periphery of the lake was habitated and many interesting relics and monuments of the past have been found in these areas; mostly now under water or in ruins.

Legend Narrated to Zain-ul-Abidin: Historian Jonaraja, who updated Rajatarangini from 1150 AD to 1459 AD, states that King Zain-ul-Abidin was anxious to build a monument, as had never been built before by any king. After much deliberation he decided to construct an island-palace in the middle of the Mahapadamsar (Wular Lake), but appreciating mammoth magnitude of the task, he sought the advice of wise men of his time regarding ways and means of its accomplishment. They all encouraged his efforts by narrating the legend, which though starts with Mahapadma as in Nilamat Puranam, but differs in content and sequence of events. This legend starts with ancient name of the lake of Mahapadamsar, named after great Serpent Deity Mahapadma, a city of ancient times presided over by the snake deity. Passage of time and the security given by beneficent rule, brought luxury and vice among the citizens, which grew with such an alarming rapidity that Mahapadma resolved to destroy the entire city, including its inhabitants. But, among the residents of the doomed city was a humble and virtuous potter, whom the deity (Mahapadma) resolved to spare. He appeared to him in a dream, warned him of the impending fate of the city and told him to save himself. Next morning the potter related the warning to the citizens, but was laughed at. As soon as the potter left the city, the waters began to rise until the entire countryside was overwhelmed by one tremendous deluge. To quote from Jonaraja's Rajatarangini (Translated); "The terrified children who stood, at first when the water was low, at the feet of their mothers, soon, as the water began to rise higher, got into their laps, then clung to their breasts, next jumped upon their shoulders, and finally sat upon their heads, as if they were their embodied vital breaths. The flood covered the quaking limbs of women as if it were an affectionate lover embracing his beloved whose limbs are trembling with emotion." After Mahapadma had wreaked vengeance upon the sinful city, he established his permanent residence in the newly formed lake. "The Lord of the Snakes was in reality Kaliya, who, being trampled upon by the feet of Krishna, bore the mark of a lotus on his head, and from that time onwards bore the appellation of Mahapadma and the lake as Mahapadamsar." Zain-ul-Abidin's wise men then wound up their story by an assurance that he (Zain-ul-Abidin), being an incarnation of Hari (Shiva), could do as he pleased in the domain of his vassal subject Mahapadma and that his efforts would assuredly be crowned with success. He, therefore, set about vigorously for accomplishment of his purpose. Large cargo boats were filled with boulders and sunk at the spot selected. The island was named Zaina Lank after him and still retains that name. He also built a small mosque at one corner of it, the ruins of which are still in existence. The legend differs from that of Nilamat Puranam, in that Mahapadma himself submerges his own city. There is no mention of city as Candrapura of King Visvagasva in this legend.

Potters Legend: Another legend is also talked about. Around 2600 BC King Sandiman of Kas'mira founded a city on both the sides of the Vitasta, at the foot of the Northern mountain ranges in Kuihama near present day Mahapadamsar. He built buildings, tall and graceful temples furnished with golden and silver images. This city was called Sandimatnagar. About six centuries later, in the reign of Sundersena (2082-2041 BC. Dates disputed), this place became a den of immorality. The people forgot God, wallowed in wine and debauchery, worshipping mammon and woman. The king sided with profligate persons. When such conditions reached a climax, a potter of this city named Nand Gupth, a man whom the people hated because of his piety, was inspired and preached against the sinful ways of the people. They mocked and laughed at him. According to the local tradition, the potter was inspired in a dream that he should tell all the citizens to leave the town and he with his family should climb the hill, but not look back till he reached the top. Next day before *Brahmamuhurat* (before dawn), with his potter's wheel on his back, he climbed the hill. When he reached halfway, he cast a look at the city but found no change. When he reached the top, the earth shook, a fissure appeared in the earth, water gushed forth and swamped the whole city. During the same earthquake a knoll of the hill at *Varahkshetra* (Varhamulla, Baramulla) near Khadanyar tumbled down, choking the outlet of the river Vitasta and consequently the water level rose high at once and drowned the whole city together with its king and the inhabitants. This caused a flood to deluge the valley also. This submerged city is now the site of Mahapadamsar (Wular Lake). The potter, however, found half of his potter's wheel turned into gold. The place on the hillside where the potter had stopped was named Shukracharya. The hillock, on the top of which is the shrine of Baba Shukur Din, is called *Krala Sangor* (potter's hillock), also called *Ziarat* of Baba Shukur Din, also referred as *Shukur Sabun*, a Sufi saint. The name Sandimatnagar, in this legend, bears somewhat close resemblance to the place of Sadangula, which was given away to third Mahapadma (Verse 988-89 Nilamat Puranam). There is one major lacuna in this legend. Use of 'nagar' with Sandimatnagar in pre BC era is not supported by any document, legend, place name, etc. in Kas'mira. The name of the place called Shukracharya appears to be of later date, named after Baba Shukur Din, a sufi revered both by Brahmins as well as Muslims.

Bosangiri Legend: There is also a well-chronicled story that there was a big town where Mahapadamsar (Wular Lake) stands, where King Prahlad had built *Prateshwara* temple and was called *Bosangiri* (Between Khuihama and Sopore on a hillock (*Giri*) called *Bosan*), which got submerged. Other name of the Bosangiri hillock given in later Kas'mira chronicles is mentioned as *Sherehkot.* Inspite of best efforts it has not been possible to establish full identity of the King Prahlad. He is not mentioned by Kalhan and hence has to be post 1150 AD. King Jai Simha reigned upto 1155 AD and was succeeded by his son Parmanuk (1155- 1164 AD). Parmanuk has been described variously in many chronicles; Parmanuk in Jonaraja's *Rajatarangini*, Parmandi, Parmanda Deva in Tapar Inscription (S.P.S. Museum, Srinagar), Parma Deva and Para Deva in the coins etc. It is likely that he was King Prahlad, who constructed the temple during resurgence of Shaivism in Kas'mira and at a time when Shaivism was at its peak A large assortment of architectural fragments of a temple; such as fluted columns, stones from pilasters, jambs, etc. are scattered round about on an island in Mahapadamsar, which tends to prove that there was a temple on the island also. This hypothesis is further strengthened by the presence of a big Shiva Linga, which is partly submerged, on the East side of the island. There are indications to show that there were series of steps on all sides leading down to the water, though the principal landing seems to have been on the eastern side. The direction of stairs are important, as they are towards the main lake, indicating that at the time of the construction of the temple, the level of Mahapadamsar (Wular Lake) was much below the stairs, which may have been used to enter the temple. It also indicates that the area around and on the sides of the stairs was dry.

However, R C Kak, in his book "*Monuments of Kashmir*" attributes construction of a temple on an island nearer to the submerged temple to Zain-ul-Abidin; "for none of his successors on the Kashmir throne was capable of such a colossal task." Jonaraja wrote Rajatarangini covering 1150 to 1459 AD period, when he was alive during Zain-ul-Abidin's time and covered each and every event of Zain-ul-Abidin in great detail till 1459. Same was the case with Shrivara, who carried Rajatarangini till 1487 AD, 17 years after the death of Zain-ul-Abidin. Both of them and Shah Nama, which gives paeans of the King, do not mention about the construction of the temple, which would have been a major event of Zain-ul-Abidin's reign. Jonaraja vividly covers Zain-ul-Abidin's visit to Mahapadamsar and his construction of a palace but is silent on any construction of the temple. The temple has had to be an effort of a Hindu King, without any doubt. Interestingly Mahapadamsar (Wular Lake) and existence of this temple figures during Zain-ul-Abidin's time also. Jonaraja does mention about Zain-ul-Abidin's intention to raise a monument as never before; a *Lank* (Island) created in Mahapadamsar (Wular Lake), as he had done in Dal Lake (*Ancient Name Dalla*), would be a feat by itself. He ordered the boatmen and the divers to locate a spot of minimum depth in Mahapadamsar (Wular Lake), where it could be raised without much effort. All of them suggested the spot where the temple existed, as when water receded in the lake to its lowest level in winter, the stones of the temple became visible through the crystalline waters of the lake. He took a boat and personally examined the spot and ordered the divers to make an attempt at finding any relics inside the temple in the water. The divers plunged into the lake and with utmost care made their way into the temple, where from they pulled out two bronze idols. Zain-ul-Abidin then selected the very site for developing an island and a palace, now in ruins. It is apparent that the two idols had to be that of God and his consort (*Shiva* and his consort Parvati; as Shiva is also called *Partheshwar, Prateshwar*). It has not been possible to find final disposal of these idols, but these could possibly have been installed in nearby town of Suyapur (Sopur, Sopore) in a *Mandir* or a new *Mandir* constructed. None of the *Mandirs* in the area have bronze idols of such antiquity nor is the location of these idols known, however, legend in Sopore says that the *Shiva* temple constructed on the banks of Vitasta (Wyeth -Jhelum) dates back to time when idols were found from Mahapadamsar (Wular Lake). Zain-ul-Abidin built 'Zain Lank' near the ancient *mandir* and built a palace called *Zoon Dub* (Moon Balcony) but was normally referred as *Razdan; Raz* or *Razah* – King; *Dan* – Hearth. The ruins of this palace still exist on the Southern edge of the lake. Admittedly Zain-ul-Abidin was tolerant but not to the extent quoted. He did not allow reconverting of *Masjids*, which had been converted from *Mandirs*, though he allowed some of the temples to be rebuilt by the community and not by him.

Mahapadamsar To Wular, Archaeological and Geological Finds

Mahapadamsar Name Dating from Nilamat Puranam: Kalhan in Rajatarangini has started the history of Kas'mira from just before the great Mahabharata war and the first King mentioned by him is Gonanda I (2448 BC - date disputed. For correct eras read Chapter 10). On Gonanda I being killed, Lord Krishna crowned his pregnant queen and her son later became the King under the name of Gonanda II. It can be assumed that Gonanda II, as per Kalhan's assessment, reigned during early part of 25th Century BC (2425-2400 BC. Again dates are disputed. Actually the era comes to 31st Century BC). The conversation quoted in Nilamat Puranam pertaining to Mahapadama is between King Gonanda II and sage Brhadasva; so the antiquity of the event of naming the lake Mahapadamsar should roughly be pre this period. There may be doubt of antiquity and date of events, merely based on ancient scriptures or as quoted in Rajatarangini. A detailed and extensive archaeological survey of Kas'mira valley during the last century (20th Century) has revealed Neolithic (of the later or more advanced Stone Age) settlements in Kas'mira and that too widely distributed from Anantnag to Pampore, Gurhoma Sangri near Mahapadamsar (Wular Lake) and many other places, with high density of settlements in Southern Kas'mira. These surveys show that the valley was pulsating with the Neolithic people and their descendants as the time elapsed; Neolithic people around 2600 +- 200 BC, hand made pottery introduced round about 2400 BC, Iron around 1800 BC followed by Megalithic period (1600 ± 200) with introduction of rice. These Neolithic settlements are none other than that of original inhabitants of Kas'mira; the Nagas and later in Megalithic period by *Manus* (Aryan Saraswat Brahmins of Kas'mira) in the later centuries, in fact with significant gaps.

Nilamat Puranam, in the narration between King Gonanda II and sage Brhadasva, categorically calls it Mahapadamsar. The appellation of Mahapadamsar could not have come to Kas'mira during the Buddhist period (500 BC – 6th Century AD), as it is a Brahmin appellation. Therefore, it has to be pre 500 BC. Archaeological evidence of Neolithic period (Of the later or more advanced Stone Age; that of Nagas) found in the area dates around 26OO ± 200 BC. It is not that all the Neolithic settlements date back to the initial period. They came in a trickle and this continued for nearly thousand years. The settlements found are either the abandoned ones or destroyed by the vagaries of nature and thus have come to light. There would have been more such settlements, which continued for further centuries and developed along with the Megalithic settlements (1600 ± 200). The naming of Mahapadamsar during Megalithic period (Advanced stage of lithic (stone) period) is relevant, dating to about 1600 ± 200 BC. These settlements dating to Megalithic period are that of *Manus* (Aryan Saraswat Brahmins of Kas'mira). Thus, the settlements of Nagas in Kas'mira started during the Neolithic period (2600 ± 200 BC), peaked around the beginning of Megalithic period (1600 ± 200); for nearly thousand years. This period also saw *Daitayas* and *Pis'acas* also settling down in the valley, though in different directions and away from the Naga settlements. The Aryan settlements, again, like Naga settlements, have started around 1600 ± 200 BC and peaked around 1300 BC. From various excavations it has been seen that Neolithic settlements were topped with megalithic settlements proving that Nagas and *Manus* (Aryan Saraswat Brahmins of Kas'mira) had established their settlements alongside at many places.

9th Century Suyapur (Sopur, Sopore) town has been named after Suya, at the point where river Vitasta leaves Mahapadamsar basin. Suya, a great engineer during Utpal Dynasty (9th Century), cleared obstructions in Vitasta from *Sar* (Wular Lake) basin at *Varahkshetra* (Varhamulla, Baramulla). After Suya's effort, it is claimed that the *Sar* (Lake) was named as Mahapadamsar, named after then ruler Avanti Varman (Utpal Dynasty; 855- June 883 AD also called Mahapadama (The devotee of the lotus feet; Vishnu), hence name Mahapadamsar. (Avanti Varman founded Avantipur; built two temples of Shiva and Vishnu, now in ruins). However, Mahapadamsar appellation quoted in Nilamat Puranam is ante Avanti Varman, therefore, the appellation name attributed to Avanti Varman does not hold ground. The name could have found origin from Mahapadam (*Maha*-Giant; *Padam* - Feet) or Lord Shiva (*Mahadev*), also referred as *Neelpadam.* Surprisingly the lake as seen from the mountains around, looks like a Giant (*Maha*) Foot (*Pada*).

Mahapadamsar is referred as Bolor by Al-Beruni (960-1031 AD), an Arab Scholar who came to Bharatvarasha with Mohammad Ghaznavi in the beginning of 11th Century, visited Kas'mira in 1030 AD and has written about Kas'mira in his book. Al-Beruni stayed in India for a number of years, wrote a book, which gives account of social, political and economic conditions of then India. Al-Beruni is also credited with giving a new appellation to Bharatvarasha, for the first time, in recorded travelogue; *Land of Snake Charmers.* He was killed in a battle in 1031 AD; just a year after visiting Kas'mira in 1030 AD. In his description of the position of Goddess Sharda's shrines at Shardi "in 'Inner Kas'mira' about two to three days journey towards the mountains of Bolor." Bolor referred to by him in his chronicle has been interpreted as the mountains overlooking Mahapadamsar; 'Wulor' or 'Wular Lake'. The phonetics of 'Wulor' in Arabic is somewhat closer to 'Bolor'. Al- Beruni visited Kas'mira when Shavisim, religious fervour and new language *Upbrahmbasha* was high and name is attributed to Sanskrit/ *Upbrahmbasha.* The lake, with its big dimensions and the extent of water, gives rise to high leaping waves in the afternoons, called Ullola in Sanskrit; meaning stormy leaping, high rising waves. 10th to 12th Centuries saw resurgence of Shavisim in Kas'mira and scholars from Bharatvarasha visiting Kas'mira, who could not continue their religious inclinations in their places due to various reasons including advent of Islam, even settling down and found Kas'mira an ideal place. Many of these scholars were from South and coastal areas. Being familiar with sea, they would have been impressed with the dimensions of the lake and the high leaping waves and may have been instrumental in coining word Ullola for Mahapadamsar. Its corrupted form saw its transition as 'Bolor' by Al-Beruni and over the centuries corrupted further to 'Wulor' or 'Wular'. This appellation finds way in many chronicles of 15th Century including accounts concerning Zain-ul-Abidin.

The origin may also be attributed to a Kashmiri word 'Wul', which means a gap or a fissure, appellation that must have come also during this period. The word Wul (Gap or fissure), is also indicator of its origin to a fissure or gap created. If the progression of languages in Kas'mira is analysed, it will be found that during the first millennium AD *Upbrahmbasha* gave way to Sharda script at the end of first millennium, Kashmiri language slowly emerged from *Upbrahmbasha* at the end of 11th Century. Wular for Wul possibly became common around 12th Century. Thus the appellation Mahapadamsar must be dating during the period of *Manu* settlements

(1600 ± 200 BC) and remained through 6th/ 7th Century AD and can be traced upto 10th Century, without any change.

Temples and Architectural Remains in Mahapadamsar: In the domain of architecture, the charm of Kas'mira, apart from its magnificent natural scenery, lies in its temples and fine arts. Wrote one European art critic: "Ancient India has nothing more worthy of its civilization, than the grand remains in Kas'mira, the massive, the grotesque the elegant in architecture, may be admired in many parts of India, but now here is to be seen, the counterparts of the classically graceful, yet symmetrically massive edifices of Kas'mira, and in beauty, and position are immensely superior." The rivers and springs of Kas'mira have also been held sacred and over the period thousands of temples had come up over the ages along the banks of rivers, rivulets and springs. We have many temples along the Vitasta banks in Srinagar, Suyapur (Sopur, Sopore) and *Varahkshetra* (Varhamulla, Baramulla). Some of the lakes big or small too have temples either on their banks or now inside the water.

Like Manasbal Lake has a temple closer to its Eastern Bank, which was surrounded by water and has recently been so reclaimed that whole of the temple is now visible from the banks. Surely when this temple was constructed, the water of the lake must have been much below the base level of the temple, indicating a geographical phenomenon of increased water level after the temple was constructed. Mahapadamsar too has ruins of many such temples, many submerged deep inside, and it is folklore that when the water of the lake reduces one can see top of a temple emerging above the water level. Jonaraja giving account of Zain-ul-Abidin's visit to Mahapadamsar (Wular Lake) mentions about it. In 1874, Dr. Vincent-Smith discovered on this island a stone slab bearing Persian inscription that mentioned the name of Zain-ul-Abidin and date A.H. (Al Hijri; Muslim Calendar 847 (1442-43 AD).

The place where the island was reclaimed had a temple, built earlier. A large assortment of architectural fragments of temples, such as fluted columns, stones from pilasters, jambs, etc are scattered round about the site, which proves that there was once a temple on the island. This hypothesis is further strengthened by the presence of a big Shiva-linga, which is partly submerged, on the East side of the island. There are indications to show that there were series of steps on all sides leading down to the water, though the principal landing seems to have been on the East side. The other structure on the island is a small domed chamber of brick masonry. This is partly built of temple materials. The string courses on top of the walls consist of projecting wooden beams and entire surface of the chamber seems to have been coated with painted plaster. Externally the walls were adorned with shallow arched recesses, typical of a temple in Kas'mira, built of large blocks of limestone, similar to those used in the mediaeval temples of Kas'mira. Even the mouldings are similar to those found in ancient temples. This also indicates existence of another temple, which may have been demolished by earlier Muslim kings and material or part of a converted temple. A small mosque built by Zain-ul-Abidin is at one corner of the island, the ruins of which are still in existence. On the Northeastern shore of the lake is situated the village of Garur, where there is a temple of mediaeval period. It is 4 feet 2 inches square internally, and seven feet three inches high from basement to cornice. The roof, undoubtedly pedimented, has disappeared and the base is buried underground. The temple faces Northwest and stands on the bank of a spring. The steps, which lead down to the water, are missing; may have been washed away by the swirling waters entering Mahapadamsar during floods. There is a small pointed niche in the walls, which contains a sculptured relief bearing a three-headed Shiva. The other two figures of this sculptured relief cannot be identified. These remains, pertaining to medieval period, point out either to the extension of the city, now a lake, which may have existed right up to this area or alternatively shifting to this area after the old area was submerged.

Geological Indicators: Over millions of years ago a revolution in the physical geography of Bharatvarasha occurred with series of earth movements and as a result of the lateral thrusts Himalayas were born. In the process several plications, fractures and over thrusts resulted, known as the Main Boundary Himalayan Range, estimated to have sprung sixty million years ago. Subsequent to the formation of the continental landmass and upliftment of the Himalayas, there were further occurrences in Kas'mira, which resulted in the uplift of the Pir Panjal, giving rise to a vast lake in the Kas'mira called the *Karewa* lake (*Satisar* of the Nilamat Puranam). Proof of this phenomenon is also confirmed by the finding of fossilized fruits of water nut (*Trapa bispinosa*) at Botapathri near Gulmarg and other places at an altitude of over 3000 meters; which grows only in water and that too not above altitudes of 1700 meters (Approximately 5500 Feet). Opening of a geological fault finally drained this lake out, when it emerged as the Vitasta after which clay deposits in the exposed lake sediments in the valley called Karewas (*Uddars* in *Kashmiri*) remained. Thus mythological traditions supported fully by research of geologists confirm that the valley originally was a huge lake and its waters were blocked near *Varahkshetra* (Varhamulla, Baramulla) and fault opening out at Khadanyar (Baramulla), which presumably occurred about 85,000 years ago; a remarkable coincidence between the legend and the scientific facts! Read Nilamat Verse (Translated) "O best amongst the kings, the goddess Uma is the same as Kas'mira. What was formerly, an enjoyable, heart-enrapturing lake for six Manvantaras….." With reclamation of marshes and small water bodies, settlement and extension of agriculture, tree vegetation got firmly established by the time and after the advent of man. In the words of Sir Francis Young Husband, "The huge lake must have been twice the length and three times the width of the lake of Geneva, completely encircled by snowy mountains as high, and higher than Mount Blank, while in the immediately following glacial period, mighty glaciers came wending down to the Sindh, Lidder, and other valleys even to the edge of water." This is perhaps the only known find of such a settlement in Bharatvarasha. However, the five fresh water bodies, the Dal (Dalla*)*, Nagin, Anchar, Manasbal and the Mahapadamsar (Wular), formed mainly during the recent geological period and are not the remnants of the *Karewa* Lake (*Satisar*).

Dating of Events: There may be doubt of antiquity and dating of events on the reason of scientific proof of habitation of the valley. A detailed and extensive archaeological survey of Kas'mira valley during the last century revealed Neolithic settlements (2600 ± 200 BC) in Kas'mira and that too widely distributed from Anantnag to Pampore, Gurhoma Sangri near Mahapadamsar (Wular Lake) and many other places. Silt beds, pits have been discovered in sections, indicating a settlement of early Pit dwellers whose date has tentatively been fixed at around 2800 BC confirming presence of Neolithic followed by Megalithic (1600 ± 200 BC) people. These surveys show that the valley was pulsating with the Neolithic people and their descendants as the time elapsed. The Neolithic culture is indicated by the discovery of ground and polished stone axes, hoes, pestle, and bone implements. As per the survey, including carbon dating of Burzhom excavated sites, various other artefacts of that era, it has been found that Neolithic people came to the valley around 2600 ± 200 BC; hand made pottery introduced round about 2400 BC, Iron around 1800 BC and rice also came to Kas'mira with Megalithic period (1600 ± 200 BC). Some of the Neolithic sites, first excavated at Burzahom under the shadow of the Mahadev peak, 16 kilometres Northeast of Srinagar were found capped by later Megalithic complexes, beginning 1600 ± 200 BC, which indicates continuity of dwellings by Nagas and *Manus* (Aryans) of these sites including that of Mahapadamsar during both periods. Interestingly the founder of Kas'mira's hermitages described as in these Verses roughly are the areas were Neolithic (Naga) and Megalithic *Manu* (Aryan) settlement traces have been found (Translated); "See, O king, these are those peak - Brahma, Visnu, and Mahesvar. That which is Naubandhana peak is S'ankara (Mahadev peak!). The one on its right side is celebrated as Hari and the left one as Brahma. ..... To the north of that which is proclaimed as Visnupada in Kramasara, Brahma - the best of the gods - himself erected a hermitage. The venerable sage Kas'yapa constructed a hermitage in the western half. Mighty Mahadeva himself erected a hermitage at the spot where Visnu stood and obtained victory at that time (Verses 184-188)."

The artefacts excavated at Gufkral, near Tral, include stone and bone tools indicating dependence on wild game; a characteristics of tribals, aborigines; in this case Nagas. From the data collected at various excavations it is established that in the Neolithic period (Nagas), the early man of Kas'mira, took up agriculture on limited scale but depended on fishing and hunting. Cultural level similarity has been seen with the present areas of Punjab, Pakistan and Bharatvarasha and not with Mongoloid or Central Asians. The earliest level of Burzahom is dated to 2400 to 1800 BC, at Gufkral to 2400 BC; stage man had not come up in cultural evolution. Even though the archaeological site at Gufkral has given enough evidence of human culture going up to the stage of "Prolific temple building and flourishing sculptural art", yet no structure going to 1300 BC has so far been discovered archaeologically. The earliest such structures at Harvan near Srinagar, assigned to the Kushans (1st Century BC/AD) and 4th - 5th Century AD. Similarly the Buddhist establishment at Ushkur (*Huviskapura)* near Baramulla is of the Gandhara period (4th - 5th century AD). Kalhan in his Rajatarangini states that a large settlement or a city was located around Gopadari, the present day Shankaracharya hill in Srinagar. From about 1300 BC to about 100 BC no evidences of any large-scale human settlements have been found archaeologically, which indicates settlements of Nagas and Aryans (*Manus*) in smaller distributed groups.

Early Human Settlements in Kas'mira: We now come to yet another interesting subject that of appearance of the Neolithic man. These by all accounts are Nagas of more advanced Stone Age. From various artefacts, excavations, archaeological surveys it has been found that *Manus* (Aryans) were Advanced stage of lithic (stone) period. There is frequent mention that appearance of humans started about 5000 to 6000 years ago, era which bears an extraordinary correlation with the *Laukika* or *Saptarishi* era according to which the current year is 5088 (2012). This assumption has not been supplemented by any excavations, scriptures; neither in Kas'mira nor in Bharatvarasha. *Laukika* or *Saptarishi* almanac is followed even today in Kas'mira and many parts of Bharatvarasha. How this calendar was evolved and used even today will remains a mystery, which has been somewhat unfolded in Chapter 10.

In Bharatvarasha excavations at Harappa and many other places have been at their height between 2600-2500 BC, which collapsed around 2000-1800 BC and the first in the series are Harappan Civilization. The height of the civilization also coincides with the Neolithic man in Kas'mira. This evolution of Neolithic man (Nagas) in Kas'mira, as per research, seems to be a sudden outburst and does firmly indicate that Neolithic culture was evolved in the valley around 2600 ± 200 BC. This indicates the origin of the Nagas as the tribes of Northern India and that the Naga Kings where from the stock of original inhabitants of Bharatvarasha and Kas'mira. Even the Naga King's can be identified as; Gonandas from a stock of other than Pandavas, while Janmejaya is descendant of Pandavas. It is apparent that in Kas'mira descendants of Nagas ruled Ka'smira as Kings in later centuries.

In Nilamat dialogue same sage Brhadasava also figures with King Nila, when he tells him of his (Brhadasava's) curse to Visvagasva (The King of Mahapadamsar) before Mahapadama turned it into lake. This must be analysed in view of the fact that traces of human settlements of later period of Harappan civilisation have also been found in Kas'mira as well as plains of Jammu, Himachal Pradesh and Northern parts of undivided Punjab. Subsequently conservative dating of Aryan Immigration to Indus valley is given in 2000-1800 BC, Saraswati Bank settlements somewhere around 1800-1600 BC, composition of Rig Veda around 1800-1600 BC and settlements of Ganges Valley around 1600-1000 BC.

The settlements of Naga's in Kas'mira started during the Neolithic period (26OO ± 200 BC) and peaked around the beginning of Megalithic period (1600 ± 200); nearly for thousand years. This period also saw *Daitayas* and *Pis'acas* also settling down in the valley, though in different directions and away from the Naga settlements. Verses 984-985 gives out the Naga Kings in charge of various directions except the West (Translated); "Bindusara for East, Srimadhaka for South and Uttarmanasa for North." This indicates grouping of hamlets, direction wise, and for coordination separate Naga heads were designated. Absence of a Naga being nominated for West indicates that the (Nagas) hamlets did not exist in the West and the area possibly occupied by *Daitaya's* and *Pis'acas.* The Aryan settlements, again like Naga settlements, must have also started around 1600 ± 200 and peaked around 1300 BC. It may be of interest to know that all the settlements of humans (Nagas, *Daitayas, Pisa'cas* and *Manus*) were vibrant and only Aryan (Manu) settlements co-existed with Nagas; mostly in the Southern portion of the valley. This is the reason for mixing of religious and cultural rituals of the two and finding mention in Nilamat Puranam. The other two settlers (*Daitayas, Pis'acas*) did also exist but in different directions in Northern and Western areas and there was little or no interaction with Nagas and Aryans. It is not that Nagas disappeared suddenly. Slowly but steadily they too mixed with Aryans, in terms of habitation and cohabitation. Whereever this happened the settlements flourished in more density of humans. There is evidence of some isolated Naga settlements which continued as such till about 6th Century AD. Physical characteristics of Nagas can still be found amongst the denizens of certain hamlets in South Kas'mira; Antimony colour skin, short statured women, differing physical characteristics of face and nose, so different from Aryan race.

Evolution of Vitasta, Chronology of Mahapadamsar and Dating of Settlements

Evolution of Vitasta: Nilamat Puranam mentions that Kas'yapa having drained Satisar, made Goddess Uma to take the form of Vitasta. Geologically there is no denial of the fact that Kas'mira, many thousand years back, was a vast lake and was drained giving rise to *Karewas* (*Uddars* in Kashmiri. Numerous significant sloping high grounds). The drainage of the lake would have been along fault lines and once the *Karewas* settled and dried up, water from the mountains flowed down towards the *Karewas* and formed various streams, rivers, rivulets; many termed as holy rivers in Nilamat Puranam. Over a period of many centuries, rivulets, rivers, etc. that flowed in between *Karewas* formed a riverbed for water to flow. The river course of Vitasta, if carefully analysed, is through these gaps in *Karewas;* a natural phenomenon of water to find route through low lying ground. Again in the formation of this riverbed between *Karewas*, Nila Kund (Verinag) is the beginning point. The source of Vitasta is in the shadow of Pir Panjal range, in the form of a spring, which lets out the water through a naturally formed subterranean duct starting from Vyethvettor. The water of Nila Kund spring, as it flows through this bed, is joined enroute by other rivulets and streams. So technically and geographically Vitasta, starting from Nila Kund, is the mother river, as mentioned in Nilamat Puranam. This geographical phenomenon must have taken shape over millenniums and completed pre 3000 BC, though it is difficult to fix exact time frame. Name Vitasta finds mention in Rig Veda (Rig Veda 10: 75: 5); possibly associated with the time of Neolithic man (Harappan Civilisation – 2600 ± BC) (Naga's) in the valley. This name later percolated to Aryans, when they immigrated to Bharatvarasha and firmed in, to be mentioned in the *mantras* of Rig Veda.

The riverbanks of the entire length of Vitasta would indicate its basic top water level is much lower than its river bank. This can be attributed to the fact that at some time the flow of the river was much more than what it is now and confirms geographical obstructions in its flow existed somewhere down the line. We have one such recorded event of such obstruction in 9th Century during the reign of Avanti Varman (Utpal Dynasty; 855- June 883 AD), when Suya cleared the obstruction. Chroniclers record that near Yaksadara (Dyargul – near *Varahkshetra* (Varhamulla, Baramulla)), large rocks had rolled down from the mountain, lining both banks, obstructing Vitasta. Suya dragged out the rocks and the level of the river lowered and regulated the water of Vitasta. There is also earthquake having rocked the valley in earlier times, thus making faults and drainage lines. Before joining Mahapadamsar (Wular Lake), Vitasta course is full of turns, curves and this course keeps its pace in check but nowhere during its course turnings are acute. Mythical Saraswati River is reported to have dried up finally around 1200 BC, attributed to creation of geographical faults in the Northern Belt of Bharatvarasha, including Kas'mira. The dating coincides with Vedic Period (1600 BC) along Saraswati Ashrams, indicating that Saraswati River existed at that time. This fault may be either due to movement of Continental Plate or an earthquake, which forced many rivers to realign and absorb the waters of Saraswati. Many other fresh water bodies were also formed during this geographical change. Now for some distinct geographical features of the river pertinent to Mahapadamsar (Wular Lake).

- At present Vitasta enters Mahapadamsar (Wular Lake) from the direction of South at a place called Banyar, water of Manasbal Lake joins Vitasta near a place called Nesbal; some distance short of Mahapadamsar.
- Vitasta exits from Mahapadamsar towards Suyapur (Sopur, Sopore) in the Southwest; near Tarzoo. The angle of exit is nearly perpendicular to inlet point; normally this does not happen in the course of a river.
- Between the entry and exit of the river, there are marshes and huge Haigam Jhil (Lake).
- The exit course of Vitasta from Mahapadamsar has hillocks on the Northern side, which has compelled the exit course of the river to skirt it. Such an angle of entry and exit of Vitasta has nowhere been observed in its 84 miles (135 kilometres) in Kas'mira.
- The marshes, low lying areas and Haigam Jhil (Lake) are a major indication that Vitasta's course in this area was through Haigam Jhil, continuing its further course from the Northern edge of Haigam Jhil to join its present course near Suyapur (Sopur, Sopore). These indicators are that Vitasta subsequently changed its course to enter the lake. The exit of the river thereafter is along the grain of the ground; dictated by the hillocks in its North.
- Geographical features of Vitasta, in the vicinity of Mahapadamsar, will give indications of the time frame and evolution of Mahapadamsar, correlating it with scriptural evidence.

Physical Features of Mahapadamsar (Wular Lake): Asia's biggest fresh water lake, at present, is 13 miles long (20.8 kilometres) and 6 miles (9.6 kilometres) wide; an area of nearly 200 square kilometres. The maximum depth of the lake is 40 Metres (133 feet); this bottom level is considered as the lowest point in the valley of Kas'mira. Compare this when the lake was formed; one Yojna by one Yojna. To the North, Northeast right up to Southeast of the lake are mountains while Southern portion is plain and low-lying. The area of the lake, if dry, would look like an extensive deep bowl with tiered levels, like in *Karewas* (*Uddars*). These physical features of Mahapadamsar, narration in scriptures, chronicles, geographical and archaeological evidence will enable formulating the evolution and chronology of Mahapadamsar.

Evolution of Mahapadamsar (Wular Lake): It has been geographically established that five major fresh water bodies; the Dal (Dalla from which water flows into *Mahasarit (Chonth Kol)*), Nagin, Anchar, Manasbal and Mahapadamsar (Wular) were formed mainly during the later geological period and are not the remnants of the *Karewa* lake (*Satisar*). There are other geographical, physical features of Mahapadamsar, as available today, from various scriptures; Nilamat Puranam in particular, chronicles, folklore and legends. Each one of them has certain relevance for evolving chronology of the evolution of Mahapadamsar (Wular Lake). Read above

- When Sadangula, as per Nilamat Puranam, was forced to leave the area it was dry and was a 'city named Candrapura, of the king Visvagasva', which later got submerged.
- As per legend Mahapadma converted it into a *sar* (Lake). This is supposed to have taken place when both Nagas and Kasyapa had settled Aryans in Kas'mira.
- The dimensions of Mahapadamsar as given in Nilamat Puranam are much bigger than exisiting dimensions. The changes in dimensions can be attributed to environmental changes over the millenniums.
- In 9th Century Suya cleared obstruction at *Varahkshetra* (Varhamulla, Baramulla), which indicates that there had been obstruction in the river Vitasta and after his effort the water level came down. Therefore, there has to be increase in length and breadth of the lake between 4th/5th Century BC and 9th Century AD. No scripture has mentioned or dated any natural calamity during this period causing river obstruction.
- When water level goes down in the lake; otherwise or during winter, top of a Temple is seen. The chronicler of Zain-ul-Abidin (Jonaraja) has also confirmed this. This is *Prateshwara* temple built by King Prahlad (12th Century). Finding of idols inside the submerged temple indicates that the water level was much below the level of the base of the submerged temple, which rose suddenly and gave no chance for retrieval of these idols. This indicates natural calamity, when the water of the lake rose suddenly; somewhere between 10th (After Suya) and 12th Century. Again there is no mention of any natural calamity in any scripture or chronicle.

Chronology of Mahapadamsar (Wular Lake): In 21st Century, with the advancement of science, it is difficult to propound theories based only on scriptures, folklore, chronicles, unless supported by scientific proof. Religious scriptures are mostly later works, having been preserved as *Shruti* (voice heard) and *Smriti* (remembered) and finally compiled at later stage. Nilamat Puranam is one of the oldest scriptures, which Kalhan has also mentioned in his memorable Rajatarangini and restructured contents from Nilamat Puranam.

- Vitasta River finds mention in Rig Veda and thus geographical phenomenon of its birth is pre Rig Veda and pre 3000 BC. Vitasta name is pre Vedic era.
- During Neolithic period (2600 ± 200 BC) Mahapadamsar was not a lake but a low lying plain of the valley.
- The area of Mahapadamsar surrounded by mountain range from North to South-East, must have looked like a vast deep bowl, with tiered rising segments of land.
- The evolution of Mahapadamsar in its form, as described in Nilamat Puranam, appears to have taken place during Megalithic period around 1200 ± BC, the time when Aryans had settled in Bharatvarasha and had moved to other areas including Kas'mira. This can also be when the mythical Saraswati River dried up due to a Geographical Fault or an Earthquake (Read earlier).
- Once submerged, the habitation settled on the tiered dry area around the lake extending right up to Garur, close by. This state of the lake remained so till 4th or 5th Century when Nilamat Puranam was written (At best end of BC era). The time when other water bodies of Kas'mira (Dal Lake, Nagin, Anchar and Manasbal were formed could be also during this period (1200 ± BC) or later.
- Being an old and ancient habitation area, settlements sprang up again including Prateshwara temple built by King Prahlad (12th Century).
- The water rose again, as the tributaries to Mahapadamsar had increased including Vitasta and one of those days' flash floods increased the volume of water input, submerging the temple. Finding of idols inside the submerged temple indicates that the water level was much below the level of the base of the submerged temple, when the temple was constructed, which rose suddenly and gave no chance for retrieval of these idols. This could have been between 12th and 14th Century.
- The frequent events of Mahapadamsar had forced the habitation to settle at safer places. However as a religious fervour another temple was re-constructed on the islands formed. Garur can also be part of this segment.

Nilamat and Kas'mira: A reading of Nilamat Puranam has been curtain raiser to the history of Kas'mira, Sindhu (Sindh), Vitasta and Mahapadamsar. In recent years archaeological and geological survey reports on Kas'mira and various sites of Kas'mira appeared. Question was correlating details known from Sacred Scriptures (Nilamat Puranam in particular) with the scientific data, to make it convincing and prove their relevance. Admittedly survey reports give closer time frame than that from scriptures. This is mainly due to events that occurred centuries earlier remembered and compiled at a later stage. In this aberrations do take place in time frame or events, not that they do not in scientific surveys. An effort has been made to correlate events leading to the naming of Kas'mira, Vitasta and Sindhu (Sindh), time frame of human habitation and finally evolution and chronology of Mahapadamsar as under:

- Name Kas'mira is attributed to Prajapati, who is called Ka and Kas'yapa is also Prajapati. "Built by him this country will be called Kas'mira. Because water called Ka was taken out by Balarama (the plough-wielder)…."
- Though appearance of humans in Kas'mira is attributed to about 5000 to 6000 years ago, correlating with *Saptarishi* [5080 (2004)], Survey, carbon dating has, however, found that Neolithic people (Naga's followed by others) came to the valley only around 2600 ± 200 BC. Many of these settlements were capped by later Megalithic people (*Manu's* (Aryans)), dating 1600 ± 200 BC.
- Nilamat Puranam uses terms Nagas, *Daitayas, Pis'acas* and *Manus* (Aryans), appearing in Kas'mira, till finally Aryans prevailed. These races can be identified as the people, in that order, during Neolithic (Nagas, *Daitayas, Pisacas*) and Megalithic period (*Manus* (Aryans)).
- The time of appearance of humans in Kas'mira is taken as a sudden outburst during Neolithic period. The origins of original inhabitants or aborigines (Nagas) of Kas'mira can be attributed to then Bharatvarasha. These verses of Nilamat Puranam (345-50) indicates King Nila of *Krishna Yoni* (Dark Skinned); "Seeing in their midst, Nila, resembling a mass of black antimony……." and; "O Nila of dark blue complexion, O lord of the gods, O king of the Naga's (Verse 353)". Nila is also depicted as son of Kas'yapa.
- It is apparent that *Daitayas* and *Pisacas* are later entrants to Kas'mira after Nagas. This could be possibly at the end of the Neolithic period (Before 1600 ± BC).
- Initial group of Megalithic period are *Manus* (Aryans), their immigration keeping pace with their movements in Bharatvarasha and in Kas'mira during Megalithic period 1600 ± 200 BC.
- Geographical phenomenon of formation of Vitasta must have taken place pre 3000 BC, though difficult to fix time frame.
- Nilamat Puranam Legend lucidly covers the events leading upto creation of Mahapadamsar (Wular Lake). Apparently area of Mahapadamsar was a low lying plain of the valley. The event of the formation of initial Mahapadamsar and naming can be dated to 1200 BC (During Megalithic period). This cause is likely to be an earthquake or a geographical fault, when the area of Candrapura caved in.

- Dal (Dalla), Nagin, Anchar, and Manasbal were formed during the later geological period (1200 BC) and are not the remnants of the *Karewa* Lake (Satisar).
- Suyapur could well have been called Visvagaspura during ancient times prior to 9th Century.

In this chapter effort has been made to validate Geographical and Archaeological data with that of Nilamat Puranam or may be vice-versa. It has amply been proved that while time frame in our scriptures was not quoted in the today's time data/scale; the events had definite co-relation with actual happenings. May be that natural events have been turned into mythical ones, or may be these mythical happenings did occur due to higher spiritual power of our ancestor sages. Who knows! Nilamat Puranam, our sacred scripture, comes out tall, with its contents, the rhythm and the events. Only our ancestors were capable of creating such an epic. This chapter has taken into consideration certain scientific data in terms of excavation and assessment reports of Archaeological Survey of India pertaining to Harappan Civilisation, Aryans, Neolithic and Megalithic sites in Bharatvarasha; Burzhom, Gufkral and Gurhom Sangri (All in Kas'mira). In addition Geographical Survey reports of Bharatvarasha and Kas'mira, Evolution of Himalayas etc have been incorporated at appropriate places.

Gopadiri Temple (Shankracharya). Gopadiri *Agrahara* (*Jagir*) attached to the Temple is now called Gupkar

Huska Era Coin

Nila Kund (Nil Nag, Verinag). (The Shape of the Nag was turned into Octagonal one During Reign of Jehangir)

Jehangir–Mughal Miniature Painting by Bichitr, c. 1625 AD

River Vitasta (Wyeth-Jhelum) Meandering Through Pravarpura (Srinagar) City

Mahapadamsar (Wular Lake) as seen from a Hill Top West of the Lake

Temple Inside Manasbal Lake
(Photograph Courtesy Rohit Kaul–June 2012)

Temple Side Arches of Sun Temple at Martand

3

Ancient, Hindu Rule and Advent of Islam

Those who act kindly in this world will have kindness

- *Quran 39.10*

Ancient Rule

Chronology of Early Settler Kings: From assessment of verses of Nilamat Puranam as well as Rajatarangini, chronology of Kings amongst early settlers, due to absence of authentic data, could possibly be as under and different from dates ascribed to them in Rajatarangini (For detailed calculations read Chapter 10):

- Gonanda I. Coronation - Roughly 3179/3180 BC.
- Gonanda I killed and Damodar's Coronation - Roughly 3149 BC.
- Gonanda II Coronation to be around 3142 BC.
- The known Chronology of the Kings of Kas'mira starts from 3179/3180 BC . Historical narrations by our scholars including Kalhan have so far been quoting 653 Kali Samvat (2448 BC) in all references to the Kings of Kas'mira; out by nearly 730 years.

In Rajatarangini chronology, apart from some King's known to be of Naga lineage, on a fair estimate names and deeds of nearly additional fifty Kings and not only thirty five kings as mentioned by Kalhan, totalling nearly eighty five Kings, have been lost. These could well be distributed; more than thirty five Kings after Damodara II (including Harandev and twenty three of Pandav lineage), between Kings Surendra and Godhara (latter belonging to another family indicating change in dynasty; probably Nagas), in the list of Kings recorded by Helaraja, Chavillakara and finally includes Indo–Greek rulers after Ashoka's Maurya Dynasty and before Kushan rule.

Pre Historic–500 BC: While few rulers/reigns of Pre Historic BC and early AD era can be established from the analysis of Nilamat Puranam and Rajatarangini, with reference to the rule of Kings between 3000-500 BC, the religion and system of rule prevailing then cannot be accurately figured. With the immigration of Aryans to Kas'mira, they brought rich tradition of Vedic Religion, which was at its infancy and turned into Brahmanism later. A Kashmiri clan is specifically quoted in *Mahabharata* and Nilamat Puranam quotes few kings, Gonandas and Yasomati, around the time of *Mahabharata* War (3137 BC). Between 3000 BC and 1000 BC, reign of three Kings can be identified; that of King Sandiman (2629-2564 BC), King Sunder Sen (2082-2041 BC) and King Nara (1048-1008 BC). There is no mention of Gautam Buddha's (May 623-547 BC) rule of Kas'mira, before he abdicated, but fifty years after him i.e. around 500 BC Buddhism had spread, as a toe hold, in Kas'mira. There is no mention of any religious influence by Adi-Shankara (of 5th Century BC) or Mahavira (599-527 BC).

Ashoka and Early AD Era: Verses 709-710a of Nilamat Puranam holds Buddha as the incarnation of Vishnu and as such it is fair to assume that *Vaishnavism* preceded Buddhism in Kas'mira and Buddhism was admix of *Vaishnavism* and Buddhism propounded by Gautam Buddha. King Gopaditya (417-357 BC), who established *Gopadiri Agrahara* (*Jagir*) (Gupkar - Shankaracharaya) was a *Vaishnavite* King, when Buddhism had not fully established and had a mere foothold in Kas'mira. Emperor Ashoka (273-232 BC) having spread Buddhism and extended rule over Kas'mira is well chronicled. Many believe Ashoka did come to Kas'mira but it is not so. In fact artifacts, Viharas or any relics of that period do not confirm his visit nor is their any evidence to this effect. Spread of Buddhism in Kas'mira is attributed to his *Bikshus,* specifically ordained and given this task by him. Ashoka's adviser Moggaliputta Tissa sent Majjhantika, his disciple, to preach Buddhism in Kas'mira (3rd Century BC).

As part of Ashoka's reign scholars attribute naming of Srinagar to him and associate it with his visit to Kas'mira. During Emperor Ashoka's rule over Kas'mira, a city, capital, under the name of Grinagari between Zabarwan Hills on the Eastern side on the banks of Dal Lake and Pandrethan, on the Southern outskirts of the present day Srinagar City, next to cantonment was founded. Girinagari name is derived from the hills around which the city (Girinagari) skirted; Giri meaning - Hill/Mountain; Nagari –Town; meaning town skirting hills. This is also confirmed by archealogical finds attributed to Emperor Ashoka's time in the belt of Pandrethan–Zabarwan. But in no way it indicated Ashoka's visit to Kas'mira or naming of City of Srinagar by Ashoka. Pandrethan is corrupted name of Puranadhishthan (old Capital), as it appeared to be capital of Kas'mira during his rule and few more centuries later. About five centuries later an extention of Girinagari was made and called Sri Nagari. Gradually the younger city, Sri Nagari, not only deprived its older rival of all its importance but also Ashoka's city Girinagari came to be known simply by the appellation of 'Puranadhishthan'. This name was still in use as early as the time of Huen Tsang, who visited Kas'mira in 631 AD. It is erroneously thought that Girinagari later came to be known as Sri Nagari. According to Kalhan, Magadh King, Ashoka (different from Ashoka the Great), who annexed Kas'mira in 250 AD, built new city of Sri Nagari, five kilometres from the present day Srinagar city, which stretched from Harvan, East edge of Dal Lake to Zewan, further South of Pandrethan. Scholars feel, erroneously though, that Kalhan was wrong in his assessment and Ashoka of Magadh was no other than Emperor Ashoka, Mauryan dynasty. Kalhan was not wrong as while describing Emperor Ashoka, he specifically mentions Ashoka's foundations and works. Like in Verse 102 King Ashoka is referred to; "embraced the doctrine of Jina, covered *Susalaletra* (Village of *Hukhlitr*) and *Vitastatra* (Vithvutur village near Verinag) with numerous Stupas." In fact King Jaluka, believed to be Emperor Ashoka's son or his representative, foundations in the valley have also been elucidated by Kalhan in detail (*Bhutesara* (Naran Nag); *Jyesthrudra* (Girinagari)) and one finds no reason as to why if Emperor Asoka had founded Sri Nagari, Kalhan would refrain from attributing foundation of the city to him and would have described it in detail, as in the case of Pravarpura. The mere fact Kalhan chose to attribute founding of Sri Nagri to Ashoka (Magadh King around 250 AD) with a single simple verse clearly indicates that Emperor Ashoka founded Girinagari and not Sri Nagari. The question remains as to why only five centuries later a new town named Sri Nagari was founded by Magadh King. From all accounts the capital Girinagari was away from Vitasta (Jhelum) and was skirting water bodies to its East and administratively city had to have a suitable accessible area fit for a capital between the river and water bodies. It gains credence that it is during this period Buddhism had started to wane and there was renaissance of Brahmanism and worship of Goddess Sri. Her *yantra Sri Chakra* had gained momentum in Bharatvarasha and with the annexation of Kas'mira many temples in the name of the goddess Sri were founded in Kas'mira. Thus, the name Sri of the goddess and *Nagari* (City) and new city called Sri Nagari; City of Sri, seems to have been the central seat till about 6th Century and away from Girinagari (Puranadhishthan). Even in Nilamat Puranam word Sri finds mention pointing to Sri Nagari as the abode of Hari. Verse 1-2; 'Having paid homage to the god Hari - the abode of Sri, the giver of boons, the highest lord, the master of three worlds, the finder of cow (earth), the imperishable and the unchangeable'. The reason that Magadh King Ashoka had only remotely annexed Kas'mira, is enough not to include him as the King's of Kas'mira in Rajatarangini.

Two centuries later Pravarsena II moved his capital farther down the river Vitasta (Jhelum, also called Wyeth), calling it Pravarpura, which continued to be called so till about end of 12th Century. All over cities then were called 'Pura'. Gradually this younger city, Pravarpura, deprived its older rivals (Girinagari-Purandishthan; Sri Nagari) of all their importance and generally became the seat of Kings. Admittedly name of the city, Purandishthan, and not recent name Sri Nagari, continued to be talked about and was also in use as early as the time of Huen Tsang. The reason seems to be that both the capitals, Purandishthan and Sri Nagari, were contiguous and Purandishthan seems to have continued to be the capital even after Sri Nagari was founded. During the later centuries focus shifted even from Pravarpura, though for a little while. Lalitaditya (7th Century) established another new capital Parihaspura; Jayapira (764-795 AD) tried to construct new capital Jayapura and Avanti Varman (Utpal Dynasty; 855- June 883 AD) during his reign shifted the focus away from Pravarpura to Avantipur and Martand. Pravarpura name bounced back and was in use during 10th Century and finds mention in the first verse of the *Vartika* on "*Malini Vijaya*" where it has been specifically laid down; "The *Kashmirian* Abhinav Gupta in the East of the city (Sri Nagari) known as Pravarapura composed *Vartika* as the very first verse of "*Malini Vijaya.*" Thus, three names for current day capital Srinagar were in use at one time or the other; Girinagari (Purandishthan), Sri Nagari (Srinagar) and Pravarpura. It is after installation of idol of *Sarika* (Sharika; Chakreshwari) at Sarika Parvat around 12th Century, Pravarpura, the seat of administration moved closer to Vitasta and Sri Nagar (Sri Nagari) name resurfaced and Sri Nagar (Srinagar) city came into prominence. From all the accounts, the seat of the Kings then on remained in the central part of the city Sri Nagar (Srinagar). Incidentally *Baharistan-e-Shahi*, a Muslim history of Kas'mira written during 1593-1614 AD, refers to Srinagar as *Shahr-e–Khaas* (City of Kas'mira), which became *Shahr* for rural people, while referring to Srinagar, even today.

After Ashoka's Maurya Dynasty and before Kushan rule, for nearly two hundred years, Kas'mira was ruled by Indo-Greek Kings or their representatives before Kushans arrived in 1st Century AD. This is also confirmed by finds of silver coins of Indo-Scythians on the banks of Vitasta (Jhelum) in the hills between Baramulla (Varhamulla) and Jhelum, which later influenced the design of coins of later Kas'mira Kings. Indo-Greek rule also gave unique architectural and sculptural design of old Kas'mira temples. One of the famous Greek rulers was a Greek General Meanander (175-150 BC), who converted to Buddhism and is considered as one of the finest rulers of Kas'mira.

Buddhism given impetus by Ashoka, continued till end of 100 AD with Kushan dynasty; Kushan King Kanishka (100 AD), Huska, Juska, Abhimanyu,

Vibhisana I, Indrajit, Ravana, Vibhisana II as per Rajatarangini. Kushan King Kanishka's reign is well chronicled from 127 -151 AD, though these dates are still disputed. Kanishka is believed to have reigned for 23 years and started Saka Samvat dating it to 78 AD, which some chroniclers say is the year of his coronation and thus disputing the dates of 127-151 AD. Kanishka's empire was vast, extending from Southern Uzbekistan and Tajikistan, North of River Oxus (*Amu Darya*) in the Northwest to Northern India as far as Mathura, Patliputra (Patna) and also included Kas'mira, where there was a town Kanishkapur, named after him, closer to Baramulla where there is still base of a large *Stupa.*

Buddhist Stupa Near Baramulla-1868 AD-Courtesy John Burke

Huen Tsang (7th Century; 631 A D) records that during Kanishka's reign Kas'mira was linked with a vast empire of extended Bharatvarasha. He organised fourth and last Buddhist Council, attended by about five hundred Buddhist scholars, at Kundal Vanvihara (Also *Shadarhatvana* (Harvan) (Kas'mira)). History mentions that Ava Gosha was a famous Buddhist Scholar of Patliputra (Patna) and Kanishka 'invaded' Patliputra to get his services for organising Fourth Buddhist Council at Harvan (Kas'mira)). Ava Gosha wrote *Buddhacarita,* a verse compendium of Buddha's teachings and first of Buddhist scriptures written in the Kas'mira and settled in the valley after the Fourth Buddhist Council. Majority of Historians place the location of this council as Harvan in Kas'mira. However, archaeological finds indicate Jallandhar. The differences are due to the fact that most of the history pertaining to Kanishka is shrouded in mystery. Even today the dates of his reign, areas he controlled, coronation date etc are hotly debated. A peep into Kanishka's time is necessary to give an idea of his empire and reign. Kanishka needed three capitals; Purushapura (Peshawar, now in Pakistan), Bagram (In Afghanistan) and Mathura (Bharatvarasha) to control his vast empire, which comprised of Bactria (Modern Afghanistan), part of Central Asia (Tajikastan) and Northwestern India (Pakistan) and Northern India including Kas'mira till Patliputra (Patna). Kanishka, King of Kushans, a Central Asian tribe, was forgotten few decades after him, but the coins and structures the dynasty left behind testify to the glory of Kushans. Kushan is derived from *Kuei Shand*, the clan that took control of the *Yuezhi* tribe and launched the push into Bharatvarasha. Kanishka a Zorastrian, embraced Buddhism during the middle of his reign. He personally seems to have embraced both the Persian Cult of Mithra and Mahayana Buddhism. It is mentioned that Kanishka donated entire Kas'mira to *Sangha* (Collective Buddhist Organisation), built many Viharas and raised Stupas (Buddhist Monuments) all over his domain. Kanishka's coins portray images of Indo-Aryan, Greek and Iranian divinities, which from the beginning of his reign bear legend 'Coin of Kanishka, King of Kings' in Greek. Later coins bear legends in Bactrian (Central Asian Dialect) and Iranian. His ancestors seem to have embraced Hinduism; his father Vima Kadphises, who made Kushans a strong power in Northern India, proclaimed himself as *Mahishwara* on his coins. Kanishka and his descendants called themselves *Devputra*, who ruled Aryavarta. The Kushan empire decline in Bharatvarsha began with the death of his descendant Vasudeva I and gave way to mighty Guptas in fourth Century. In Rajatarangini Kanishka's descendants are mentioned as Huska, Juska etc. and not Vasudeva I, as is chronicled in Bharatvarasha. From this and details of Kushan Dynasty given in Rajatarangini, it appears that later rulers of Kushan Dynasty after Kanishka do not appear to be his direct descendants though they may have been related or from the same tribe. It appears that Kanishka's rule in Kas'mira had come to an end with the rule of Vibhishana II, as chronicled in Rajatarangini.

Buddhism continued for a while, till about 300 AD, in Kas'mira. Buddhism thereafter was on a downslide. Later chronicles mention a Magadh King, Ashoka (different from Ashoka the Great) annexed Kas'mira in 250 AD and built new city of Sri Nagri (earlier). This King Ashoka had built a 'stupa' in today's Badgam, relics of which have been found. This city Sri Nagri later got the name of Srinagar with extended areas, though it cannot be placed as to the era in which transition of the name to Srinagar came about. It was during Dogra rule Srinagar name replaced name of *Shahr*.

In 515 AD, Mihir Kula (515-550 AD), a Hun General, also called terrorist king, ascended the throne. He devastated Viharas, Chaityas and Mutts and killed Buddhists ruthlessly. Later till beginning of 7th Century Gonanda dynasty gave Kas'mira two notable rulers; Meghavahan and Pravarsena II. This was the beginning of a pure Hindu rule. Meghavahan, a pious and a strong ruler with Buddhist leanings, stopped killing of animals and birds throughout his Kingdom and undertook conquest of many nearby countries solely for the purpose of stopping animal slaughter. The next great King was Pravarsena II (6th Century AD), a staunch believer in Brahmanism, conqueror who extended the boundaries of Kas'mira in all directions and ruled for 60 years. Pravarsena II installed *Sri Chakra* at Chakreshwar (Hari Parvat), established his capital down town of present Srinagar along river Vitasta, calling it Pravarpura. After Pravarsena II for next century the rule was indifferent by weak rulers, who hardly made any contribution to be talked about.

Hindu Rule

Hindu Dynasties - Karkota Dynasty (631- 855 AD): In 631 AD Karkota Dynasty rule was founded by Durlabh Vardhana. Huen Tsang, the great Chinese pilgrim entered Kas'mira during Dulabh Vardhana's time (631 AD) and notes that entry of all outsiders, except Hindus, was banned. Durlabha Vardhana established roots and most importantly brought *Vaishnavite* Philosophy to Kas'mira, which flourished further during the rule of Lalitaditya Muktapira (724-761 AD). Lalitaditya, the third son of Karkota King Partapaditya II, succeeded his brother Tarapira in 724 AD. Amongst the Kings of Kas'mira, of all the times, Lalitaditya Muktapira is considered greatest ruler of Kas'mira and equated to Samudra Gupta of Bharatvarasha. Narration of his numerous expeditions will fill pages, as he successfully led numerous expeditions to many Asian and Bharatvarasha Kingdoms of that time, which included Tibet, Iran, Ladakh, Punjab, Kannuj, Bihar, Gauda (Bengal), Kalinga (Orissa), parts of South India, Malwa, Marwar and Gujarat. He also broke the power of Arabs in Sindh (Pakistan). His expedition to Sindh can best be judged by passage from a letter by Dahar, the King of Sindh to Mohammad Bin Qasim, first Muslim invader of Bharatvarasha, in 712 AD; "........If I had sent against you the King of Kashmir on whose threshold the other rulers of Hind had placed their heads, who sways the whole of Hind, even the countries of Makran and Turan..." His victories created a feeling of pride amongst denizens of Kas'mira, who include his name in the daily worship and special *Pujas* till this day (His name is still mentioned in Kas'mirian *Puja* on *Shivratri*). Kalhan, the great historian, records that even in his time (12th Century) victories of Lalitaditya were celebrated throughout Kas'mira. Al-Beruni, who accompanied Mohammad Ghaznavi in his Indian campaigns, specifically mentions in *Tahqiq-i-Hind* that Kas'miris observed second of *Chaitra* (Feburary/March), as the day of victory, in the memory of the expeditions of Lalitaditya.

Lalitaditya Muktapira was equally a great builder; he built very fine and massive temples including world famous Sun Temple at Martand, new capital close to Kheer Bhawani (Tulla Mulya (Tul Mul)) naming it Parihaspur (City of Pleasure). He was also known as Mukhtapira; even 'Sharda' Mukhtapira in later chronicles. Though himself a Vaishnavite Hindu, he erected a massive Buddhist Vihara at Parihasapur, though Buddhism had started to wane in the valley by then.

Lalitaditya built a new capital under the name of Parihaspura (City of Pleasure), near Mansbal. Throughout Kas'mira many temples were built by him including world famous Sun Temple at Martand (Mattan). After his death, mostly weak rulers ruled Kas'mira, except his grandson Jayapira (764-795 AD). Jayapira's expeditions were few in comparison, but he too tried to construct a new capital Jayapura, closer to Parihaspura. He is known for confiscation of *Jagir* lands of Tulla-Mulya (Tulla Mulya) *Agrahara* (*Jagir*) and taxes imposed on parts of *Agrahara*. For this he was cursed by one of the Brahmins of Tulla Mulya, named Atal. Few days later a heavy pole of the throne's canopy fell on Jayapira and after a few days later he died and his death was attributed to curse of the Brahmin Atal of Tulla-Mulya. With the death of Jayapira, rule of Karkota dynasty slid further and the vast Kingdom of Lalitaditya disintegrated and was constricted to areas around Vitasta Basin. Just before end of the dynasty, Ajitpira (813-850 AD) ruled Kas'mira but closer to his death the kingdom had shrunk further, inspite of his efforts during 38 years of his rule. By 855 AD a new dynasty, Utpala, took over the rule of Kas'mira.

Utpala Dynasty (855-939 AD): It was around 855 AD that Karkota rule ended, and a new Utpala Dynasty under Avanti Verman (855-883 AD) assumed power in Kas'mira. Avanti Verman recovered Kas'mira from utter political and economic disorder and rose to great heights in the realm of philosophy, art and literature. There was an outburst of literary activity on a grand scale. The most important foundation of the King was his capital city of Avantipur, which he embellished with two temples; one dedicated to Shiva and other to Vishnu. Both of them are in ruins now, but even then, they stand as the most imposing monuments of ancient Kas'mira. Avanti Varman, the first King from Utpala Dynasty, is termed as the first fully Vaishnavite King of Kas'mira, who built the shrines of Vishnu Avantisvamin, even before he became a king. Avanti Varman during his reign shifted the focus away from Pravarpura to Avantipur.

It was during Avanti Varman's time Kas'mirian Suya with his singular thinking regularised the flow of Vitasta (Jhelum) at the outlet of Wular Lake near the present town of Sopore, which got its name from Suya; Suyapur. Avanti Varman died in a temple on the Dal Lake, when a fatal disease caught him, and in the words of Kalhan; "listening to the end to the song of the

Lord and thinking of the residence of Vishnu (Vaikuntha) he cast off his earthly life with a cheerful mind." Avanti Varman was succeeded by his son Shankar Varman (883-902), an ambitious and oppressive ruler. He conquered neighbouring kingdoms including Gujarat, which was then under the rule of a Muslim and led an expedition to Kabul. He founded the city of Shankarpura, now known as Pattan. During the reign of Shankar Varman the struggle between the Brahmins and other castes such as *Kayasth's,* reached a climax, but power of Brahmins was broken by Shankar Varman. With the death of Shankar Varman, his son Gopal Varman (902 to 904 AD) succeeded him. During short three year rule of Gopal Varman, an expedition under a general, Prabhakar Deva, was mounted towards Kabul, who successfully installed an amenable King on Kabul throne. However, within Kas'mira general disorder had set in, which threw into prominence turbulent Kas'miri tribe, Tantrins (Tantray's), who set up one king after another, until Chakra Varman (922-933 AD) with the help of 'Damaras' and 'Ekangas' broke their power. 'Damaras' were the feudal barons and 'Ekangas' the Kings Bodyguard. When Chakra Varman was killed by Damaras, the decline of Utpala dynasty had already set in and by 939 AD Utpala dynasty ceased to exist. A Brahmin King, Vyasaskara Deva (939-48 AD), was placed on the throne by Damaras, who ruled for a period of about a decade. This short rule was followed by a brief spell of 54 years by Gupta Dynasty.

Gupta Dynasty (949-1003 AD): The dynasty was started by Parva Gupta, who ruled for a year plus and on his death the throne passed on to his son Kshema Gupta. In 950 AD, Kshema Gupta a man of mediocre ability, ascended the throne of Kas'mira and married princess Didda, daughter of the ruler of Lohara (Poonch) and grand daughter of the Bhima Shahi King of Kabul. Bhima is described by Al-Beruni as the Brahman King to rule Kabul. During Kshema Gupta's time Didda was de-facto ruler of the state, as she was very dominating and exercised immense influence over her husband. On the death of Kshema Gupta in 958 AD, Didda became the regent (958-972 AD) of their minor son Abhimanyu II. Before her, two other women had been regents of Kas'mira; namely Yasomati (Regent for her minor son Gonnanda II- Pre BC Era around *Mahabharata* War)) and Sugandha (Regent 904-906 AD after death of Gopal Varman). In 980 AD, Didda after killing of her grandson ascended the throne in collusion with a peasant named Tunga. Didda led a very immoral life and was unscrupulous and literally became paramour of Tunga. Inspite of these drawbacks, she firmly ruled Kas'mira. It was during her time, Mohammad Ghaznavi tried twice to capture Kas'mira but strong fort at Lohara (Poonch), proved impregnable forcing Ghaznavi to abandon the expedition. As her children and grandchildren had died, she by her machinations settled the succession to the throne in favour of Sangram Raja, son of her brother Udai Raja, the ruler of Lohara (Poonch). After her death in 1003 AD, Sangram Raja ascended the throne, as planned and thus started the rule of Lohara Dynasty of Poonch.

As per later research of above dynasties in AD era, there are clear indications of Naga Kings having ruled Kas'mira. These are Kârkota Nâga and Utpala dynasties of Kas'mira (631 to 1003 AD), with attributed lineage to the founder of the Nâga dynasty, suggesting indigenous family. Karkota Naga Kings (631 – 855 AD) were; Durlabha Vardhana; Pratipâditya (Durlabhaka); Candrapîda;. Lalitâditya Muktâpîra (724-761); Jayapira (764- 95 AD). Karkota Naga dynasty was followed by another Naga lineage dynasty (Utpala dynasty) Avanti Varman (855-883), Shankar Varman (883-902 AD) and Diddâ (Khasa princess who kills off her grandsons) exercisd power from around 950 and ruled with the peasant Tunga from 980-1003 AD.

Lohara Dynasty (1003-1273 AD): During the reign of Sangram Raja (1003-1028 AD) it is recorded that the Kas'miri's crossed river Toushi and destroyed detachment of soldiers sent by Mohammad Ghaznavi but had to withdraw due to stiff resistance. It is at this time Punjab passed into Muslim hands and most of the tribes on the borders of Kas'mira embraced Islam, who even after their conversion, continued to come to Kas'mira as traders, tourists and some for furthering the cause of Islam. However, even with this increase in visits of Muslims there was no effect on the polity of Kas'mira. Sangram Raja was succeeded by his son Hari Raja (1028 A D), who had just a year of rule and on his death Ananta (1028-1063 AD) took over the throne.

During Ananta's reign Damaras, the feudal lords, rose in rebellion, but were ruthlessly crushed. It is during this time an expedition to neighbouring Chamba, through which road to Eastern Punjab passed, was mounted successfully. However, expedition to Hazara (NWFP- Pakistan), which connected Kas'mira with Western Punjab and Afghan territory failed. Due to Ananta's expedition his fame spread and Princess of Jallandhar area, Suryamati, was married to him. She was a brave queen and accompanied Ananta on many expeditions. *Kathasaritsagara* (Ocean of the Streams of Stories) famous Sanskrit 11th Century collection of Indian legends, fairy tales and folk tales as retold by a Shaivite Brahmin named Somadeva. Nothing is known about the author other than that his father's name was Ramadev Bhatta, an Aryan Saraswat Brahmin of Kashmir. The work was compiled for the entertainment of the Ananta's queen Suryamati. *Kathasaritsagara* consists of 18 books of 124 chapters and approximately 22,000 Shlokas (distichs) in addition to prose sections. The complete translation into English is by C. H. Tawney (1837–1922), published in two volumes (1300 pages in all) in 1880 and 1884 AD.

After the death of Ananta, Kalsa ruled for 26 years (1063-1089 AD). There was no let up in the activities of Damaras and Kas'mira passed through a difficult phase.

From 1089 to 1101 AD, Harsha ruled Kas'mira. Versed in many languages, a good poet, lover of music and art, he started his rule in a remarkable way and became famous in Northern India. Kings prior to his accession relied solely upon their Ekangas (Body Guards) and Tantrin (Tantray) soldiers, but for the first time in the history of Kas'mira, Harsha enrolled Muslims in his army. Muslim soldiers were grouped in a lot of hundred, each under a Muslim commander. From this time, with their fighting qualities and royal patronage, Muslim soldiers became powerful factor in the political scene of Kas'mira. During this time people suffered from famine, plague and a sizeable section of citizens became victims of these calamities. Harsha embarked upon a policy of exorbitant taxation and even robbed the temples of their valuables. This created a great deal of resentment amongst people, nobleman and the army, which led to a general uprising under two nephews, of Harsha; Uchchala and Sushala. Harsha along with his son Bhoja were murdered with the help of Damaras and the kingdom passed on to two brothers, Uchchala and Sushala, in turn. Uchchala (1101-1111 AD) soon fell out with Damaras, as he could not fulfil their extravagant demands and dealt a crushing blow to them. In the reign of Sushala (1111-1128 AD) who followed Uchchala, Damaras again rose in rebellion. They attacked and plundered the city of Pravarpura (Srinagar) and reduced the king to such a plight that he had to flee for his life to Poonch. Bikhshachara, a distant cousin of Sushala, was selected for the kingship by the rebellious nobles and supported by Muslim of the Royal Army. Finally these soldiers were destroyed by Sushala in a short time. The Turshkas (Muslims) gone, Bikhshachara was defeated and Sushala regained his power. However, at the end both, Uchchala and Sushala met the same fate as that of Harsha; killed by those very people who had supported them to become kings.

Later Period-Lohara Dynasty: This is the time Lohara (Poonch) Dynasty descendants re-appeared and Jai Simha's (1128 - 1155 AD) ascended the throne. During his reign, there was general disorder because of the preceding civil war and political unrest created by rebellious warring chiefs, but Jai Simha coped with it and even defeated a detachment of foreign troops, which were about to raid Kas'mira. Another tribe known as Lavanyas (Lones) now came into prominence, still Jai Simha was able to maintain his firm rule for 27 years in comparative safety. The King repaired and restored many temples and shrines and many other such foundations were laid during his reign. The people after a long time heaved a sigh of relief. The first known Muslim to have settled in Kas'mira (Many Muslims visited Kas'mira like famous chronicler Al-Beruni in 1030 AD) was a Syrian, named Hamid, who accompanied son of Sindh ruler to Kas'mira, when Arabs conquered Sindh during the reign of Jai Simha. The last seven years of Jai Simha's rule were exhausted in obstructing Muslim incursions, for which he also sought the help from neighbouring Hindu chieftains. After him his son Parmanuk (1155-1164 AD) ascended the throne. Due to Parmanuk's incompetence, vassals of Kishtwar, Rajapuri (Rajauri) and others on the outer fringe of Kas'mira declared independence and the kingdom constricted in area. Thereafter Vanti Dev (1164-1171 AD) and Bopa Dev (1171 - 1181 AD) ascended the throne, one after another, and the conditions in Kas'mira deteriorated further due to their incompetence. They were followed by Jassaka Dev (1181 - 1199 AD) and later by his son Jag Dev (1199 - 1213 A D), who tried his best to stem the rot and halted the disintegration of the state. Unfortunately Jag Dev was poisoned to death by Padma, the commander of the gate guards. His son Raja Dev (1213 - 1236 AD), who had fled to Kishtwar on the death of his father was brought back and acknowledged as the ruler by the entire Kashmiri population. He rehabilitated Lavanyas (Lones) and made them his strong allies, but could not arrest the erosion that had seeped down into the very fibre of society and was vanquished by the chieftain of Lar (Near present day Gandherbal) Baladhya Chandra, who grabbed half of Pravarpura(Srinagar). Brahmin population did not take kindly to Raja Dev's weak-kneed policy, consequently revolted but were dealt with an iron hand. They were persecuted so vehemently that they opted for changing their caste even.

Fort on the Banks of Vitasta (Jhelum) Built by Lohara's The Fort was in Ruins and was Rebuild as Chieftain's Palace During Dogra Rule and usually referred to as Roop Singh Building on the side of Badiyar Bala Ghat

Sangram Dev (1236 - 1252 AD) Raja Dev's successor put in hard labour to reclaim the lost territories from neighbouring chieftains but his younger brother Surya Dev fell out with him, thus effecting the expeditions. Finally Surya Dev was taken prisoner and killed. During the absence of Sangram Dev, while he was on expeditions, 'descendants of Champaka' (Champaka

Kashmiri nobleman and father of Historian Kalhan), together with Damras unleashed a reign of terror and Sangram Dev had to seek asylum with the ruler of Rajapuri (Rajauri). Sangram Dev later returned incognito, collected his forces and regained his throne. Though he forgave Champaka's, being Brahmins, but they finally killed him. His son Ram Dev (1252 to 1273 AD) avenged the murder of his father by putting to sword all those who had colluded with each other and killed Sangram Dev. The Vishnu temple at Kakapora was renovated by him, which had earlier been mistakenly desecrated. During the reign of Ram Dev some Bhattas (Brahmins) who had helped in his investiture as king, having been insulted by him, conspired to install somebody from amongst *Khashas* (People living closer to *Chandrabagha* River (Chenab)) on the throne of Kashmir. The conspiracy leaked and an orgy of plunder, destruction and killing was let loose. Many to save themselves cried "***Na Bhatto Aham***" (In Kas'miri -'Na Bhattu (I am not a Bhatta). This is the first onslaught recorded in history against the Bhatta's of Kas'mira. Ram Dev had no son of his own, hence adopted a Kashmiri Brahmin boy Laxman by name and named him Laxman Dev, who on his death ascended the throne. Thus, in 1273 AD technically rule of Lohara Dynasty came to an end.

First Kas'mirian Brahmin King and After (1273-1320 AD): Laxman Dev occupied the throne (1273-1286 AD) and **became the first Saraswat Brahmin King of Kas'mira**. But it proved to be crown of thorns for him, as though he being *Kshatriya* King, he could not get over his Brahmanical outlook. To add to his woes, during his reign Turk Kajjala invaded Kas'mira and Laxman Dev was uprooted. His wife Ahila constructed a *muth*, which was called *Ahlmar* (Present day *Gund Ahlmar* near Ganpatyar). On his death his son Simha Dev (1286 -1301 AD) ascended the throne. Sangram Chandra, a feudal lord of Lar, in collusion with the Turk invader Kajjala made Simha Dev flee to the Liddar Valley (Pahalgam), which now became his nominal state. When Sangrama Chandra died, Simha Dev re-entered Pravarpura (Srinagar) and set the house in order. Like his father, Laxman Dev, Simha Dev was a devout Hindu and constructed many shrines, prominent amongst these was the temple of 'half lion, half man' (*Nara Simha*) near Bandipore. However, he later on fell in bad company and had illicit relations with one courtesan by name of Idagali. One Darya (Khan) who was in the Royal Treasury got Simha Dev assassinated by one Kama Samuha. This was the first major political assasination carried out under the orders of a Muslim. This very assassinator, Kama Samuha, became a King maker and installed Suh Dev (1301-1320 AD), brother of Simha Dev, on the throne. During Suh Dev's reign a sizable number of fugitives and Muslims came to Kashmir for seeking employment here. Suh Dev obliged them readily, least knowing that he was digging his own grave and working unconsciously for the dissolution of Hindu rule. It was during his reign Shah Mir arrived in Kashmir in 1313

AD and the Suh Dev allotted a *Jagir* to him. On Suh Dev's death his brother Udyan Dev ascended the throne but fled to Kathwar (Kishtawar), when Zulchu invaded Kas'mira, which paved way for Rinchen to take over the reigns of Kas'mira (1324-1326 AD). On the death of Rinchen, with the efforts of Koteh Ren, Udyen Dev was re-installed as King and Koteh Ren married Udyen Dev. Udyen Dev died in 1341 AD and Shah Mir ascended the throne in 1342 AD.

Advent of Islam-Rinchen and Shahmiri Dynasty (1324–1555 AD)

Advent of Islam: Continuation of this narration will be incomplete without details of advent of Islam, role of then rulers and preachers. Indirectly these events throw more light on the process of our honorific, names, surnames etc.; which came in stages to Kas'mira from mid of first millennium and got modified during Muslim period. Majority of Kashmiris converted to Islam not by a planned invasion but by the efforts of Muslim *Sufi's* and Islamic preachers, who were given honourable receptions by then Kas'mira rulers. What accelerated the conversion was indifference of then rulers, inner strife and even doubtful character of the Kashmiri Kings. Things started worsening during the beginning of 11th Century, in-spite of King Harsha's achievements and by the time of Jai Simha (1128-55 AD), this acute slide continued. *Trushkas* had started coming to Kas'mira, in a trickle, with their selected followers and slowly settled down. *Trushkas* is the name given to Muslims invaders in Kalhan's Rajatarangini. Actually most of the Muslim invaders were from Central Asia and were dubbed as *Turkmens* or *Turks* or *Turki*. *Trushkas* apparently is adapted form of these, which also means invaders in *Upbrahmbasha*. The first known Muslim to have settled in Kas'mira (Many Muslims visited Kas'mira like famous chronicler Al-Beruni in 1030 AD) was a Syrian, named Hamid, who accompanied son of Sindh ruler (Now in Pakistan), named Jaisingh, when Arabs conquered Sindh during the reign of Jai Simha of Kas'mira. Jai Simha presented him (Jaisingh) an estate, as he had lost his kingdom. After death of Jaisingh (of Sindh), Hamid became the owner of this estate. He then started propagating his religion among his friends and acquaintances, taking advantage of his status and influence. King Jai Simha turned blind eye to this blatant violation. This was the first known settlement owned by a Muslim in Kas'mira. In Rajatarangini, Kalhan has been critical of Jai Simha for many reasons and it is apparent that this could also be one of them, as he (Kalhan) mentions soft stand of Jai Simha towards *Trushkas* (Muslims). As the time passed, help to *Trushkas* by then rulers of Ka'smira was a deliberate effort to counter co-religionist opponents and that is how Muslim mercenaries even found their way into the army of then Hindu rulers. However, it was handful of Muslims *Sufi's* and Islamic preachers, pairing with then rulers, who changed history and demography of Kas'mira; preachers like Bul Bul Shah, Mir Ali Hamdani (Shah-e-Hamdan) and Mir Shams-ud-din Iraqi. The rulers and their minions who helped these preachers, directly or indirectly, were Suh Dev, Rinchen, Koteh Ren (Also called Kota Rani), Shah Mir (As a ruler), Sikandar But Shikan and his son Ali Shah, Hassan Shah Fateh Shah (15th and 16th Century respectively) and Musa Raina.

Bul Bul Shah And Rinchen: Bul Bul Shah, who started the advent of Islam in Kas'mira, was a *Sayyid* of then *Turkistan. Sayyid's* are priestly class of Muslims and in Kas'mira their descendants were then nicknamed as *Muslim Brahmin's*. He paid his first visit to Kas'mira in 1286 AD, during the reign of Simha Dev (1286-1301AD) but returned to his native country; Turkistan. The state of affairs in Kas'mira deteriorated during the reign of Suh Dev (1301-20 AD) and many foreigners apart from Bul Bul Shah, mainly Muslims, came to Kas'mira. Suh Dev went out of his way to receive them, including Bul Bul Shah, whom he received at Varahamulla (Baramulla) and gave him gifts. For some time things did not go Bul Bul Shah's way till Rinchen, a *Ladakhi* runaway, was thrown up as a rallying point in Kas'mira against the monarchy. Rinchen became King in 1324 AD, was not admitted to Brahmanism and Bul Bul Shah converted him to *Shia* faith in 1325 AD. *Bulbul Lank* (Lankar) locality, in downtown Srinagar, is named after Bul Bul Shah and Rinchen, as a gratitude, constructed first *Khanaka* in the valley in his honour in the same locality. *Khanaka,* is different from *Masjid* in terms of name, design and has architecture of Central Asian design, with tiered wood roof to cater for vagaries of snow and cold weather.

Rinchen, claimed to be a Tibetan Prince, which is doubtful, as during 14th Century AD Tibet had no principalities and the religious Lama's called *Rimpoche's* held sway. To come to Kas'mira Rinchen had to pass through Ladakh and if so he could have settled in Ladakh rather than in Kas'mira. It is, therefore, fair to assume that he was a *Ladakhi*, 'assumed' to be a prince of a small principality or heading a small clan. After the death of Suh Dev in 1320 AD, he settled as a refugee in Kas'mira and yielded considerable power by his deeds, amidst anarchy during the period 1320-24 AD. Zulchu (Zulkadur Khan), a Mongoloid chieftain, invaded Kashmir in 1321 AD with a 70,000 strong army. Suh Dev's brother Udyen Dev, on the throne, fled to Kathwar (Kishtawar) and the inhabitants were at Zulchu's mercy. Zulchu and his band killed and took away thousands of men and women as slaves but due to adverse weather conditions perished enroute. The land of Kas'mira became barren, as there was no one left to attend to them, starting a Kas'miri saying; 'Yeti vowe Zulichen Gassa (Here Zulchu cultivated grass)'. Rinchen, together with Ram Chand, Chief of Suh Dev's Army, drove off Zulchu and gained respect amongst the population. The people had lost faith in the ruler and found Rinchen a strong man, who could establish peace. Rinchen had previously also repulsed attack by *Khasha* tribe (Inhabitants who lived between Vitasta and *Chandrabagha* (Chenab River) were called *Khasha's*). Without any serious opposition, Rinchen seized the throne and became undisputed King in 1324 AD, though Ram Chand, then Commander-in-chief of the late king Suh Dev, put in feeble resistance and was killed. Not a ripple was created. So much so Rinchen married Ram Chand's daughter Koteh Ren, also called Kota Rani (Many noble men were called Renu, while their womenfolk were called Ren). Ram Chand Renu family was from Lar, near *Gandarbal* and Koteh Ren became a turning point in the history of Kas'mira by becoming wife of a ruler, who had killed her father and later converted to Islam. Rinchen, as King, approached one *Devaswami*, a *Shaivite* saint and scholar, requesting admittance to the fold of Brahmanism. He (*Devaswami*) flatly refused his admittance to Brahmanism, as he was *Bhautta* (*Botta*-generally refers to Buddhist people from Ladakh) and there was no precedence of converting people of other faiths to Brahmanism. Ironically this assertion of *Devaswami* does not hold ground as Brahmins, who had converted to Buddhism had returned to the Brahmanical fold during the first part of the first AD millennium. Rinchen eager to identify himself with people of Kas'mira, approached Bul Bul Shah, who readily admitted him to Muslim *Shia* faith in 1325 AD, including Ravan Chand (younger brother of Koteh Ren) and many others. The story goes that Shah Mir, who also had risen in the hierarchy and had worked alongside Rinchen, one night suggested to Rinchen, that they go for a morning walk and the person who meets Rinchen first would be a 'truthful' and it is better to adopt his religion. Next morning the first man to meet them was Bul Bul Shah. The other story is that Rinchen, having been spurned by Brahmins, hardly had any option and decided this methodology on his own. He enquired from the first man he met as to who he was; 'I am a *Garibham* (Stranger)' was the answer; the man who answered was no other than Bul Bul Shah.

On conversion Rinchen took the name of Malik Sadar-ud-din, became first ruler of Kas'mira to be converted to Islam and launched vigorous campaign of converting Brahmins of Kas'mira to Islam. Shah Mir, who was around, was made one of his chiefs and became a close associate. Rinchen got a son from Koteh Ren, named Haidar Khan by Bul Bul Shah. Rinchen just before his death in 1326 AD, entrusted care of his son Haidar Khan to Shah Mir. It is not chronicled if Koteh Ren had converted to Islam; it appears she did convert to Islam. This is also confirmed by the fact that her brother Ravan Chand too had converted to Islam and she allowed her son to have a Muslim name; Haider Khan. It is also pertinent to note that Rinchen had been spurned for conversion to Brahmanism and instead converted to Islam and would have ensured that his wife (Koteh Ren) too converts to Islam. It may be argued that her name did not change but women converted to

Islam during this period seldom changed their name. On the death of Rinchen, with the efforts of Koteh Ren, then widow of Rinchen, Udyen Dev was re-installed as King and she married Udyen Dev. May be she reconverted at this time, which is probable. Udyen Dev had no other option but to accept her offer of marriage to re-ascend the vacant throne, vacated by him in 1320 AD. Udyen Dev died in 1341 AD, leaving behind a minor son. After his death, Koteh Ren (Kota Rani) held the reins of kingdom, as regent, for just five months. Udyen Dev can be termed as last Brahmin King of Kas'mira before Maharaja Gulab Singh took over reigns in 1846 AD. The distinction of being last Hindu ruler is being wrongly conferred to Koteh Ren, who was only a regent of her Muslim son Haider Khan (1326 AD for a short time till Udyen Dev re-ascended the throne) and on Udyen Dev's death regent of her minor son from Udyen Dev (1341-43 AD), had married a Muslim (Rinchen) and in probability had converted to Islam. Of late some Kashmiri scholars and writers keep her on a higher pedestal clubbing her with Lal Ded and others for guarding the community. As the history will reveal, she for her lust of power was another main step to push Kas'mira to Islam. Shah Mir, Rinchen's confidante, in the meantime had become rallying point, while Koteh Ren tried her best to 'establish herself' on the throne, was defeated, outwitted, married Shah Mir and was finally executed.

Shah Mir: Shams-ud-Din Shah Mir, Shah Mir for short, runaway descendant of rulers of Khorasan (Swat- NWFP) where living had been made difficult because of invasions of Taimur, came to Kas'mira in 1313 AD during the reign of Suh Dev with a group of *Sayyids* and found Kas'mira a safe place. He received protection and facilities for carrying out religious preaching, indulged in political intrigue and remained safe from Taimur's terror. Shah Mir's grandfather (or ancestor), a *Sufi* saint, had predicted that his grandson, Shah Mir, would become ruler of Kas'mira; "My son Tahir will be given a son named Shah Mir, who will become the ruler of Kashmir and assume the title Shams-ud-Din. The kingdom of that region and the government of those lands will remain entrusted to and confirmed in the hands of his descendants for a long time." According to Jonaraja, who wrote Rajatarangini after Kalhan covering 1150 to 1459 AD, 'Goddess *Mahadevi* came to *Saimira* (Shah Mir) in a dream and told him that he would become king of Kashmir, which will remain with his descendants for a long time'. That is what happened; a long spell of *Shahmiri* reign, though veracity of the dream, as recorded by Jonaraja, is doubtful. After death of Rinchen, Koteh Ren appointed Shah Mir as Chief of the Army. When another Turk, Achala, invaded Kas'mira in 1331 AD, Udyen Dev again fled to Kathwar (Kishtwar) and Shah Mir rose to the occasion and thereafter went all out to achieve his ancestor's prediction. Jonaraja writes that during the disturbances created by Achala, people found a protector in Shah Mir. There was no change in Shah Mir's plans to usurp power, even after return of Udyen Dev and his plans took concrete shape once Udyen Dev died in 1341 AD. Koteh Ren, in order to keep power, tried to keep together her flock and was even ready to compromise with Shah Mir. In 1342 AD Bikhshana Bhatta, Koteh Ren's Chief Vizir and Malik Avtar (Brother of Koteh Ren) were sent to negotiate peace with Shah Mir, but were mercilessly murdered, as soon as they entered Shah Mir's residence. Another story of this incident goes thus; Shah Mir feigned illness and his collaborators made it known that he was about to die. As a matter of courtesy, Koteh Ren, deputed Bhikshana Bhatta and Malik Avtar to call on him and enquire about his health and were murdered as soon as they entered his residence. Inspite of this, Koteh Ren compromised with Shah Mir and one night slept in the same bed and was handed over to executioners next day. Jonaraja denies that Koteh Ren and Shah Mir were married and writes that; 'Saimira (Shah Mir) shared her bed for one night and then put her in prison. Hasan, Muslim Historian (Different from *Mulla Hasan Qari*), gives the same story, but with a slight difference in detail. According to him; 'She was compelled by circumstances to agree to his proposal (of marriage). On the day of their marriage she clad herself in gorgeous robes; but stabbed herself by ripping open her bowels and said to Shah Mir; 'This is my acceptance'. The suicide story is most improbable, probably to protect the honour of Shah Mir, for he would have been accused of adultery under Islamic covenants.

History will indicate that Koteh Ren was ambitious and would have done anything to remain in power; she married, after Rinchen's death, Udyen Dev. She could have got Shah Mir murdered, after he had murdered her emissaries, but opted for a compromise; marriage being most helpful to her. Her compromise in no way should be construed as a sacrifice, for she did it for her own greed and not for the love of Kashmiri Brahmins. Shah Mir, however, knew that she and not him would yield power and clipped her wings forever by executing her. Shah Mir ascended throne in 1343 AD, assumed the title Shams-ud-Din, and by coercion, taxation, laws, and intermarriages between the two communities, Muslims and Brahmins, broke the resistance of Brahmins and this way his contribution to Islam was enormous. His son married daughter of a Brahmin, daughter Guhara married off to a Brahmin Damara (Feudal lord) to obtain Damara support. Jonaraja comments; 'Damaras wore daughters of Saimira (Shah Mir) as garlands and did not realise that they were the she-serpents of deadly venom'. Shah Mir ruled for three years and five months and died in 1345 AD and and his reign was the beginning of rule of Shahmiri Dynasty for next 213 Years. He had two sons; Jamshid and Alau-u-din and was succeeded by his elder son Jamshid, who ruled for a year and two months, after which he fell out with his brother Alau-u-din. In an armed confrontation, which ensued in the village of Avantipur, Jamshid suffered a defeat, following which Alau-u-din ascended the throne in 1347 AD. Alau-u-din's rule lasted twelve years and eight months. He founded the locality of Alau-u-din Pora, where he himself lived and died in 1359 AD. His eldest son Shihabu'd-Din succeeded him and ruled for nineteen years (1359-78 AD), during which he was mostly busy in subjugating and annexing adjoining territories to his kingdom; Buhlr, Gilgit, and Dardu (Dardistan – North of Kishanganga River). This kept him away from Kas'mira. His next expedition was to Tibet, which was then under the suzerainty of the ruler of Kashghar. Although the troops of the ruler of Kashghar outnumbered the Shihabu'd-Din's forces, Kashgharian army was routed and their soldiers dispersed helter-skelter. The victorious Shihabu'd-Din then proceeded via Tibet to conquer Nagarkot (Nepal). Later under Malik Chander, a Damra General of Shihabu'd Din, Kathwar (Kishtwar) was conquered and thus whole of the mountain range upto Jammu was under Shihabu'd-Din's control. Towards the end of his life, he was infused with a zeal for demolishing idol-houses, temples and idols and destroyed the massive temple at Bijbehara. In fact, he had plans to destroy all the temples and put an end to the entire community of Aryan Saraswat Brahmin's of Kas'mira, but death in 1378 AD intervened and was succeeded by his brother. Qutab-ud-din, who founded Qutab-ud-din Pora and made it his residential headquarters. Here he built himself a lofty palace, the like of which had not been built by his predecessors, except the Palace at Andarkot.

Sikandar - Suha Bhatta - Ali Shah and Shah-e-Hamdan: Bulbul Shah was followed by *Sayyid* Jalalud-Din of Bukhara and Sayyid Taj-ud-Din, the cousin of Mir Ali Hamdani (Shah-e-Hamdan). Sayyid Taj-ud-Din was accompanied by his two disciples Sayyid Masud and Sayyid Yusuf. There also came Sayyid Hussain Simnani the younger brother of Sayyid Taj-ud-din. It is said that Taj-ud-Din and Sayyid Hussain came to Kas'mira under instructions from Mir Ali Hamdani, preacher (*Sayyid*) from *Hamdan,* to find if the country could give them protection against the attacks of Timur. Mir Ali Hamdani (Shah-e- Hamdan) first came to Kas'mira in 1372-73 AD and picked up conversion threads left by Bul Bul Shah, what is called *Nizam-e-Mustafa* (Absolute and total adherence to *Sharia* and covenants of *Quran*) and by 1378 AD Kas'mira had nearly been fully Muslimised. At the time of his third visit (1383 AD), he came with about seven hundred *Sayyids* and another three hundred came with his son, Mir Mohammed Hamdani. They had been forced to move out due to atrocities by Timur, then ruler of Persia who was suspected of contemplating a wholesale massacre of the whole lot of the *Sayyids*. In 1384 AD Mir Ali Hamdani (Shah-e-Hamdan) was reluctant to stay in Kas'mira, as the ruler, Qutab-ud-din, had failed to propagate Islam in accordance to his wishes. Actually the reason was that though he was allowed implementation of Islamic faith as per *Quranic* interpretation, conversions of Brahmin's, demolition of their places of worship, his *Sayyids* followers were given short shrift for they indulged in intrigue of their own, mostly against the Sultan (King). He left Kas'mira via Varahamulla (Baramulla)

A 19th Century (1877 AD)
Sketch Painting of Khanaka-i-Maula (Shah-e-Hamdan Mosque)

for a pilgrimage to Mecca and died enroute at Paneri (Swadgir; Swat – NWFP (Pakistan)) in the same year (1384 AD). During his time most revered *Kalishri* temple (*Kali* temple on the banks of Vitasta near *Zaina Kadal,* Srinagar) was demolished and converted into an estrade (Platform) on which he recited *Quran* and offered *namaz* five times a day. In 1389 AD then King Qutab-ud-din (Area around Ali Kadal known as Qutab-ud-din-pora is named after him) died and his eldest son Sikandar succeeded him. Qutab-ud-din had married a Brahmin girl (*Su Bhatta*) who had borne him a son, named Sikandar. Sikandar, another descendant of Shah Mir, was ready for further onslaught on Brahmins. Sikandar (1389-1413 AD) has been given addendum of *But Shikan* (Iconoclast, Idol Destroyer) in chronicles and history, for his destruction of places of Brahmin worship, forceful conversion and killings. At Mir Mohammed Hamdani (Shah-e-Hamdan's son), who had stayed back, Sikandar constructed *Khanaka* on the erstwhile site of *Kalishri* temple, named it *Allah-u-Dinpur,* renamed later as *Khanaka-i-Maula*. It is a folklore that Lal Ded (Born 1320? – Died 89?), hid herself in a *Kandur's Tandoor* (Bakers oven) when she saw Mir Ali Hamdani (Shah-e-Hamdan). Legend says that she hid herself saying 'Here is a *man* going' and came out fully decked up. This *Lal Vakh* gives the reason as to why she had started roaming around naked, which many scholars assert that it is a philosophical *Vakh* and not indicative of her roaming around naked. "Goran vo'num kunuy vatsum, Neybra doupanam anndaray atsun; Suy gav Lali mey vaakh ta vatsun, Tavay mey hyotu nagay natsun." (Guru gave me only one percept, withdraw from worldly ways and look deep within, this percept became dictum for Lala and that is why I roam naked). Indirectly *Vakh* indicates that the standing of the 'men' of that time was so low that she did not consider them as 'men'. Lal Ded could have performed this miracle to indicate to *Hamdani* that had *Sayyids* (Hamdani and his followers) purity and spirituality, they could have borne Timur's test for *Sayyids* and not migrated to Kas'mira. The other reason could be reverence to a man, whom she considered pious; it is a fact that Lal Ded was soft to Islamic Preachers and *Sufis*. It is said that by the time the two had met, she had achieved exalted spiritual standing. Some chroniclers are of the opinion that the two, Lal Ded and Shah-e-Hamdan, never met; as recorded in *Waqiati Kashmir* in Persian; *Nazd-I arbab-i tahqiq sabit na shud,* meaning 'Held not proved by research scholars'. It is improbable that they did not meet though they were in the same area for nearly twelve years (1372-84 AD). Apparently it is an effort by chroniclers not to expose either of them to a comparison.

To add to Sikandar tyranny, a Kas'mira Brahmin named Suha Bhatta (Also referred as Suha Dev Bhatta, Saha Bhatta (Suh Bhatt)), Chief of Army, converted during Sikandar's reign and took the name of Saif-ud-Din (Meaning 'Sword of Faith'). He was then appointed Chief Vazir and became leader of Muslim converts and joined Sikandar and Mir Mohammad Hamdani (Shah-e-Hamdan's son) against Brahmins. He, Saif-ud-Din - Suha Bhatta, had his own axe to grind; to take revenge against his previous co-religionists, who had given him a short shrift after conversion. He (Suha Bhatta), with Sikandar, planned obliteration of all the traces of Brahmins in Kas'mira.

Muslim Historian Hassan (*Tarikh-i-Kashmir*) writes "this country possessed from the times of Hindu Rajas many temples which were like the wonders of the world. Their workmanship was so fine and delicate that one found himself bewildered at their sight. Sikandar goaded by feelings of bigotry destroyed them and levelled them with the earth and with their material built many mosques and *Khanakas*. In the first instance he turned his attention towards the Martand temple built by Ramdeo (Ram Dev (1252-73 AD)), on Mattan Kareva. For one full year he tried to demolish it but failed. At last in sheer dismay he dug out stones from its base and having stored enough wood in their place set fire to it. The gold gilt paintings on its walls were totally destroyed and the walls surrounding its premises were demolished. Its ruins even now strike wonder in men's minds. At Bijbehara three hundred temples including the famous Vijveshwara temple which was partially damaged by Shihabu'd Din (Elder brother of Qutab-ud-din, father of Sikandar) were destroyed and with the material of the latter a mosque was built and on its site a *Khanaka* which is even now known as Vijveshwar *Khanaka*."

Significant details chronicled about the conversions under Sikandar is that three *Kharwars* (one *Kharwar* is approximately eighty kilograms) of ceremonial thread (*Jenev*; then called *Zunnar*) were burnt. Hassan further on says that "Sikandar meted out greatest oppression to the Hindus. It was notified in the city that if a Hindu does not become a Muslim, he must leave the country or be killed. As a result some of the Hindus fled away and some accepted Islam and many Brahmans consented to be killed and gave their lives. It is said that Sikandar collected by these methods about three *kharwars* (six maunds – nearly 240 kilograms) of sacred threads from Hindu converts and burnt them. Hazrat Amir Kabir (Mir Ali Hamdani (Shah-e-Hamdan)) who was a witness to all this orgy of brute passion and vandalism at last advised him to desist from the slaughter of Brahmins, and told him to impose *Jazia* instead of death upon them. All the Hindu books of learning were collected and thrown into Dal lake and were buried beneath stones and earth." Ironically the woman who gave birth to Sikandar was a Brahmin named *Su Bhatta* (Possibly named Su Bhatten). Sikandar built the locality of *Navato* (Nowhatta; also called Iskandarpora) for his palace and a lofty and imposing *Jami* mosque (Jamia Masjid) in the middle of the city, where Eid festivals are celebrated and congregations held, destroying *Maha Shri* temple built by King Pravarasena II (6th Century AD) and another one built by Tarapira (7th Century). The material from these two temples in the vicinity of the masjid was used for constructing *Jami* mosque (Jamia Masjid). During Sikander's reign he made all the efforts to glorify his reign and rise in esteem amongst *Sayyids* and the convertees. Apart from destruction of temples throughout the valley, construction of many masjid's, he even got coins minted in the name of God (Allah) with his emblem on the obverse. Sikandar died in 1413 AD and was succeeded by his son Ali Shah.

Coin from Sikandar's Reign

Ali Shah (1413-19 AD), during his short reign of about six years, continued with persecution, conversions with greater vigour and enforced *Jazia* for the stay of Brahmins, as was done during his father's reign of 24 years, assisted by Sikandar's protégé Suha Bhatta (Saif-ud-Din). While Sikandar's reign was of large-scale forceful conversions, Ali Shah's draconian laws, killings, destruction of religious places, scriptures and conversions forced exodus of a big magnitude. Jonaraja, in his Rajatarangini (1150 to 1459 AD) calls it '*Chandh-Dandh*'; which in Sanskrit means 'violent, cruel and horrible punishment'. As the easiest way out many Aryan Saraswat Brahmins of Kas'mira converted to Islam, those valuing self-respect and religion killed themselves and quite a number left Kas'mira. This was the first exodus of the Brahmin community. Only 'proverbial' eleven families (*Kaah-Ghar*) remained. *Kaah-Ghar* acronym was more proverbial than indicating total number of Aryan Saraswat Brahmin families left in the valley. Though numbers had dwindled due to conversions, fair concentrations of Brahmins continued in other specific parts of the valley and on the fringes of geographical limits of the valley. This is also borne by the facts that barely eight decades later 24000 more Aryan Saraswat Brahmin's were converted again (Mir Shams-ud-Din Iraqi's and Musa Raina's time). Such fast proliferation of Brahmin's could not have been possible by only *Kaah-Ghar's* (Eleven Families). The acronym was coined as out of a big concentration, in the interior of then city, closer to present day Batyar/Zainagir, only ten to eleven families stuck to their religion/home, surrounded by clusters of Muslims and convertees. This is based on the antiquity of certain religious places and can even now be fixed by various Muslim associated religious and other places in the area; *Suha Yarbal* (*Suh Yar* - Waterfront named after Suha Bhatta - Saif-ud-Din), next to *Ali Kadal* bridge and *Ali Kadal* bridge constructed during Ali Shah's reign and named after him.

Sultan Zain-ul-Abidin–Badshah: After nearly six years of draconian reign like his father Sikandar, Ali Shah finally planned a *Haj* in 1420 AD for thanksgiving for the job done by him for Islam and appointed his younger brother Ghiyas-ud-Din (Shahi Khan) to look after Kas'mira in his absence. Shahi Khan (Ghiyas-ud-Din) ascended the throne under the name of Sultan Zain-ul-Abidin. The title Zain-ul-Abidin was conferred upon him by his elder brother Ali Shah, who in turn was given jewels and horses by Shahi Khan, presumably to enable him to meet the expenses of outfit and transport for *Haj* pilgrimage. But Ali Shah's Hindu father-in-law, King of Jammu, induced Ali Shah to abandon *Haj* pilgrimage and return from Thatta to Kas'mira with a contingent of the army of his father-in-law from Jammu and returned to Kashmir via Pakhli to resume kingship. Shahi Khan resisted him, but was defeated and Shahi Khan fled to Madra (Punjab) where Jasrat Khan Ghakkar (Khokkars- Raja Jasrat of Punjab, Northeastern of present Punjab was then called Madra) gave him shelter. Together they raised a large army, and in the second battle fought between Ali Shah and Shahi Khan, Ali Shah was captured by Khokkars and died at Chadura, hills of Badgam. The victorious Shahi Khan marched on to *Shahr-e- Khaas* (Pravarpura- Sinagar), where he was warmly received by the people. Shahi Khan (Ghiyas-ud-Din) ascended the throne again in 1423 AD under the title of Zain-ul-Abidin (1420-1474, with brief break in between) and was named Badshah (The great King) by his subjects during his reign. Zain-ul-Abidin extended his kingdom over Gandhara, Northern portions of Madra (Punjab), parts of Sindhu (areas around Sindhu (Indus) River) and Rajapuri (Rajouri). He defeated king of Udbhandapura (Ohind) several times. He also brought Guge in Ladakh, then called Bhotta Desh, under his control. Jasrath, the Khokkar chief of Sialkot, who had helped Zain-ul-Abidin to defeat his brother Ali Shah, defeated Maladeva, the king of Madra (Punjab) with Zain-ul-Abidin's help.

After continued onslaughts on Brahmins from mid 14th Century till the defeat of Ali Shah from the hands of Shahi Khan, there was no hope of any respite from the tyranny of the Muslim rule in 15th Century to Bhattas. One of the reasons of Ali Shah's defeat was tyranny and his successor, Shahi Khan (Zain-ul-Abidin), was aware of it. He was around when his brother had unleashed tyranny and Shahi Khan (Zain-ul-Abidin) had understood the negative aspects of such measures. Even then, during initial period of Zain-ul-Abidin's reign, there were no indications of his being softer or harsher than his brother. *Sayyids* were still holding power and in fact Shrivara mentions that the king was married to one Vodha Khatun of *Sayyid* family. With this alliance there was continuity in the power held by *Sayyids*. The time and circumstances could possibly change attitude of Shahi Khan (Zain-ul-Abidin), which it did. In later years he gave a life line to Aryan Sarswat Brahmins of Kas'mira by his conduct and benevolence, discussed separately. Kas'mira Brahmins were literally reborn during the rule of the benevolent King. This was the rebirth of Brahmins in Kas'mira, not for long though.

For his secular reign Zain-ul-Abidin was condemned as one who had revived idolatory, allowing Brahmins to pursue their religion, called *be-din* (Without Islamic religion, literally meaning infidel (*Kafir*) and encouraging infidelity (*Kufur*) by allowing them to come back to their ancestral land. His popularity went down when he protected the gold image of Buddha from destruction at the hands of vandals. A lot of resentment got generated against him when he got Sayyid Ali, a *Sayyid* preacher, paraded through the streets for killing a *yogi*, dressed in saffron robes. His allowing reconstruction of old temples, destroyed during his fathers time, was stiffly opposed by *Sayyid* preachers and zealots, who accused him of undoing things his father had accomplished with zeal for Islam. Inspite of the resentment of Muslims as well as *Sayyid* preachers, he was in firm control of his kingdom. Brahmins of that period claimed that in his death they had lost an incarnation of God

Vishnu (Narayan), who had granted them a new life. For his being benevolent towards Brahmins, Muslims called him 'Bhatta Shah', the King of Brahmins, in disdain and out of sheer disapproval of his benevolence towards Brahmins. The Sultan himself was adept at writing verses and possessed a poetic sensibility. He adopted 'Qutb' as his pen-name and has left behind a compendium of his verses. Here is a verse from his composition; (Persian) 'ay begird-e sham'-i vaz lab-i shirin-i tu shorist dar har khanehi ?'

During the last days of Zain-ul-Abidin's reign, his three sons, Adam Khan, Haji Khan and Bahram Khan rebelled against him but he took energetic measures to crush them. In fact he banished his elder son Adam Khan and was succeeded by his son Haji Khan, who took the title of Haidar Khan. A new Kas'mira calendar was started by Zain-ul-Abidin from 1420 AD, though no longer in use. It was coined on his completing 50 years of his reign and started from the date of his ascending the throne. During his 54 years reign, though interrupted initially, between 1420-1423 AD, Zain-ul-Abidin enforced system of responsibility of the village communities for local crimes, regulated price of the commodities and stabilized the currency which had been debased during the reign of his predecessors. He undertook a large number of public works and founded several new cities, built many bridges and dug many irrigation canals. It was during his time Zaina Kadal, one of the major bridges, was constructed across Vitasta (Jhelum) and named after him. Chroniclers, however, aver that during his rule forced labour (*Begar*) continued.

As about Badshah's endeavor of constructing canals or *Kols*, as they are called in Kashmiri, the Sultan constructed Lal *Kol* at Sopur, Zainagir *Kol* at Wular Lake, Nallah *Puhur* at Sopore, *Shah Kol* and the *Nallah Mar* in *Shahr-e-Khaas* (*Shahr* for short. Muslim name for Pravarpura (Srinagar)). These bodies were dug uniformly, stone embankments constructed and with crossing places. Apart from being used for irrigation, they were also means of inland waterways during those days and were functional as recent as 1960's. *Nallah Mar* has a history. Water from Dal Lake, called Dalla in ancient times, flowed into a water channel called *Mahasarit* and entered Vitasta (Jhelum) near Sher-Garhi Royal Palace, 500 metres west of of famous Gaw Kadal near Basant Bagh. This confluence was considered sacred place by Aryan Saraswats and a temple was built on the right bank of the confluence, which still exists. In ancient times this confluence was named *Mahasaroor* and historian Shrivara in his Rajatarangini called it *Marisangam*, which over centuries became *Mari* and finally became *Mar*. The temple had a vast open orchard on the East of it called Basant Bagh (Spring Garden) and was frequented by people during *Sonth* (Spring). Pandit Parmanand, Accountant General of the State during Maharaja Hari Singh's rule had constructed his house next to this temple. Water of Dalla (Dal Lake) and

Gateway of enclosure once a Hindu temple of Zain-ul- Abidin's Tomb in Srinagar. Probable Date of construction of temple 400-500 AD Photo Courtesy John Burke-1868

Mahasarit had created a vast swamp East of Srinagar City, which was linear, extending right upto present day Safa Kadal. In fact, this swamp had literally created isolated hamlets on the Eastern side of the city. Over the centuries development and construction of canals diverted the swamp water and the land became habitable. From *Mahasarit* (now called *Chonth Kol*), four more branch canals were constructed like the Kawdara *Yarbal* and the Daulat *Kol*. This had a length of three and a half miles. Aali Masjid constructed by Ali Shah, brother of Zain-ul-Abidin, at *Eidgah*, was also fed by the canal as it snaked to adjoining Achan, which extended further and drained into Anchar Lake. Another branch canal was from *Braya Kuj* (*Gund Ahlmar)* to Rainawari and yet another running from *Baba Pora* (Habba Kadal) right upto *Eidgah*. A later addition to these *Kols* in the city is the one from Sher-Garhi Palace to Chhatabal Weir. These *Kols* apart from being used for movement of smaller boats, had bigger boats as dwellings and even those could navigate through the *Kols* in earlier times. These *Kols* were the main routes for moving from one place to another within the city or even to places connected with Vitasta (Jhelum), for these *Kols* had branches which emptied into Vitasta. Many smaller brick mortar bridges were constructed over the centuries over these *Kols* for movement from one hamlet to another. Most of these canals have now been turned into roads or have dried up. *Nallah Mar* project in downtown Srinagar was filled and converted into a circular road after 1950. The bridges constructed, over these *Kols* and Vitasta (Jhelum) then were of raw small bricks, arched and fixed with mortar. These bridges used to get damaged during floods and most of the time water used to overflow these bridges. These were replaced with wooden bridges during Afghan and Dogra Rule and in Srinagar (Pravarpura) seven bridges existed over the Vitasta (Jhelum). While *Ali Kadal* details have been enumerated above, interestingly first bridge, *Nav Setu* boat-bridge (*Nav* – Boat; *Setu* – Bridge) crossing over Vitasta (*Wyeth*) was built by King Pravarasena II (Gonanda Dynasty) in 6th Century AD at some distance from *Maksikasvamin* (Maisuma), closer to present day *Badshah* Bridge (Kalhan's Rajatarangini Verse 354 Book III). Majority of the population was then restricted to the East side of Vitasta (*Wyeth*) and people used boats to cross the river. *Zaina Kadal* was named after Zain-ul-Abidin, *Ali Kadal*; named after Ali Shah (1413- 19 AD). *Safa Kadal*; (orginally called *Saifa Kadal*) by Saif-ud-Din (Suh Bhatt-Chief *Vazir* of Sikandar and Ali Shah), who wanted access to his residence, *Suh Yar*, from either side of the river. Then *Fateh Kadal* during Fateh Shah's rule (1486-93,1503-14 and 1515-17 AD), who wanted *Khanaka-i-Maula* (Kalishree Temple) and *Pathar Masjid* (Stone construction of an old *Baudh Vihara*, converted into a Mosque) to be connected. Yusuf Shah Chak (1576-82 AD) constructed *Habba Kadal* and named after his wife, Habba Khatoon. *Amira Kadal* was constructed by Afghan Governor Amir Khan, who also constructed old Sher-Garhi Palace. The bridge was constructed to connect Sher-Garhi Palace with eastern portion of the city. Houses constructed on either side of this route on Eastern side were referred as *Amira* (*Amra*) *Kadal* while on the other side are called Hari Singh High Street after Maharaja Hari Singh.

20th Century Beginning Photograph of a 400 Year Old Setu (Bridge) over an Inland Waterway in Down Town Pravarpura (Srinagar)

Return, Conversions and Exodus

Return : Gratis Shriya Bhatta (Shri Bhat): Zain-ul-Abidin was a learned man, who knew Persian, Sanskrit and Tibetan. On his orders the *Mahabharata* and Rajatarangini were translated into Persian. He was known for his religious tolerance and called back the Brahmins who left Kashmir during his father's reign and abolished the *Jazia*. He allowed Hindus to built their temples and follow their personal law according to the *Dharmashastras*. Temples which had been destroyed totally during the reign of Sikandar were re-built and re-habilitated by him including Jyesthwara (Zethyr) temple on the outskirts of the city overlooking Dal Lake. He stopped the killing of cows and passed some restrictive regulations about eating beef. He re-introduced the grant of stipends to the learned Brahmins. The place of settlement of those Aryan Saraswat Brahmins of Kas'mira, who had migrated to Bharatavarsha had itself been active between the marauders and defenders. As the word spread of the benign rule of Sultan Zain-ul-Abidin (Shahi Khan), they opted to return to their roots, around 1430 AD. Many families returned to the valley, probably around 1450 AD. Credit for their return goes entirely to Shriya Bhatta, commonly referred as Shri Bhat, who cured Zain-ul-Abidin from a poisonous boil. Jonaraja, the historian, records Shriya Bhatta's feat thus; "As flowers are not obtainable in the month of *Magha* (February) on account of the mischief by snow, even so physicians who knew about poisons could not at that time be found in the country owing to Governmental oppression. The servants of the King at last found out Shriya Bhatta who knew the antidotes of poisons and was well versed in the art of healing, but out of fear he, for a long time delayed to come. When he arrived, the King gave him encouragement and he completely cured the King of the poisonous boil." As a *gratus* Shriya Bhatta requested Zain-ul-Abidin to be kind to Brahmins of Kas'mira and allow those who had left to return. Zain-ul-Abidin agreed and also gave land to returnee families in Zainagir/Zainapur (Between *Ali Kadal* and *Zaina Kadal*; remembered as 4th and 5th Bridge). He even allowed many Brahmins from Bharatvarasha to settle in the valley. Bhattas (Bhat's; Simha, Ruppa, Karupar) held most of the ministries during his rule and contributed significantly, apart from Shriya Bhatta (Shri Bhat), Shrivara (Historian); while Kaulas (Madho, Ganesh, Gopala) held important administrative posts during the reign.

By now Persian had become the official language and the desire of Brahmins to share assignments in the Sultan's administration with others could not be fulfilled without study of Persian. They took to study of Persian and in a brief span of a few years acquired mastery over this language. This is well chronicled; Avtara Bhatta remembered *Shah Nama* (in Persian) by heart and used to recite it to Zain-ul-Abidin. Sanskrit and religious ceremonies were not forgotten, being distinctive features to keep separate identity of the community. Even then the community members were mostly addressed as Bhattas or Bhat and surnames Kaul (Kaula), Renu, Razdan, Malik, Raina were found amongst the gentry, though not common. Some of them were in constant attendance on Zain-ul-Abidin, the Sultan, whom they described as '*Suratrana Shri Jainulavadena*'. He listened to recitations from Nilamat Puranam and other *Shastras*, such as *Vashishta Brahma Darshna*. Shrivara in his history 'Zaina Rajatarangini' records; 'The king heard me recite the *Vashishta Brahma Darshna* composed by Valmiki, which is known as the way to salvation and when he heard the annotations he was pervaded by a feeling of tranquility. He remembered them even in his dreams.' A short description of other Brahmins who rose high in his reign are; Sadasheo Bhatta (Bayu) the royal astronomer and astrologer; Tilkacharya, Buddhist scholar. Soma Bhatta a high dignatory, who held distinguished position and was in charge of the Translation Department started by the King. There were others also who were given strictly confidential diplomatic missions to execute. In short, the Aryan Saraswat Brahmins carved for themselves a place in the body politic.

Transition During Benevolent Rule: Zain-ul-Abidin had established a translation department, where important works were translated from Sanskrit and Sharda into Persian and vice versa. This opened the portals of Sanskrit and Sharda (*Sidhamatrika*) learning to Muslim savants also, while Bhattas learnt Persian. Many religious, poetic and devotional scriptures and philosophies of 10th to 14th Century AD were retrieved, rewritten and few translated into Persian. *Mahabharata* and Rajatarangini were translated by Mulla Ahmad for the first time into Persian under the supervision of Soma Bhatta. Copies of Vedas and *Shastras* were procured from Bharatavarsha and translated into Persian and many Arabic and Persian books were translated into Sanskrit. However, there were many who criticised Zain-ul-Abidin for his favours to Brahmins as recorded in *Baharistan-i-Shahi*; "He (Zain-ul-Abidin) helped the community of the misled idolaters to prosper. In every village and town, blasphemous customs connected with spring (*Nag*) or temples were revived. He ordered that in every town and locality, celebration of special feasts and festivals by the infidels be revived in accordance with the customs prevalent in the past. He himself attended many of these festivities." It is chronicled that Zain-ul-Abidin visited *Amaresvara*, present-day *Amburher* near Srinagar, as Jonaraja does not describe the *Amaresvara* (*Amarnath*) *Linga* in great detail, as he did with Sharda Temple at Shardi during Zain-ul-Abidin's visit. There is lot of mention about Amaresvara quoted by Kalhan in Rajataranagani as referring to Amarnath. Though he mentions many places in the verses, which are common with present day Amarnath, he qualifies verses with giant buildings and mutts. No traces of buildings and mutts have been found at Amarnath. The reference by Kalhan is, therefore, to *Amburher* near Srinagar (Adjacent to Vichar Nag) and so is reference to the visit of Zain-ul-Abidin.

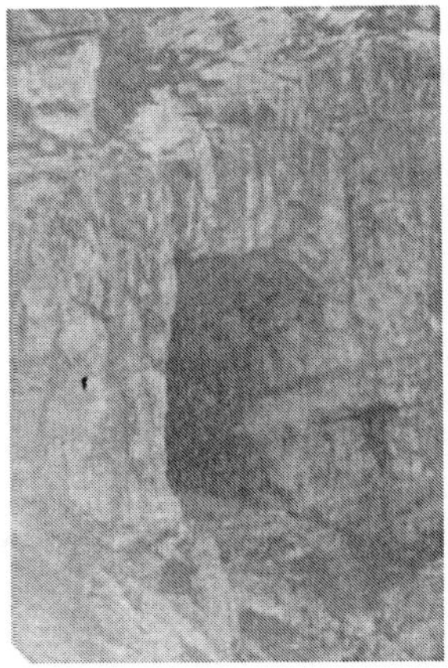

Entrance To Amarnath Cave

None of religious scriptures/treatises translated into Persian during Zain-ul-Abidin's period have been traced except Jonaraja's updation of Rajatarangini (Upto 1459 AD). Even later translations of Sanskrit histories, scriptures into Persian including Prajya Bhatta's Rajatarangini (Covering 1486-1513 AD) have been lost. *Baharistan-i-Shahi*, a chronicle in Persian, includes history of Brahmin period based on Sanskrit and Sharda chronicles of that period. Kashmiri, a variant of *Nastalique* (script used for Persian and Urdu languages) was adopted with a few modifications, as a script for Kashmiri tongue also appeared as language of the common people, though it had an appropriate and precise script of its own in Sharda.

Old Photograph (Beginning 20th Century) of an Inland Waterway Constructed During the Reign of Zain-ul-Abidin

A systematic literature in Kashmiri of this period starts from '*Mahanay Prakash*' written in 13th Century by Siri Kanth in *Vakh* form, style of which was later used by mystic Lal Ded to convey her *Vakhs*, referred as Lal *Vakhs*; a mix of *rishi-sufi* cult sayings. Lal Ded was disciple of Sidhi Kanth (Also Siri Kanth, Sidhi Sri Kanth, Sidha Mol) and from all accounts; name, era and mastery over *Vakhs;* Sidhi Kanth is same as the author of '*Mahanay Prakash*'; master in *Vakh* form of writing. He was also the family priest of Lal Ded's parental family. Probably Lal Ded carried his mastery in *Vakhs* to convey her mystic sayings; called Lal *Vakhs*.

Many returnee families settled for a short while in Zainagir/Zainapur before circumstances forced them to move out again. They, from all accounts, had got recognition of their administrative and literary acumen during their short sojourn outside and got similar assignments on return to the valley. In fact, their land and other assets, left behind were returned. During exile they had picked up Persian and were well versed with Sanskrit and *Upbrahmbasha* variants also, as used in the plains of Bharatvarasha. With knowledge of many languages they found their way into various departments established during the reign and continued their scholarly profession. It did not last long. On the demise of Zain-ul-Abidin in 1474 AD, the sword of conversion again hanged over them. *Baharistan-i-Shahi* (Persian) (Unedited translation from Persian to English) describes benevolence of Zain-ul-Abidin, with disdain, thus; "Whereas the Sultan showed considerable favour and regard to the Muslim nobles and their learned men, he also undertook the re-construction of the monuments of the infidels and the communities of the polytheists. He popularised the practices of the infidels and the heretics and the customs of idol-worshippers and the people ignorant of faith. All those temples and idol-houses of the infidels, which had been destroyed totally in the reign of Sultan Sikandar, may God bless his soul, were re-built and re-habilitated by him (One such temple was that of Jyesthwara - Zethyer). Most of the unbelievers and polytheists, who had fled to the lands of Jambu (Jammu) and Kathwar (Kishtwar) because of the overwhelming strength of Islam, were induced by him to return to Kashmir. The sacred books of the infidels and the writings of the polytheists which had been taken out of this country were brought back, and thus the learning of the unbelievers and the customs of the polytheists were revived by him." During Zain-ul-Abidin's reign, he took steps to improve the general quality of life of his subjects in which his Bhatta ministers (Bhat's; Simha, Ruppa, Karupar) contributed significantly.

Mir Shams-ud-din Iraqi and Musa Raina: Pressure on Saraswat Brahmin's of Kas'mira to convert to Islam, after the death of Zain-ul-Abidin (1474 AD), resurfaced with indifferent rule of his son Haider Shah (1474-76), with a clique headed by Shams Chak, Shringhar Raina and Musa Raina holding the real power. Though *Sayyids* had yielded power before Zain-ul-Abidin's rule, they did not get much of the power and say during his reign. With his death *Sayyids*, who had been responsible for destroying the religious fabric of Brahminism in Kas'mira, came back to yield power during Haider Shah's brief rule and started reasserting themselves. By the time they could act assertively, Brahmins had gathered some guts and sparks of revolt were seen and they even damaged *Masjid* constructed at the site of *Kalishree* (*Maha Kali Temple*). Haider Shah, given to drinking carouses could not bear 'rebels' damaging the Mosque of Shah-e-Hamadan, issued decree, on the advice of his barber, to 'chop off the noses and ears of all Kashmiri Brahmins, wherever they be and whatever their status be'. Brahmins working in the court of Haider Shah were not spared either. They were subjected to the same treatment. Thousands braved this savagery and brutality, but many cried in pain "***Na Bhatto aham*** **- I am not a Bhatta**" to save themselves. This savagery was accompanied by loot, rape and arson. "Nona Deva, Jaya and Bhima and others were maimed.... They struggled and finally jumped into the Vitasta river..." mentions Shrivara in Zaina Rajatarangini. On his death Haider Shah was succeeded by his son Hassan Shah (1476 - 84 AD), a great lover of music, musician who handled many instruments, a great Sanskrit scholar and well-versed in the Brahamanic Philosophy. He started his governance with promise and 'revived the laws and practices' which were in vogue during the time of his father, Zain-ul-Abidin. Hassan Shah became addicted to wine, neglected affairs of the State and after some time his power weakened as powerful factions, who had come up, took advantage of Hassan's addiction to wine and music. These powerful factions started intrigue with a definite class basis, each trying to gain as much power as they could, which ultimately resulted in a civil war, seeds of which had been sown during his time. The most powerful faction was that of the *Sayyids*. Hassan Shah's queen, Hayat Khatun, daughter of *Sayyid* Hasan-ibn- *Sayyid* Nasir Baihaqi, also known as *Sayyid* Hassan Baihaqi bore him two sons, Mohammad Khan and Husain Khan. Just before his death Hassan Shah had expressed a desire that in preference to his minor sons, one of the two other princes of the royal blood should be installed on the throne and his son Mohammad Khan should be nominated as heir by succeeding prince. Hassan expected establishment of a strong rule with out any chances of clashes between various factions. His father-in-law *Sayyid* Hassan Baihaqi, at the time of Hassan's death was a minister of his son-in-law. Baihaqi regardless of the instructions given by the late king, installed Mohammad Khan, his own elder minor grandson (son of Hassan Khan), a boy of seven years, on the throne. There are indications that Hassan Shah had been poisoned by *Sayyids*, for his views on succession after his death.

Conversions and Killings: In the meantime Mir Shams-ud-din Iraqi, of the *Sufi* order of *Naqshabandi's* had arrived in 1477 AD, stayed in Kas'mira for about eight years and was exiled in 1484 AD. Mir Shams-ud-din Iraqi initially had very few followers and literally had no support in Kas'mira. He, therefore, took refuge under the wings of another Muslim preacher, Sheikh Ismail Kubravi, who had shown lots of zeal for furthering the cause of Islam in Kas'mira and yielded considerable influence amongst the Muslims. This did not last long as Mir Shams-ud-din Iraqi sided with another Muslim preacher Baba Ali Najar, who also wielded lot of influence over the Kashmiri Muslims. On the death of Baba Ali Najar, Mir Shams-ud-din Iraqi managed to boost up his followings. His second visit came in 1496 AD, during the reign of Mohammad Shah, when Malik Musa Raina, then Chief Vazir, held almost all administrative authority and for next few decades Musa Raina became most dreaded tyrant, working under the instructions of Mir Shams-ud-din Iraqi.

Musa Raina, before conversion named Soma Chandra, a notable Kashmiri Brahmin, converted to *Sunni* faith but later at the hands of Shams-ud-din Iraqi underwent second conversion to *Shia* faith. He was bestowed with title of Malik, made Chief *Vazir* and granted a *Jagir*. Since the reign of Sikandar, no ruler or *Vazir* in Kas'mira worked as much for the propagation of Islamic faith as Malik Musa Raina; a convertee. Mir Shams-ud-din Iraqi, with Musa Raina's help, used forcible methods for conversions; *Sunnis* forcibly converted to *Shia* faith or killed in-spite of Fateh Shah, then Sultan (1510-19 AD); in spurts) being a *Sunni*. Mir Shams-ud-din Iraqi constructed a *Khanka* at *Zadibal*; which remains the centre point of *Shia* concentration even to this day. Bhattas were his main target; about 24000 were forcibly converted to *Shia* faith, many killed or forced to migrate to Bharatavarsha; leaving their hearth and home. Under his and Musa Raina's instructions religious scriptures from Atri Gupta (7th Century AD) onwards, as many as eighteen big temples were destroyed, property confiscated and those allowed to live had to pay revived *Jazia*. He (Mir Shams-ud-din Iraqi) had issued orders that everyday 1,500 to 2,000 Brahmins be brought to his doorstep, their sacred thread (*Zennev – Zunnar*) removed, administer *Kalima* to them, circumcise them and make them eat beef. Thousands of Brahmins braved this savagery and brutality by killing themselves, some migrated but there were many others who cried '*Na Bhatto Aham*' ('I am not a Bhatta'), in pain and agony to escape death. This period brought spate of conversions to *Shia* sect of Islam, second exodus and *Nasdiq* language (A variant of Arabic) as the vehicle of reading Islamic religious scriptures. However, there were sparks of revolt; ruling Muslim factions fought each other, bringing some respite for a while, but renewed disturbances for a longer period. Fed up Brahmins desecrated certain converted *Khanka's*. Muslim Historian Hassan (Tarikh-i-Kashmir) writes; "The patience having reached the breaking point, they (Sic; Brahmins) rose in a body and set fire to some mosques which were built with the material of the temples once demolished by Sikandar." Shams-ud-din Iraqi reacted thus to this revolt; 'This community of Idolaters (Brahmins) has, after embracing and submitting to the Islamic faith, now gone back to defiance and apostasy. If you (Musa Raina) find yourself unable to inflict punishment upon them in accordance with the provisions of *Sharia* and take disciplinary action against them, it will become necessary and incumbent upon me to proceed on a self-imposed exile and in that case you shall not stand in my way at the time of my departure' (translated from Persian).

As a result of Shams-ud-din Iraqi ultimatum, massacre took place on 10th of Har (Asadh) June 1518 AD. Musa Raina, organised a band of *Gazis* (Fighters) under the leadership of a Chak warrior to loot and murder Brahmins sticking to their faith. They were also entrusted with the specific task of destroying Brahmin families and their schools. *Baharistan-i-Shahi* which enjoys the status of being the first fully detailed history of Kas'mira in Persian, written anonymously in 1593 AD and completed in 1614 AD, records this retribution as such (Translated from Persian); 'Since the above-mentioned Malik (Musa Raina), prior to his assumption of power and authority, had promised him that he would never deviate from or disregard his (Shams-ud-din Iraqi) wishes and injunctions, therefore, in deference to his wishes, he held consultations with his counsellors and administrative officers, and decided upon carrying out a wholesale massacre of the infidels. Their massacre was scheduled for the days of the approaching 'Ashura' (10th Day of Muharram). Thus in the year AH 924 (Al Hijri; Muslim Calendar) (June 1518 AD), corresponding to 94th year of Kas'mira calendar, during the 'Ashura, about seven to eight hundred infidels were put to death. Those killed were the leading personalities of the community of infidels (Brahmins were called Kafirs (Infidels)) at that time: men of substance and government functionaries. Each of them wielded influence and sway over a hundred families of other infidels and heretics. Thus the entire community of infidels and polytheists in Kas'mira were coerced into conversion to Islam at the point of the sword."

Mir Shams-ud-din Iraqi did not even have confidence in convertees to Islam, who had to suffer his wrath. Mir Shams-ud-din Iraqi had observed them chanting *mantras* by placing their haunches on the hand written copies of the Muslim religious books and also bowing before idols. Religious fiat (*Fatwa*) was issued by him and executed by Musa Raina, which led to the setting up of camps for the forcible circumcision of these convertees. With a further view to brutalise and deculturise them, they were forced to eat beef. Some convertees led by Kazi Chak launched a campaign against Musa Raina for his anti-Brahmin activities to overthrow Musa Raina from political power. The campaign ultimately led to the assassination of Malik Musa Raina in 1519 AD. During the course of rivalry between Malik Musa

Raina and Kazi Chak, a daring Brahmin Nirmal Kantha, reconverted Brahmins forcibly converted to Islam. The attempt proved disastrous for Nirmal Kantha and the convertees, who were all executed. Shams-ud-din Iraqi in his quest to destroy all connected with Brahmanism vandalised a wing of Vishnu temple at Buniyar in Varhamulla (Baramulla) and led crowds to vandalise, destroy and burn temples in the city. Mir Shams-ud-din Iraqi after the massacre proceeded to Tibet (May be Ladakh) for similar conversions and it is certain that during this period he targeted Kargil; where *Shia* Muslims are in a majority till this day. He 'probably' died in the same year (1518 AD) on his return journey to Kas'mira.

The extent of persecution of Brahmins by Musa Raina was as much as that of Sikandar and is best narrated in *Baharistan-i-Shahi*; (Translated from Persian); "After Sultan Sikandar, God's peace be upon him, no one among the Muslims who wielded authority over this country rendered as much service to Islam by its propagation and advancement as Malik Musa Raina did. Nobody was able to make as organized an effort as he did towards the advancement and furtherence of the Mohammadan religion." The death of Fateh Shah recorded in the chronicle *Baharistan-i-Shahi* thus ; "During the whole period for which he held the reins of the government, he (Fateh Shah) was always guided by Amir Shamsu'd-Din 'Iraqi's instructions, directives, and commands. It was during this regime that Amir Shamsu'd-Din 'Iraqi ordered Malik Kaji Chak to reconstruct the *khanqah* of Amir (*Sayyid* 'Ali Hamadani). During this period Fateh Shah reigned over Kashmir. On the day they were laying out the plan of the structure of the *khanqah*, an altercation took place between Amir Shamsu'd-Din and Fateh Shah with the result that, a few days later Fateh Shah was deposed and expelled from the country. Mohammad Shah was recalled and put on the throne. Fateh Shah never came back to Kashmir. Malik Shankar Raina, too, was languishing in the Indian mountains at that time. In AH 925 (AD 1519) both Fateh Shah and Shankar Raina died somewhere in the mountains of India (probably somewhere in Nowshehra mountains and the cap of Hamadani which had remained in the possession of the Sultans from the times of Qutab-ud-din was buried with the dead body of Fateh Shah)."

Death of Mir Shams-ud-Din Iraqi became a rallying point for *Sunnis* and remnants of Brahmins to revolt against *Shias*. *Sunnis* plundered and persecuted *Shias*, destroyed their houses, burned their *Khanakas* and desecrated the grave of Shams-ud-din Iraqi. This enmity between two sects exists till this day and predominantly in down town Srinagar. Brahmins decided to recommence pilgrimages to various religious places including Sharda, Gangabal (*Harmukh Ganga*) etc., which may not have been possible if Iraqi or Musa Raina were alive. This confirms that both of them died before *Ganga Ashtmi* of the year 1519 AD.

As if this was not enough, in 1519 AD nearly ten thousand Kashmiri Brahmins died during pilgrimage to *Harmukh Ganga* to immerse ashes; possibly of those who had been massacred a year before. 'They rose at midnight on top of *Mahalesheh Marg*, meadow closer to *Harmukh* Lake, following a call from '*the invisible*', moved along a wrong track leading to a steep precipice from which they fell down; one after another'. The dead included men, women and children. The poet historian Suka says that "Ganga (*Harmukh Ganga*) was oppressed with hunger, as it was after a long time that she had devoured bones. She surely devoured the men also who carried the bones." '*The invisible*' theory may not be true, as precipices surround *Mahalesheh Marg* and weather during this period is adverse due to monsoon, which could have resulted in this disaster by landslides and early snowstorms. There have been many more such catastrophes in subsequent centuries, though not of this magnitude. The massacre in 1518 AD and deaths in 1519 AD, after sometime, started collective Brahmin community *shradha* ceremonies at various designated places, for those who lost their lives. This custom continued even in 1950's and *Shradha's* used to be performed at Khoromoh.

Exodus: Nineties of the last Century (20th) saw major migration/exodus of Saraswat Brahmins of Kas'mira for the third time; First exodus was during the rule of Sikandar *But Shikan* and his son Ali Shah, Second at the end of 15th and beginning of 16th Century during Mir Shams-ud-din Iraqi's foray in league with Malik Musa Raina. Admittedly there have been more conversions and smaller exoduses during the remaining period of the second millennium. But those who left during the two exoduses and returned, earned a place of pride for their clan/family in the valley. Such families remained obscure due to various reasons; tyranny, nepotism, unsettled conditions and even lack of concern by the community.

Role of Convertee Brahmins: The above narrations bring home glaring instances of Brahmins converting for the lust of power and then becoming tyrants of the highest order; Suha Bhatta, Ravan Chand (Koteh Ren's Brother), Soma Chandra (Musa Raina) and many others. Ironically the Hindu rulers had more trust in the mercenaries and Muslim preachers than their *praja* (Subjects). Many Brahmins, mostly senior functionaries of the reign, remained untouched initially, yet they helped the rulers and convertee functionaries to torment the poorer segment of Brahmins. Very few of these had courage to stand up and it was the lower segment of Brahmins who revolted in 1518 AD, which talks volumes of their grit, even though some of their co-religionists were divisive and even helping tormentors, inspite of being outnumbered. These exoduses bring home travails and triumphs of our ancestors, community, who maintained their identity in and outside the valley, persevered and survived against all odds and finally achieved places of pride in the community and Kas'mira as a whole.

Sayyids, Intrinsic Civil War and End of Shahmiri Dynasty

***Sayyids*:** Bul Bul Shah, who started the advent of Islam in Kas'mira, was a *Sayyid* of then *Turkistan. Sayyids* are believed to be descendants of *Paigambra* (Prophet-Peace be on Him)) of Hashimi line, priestly class of Muslims and in Kas'mira their descendants were nicknamed as *Muslim Brahmins*. Bul Bul Shah paid his first visit to Kas'mira in 1286 AD, during the reign of Simha Deo (1286-1301 AD) but returned to Turkistan. This was the first flux of *Sayyids* into Kashmir. Many more followed during the later years during the reign of Rinchen and Shah Mir. This was followed by Mir Ali Hamdani (Shah-e-Hamdan), a preacher from *Hamdan,* who first came to Kas'mira in 1372-73 AD and picked up conversion threads left by Bul Bul Shah. He went back and made another trip to Kashmir. He at the time of his third visit (1383 AD) brought along 700 *Sayyids* from *Hamdan*. They continued to hold positions during the rule of Sikandar (1389-1413 AD) and in fact became main force for implementation of the fiats (*Fatwas*) of Mir Ali Hamdani (Shah-e-Hamdan), orders of Sikandar and his Chief Vazir Saif-ud-Din (Suha Bhatta). Even Zain-ul-Abidin had given them very high seats in the court. Apart from strategic preaching positions, *Sayyids* had cornered high positions and obtained tremendous privileges and favours for themselves and their kinsmen. They too married in royal and noble families. This resulted in their use of their position and powers.

With the position of power they held Kas'mira during this time had reduced to a state of bankruptcy. *Sayyids* considered it below dignity to give converted Muslims equal status, as envisaged in Islam. Out of disdain they called them '*Brahmanzadas*' (Sons of Brahmins) to spite them. Shrivara has amply expressed his impressions thus; "Accepting bribes by them (*Sayyids*) was virtuous, oppressing people was wise and indulging in drinking and sex was happiness". In such a state Muslim nobility was side-lined, utterly ignored in matters of politics and religion, humiliated and disrespected. In this state Muslim nobility rose in revolt against *Sayyids* resulting in utter chaos and anarchy. But *Sayyids* suppressed the revolt with firmness. This was the first sign of imminent Civil War within the Kingdom, which was further fuelled by other circumstances.

Having put down the Muslim nobility revolt, *Sayyids* cast off the robes of religious friars and freely began dabbling with politics and had become a force to reckon with during the reign of Hassan Shah (1476 - 84 AD). Hassan Shah's wife Hayat Khatun was, daughter of *Sayyid* Hasan ibn *Sayyid* Nasir Baihaqi, also known as *Sayyid* Hassan Baihaqi. Shrivara says; 'it was owing to the good luck of their daughter (the queen) that the *Sayyids* obtained wealth and greatness but they regarded the people of Kashmir scarcely even as grass. The king bent upon furthering the interests of *Sayyids* acquiesced in orders whatever they were, that were issued by them for their own selfish ends. They were busy in creating factions and the king was fore-bearing...". In the closing year of Hassan Shah's reign their power had grown immensely. Their ranks were further augmented by the arrival of bands of their outside helpers, kinsmen from Persia. An incident indicates their ruthlessness and animosity towards Brahmins. *Sayyids* were fond of hunting and did not spare even those places which because of their sanctity were treated as sanctuaries. A *Muni* by name Vaisharana, who was held in high esteem, lodged a mild protest against trespass on his land. The result was that not only he but all the Brahmins residing in the locality were made to pay a heavy toll of suffering. Women-fòlk were raped and sold to fanatical zealots. Many women committed suicide by jumping into river or wells. Brahmins still adhering to their faith were put in fetters and their eyes gouged out, body-limbs cut off or beheaded and their bodies thrown on road-sides as display of terror. Decapitated heads were put on a pile of wood and coals on the banks of the Vitasta (Jhelum) and burnt for the people to watch the grisly scene. *Sayyids* even beheaded a renowned physician, *Bhuvneshwara* by name and to instill fear, threw his decapitated head on the road-side.

Downfall of *Sayyids*: The embers of the struggle between the *Sayyids* and the indigenous Kashmiris were smouldering under an external surface of seeming peace, when Hassan Shah died in 1484 AD. After Hassan's death Baihaqi installed Mohammad Shah on the throne and himself became the regent, with all powers in his hands. Envious, Muslims created opposing faction. The intrinsic war within the dynasty and the country had begun. *Sayyids* were in power, they had money and men at their disposal. As against them the opposing faction was not so well equipped. But somehow or other the Muslim leaders enlisted the support of Paras, the king of Jammu who was passing his days in Kashmir as a fugitive along with a small force, took the initiative and fired the first shot. A night attack was made, *Sayyid* Hassan Baihaqi was killed with thirty other *Sayyids*. His son *Sayyid* Ali collected his supporters and gave battle to the Muslim insurgents. After having won some preliminary successes the *Sayyids* were completely routed. Scores killed and many others went into hiding, and those who were caught were banished along with *Sayyid* Ali. The power of *Sayyids* was completely broken along with the pricking of the bubble of their prestige. With the elimination of the *Sayyid* influence the Kashmiri party thought that they could hold the boy king (Mohammad) as a pawn in their hands for furthering their own interests.

Jahangir Magre, of Magre faction, had worked for the downfall of the *Sayyids* and wanted to centralize all power in his own hands. Jahangir Magre, a great Kashmiri general whose power was sought to be broken by the *Sayyids*, had gained an audience with the king and spoke to the king in unreserved terms thus: "these *Sayyids* O ! king, were once exiled but have been brought back. You have yourself brought this curse on this peaceful country......... The *Sayyids* have further been encouraged by the Turshkas with hopes of support and they should always be feared. They are eager for the kingdom as vultures are for meat. It is not fit, O my master! that you who have many ends to accomplish should devote himself exclusively to one... I am going away for the safety of your kingdom as well as of myself. The country is ruined and you ought to save yourself somehow." Reference to Turshkas (Turks) actually is indicative of powere struggle between foreigners and Kashmiris. As against him another group under the leadership of Tazi Bhat took the side of Fateh Shah, who was one of the two princes nominated by Hassan Shah to succeed him. Fateh Shah attacked Kashmir but was defeated by Jahangir Magre who freely availed the assistance of the exiled *Sayyids* who were now content to play the second fiddle under Jahangir. But Fateh Shah again made bold attack and this time with success. With Fateh Shah's success, another clique of the Kashmiris headed by Safdar came into prominence with Safdar as the Chief Minister.

Intrinsic Civil War: Not long after this party also divided itself into factions and thus started the civil war. Mohammad Shah and Fateh Shah were their pawns and these factions sided with one of the prince. In reality they had their own designs; to gain absolute power. Mohammad Shah was now replaced by Fateh Shah in 1493 AD and ascended the throne. Between 1484 AD and 1528 AD, Mohammad Shah ascended the throne five times (1484-86, 1493-1505, 1514, 1517-28 and 1530-37 AD). Fateh Shah was no less and he ascended the throne many times (1486-93, 1503-14 and 1515-17 AD). Fateh Shah became ruler for the last time in 1515 AD and in order to eliminate the chances of bickering and quarrels breaking out amongst his own supporters divided the country in four parts, out of which he reserved only one for himself. The rest parts were controlled by different warlords/clans. The fourth term of Mohammad Shah (1517-28 AD) was briefly interrupted by Ibrahim Shah (1928 AD) and Nazuk Shah (1529 AD).

Forays by Babur and Sher Shah Suri: Abdal Magray, head of Magray Clan, approached Babur (Reign 1526-1530 AD) to invite him to invade Kashmir. Babur deputed his Generals Ali Beg and Muhammad Khan to assist Abdal Magray. Abdal Magray with Babur's troops entered Kashmir via Havel but were repulsed by troops under Kazi Chak on behalf of then King Ibrahim Shah. Kazi Chak thus became powerful, was appointed as the Chief Minister of the succeeding ruler. This raised them high enough in popular esteem and amongst the factions they were leading in power struggle. During this period Sher Shah Suri (1540- May 1545 AD) also tried to get the suzerainty over Kas'mira but failed. Actually ambitious to gain power, Kazi Chak went to Sher Shah Suri for assistance but after some initial success failed. Kazi Chak died in 1544 AD.

After Mohammad Shah's death in 1537 AD, till 1555 AD, Shamsu'd-Din (1537-40 AD), Ismail Shah (1540 AD), Nazuk Shah, second time (1540-51 AD when Mughul General was the real power holder), Ibrahim Shah (1551- 54 AD), Ismail Shah second time (1554-55 AD) and finally Habib Shah (1555 AD) were the rulers. They were figureheads only, while the real power initially was with *Sayyids* and then passed on to various factions; Chaks, Magre's, Muslim Noblemen.

Mirza Haider Dughlat's Moghul Invasion, Chaks and Magrays: While Kashmir was going through the civil war, Tartar invader and Mughal general, Mirza Haider Dughlat, a cousin of Babur made his first raid into Kashmir from Turkistan with an army from Kashgar from Zojila pass in 1533 AD Mohammad Shah the then Sultan (King) had to acknowledge suzerainty of Said Khan of Kashgar. Matters did not end here, Mirza Haider Dughlat invaded the valley second time in the name of Humayun, during the latter's exile from Hindustan. Dughlat was soon able to establish his ascendancy in the valley and like Dulchu, killed, looted and plundered the people and made women and children their slaves. In October 1540 AD Magrays, assisted Mughal troops, who entered Kas'mira, while Kazi Chak together with his sons also moved into Kas'mira. Mirza Haidar Dughlat continued with his foray and at this stage Kas'mira was divided into three parts; one was given to Abdal Magray along with administrative authority, second to Chaks and third to Mirza Haidar Dughlat. In due course of time Mirza Haidar Dughlat virtually took over the reigns of the valley for more than a decade (1541-51 AD). Nazuk Shah, then ruler became almost a puppet in his hands. Mirza Haider Dughlat appointed Moghuls on high posts and the *Jagirs* of Kashmiri noblemen were confiscated. He, however, encouraged Kashmir Art and Crafts and trade and commerce began to thrive in the valley. Mirza Haider Dughlat died and following inscription on his tombstone gives the date of his death; AH 958 (1551 AD). Historians have given contradictory statements about Mirza Haider Dughlat, Moghul General's end: struck by an arrow during battle; from fatal blow of lance; killed by accident; murdered by a butcher with an axe. Daulat Chak, Ghazi Chak and other Chak's who had opposed and fought Mirza Haider Dughlat wanted to throw his dead body to dogs, but *Sayyid* Mohammad Baihaqi, Husain Magray of Magray Clan, and people of Sunni faith lifted the dead body five days after he was murdered and buried it in the *Mazar-i-Salatin* on the left side of the grave of Sultan Zaina- ul-Abidin. The chronogram inscribed on the tombstone of Mirza Haider Dughlat, who made the first Mughul foray into Kashmir reads; (Persian) *'Shah-i Gurkan Mirza Haider akhir...be mulk-i shahadat zadeh kus-i shahi...qaza-e ilahi chunin bud tarikh..shudeh bahr-i waslash qaza-i ilahi'*. The use of word *shahadat* (Sacrifice-Martyr) clearly indicates that he was killed during battle.

End of Shahmiri Dynasty. The last Shahmiri ruler, Sultan Habib Shah (1555 AD), a weakling was deposed by his commander and nobles raised Gazi Shah Chak, a prominent Chak of the time on throne. He was direct descendant of Lankar Chak, who had come to Kashmir towards the close of Hindu rule. This era became a tainted page in the history of Kas'mira and end of Shahmiri Dynasty which had ruled for 213 years (1343- 1555 AD), but clans of Chaks (Warlords and prominent Muslim clan) were in the forefront in the power struggle. Many Historians refer to Shahmiri Dynasty Rule from 1339 to 1561 AD, but from the Chronology of the Kings of Shahmiri Dynasty from most authentic sources of that time, the dynasty ruled from 1343 (Shah Mir) to 1555 AD (Habib Shah) (213 Years), Chak Dynasty from 1555 to 1586 AD (31 Years) though from 1586-89 AD Moghuls were busy annexing Kas'mira completely.

Bhattas During Civil War: During this civil war, which lasted for a number of years, the worst features of human nature came into prominence. Both Mohammad Shah and Fateh Shah lost and regained the throne no less than four times. During these days Kas'mira was plunged in a worst phase of lawlessness. Roads were totally unsafe, trade was quite at a standstill and agriculture neglected. People fell from their morals and even Brahmins did not remain untouched. Shrivara recalls the situation thus; "people are now fond of blameable practices and are ashamed to follow the *Shastra* which was followed by their fathers and grand-fathers. Men of four castes had graced the kingdom in former days but lately the people had gradually adopted blameable practices and the ceremonies prescribed for special days in the *Puranas* came to be forgotten. Why should not the people whose customs are bad suffer calamities?" The civil war, however, brought some sense to Bhattas to preserve their religion. With civil war raging all round, Bhattas took to the peacetime occupation of writing books on history, philosophy and poetry. Practically there was only one caste, Bhatta, that of the 'Brahmin' which represented Brahmanism in Kas'mira. In 15th and 16th Century when Islam made sizeable inroads into the community, just essential measures had then been taken to preserve their entity and religion to the extent they could. Bhattas did not forget Sanskrit learning and their religious ceremonies, because this was the only distinctive feature to keep them alive as a separate group. They separated spiritual and temporal seats and were divided into two sub-castes, the *Karkuns* (Derived from word *Karinda* (Persian-literally meaning white collar worker who studied Persian and entered Government service) and the *Bhasha Bhatta* or *Bhacha Bhatta* (Those who studied *Bhasha*-Religious Language i.e., Sanskrit/Sharda) who took charge of the religious affairs of the community. Daughter's son was made to study *Bhasha* (*Language/scriptures*) to administer religious needs of his maternal family. Since grandchildren were very young to learn *Bhasha*, they were called *Bhacha* (Kids) thus *Bhacha Bhatta*. This system started a chain of future generations of *Bhasha Bhattas* and also started bringing daughter's husband into the fold and if one carefully scrutinises *Kulawali* of *Bhasha Bhattas,* you will find *Gar Zamtur* (*Ghar Jamai*) ratio high and more prevalent amongst them. This system introduced one more asspect of giving respect to our family Guruji (*Gor*). Irrespective of anything Guruji (*Gor*) was given pride of place when he visited the house of the host (*Yazman*). It was because of the fact the Gurujis (*Gor*) basically belonged to daughters-in-law family, hence the special respect, which is adhered to even to this day.

Chak Rule (1555-1586 AD)

Chak Clans: There were two prominent Chak Clans which came into limelight during Shahmiri Dynasty, resulting finally in establishment of Chak Rule by one of the clans. Both were inhabitants of Dardu (Dardistan, Called Drava in olden days and people were called Dards). Dards have a long history; Ptolemy in his book '*Almagast*' has used the word Daradrai for Dards of the Western Himalayas. Before embracing Islam, they were the followers of Buddhism and Hinduism. At present their major concentration lies in Dardistan (Dardesa); the area to the North of Kas'mira Valley, Gilgit and Askardu especially Neelam Valley; Shardi (Chilas, Naili, Neelam), Upper Kishanganga (Kel, Seri), Gurez and Tilel Valley (North of Kishanganga River) in Pakistan Occupied Kashmir (POK).

The first group of Chaks of Trehgam (Near Kupwara) originally were inhabitants of Gilgit and trace their ancestry to a group of Aryans, belonging to the Dardic descent. Chaks had entered the borders of Kas'mira during the hegemony of Shah Mir. They were represented by Shams Chak son of Helmat Chak who settled down in the town of Kupwara and their relations with Chaks of Trehgam were distant, bordering on mutual distrust and hostility. Shams Chak later entered the service of *Sayyid* Mohammad Baihaqi and changed sides to serve under one Malik Nowroz Itoo, son of Ahmad Itoo (Guardian of younger minor son of Sultan Hassan Shah (1476 - 84 AD). Before long Shams Chak, fearless by nature, displayed exceptional feats of bravery in many battles and wielded full authority during the days of Chief Vazir Malik Saif Dar.

The second clan of Chaks was that of Lankar Chak (Alamkarcakra), who was founder of the house of Barshal in Dardu and he too had come to Kas'mira during the reign of Suh Dev (1301-20 AD). It was actually Ram Chand, chief of the Kashmiri Army of Suh Dev, who provided shelter to Lanker Chak and his followers, who had been defeated in their native land by the forces inimical to them and settled down in Trehgam. Pandav Chak, Husan Chak and Kazi Chak were the descendants of Lanker Chak. Though majority of both the clans had converted to Shia faith by Mir Shams-ud-din Iraqi. yet to avoid threat to his power, Musa Raina, himself of Shia faith, felt threatened and broke the power of Chak Clans as a group. Kazi Chak assisted by many disillusioned converters launched campaign against Musa Raina as a ploy to overthrow Musa Raina, which finally led to assassination of Musa Raina in 1519 AD. However, with the death of Kazi Chak in 1544 AD, this clan had a slight setback, though not for long.

Chak Rulers: Sultan Habib Shah (1555 AD) of Shahmiri Dynasty, was a weakling and Ghazi Khan Chak of Lankar Chak Clan aspired to adopt title of Sultan and ascend the throne as an independent ruler. For this he sought help from various factions and his counsellors. It is said that the behaviour of Habib Shah was so atrocious in his court that Ali Chak, a nobleman and younger brother of Gazi Khan Chak, present in the court openly declared in the court that Habib Shah was misfit as a Sultan and lifted the crown from Habib Shah's head, put it on the head of Ghazi Khan Chak and made him sit on the throne. Ghazi Khan Chak formally took over reigns in 1555 AD and thus established the rule of Chaks in Kashmir. Ghazi Khan Chak reigned for a period of nine years (1555- 1563 AD). After he was inflicted with leprosy, which made him blind, he abdicated in favour of his blood brother Husain Shah Chak and died in 1567 AD. Husain Shah Chak, on ascending the throne, ordered the eyes of Allamad Khan, son of Ghazi Khan Chak, Muhammad Magray son of Abdal Magray head of Magray Clan, be gouged out to ensure that line of Gazi Khan Chak was denied power and Magray clan kept under control. During Husain Shah Chak's kingship Akbar's envoy to Kashmir, Mirza Muqim, came with a message that the Chak Clan accept the suzerainty of Moghul King Akbar. The envoy was sent back with gifts for the Moghul King as a token of friendship but not accepting Moghul suzerainty. Husain Shah Chak was deposed in 1570 AD and Ali Shah Chak, his brother, succeeded him to the throne. In the beginning of his reign, Ali Shah Chak's kinsmen and counsellors advised him to gouge out eyes of Husain Shah Chak and imprison him, which he declined. Ali Shah Chak died in 1578 AD.

When Abdal Chak learnt about the death of his brother Ali Shah Chak, he mustered troops and decided to fight Yusuf Shah Chak, son of Ali Shah Chak and the heir, in the locality of Nowhatta. When Yusuf Shah Chak came to know of these developments, he sent his emissaries to Abdal Chak to bring home the point that he was the heir to Ali Shah, in letter and spirit and Abdal should desist from taking any precipitate action. Abdal Chak did not agree and was ready to fight the battle for power. A force under Shams Chak, launched a fierce attack on Abdal's forces and defeated them. In the course of fighting Abdal Khan was wounded and was later killed with a sword. Yusuf Shah Chak formally ascended the throne in the year 1578 AD.

Yusuf Shah Chak: Yusuf Shah Chak was gifted with a graceful body and disposition; was well versed in music, Sharda, Sanskrit, Kashmiri and

Persian poetry. His compositions were popular with the lovers of music. His verses were well-known in 'Hindustan' and Kashmir and often quoted by scholars and poets. He spent most of his time in sensuous enjoyments and sport. First term of Yusuf Shah's reign lasted for forty days, when he left the rule in the hands of one trusted *Sayyid*; Miran *Sayyid* Mubarak Shah. Yusuf Shah Chak ascended the throne for the second time in 1580 AD. Yusuf Shah Chak had married Habba Khatoon. She was a great Kas'mira poetess; mostly rendered *birah* poems (A beloved's separation) in separation from her husband; Yusuf Shah Chak, who had got her divorced from her first husband and married her. When Yusuf Shah Chak was kept by Akbar in the Imperial Court and was Commander of Bengal Moghul Army, that is the time some of the heart rendering poems were composed by Habba Khatoon. Read these: '*Nad ha Layei, Miane Yusufo Wallo*' (I am calling you, do come my Yusuf) and '*Katue Chuk Noond Bane Wallo Mashooq Miane* (Where are you Handsome man, Come home my lover) and of course '*Variven Saet Wara Chas No Chara Karu Meon Malineu Ho*" (I am not happy at my in-laws place, Do something my parental home). From the accounts including Moghul Chronicles, Yusuf Shah Chak was a tall, well-built and very handsome man and such men were generally called referred as *Noond Bane* (Tall, Well Built Handsome Man. Genesis of *Noond Bane* not known).

Yousuf Shah Deposed: In 1580 AD itself one powerful noble Abdal Bhat, with the support and consent of the commanders, installed Lohar Chak, son of Shankar Chak, on the throne in place of Yusuf Shah Chak. But in effect all power was in Abdal Bhat's hands and Lohar Chak was just a nominal King . For one year (1580-81), Abdal Bhat ruled by proxy. Yusuf Shah Chak tried to regain his throne, but failed. The result was that he turned towards Akbar (Feburuary 1556- October 1605), the Moghul King, who had brought nearly the whole of Northern India under his enlarged domain. Only rule over Kashmir eluded his vast kingdom. Yusuf Shah Chak's approaching Akbar provided a window of opportunity to Akbar's desire to have Kashmir as part of Moghul Empire. Deposed Yusuf Shah Chak went to Agra for help to regain his throne but changed his mind. He felt that this step will ultimately lead to his being sidelined or even loss of his kingdom. In the meantime a considerable number of soldiers, noblemen had joined Yusuf Shah Chak, after being disillusioned with the tactics of Abdal Bhat. With the help of deserted troops and some more local help Yusuf Shah Chak succeeded in regaining his throne. Meanwhile Akbar was angered by the behaviour of Yusuf Shah Chak and sent emissaries with Moghul Royal *Firman* (Order) that Yusuf Shah Chak must at once come to Akbar's Court at Agra and pay his respects. The emissary laid down that in case Yusuf Shah Chak agreed to proceed to the imperial court along with him, he would be shown special favours, robe of honour presented to him with an assurance that Kingdom of Kas'mira would remain with him and his power and authority would remain the same as in the past.

Moghul Forces Defeated. Yusuf Shah Chak agreed and was ready to obey the Moghul *Firman* (Fiat), but his supporters and advisers did not agree and Yusuf decided not to present himself in the Moghul Court. With this situation some of his staunch supporters turned against him and went to Lahore to meet Raja Man Singh. They pleaded for the conquest of Kas'mira by the Moghul's. Akbar, thereafter, ordered an expedition to Kashmir under Raja Bhagwandas and Shah Quli to conquer Kashmir. Chaks made preparations to meet Moghul Army. During the final stages of the battle, when victory of Chak Forces was imminent, Yusuf Shah Chak with a small band of his loyal troopers joined Moghul Army. The Chak Army knew that their victory was imminent and defection of Yusuf did not matter. The nobles and commanders installed Yakub Shah Chak, son of Yusf Shah Chak, on the vacant throne (1585 AD). To the luck of Chak Forces incessant rains cut off Moghul forces and converted their camp into a huge marsh. Chak Army inflicted heavy blow on the Moghul contingent. Bhagwan Das in this situation offered truce and entered into a treaty with Yakub Shah Chak and left Kashmir with his forces. The main part of the treaty was a promise of tribute from Yakub Shah Chak to Moghul King and in return Yakub Shah Chak would continue to hold his kingdom.

Yakub Shah Chak did not follow the victory against Moghul's with any effort to administer his kingdom or mend affairs. On the contrary he himself contributed to the prevailing disorder. Lawlessness and disorder were order of the day. Yakub Shah Chak considered himself as the custodian of Shia Faith. At that time Jama Masjid was being repaired, which was resented by him as the Masjid was the main place for worship by Sunni Muslims. Yakub Shah Chak ordered Qazi (Chief Priest) of the Jama Masjid to amend words of *Qalima* and add words praising Hazrat Ali (*Ali Vali Alla*-Hazrat Ali the heir) to highlight Shia faith. Sunni Muslims naturally resented and rose in revolt. Yakub Shah Chak let loose repression upon Sunni's, ordering ruthless killing. Qazi of Jama Masjid was killed for his refusal to make addition in the *Qalima*, his body was tied to the tail of an elephant and dragged in the city. Bhattas were also not spared, oppressed and wholesale conversion of the Bhattas planned. But for good luck of Sunni Muslims and Bhattas, Yakub Shah Chak fell ill and therefore the idea was given up. Word went round that it was the punishment by Allah to Yakub Shah Chak for daring to make additions in the *Qalima*.

Moghuls Again Invade Kas'mira: On the outcome of Raja Bhagwan Das's expedition, Akbar was livid and did not ratify the treaty between Raja Bhagwan Das and Yakub Shah Chak. He at any cost wanted to annex Kashmir. Another opportunity arose when persecuted Sunni delegation under Sheikh Yakub Sarfi and Baba Daud Khaki met Akbar. After detailed briefing of persecution of Sunni's under Yakub Shah Chak and conditions in Kas'mira, they made a fervent request to him to free Kas'mira from the clutches of insolent Chaks. Akbar agreed to their request and agreed to certain conditions; no interference with the religious affairs, no slavery and nobles of Kas'mira having been source of mischief will not form part of Kas'mira administration. Akbar, deputed his most trusted general Mir Qasim with an army of forty thousand strong to annex Kashmir. Yakub Shah Chak also collected an army of thirty thousand but at the crucial hour the major portion of his army deserted him and joined Moghul side. Yakub Shah Chak was defeated and the country passed into the hands of Moghul Empire under Akbar in 1586 AD, ending 31 years Chak rule.

Final Farewell of Yousuf Shah Chak: Yusuf Shah Chak had since fallen from grace and had been put in prison for sometime by Moghuls. He was given command in the Bengal Army, but after some time he became deranged and soon after died in AD 1591 at Jagannath Puri (Orissa). Yusuf Shah Chak's dead body was taken by his trusted *Sayyid*, Miran *Sayyid* Shah Abul-Maali with elaborate befitting ceremonies due to a king performed and was buried in pargana of Bisnak (Biswak) in Bihar. The journey from Jagannath Puri was covered in two months and on each day, alms and charities, food and *sherbet* were given en-route to the poor and the destitute and buried 'On Sunday, the 23rd of the month of Rabiu'l-Awwal AH 1000'(1591 AD)'. On being defeated by Moghul Forces, Yakub Shah Chak was taken away and kept in 'Hindustan' under the supervision of Raja Man Singh. Though Chak rule had come to an end in 1986, the last of the Lankar Chak/Gazi Khan Chak descendant Yakub Shah Chak was poisoned by some inimical Kashmiris and died in AD 1592 (A.H. 1001).

Chak Rule: Chaks were brave but fanatics, ferocious and barbarous and these qualities enabled them to dominate the last few decades of Shahmiri Dynasty Rule and finally resulted in Lankar Chak Clan coming to absolute power. However, their own base was limited to Lankar Chak Clan. There was open hostility with other Chak Clan of Shams Chak (Trehgam) and his descendants. Kas'mira at that time was on the brim of collapsing Shahmiri rule, while Lankar Chak Clan consolidated their political position through political murders, even within the clan, intrigues and decimation of upcoming forces or personalities. Both Chak Clans had converted to Shia Sect, while majority of the population was of Sunni faith, thus there was a huge gulf existing between the Chak rulers and the ruled. Their fanatical zeal for forcing Shia faith made them a despised lot. Kazi Chak, their ancestor, had affected forcible conversion of many Bhattas and Sunni Muslims to Shia faith. The Chak rule at best was dictatorial rule as long as their nobles were united and kept their places in the hierarchy. Being warriors they were poor administrators. Dissensions broke out in the reign of the first Chak ruler Gazi

Khan Chak. Chak Clansmen could not tolerate stern measures which were adopted by him in suppressing lawlessness, resulting in a serious disorder and Gazi Khan Chak had to abdicate in favour of his brother, Husain Shah Chak, who though of moderate views too had to abdicate in favour of his younger brother Ali Shah Chak. A severe famine during Ali Shah Chak's reign further weakened the Chak rule. Yusuf Shah Chak's rule, dilly dallying, depositions and Mughal invasions further weakened Chak Rule with Yusuf Shah defecting to Mughal Force at a crucial phase of the fight between the two forces and his son Yaqub Chak being crowned in his place. Yusuf Shah Chak's and Yaqub Shah Chak's final days in 'Hindustan' have been given above. Thus, was the end of Chak Clan in 1592 AD, when Yaqub Shah Chak died of poisoning in 'Hindustan', but Chak Rule had come to an end in 1586 AD when Mughul Army entered Kashmir, though it took them three more years to annex Kashmir.

Chak rulers harbouring Shia faith pursued the same policy of converting or eliminating Bhattas, who were largely reduced in numbers as a result of conversions during Shahmiri Rule.The Chaks ordered the slaughter of one thousand cows every day and *Jazia* was re-imposed on the Bhattas. Killing, butchering and marauding Bhattas was order of the day. Poverty stared them in the face as they were bereft of all means of sustenance. Historian Suka, writes; 'The Bhattas were over-powered by the religious intolerants the same way as the sun is over-powered by the grey sable clouds'. Bhattas wearing *Jennev* had to pay an annual tax to the Chak rulers. These atrocities forced Bhatta community members to take shelter in the neighbouring areas and Bharatvarasha. The Chak rule lasted for a brief period of 31 years (1555 -1586 AD). During Chak rule, Bhattas had no respite, but rule was not as tyrannical as Shahmiri's, as infighting amongst Chaks and other clans, forays by Moghuls kept them away from major nuisance.

Oh God : Move Back Again*:* Return to anarchy, tyranny and forceful conversions forced majority of Brahmins to move back to their old destination. After all they would be welcome in the plains of Bharatavarsha, where they had earned name and respect. Bharatavarsha was also going through upheaval of various battles, invasions during this period, till Babur (Founder of Moghul empire-1526 AD), Sher Shah Suri (1540-1545 AD) and later Akbar (February 1556-October 1605 AD) came on the scene. Establishment of firm Moghul rule by Akbar opened new vistas for them also; like it did for others in Bharatavarsha. They were now linked again with the mainstream in Bharatavarsha, which provided them rich and fresh field in many spheres of intellectuality, knowledge and even coveted posts in running administration. Gradually there sprang up Kashmiri colonies in Agra and Delhi, where they maintained separate identity and came to be known as Kashmiri Bhattas or Saraswat Brahmins of Kas'mira. They had variety of surnames, cross names, based on vocation etc.; mostly Kauls, Renu, Razdan, Malik, Raina etc. In course of time their *Bhacha Bhattas /Basha Bhattas* (Priests/*Purohits*) also migrated and settled alongside them. By now 'Aryan' address, which had come into disuse, had been dropped, though number of surnames had increased by adopting *Takhalus* (Honorific) as surname. These proliferated further during 18th and 19th Centuries and stabilised by beginning of 20th Century. However, Saraswat and *Gotra* oriented assertions continued.

4

Moghul, Afghan and Sikh Rule

> 'The conduct of the wise one, which is unrestricted by motive, shines, being free from pretence but not the affected calmness of the deluded person whose mind is attached.....'
>
> *Ashtavakra Samhita* xviii. 52

Moghul Rule

Star Ancestors Under Akbar and later Moghuls: Moghul rule under Akbar (February 1556-October 1605) extended to Kas'mira in 1586 AD and Akbar visited Kas'mira in 1587 AD. During his reign, his Finance and Revenue Minister, Raja Todar Mal, made revenue settlement of the valley, where land belonging to those who had left due to persecution was restored. Aditya Pandit (not a Kashmiri) was appointed to effect distribution of these lands. During his stay, Akbar participated in the festivals of Kashmiris.

On 13th of *Bhadoon* (Vikrami Samvat), also known as Vitasta *Triyodashi* (*Truvah*); celebrated as birthday of Vitasta (Jhelum-*Wyeth*), he ordered illuminations all over the city and participated in the festivities. All this was a great and a decisive step taken towards recognising their distinct existence and they came again into prominence. Akbar, as part of establishing strong seat of his Government in the valley, selected land around Hari Parvat (*Chakreshawari*). A fort was constructed around the hill and a town founded there; named *Nogar Nagar*. The place was also called as '*Nogar*', meaning 'new home' which seems to be more appropriate, as Akbar was famous to adapt local names, clichés for such ventures. A stone edict mentions the construction of this fort as such (Translated); "The foundation of the fort of *Nogar-Nagar* was laid in the reign of the just sovereign, the King of Kings, Akbar, unparalleled among the kings of the world, past or future. He sent one crore and ten lakhs (of rupees) from his treasury and two hundred Indian master-builders, all his servants. No one was forced to work without remuneration. All obtained their wages from his treasury. (In the) forty-fourth year after the accession of the Emperor (and) 1006 after the Prophet (1597 AD)."

Trade in Kas'mira flourished with outside; with Bharatvarasha and neighbouring countries of Afghanistan, Central Asia, Tibet, Ladakh. Traders from all these places visited Kas'mira. The habit of taking tea, which is now common in Kas'mira, was imbibed during this period, following contacts with Tibetan traders, who had themselves taken it up from Chinese. This is the time the families of Rainas of Budhgair/Cawdor, who had been bestowed with the title of Renu (Raina) took to financing of the trade in *Shahtoosh* wool; (Wool from Chiru Goat and now most endangered animal in the world) and *Pashmina* (Wool from *Pashmina* Goat). They would go to far off places of Ladakh area, bring caravan of wool and distribute it amongst the shawl makers, by making a *Fheri* (Going around with their wares and finally collect finished product) in far off places in Bharatvarasha and even places like Kabul, Persia etc. That is how they got the surname of *Fehrists.*

Akbar was very appreciative of efforts by the Bhatta community and Abul Fazl in *Ain-e-Akbari* records; "The most respectable class in this country Kas'mira is that of the Bhattas, who notwithstanding their need for freedom from the bonds of tradition and custom are the true worshipers of God. They do not loosen their tongue of calumny against those not of their faith nor beg nor importune. They employ themselves in planting fruit trees and are generally a source of benefit to the people." Akbar's efforts put across a signal to the other Bhatta community members in the plains to return to their roots. One of the families, which returned again, was the *Banumasi* ancestor of Historian Narain Kaul (1640 – 1712 AD).

Pandit Honorific: Kashmiri Pandit (KP) Born: This era and for sometime after Akbar, was somewhat similar to that of Zain-ul-Abidin's reign. In the Moghul Durbar, Akbar's learned Brahmins and scholars were referred to as Pandits; which was used as a generic term. Many Kashmiri Brahmins, who had migrated to the plains of Bharatvarasha were generally referred to as Pandits, for their literary and religious knowledge, as majority of them had not carried their family surnames when they migrated. This was due to the fact that during the exodus of 14th Century surnames had yet to catch up with the community in the valley and many did not have one. They had peculiar religious routines; applied *Teok* (*Tika*), morning and evening read religious scriptures and were well versed with religious activities, peculiar of a Brahmin; generally referred to as *Pandit*. This form of address was not prefixed but suffixed with the name; like Narain Kaul Pandit, Miru Pandit etc. This honorific was not only used for them but also for many others in Bharatvarasha, who had excelled in literature, art, culture and religion. For many it became surname; prevalent even today with Brahmins all over

Bharatvarasha. This honorific proliferated at local levels and did not meet the specific aspirations of separate and distinct identity for Aryan Saraswat Brahmins of Kas'mira. On representation by Jai Ram Bhan Pandit in 18th Century (Direct descendant of Chandra Bhan Pandit; a great scholar ranked with first class poets of the day and favourite of both Shah Jehan (1627-1658 AD) and Dara Shikoh) to distinguish Saraswat Brahmins of Kas'mira from the Brahmins (Pandits) of other parts of India, then Moghul King Mohammad Shah (1719-1748 AD) bestowed 'Pandit' honour title on them as a Prefix. Interestingly this prefix Pandit title was initially restricted to Saraswat Brahmins of Kas'mira living in the shrinking Moghul Empire of Bharatvarasha; more so for those connected with Mughal Durbar, in Delhi (Called then as Shahjahanabad) and Agra. Since such Kashmiris had their roots from Kas'mira, this honorific got tagged as Kashmiri Pandits (KP's). However, many artists, *Gharanas* and intellectuals were also bestowed with similar honorific; but it was different suffix of '*Pandit*' and not 'Kashmiri Pandit'. Even today we have many of this class like Late Pandit G.B. Pant, Late Pandit Ravi Shankar (Famous *Sitar* maestro) etc. During last two centuries Pandit form of address was used in the valley as a form of respect, selectively though, by Dogra establishment and Hindus, who were either visiting or were operating from Kas'mira. Thus, the Kashmiri Pandit took his birth in his modern shape, though till then the name Kashmiri Pandit was not coined to describe this community, which was described as Bhatta. Even now a Kashmiri Pandit at home describes himself as a Bhatta and it is by this name that others describe him in Kas'mira. Muslims or even Bhattas themselves, sometimes, used Bhatta form of address, in disdain, and the womenfolk referred to or called as *Bhatten*. Pandit honorific, not Kashmiri Pandit (KP), came into more usage after 15 August 1947, when Prime Minister sworn at midnight was Pandit Jawahar Lal Nehru; yet every KP in the valley was Bhatta (From here onwards Bhattas have generally been referred as Pandits).

A noted *Kashmiri* writer, however, writes; "Before grant of Pandit honorific to Kashmiris, both Hindus as well as Muslims used to be called as *Khujjah* (*Khwajah*) in the Moghul Durbar." *Khujjah* (*Khwajah*) honorific was exclusively used for Muslims and not for any Hindu or Saraswat Brahmin of Kas'mira. *Khwajah* was specific title for the learned Muslims and *Sufis* of the era, of which we have many examples; *Khwajah* Chisti, *Khwajah* Nizamudin etc. *Khujjah*, in Kas'mira, was used in later centuries for reference to learned and affluent Muslims, who had become powerful families and force to reckon with. The word *Khujjah*, of Persian origin, (*Khojeh, Khojah*) became more prevalent in Kas'mira during Muslim rule. The architect of Jamia Masjid constructed during Sikander's time was *Khwajah* (*Khujjah*) Sadru'd-Din who had come to Kas'mira from Khurasan (Persia). *Khujjah Saab* was used by Dogra establishment and Britisher's to address older, affluent and learned Muslims during last two centuries and is used even today (*Saab* is later appellation for learned man).

Pandit Honorific–Later Moghuls

Pandit Honorific Usage: There is an erroneous impression that Miru Pandit was first to be conferred with Pandit suffix, first to return to Kas'mira during Akbar's rule with a contingent of Saraswat Brahmins of Kas'mira settled outside. He is also being termed as founder of *Banumassi* Dhar clan and being from Dhar (Place in Madhya Bharat; near Indore). Miru Pandit's ancestors after migrating during the time of Sikandar /Ali Shah (14th Century), had settled in the *Brahmani* kingdom in the South during Feroz Shah's reign (14th Century). Miru Pandit returned to Kas'mira with Jehangir (1605-1627 AD) in early 1600 AD. Dhar surname and Dhar's, were around when Miru Pandit entered the valley. Miru's family was generally referred to with Pandit suffix, for their known and carried knowledge of literature and religion and he was actually in charge of Golkanda Fort (Present day Andhra) in South, while his family was at Ellichpur (Deccan). Having left the service of the Golkanda Chief, Miru Pandit came to Delhi, where he was appointed to command Noor Jehan's bodyguards and soon got a chance of showing his military skill by being part of the group, which freed Jehangir from Mahabat Khan's captivity; who had taken Jehangir as prisoner at Jhelum (Now in Pakistan). As a mark of royal favour, Jehangir took Miru with him and permitted him to settle in Kas'mira, granted Jagir and was made the Governor of Kamraj (areas of Kupwara, Suyapur (Sopore), Varhamullah (Baramulla)) and tasked to build and supervise forts on Kas'mira borders. Miru and his sons built forts at Suyapur (Sopore), Varhamullah (Baramulla) etc. and recruited people from Muzaffarbad, *Uttara* (Means Northern Area; Titwal, Kupwara, Tilel Valley and Lolab) to man his forces.

Later Moghuls: During Akbar's rule Brahmins of Kas'mira had achieved apical level of re-recognition and comfort. With his death in October 1605 AD and accession of Jehangir, the empire stepped into first step of decay. Jehangir, Shah Jehan and later Aurangzeb (1658- March 1707 AD) had little or no contribution to Kas'mira except pleasure trips and back to tyrannical ways, though not that severe. Jehangir's visits to Kas'mira were more of pleasure trip's rather than administrative. Jehangir seemed to be tolerant because of influence of his Hindu mother and Man Singh and dichotomy for Noor Jehan was a Shia but soon got tag of an iconoclastic. During Jehangir's reign Itqad Khan, Mughal Subedar of Kas'mira, further marred and tarnished Jehangir's already sullied image. The subedar, harassed and persecuted Brahmins of Kas'mira, forcing many of them to convert to Islam (Moghul Subedars (Governors) came to be deputed from Bharatvarasha, who came to Kas'mira with a retinue of their trusted men).

Jehangir's wife Noor Jehan too was against Kashmiri Pandit's and

Bhattas. On the bank of Vitasta in Srinagar city, Jehangir's queen Nur Jehan re-constructed a mosque, *Pather Masjid*, opposite Shah Hamdan's mosque. Nur Jehan had got sculptured and chiselled stones for this *Masjid,* after dismantling flight of steps, linking Shankaracharya temple to the river Vitasta, near the temple of Goddess *Tripursundari* (Now called Durga Nag). This *masjid*, an old *Baudh Vihara,* was converted into a *Sunni Masjid* during Fateh Shah's rule (1486-93,1503-14 and 1515-17 AD). Though used as *Masjid* for some time, *Sunnis* did not use this mosque after renovation by Nur Jehan, as it had been rebuilt by a Shia woman; Noor Jehan. There is also a legend that when asked about the cost of re-construction of the *Masjid*, she pointed towards the gems studded in her shoes, indicating that costs hardly made any difference to her. This angered the *Ulema* (Muslim Scholars) and they decided not to use this *Masjid*; honoured till this day. Sikh commander, Akali Phula Singh, during brief rule of Sikhs (early 19th Century) declared *Pathar Masjid* as the property of the state, as it was built out of the dismantled material of a temple of a high architectural merit. That is how it passed on as a state property till this day. One must also be clear that though Miru Pandit exercised considerable influence over Noor Jehan as well as Jehangir, with tongue in cheek, he failed to restrain Noor Jehan from dismantling the old and carved steps leading to Shankaracharya Temple.

On the death of Jehangir in 1627 AD, Shah Jehan ascended the throne and was equally responsible for indulging in iconoclastic activities in Kas'mira. Though Shah Jehan visted Kas'mira seven times, these again were pleasure trips and his religious inclination was against Brahmins. At his behest, not only number of temples were profaned and desecrated, but also ravaged and demolished. English Historian and writer Bernier records; 'The doors and pillars were found in some of the idol temples demolished by Shah Jehan and it is impossible to estimate their value'. It was expected that Dara Shikoh, eldest son of Shah Jehan, will ascend the Moghul throne after Shah Jehan's death. Dara Shikoh was considered to have secular leanings. His teacher in Kas'mira was Akhund Mullah Shah, who was contemporary of Rishi Pir. In fact, Dara Shikoh took more interest in Kas'mira than his father. Dara Shikoh built an archaeological marvel of a mosque on Hari Parvat Hill called Akhund Mullah Shah Mosque, which stands dilapidated today. The Mosque was neglected soon after Dara Shikoh was executed by Aurangzeb. Dara Shikoh also built a seminary in honour of his teacher Akhund Mullah Shah, with a terraced garden, on the shoulder of the Zabarwan Hill overlooking the Dal Lake, now called as Pari Mahal. His another marvel was the Garden at Bijbihara (Vijeshwara) on the two banks of Vitasta (Jhelum) connected by a bridge and designed unlike the Moghul Gardens. This garden at time boasted of the worlds biggest, girthwise, Chinar.

Shah Jehan's son Aurangzeb ascended the throne in 1659 AD after executing his brothers and imprisoning Shah Jehan. which had tremendous effect in Kas'mira in the years to come. It was beginning of another phase of persecution through Mughal Subedars (Governors). However, one of the Moghul Subedar Ali Mardan Khan (1650-1657 AD), just before Aurangzeb ascended the throne, was a cut above other Mughal Subedars. Ali Mardan, originally an Iranian, had taken shelter in the court of Shah Jehan, as he was reluctant to handover treasure-trove he had got in Qandahar (Kandhar - Afghanistan) to the ruler of Iran. As Moghul Governor of Kas'mira, he proved quite tolerant and felt attracted to the monistic philosophy of *Shaivism*. He was a poetic genius, had mastery over Persian language and his lofty and sublime eulogy of Lord Shiva, in Persian, and his praises galore of the Hari Parvat is laudable. Even today a locality close to Hari Parvat is known as Ali Mardan and his poems used to be sung during various religious congregations as *bhajans*.

Aurangzeb visited Kas'mira only once and granted some land to the *Pandas* of *Martand Tirtha* (Mattan) under his royal seal. Outwardly there was some religious tolerance as Akbar's rule had brought in some relief and stability, which though on waning side had some semblance. However, in Kas'mira remnants of powerful Muslim families like Shahmiris, Chaks, Magres, Rainas, Maliks, Bhats, who for nearly three centuries had been masters to shape destiny, some as convertee Muslims, fell from their high pedestal and within a short span became unknown. However, inwardly they were defiant and waiting in the wings. But there were many Muslim scholars, poets and *Sufis*. During this period Poet Ghani, a Muslim poet, more of a *Sufi* than a Muslim poet, declined Aurangzeb's invitation to visit Moghul Court. Ghani would close all doors and windows, when he was in his house and leave them ajar when he was out. His explanation was that the most precious item in his house was he himself. Rightly the inscription on his tombstone, in Persian, even quoted during last Century by Kashmiris for 'could not care' reads; '*Chy Shama Manzile Ma Ba Payi Mai*' (Translated: Like a burning candle my destination is under my feet).

Pravarpura (Srinagar) – 1861-63

Another *Sufi* saint Rishi Pir (Pir Pandit *Padshah*) by his admix of *Sufism* and *Brahminical* thoughts, had created a place across all the segments of the population of then Kas'mira. Unlike many of his contemporary *Saints / Sufis*, he had no political advisors, was not interested in mundane affairs, never converted people to his Muslim faith, yet helped men of all hues in going up the ladder of spiritual elevation. Aurangzeb, however, had not taken kindly to Rishi Pir's close relations with Akhund Mullah Shah, teacher of his late brother Dara Shikoh and ordered his detention; which remained unimplemented. The Brahmins say; 'same night Rishi Pir appeared in a dream to Aurangzeb, demanding to annul imperial order of his arrest' but fact remains that stoutly convinced of Rishi Pir's spiritual attainments, Muslims interceded to deter then Subedar from arresting him. He (Rishi Pir) had no rancour against Aurangzeb and even went to the extent of solacing him when Aurangzeb was remorse for having executed Samrad, a *Sufi*, whom Aurangzeb considered a heretic. *Sufism* was not acceptable to Islam and *Sufis* were rejected as heretics because their thought content was more or less monistic or pantheistic akin to *Brahmanism* and Buddhism, while Islam is deistic. Somehow *Sufism* thrived in Kas'mira mainly due to the fact that the believer Muslim's had *Brahmanical* base and many Bhattas also were devotees of these *Sufi's*. During this period another *Sufi*, Mansur (Sayed Ali Mansur), was beheaded when he proclaimed, 'I am the Truth'. (A locality near Raghunath Mandir is still called after this *Sufi*. This *Sufi's* utterances, in Persian, heard by me as a child still ring my ears). Aurangzeb died in the year 1707 AD.

Lal Ded's *Vakhs*, which so far had been passed on by the word of mouth written for the first time, in 1654 AD in ***Asrarul - Abrar*** **(The Secret of Pious)** by Baba Dawud Mushkati; Abul Fazl's *Ain-e-Akbari* covering Akbar's reign; Prajya Bhatta and Shuka's updated Rajatarangini and these had gained eyes and ears of the learned Kashmiris. An analysis of the Kings, after the advent of Islam in Kas'mira, will show that the Kings, who opted and were interested in updatation of Rajatarangini were only two; Zain-ul-Abidin and Akbar, both known for their tolerance and had been benevolent *Rajas* (Kings). It is also evident that *Baharistan-i-Shahi* written about advent of Islam, eulogising Muslim rulers, was critical of Zain-ul-Abidin and possibly counter to Rajatarangini. The contents were never complimentary to Bhattas or their religion. After the death of Shuka no one had updated Rajatarangini; one of the reasons being that Abul Fazl's *Aine-e-Akbari* had covered Akbar's rule. The other reason was dark era of rulers from mid 14th Century was no cause celebre to write about and equate to narration of Kalhan's Rajatarangini. From Jonaraja onwards narration was not as flowery, lacked frank expression and details of tyranny undergone by Bhattas. Many important events were either left out or put in mildly, for they too, perhaps did not want to antagonise then Kings, who had commissioned them.

End of Moghul Rule

Kashmiri Pandit Delegation to Guru Tegh Bahadur: About Aurangzeb historian Narain Kaul (1640 – 1712 AD) writes; 'through his Subedar Iftikar Khan (1671-75), a cruel and tyrannous, the Emperor being a religious bigot re-imposed *Jazia* (tax) and other levies on Bhattas'. This tyrannical order got stopped when a delegation of Brahmins of Kas'mira assured Aurangzeb that they would accept Islam 'if Guru Tegh Bahadur (1621 –75 AD; 9th Guru of Sikhs) was first converted to Islam'. The history of this time also records of a delegation of five hundred Brahmins of Kas'mira led by Kirpa Ram, a learned Bhatta, calling on Guru Tegh Bahadur at the village of Anandpur Sahib. The Guru was informed of the Mughal Governor's immeasurable hostility towards Bhattas of Kas'mira to coerce them to get converted to Islam and wanted Guru to plead their case with Aurangzeb. Guru Tegh Bahadur was categorical in informing them, that it could be stopped at the cost of a great sacrifice and was silently lending succour and moral help to them. Guru Gobind Singh, then only twelve years old, exhorted his father to undertake the sacrifice for the noble cause of preserving and conserving the religious faith of Bhattas. Guru Tegh Bahadur was already under the surveillance of the Mughals, who doubted his bonafides as a saint. Ultimately he was imprisoned and executed on 11 November 1675 at Gurudwara *Sis Ganj* (Delhi) for refusing to embrace Islam. His head was cremated at Anandpur Sahib by his son Guru Gobind Singh and other mortal remains cremated at Gurudwara *Rakab Ganj* (Delhi). On receiving the news about the sacrifice Guru Gobind Singh said: '*tilak janju raakhaa prabh taakaa keeno bado kalu mahi saaka*'.

It has been vividly recorded in the tyrannical rule of Subedars; when *Jazia* was reimposed in 1679 followed by other restrictions; 'No Bhatta should be allowed to ride a horse, wear *Jama* (Mughal dress), bear arms, participate in fairs and festivals, put on a *Teok* (Tilak mark), receive education and visit a garden'. The history further records that the conflicts in Kas'mira were not restricted to Bhattas and Muslims, but struggle between Hindu Khatri commercial class and the Muslim commercial class of Kas'mira also. Muslim traders would approach Muslim masses, inflame in the name of religion against the '*Kafirs*' (Infidel) traders. It is only after the brief incursion by Sikh Army in early 19th Century things started looking better. There was no denial that these traders flourished much to the anguish of Bhattas as well as Muslims and was one of the reasons for deep rooted hate Muslims developed against them.

Pandits Under Moghuls: There is no denial that many Brahmins of Kas'mira held high places during the reign of Moghuls but it was mainly for their acumen. Mahadeo Pandit was the *Peshkar* (Chief Minister) of Ali Mardan Khan. Judges decided affairs of administration and legal cases according to *Shastras*; one such Judge being Srikantha Pandit. Deeds were written in Sanskrit, though not grammatically polished language, but a dialect; admixture of Sanskrit and Persian, which became court and literary language of that time. Many were granted *Mansabs* (Honorary Exalted Status); Chaudhari Mahesh Shankar Das was a *Mansabdar* during the Subedarship of Saif Khan (1668-1671 AD). He laid an extensive garden on the banks of Dal Lake near Nishat Bagh, constructed a road across Dal Lake over a distance of four miles, connecting the garden with his residential house at Rainawari (*Rajanvatika)*, which exists till this day. It is learnt that this road has been developed further and is used as short cut from Hazratbal to Moghul Gardens. His garden got acclaim from then Subedar Saif Khan, himself a great builder, who remarked bitterly; '*Choudhari Mahesh bag na kard Dar Dili Saif Khan dag kard*' (Persian-Translated: Choudhari Mahesh did not lay a garden but simply created a scar in the heart of Saif Khan). Descendants of Choudharis of Rainawari should feel elated!

Kashmiri Pandits in Moghul Court: Aryan Saraswat Brahmins now known as Kashmiri Pandits had by now risen very high in the Moghul court at Delhi. Important State business was conducted through them. Pandit Jai Ram Bhan held a *Mansab* (Honorary Exalted Status). He was the head of the small community of Kashmiri Pandits who were living at Delhi and Agra and wielded enormous influence in the Moghul court. But even there the Pandits had their enemies amongst themselves. On a complaint by Raja Raushan Rai Kamboh before Qamar-ud-Din, Wazir of Emperor Mohammad Shah, Jai Ram Bhan was incarcerated and his property confiscated and his sons sent to prison. He was later on sent to Moradabad but on the way murdered at the instigation of the Raja Raushan Rai Kamboh and order communicated to Inayat Ullah Khan, then Subedar of Kas'mira, for the confiscation of the property of Jai Ram Bhan. However, Inayat Ullah Khan, had many reasons to be grateful to Jai Ram Bhan and sent word to Jai Ram's brothers to conceal whatever they possessed of value before a formal search was made of their houses. The result was that though a search was made of the houses, nothing valuable could be found there.

Moghuls and Kashmiri Muslims: The policy of the Moghuls towards the Kashmiri Muslims had not at all been favourable. Very few Kashmiri Muslims were ever given *Mansab* and the portals of the military service were closed on them. But in spite of this a rich class of industrialists dealing in shawls and other similar articles had come into existence amongst them. The rise of this class contributed largely to the weakening of the Moghul rule in Kas'mira. This class had harboured a rancour against their Moghul rulers, which was further augmented by the partiality, which the latter had shown for the Kashmiri Pandits. Now that the Moghul rule was on its last legs, the rise of Ahmed Shah Abdali in Kabul created new hopes in the minds of these

Kas'miri Muslim notables. Some amongst them wrote a letter to Abdali inviting him to depute a Subedar for Kas'mira, with assurance on their part that the country along with its Moghul Subedar, Afrasiab Beg Khan, would be handed over to him without any bloodshed. By chance this letter fell in the hands of Afrasiab Beg Khan, who thinking it inopportune to take any drastic measures against the offenders, merely produced it before them in an open Durbar with the hope that such a generous gesture on his part might prevent them from further mischief. But this yielded no beneficial results and fresh conspiracies came to be hatched up.

Moghul Rule on the Wane: While Mohammad Shah conferred Pandit Honorific on Aryan Saraswat Brahmins of Kas'mira, his Subedars were both indifferent and incapable or cowed down by religious fanatics. History records tyranny of Muhatta Khan, Sheikh-ul-Islam of Kas'mira (Muslims then had a religious head on the lines of *Mir Waiz* called Sheikh-ul-Islam) thus; 'The Empire started cracking and crumbling and as a consequence Kashmir witnessed cruel Muhatta Khan asserting his political hegemony over the head of the Deputy Governor, Mir Ahmad Khan and instructed him to execute the insensate measures against the Bhattas. Muhatta Khan (Sheikh-ul-Islam of Kashmir) deposed Mir Ahmad Khan (Moghul Subedar) and assumed the reins of government under the title of *Dindar* (Upholder of Faith). Muhatta Khan credited with a deep knowledge of Islamic laws, somehow or other found fault with the policy followed by Mir Ahmad Khan towards Bhattas and had made it plain that ascendancy of the Bhattas was intolerable from every point of view'. The tyranny was not restricted to Bhattas only but engulfed other sect of Muslims; Shias *Shia-Sunni* riots, brought untold miseries upon Shias, followed by murder of Muhatta Khan, the Muslim *Dindar*. The Subedar (Momin Khan) found he was unable to cope with the disorder rampant in Kas'mira. Two sons of Muhatta Khan were killed at the instigation of one Abdullah; a local *Rais* (Richman) and as ill luck would have it, some of the participants in the murder were *Shias;* a hated class because the *Shawl* manufacture was in their hands and the factory workers were mostly *Sunni* Muslims. The Subedar, as a stroke of policy, named Sharafuddin, son of Muhatta Khan, as successor to the office of Sheikh-ul-Islam. The son improved upon the methods of his father and inflicted various kinds of tortures; mental and physical upon the Bhattas and did not even spare Muslims who had sympathised with Bhattas. Subedar Momin Khan failed to establish order and had to make room for another Subedar, Samad Khan, who came with a strong force, captured Sharafuddin and along with his fifty confederates was hanged publicly. The orders against the Bhatta's were mercifully withdrawn and it was after an agonising period of a number of years that the Bhattas were permitted to use a turban, to put on good clothes, to put on *Teok* (*Tilak*), send their children to *Pathshalas* and to perform their religious ceremonies.

The closing years of Mohammad Shah's reign, which was greatly weakened by the attack of Nadir Shah witnessed a considerable lawlessness and disorder in Kas'mira. The Subedars refused to acknowledge the suzerainty of the Moghul overlord. There were insurrections and wars, which reduced the people to the lowest ebb of penury. Trade and commerce, art and industry died. Agriculture was abandoned and the people witnessed a huge famine. So many died of hunger and starvation that it became impossible to manage the dead. Srinagar was looted and burnt a number of times. Other towns fared no better. Fields once rich in harvests were lying desolate and beautiful hamlets which studded the country were mere heaps of ruins with no signs of life in them.

It was during these unsettled days that Mohammad Shah the Moghul Emperor died in the year 1748 AD. Mohammad Shah was succeeded by Ahmad Shah. Ala Kuli Khan was the last Moghul Subedar of Kas'mira, who took charge in the year 1752 AD and appointed Mir Muqim Kanth, a Moghul by race and a Kashmiri by domicile as his representative (*Naib Qaim Muqam*). Civil war, famine and floods had wrought havoc upon Kas'mira. Abul Qasim, son of Abu Barkat, a former Moghul Subedar was in Kas'mira and planned striking a blow upon Mir Muqim, whose phenomenal rise was envious and unacceptable. Abul Qasim came out of his retirement and collected all the discontented soldiers and raised the banner of rebellion. Deputing his brother, Nuruddin Khan with a considerable force from the side of Nawa Kadal, Abul Qasim himself launched a well planned attack on the house of Mir Muqim at Zaldagar, who fled for his life. Few more minor skirmishes decided the fate of Kas'mira and the Moghul rule came to an end and Abul Qasim became the ruler. His rule, however, lasted just three months. In the meantime Mir Muqim joined hands with Khwaja Dedamari another Kas'miri nobleman and together they sent a prayer to Abdali to conquer Kas'mira.

Afghans on the Scene: Consequent upon the murder of Nadir Shah at the hands of his own followers in the year 1747 AD, Ahmad Shah Abdali seized his vast dominion and installed himself upon the throne. Such an incident as Abdali coming to power could not pass unnoticed in Kas'mira. The result was an Afghan incursion. Afghans after meeting with some preliminary successes, the tide turned against the Afghans, and they met with a complete discomfiture and were forced to beat an ignominous retreat. Not for long, as they returned with more force duly supported by the local Muslim nobles.

Abdali had reached Lahore and during last few years his forces had made frequent unsuccessful forays and here was a golden chance. Abdali was happy to receive the request and deputed Abdulla Aishak Aqasi with a big force to conquer Kas'mira. The two armies met at Gund Niamat, a village near Srinagar and the battle raged for fifteen days. Tremendous efforts were made by Abul Qasim to turn the tide and was on the verge of success, when commander of his forces, Gul Khan Khaibri, joined Abdali's forces and the battle was decided in favour of Afghans. Abdul Qasim fell, was captured and Afghans under Aqasi made a triumphant entry into Srinagar and laid the foundation of the Afghan rule. It took some more years before Afghans were firmly established. For a period of five years (1748-53 AD) Kas'mira had lingered on as a part of the tottering Empire of the Moghuls, finally in 1753 AD passed out of the Moghul suzerainty and came into the possession of Afghan King Ahmad Shah Abdali.

Afghan Rule (1753-1819 AD)

Raja Sukh Jiwan: Having stayed in Kashmir for a period of about six months, Aishak Aqasi left for Kabul leaving behind Abdulla Khan Kabuli to carry on the administration of the country. Abdulla Khan, however, was not destined to remain for long. People had been tyrannised by Aqasi and did not expect better treatment from his successor. The rule of the Afghans too was not fully established and a conspiracy was hatched up by Sukh Jiwan Mal and Abul Hassan Bandey as a result of which Abdulla Khan was murdered and not even a faint voice was raised against Abdulla Khan's murder. So bitter was the memory of the past few months that people gladly received the news of Raja Sukh Jiwan Mal having assumed the reins of Administrator (Subedar, as Governors were called) of Kas'mira in 1754 AD. Sukh Jiwan a native of Gujarat was serving in the Army of Ahmad Shah Abdali, when he was deputed to serve under Aqasi in his Kashmir campaign. Aqasi had appointed him as *Sahibkar* to Abdulla Khan Kabuli. Sukh Jiwan soon after assuming reins of Subedarship, appointed Abdul Hassan Bandey as Prime Minister, called as *Madhurmillan*. For some time Sukh Jiwan carried on in the name of King Ahmad Shah Abdali, who too did not think of taking any serious view of Sukh Jiwan's action and issued an appointment order to him. For some time all was well till Abdali made a demand for a huge sum of money, over and above annual tribute. Sukh Jiwan could ill afford to fulfil Abdali's demand as people were already impoverished and no further burden on them could be laid and rightly refused to pay exorbitant amount. Sukh Jiwan was left with no alternative except declaring independence from Afghan rule which he did. Abdali was furious and deputed Aishaq Aqasi with a big force to bring Sukh Jiwan on his knees. The battle lasted some time. Afghan forces were offered stiff resistance resulting in their disintegration and defeat, while Aqasi fled from the battlefield. Sukh Jiwan returned to Srinagar as an independent and a victorious ruler and was given a right royal reception by the people.

Mir Muqim who was all these years in Kabul returned to Kas'mira but having found his former power and influence gone, resorted to intrigue. In a short while he succeeded, resulting in Prime Minister Abdul Hassan

Main Sun Temple Built by Lalitaditya Muktapira at Martand (In Ruins)

Carvings on Side Walls of the Sun Temple.

Ancient Painting of 16th Century Folio Retelling of the *Kathasaritsagara*

An Old Paining of Inland Water Way-Nallah Mar in Pravarpura (Srinagar)

Hari Parvat Fort Built under the Orders of Akbar (Photograph Courtesy Rohit Kaul–June 2012)

A Rare Painting of Akbar in his Old Age

Pari Mahal on the Outskirts of Srinagar overlooking Dal Lake

Stone *Khraw* (Slippers) used by Rishi Pir.
Single *Khraw* (Slippers) of the Saint is Worshipped Even Today

Bandey being sent to prison and Mir Muqim appointed in his place in 1757 AD. Mir Muqim was soon found out and Abul Hassan Bandey reinstated. Soon thereafter Sukh Jiwan left for an expedition to Sialkot and left the country in the hands of Bandey. During this period Bomba tribes rose in rebellion, which could not be controlled by Bandey. After quelling the rebellion, Sukh Jiwan divested Mir Muqim as well as Abdul Hassan Bandey of all powers and Kashmiri Pandit notable Mahanand Dhar as *Madhurmillan* (Prime Minister).

Sukh Jiwan set the administration right and took various measures to improve the lot of people, specially peasants. Many public utility projects were undertaken and learning was patronised. Poetry was encouraged. Sukh Jiwan's era was that of peace and relative prosperity and was called '*Zamana Sukh Joo (Kas'miri),* good old time of Sukh Jiwan. Some Muslim historians accuse Pandit Mahanand Dhar of inimical tendencies towards the Muslims and in their support they state that it was at his suggestion that cow - killing was made an offence by Sukh Jiwan. But the popularity of Pandit Mahanand Dhar with the Muslims was certainly at a very high level. He was instrumental in taking measures for the benefit and amelioration of the lot of the people. Mahanand Dhar's popularity with the Muslims can be gauged from the following Persian verses that were addressed by a contemporary poet, Mohammad Jan Beg to Sukh Jiwan, in which reference is made to the Pandit in most glowing terms (Translated from Persian); "Mahanand, who comes from the clan of the Dhars is your Chief Minister; you have rightly made him master of all cash, kind and administration, Saadi who is well versed in reading the mysterious working of the decrees of Fate, has said, that God certainly gives bread to all, but the condition that one has to fulfil is that he must possess wisdom, and then seek it from Dhars."

Fall of Sukh Jiwan: Rise of Sukh Jiwan was a thorn in the eyes of his enemies and few noblemen conspired to bring about his downfall and made use of a Balkhi prince who had been expelled from his own country and was enjoying the hospitality of Sukh Jiwan for a number of years. The prince made a cowardly attack upon the person of the Raja and wounded him seriously but was killed in retaliation. With Sukh Jiwan seriously wounded, conspirers extended invitation to Abdali. In 1762 AD Nuruddin Khan Bamezai, a veteran General in the army of Abdali, was deputed for re-conquest of Kas'mira. Sukh Jiwan, who had recovered by then made preparations and deployed his forces on Tosa Maidan. Just when the battle was to commence Commander of his forces Bakhat Mal, a Hindu, joined the Afghan forces. Disheartened Sukh Jiwan left the battlefield, but was caught while running away. His eye's were gouged and was imprisoned. So far Afghan rule was in bits and pieces, with frequent changes of Subedars, but now on real Afghan rule began in Kas'mira. Though Nuruddin Khan Bamezai tried his best to establish peace in country, he was outsmarted by Pandit leader Kailash Dhar, who yielded considerable influence over Durrani overlord (Abdali), got Bland Khan Sadozai appointed as Subedar in 1762 AD. In 1764 AD there was another change and Nuruddin Khan Bamezai appointed Subedar. By this time Afghan rule had established itself and Abdali required Nuruddin's services at Lahore. Nuruddin Khan Bamezai left for Lahore in 1765 AD leaving his nephew Jan Mohammad Khan to carry on the administration of the country.

Rise of Pandit Kailash Dhar: After Nuruddin Khan Bamezai had left, disorder again set in and one Lal Mohammad Khan, a Jagirdar of Berul and a trusted servant of Nuruddin Khan defeated Jan Mohammad and himself became the ruler of Kas'mira. His rule, however, did not last longer than six months, but during this period he took all repressive measures against Pandits. Abdali in the meantime appointed Khurram Khan as Subedar and Kailash Dhar as his *Sahibkar*. Both of them regained Kas'mira by use of force in 1766 AD. Khurram Khan, however, alongwith Kailash Dhar left for Kabul leaving Kas'mira at the mercy of Mir Faqirulla and his supporters, who assumed the reigns of the country in 1767 AD in his own name. As a result Afghan ruler Abdali deputed Nuruddin Khan Bamezai, a second time, for the re-conquest of Kas'mira. Mir Faqirulla was vanquished though his Bomba tribals plundered Kas'mira in a leisurely manner.

Kailash Dhar Murdered: In 1770 AD Khurram Khan succeeded in installing himself as the Subedar for the second time. He had no support base and was deposed and in his place Amir Khan Jawansher was appointed as the Subedar of the province in the year 1771 AD. With this change Kailash Dhar's power was eclipsed and was killed by Fazal Kanth in the Darbar Hall and his body thrown into close by Vitasta (Jhelum). It was tragic end of Kailash Dhar who had, in the name of the community leadership, sided with tyrants and had no morals to change side to suit his personal interest.

Amir Khan's debaucheries of a degraded character went on in an unsettled manner and amidst the turmoil news of the death of of Abdali (1773 AD) was received in Kas'mira. Taimur Shah, eldest son of Abdali, Governor of Kandahar succeeded Abdali and continued Amir Khan Jawansher as the Subedar and even bestowed the title of *Diler Jung* (Brave Warrior) on him. Amir Khan somehow conceived notions of independence and stopped the payment of annual tribute to Kabul and ceased all connection with Kabul. Amir Khan was a Shia and after the declaration of independence persecuted Sunnis to encourage conversion to Shia faith. The news about the revolt of Amir Khan took some time to reach Kabul, but as soon as the Taimur Shah, the then ruler, was apprised of it, he deputed Karim Dad Khan with a strong army for the conquest of Kas'mira. Amir Khan was defeated without great effort, his supporters having deserted him at the nick of time left the country leaving it to its own care. The victorious Haji Karim Dad Khan became the Subedar in 1776 A D. Construction of Amira Kadal and Sher-Garhi Palace, is attributed to Amir Khan Jawansher.

Rise and Murder of Pandit Dila Ram: Karim Dad Khan appointed Pandit Dila Ram as his *Sahibkar* (Chief Minister). Dila Ram came like an angel with a new message of life and for the country his presence brought about its rehabilitation. In the year 1783 AD Karim Dad Khan handed over his *Subedarship* to his son Azad Khan. There was rebellion by Bomba and Khoka tribals, which was quelled by Azad Khan. Spurred by this victory Azad Khan declared independence and took the title of Nadir Shah II. It took some time before the Kabul king came to know of Azad's rebellion and deputed an emissary to peacefully bring Azad Khan to his fold, which failed. Inevitably the two armies met at Muzaffarabad and Azad Khan came out victorious. Another expedition was mounted by Kabul ruler Taimur Shah under the command of a veteran general Madad Khan. A battle was fought (1785 AD) culminating in the victory for Madad Khan. Azad, crest fallen with no support committed suicide and Madad Khan made a triumphant entry into the city of Srinagar in 1785 AD. Madad Khan was not to remain in Kashmir for more than ten months and was succeeded by Mirdad Khan in year 1786 AD who died in 1788 AD. Mulla Gaffar Khan succeeded him but he too was recalled back after a period of only four months. Sirdar Jumma Khan Alkozai was appointed but he too died in 1792 AD and was succeeded by Mirza Khan. Mirza Khan, of a religious bent of mind, after few months left Kas'mira, became a religious recluse and installed his son Mir Hazar Khan in his place. Soon after his assuming the reins, Mir Hazar Khan declared his independence and announced that he would rule as an independent king. He was merciless and brutal towards Pandits and was satisfied not only with killing them or throwing them into the rivers and also adopted well planned methods to destroy them. A reign of terror was ushered in Kas'mira, which took its first victim in Pandit Dila Ram, who was murdered at Khanayar in the year 1793 AD. Taimur Shah, Kabul King, breathed his last and was succeeded by Zaman Khan, who confirmed Mir Hazar Khan's appointment but at the same time demanded annual tribute, which was refused.

After the murder of Dila Ram, a systematic process was adopted for the extermination of the whole lot of the Pandits. A regular Kashmiri Pandit hunt was mounted and various methods adopted for their killing. "Thousands of them were killed by ordinary and known methods. Many more were put in sacks and drowned in the Dal Lake, and those who survived were harassed in such a manner that they forgot even Faqir Ullah's *zulum* (Cruelty)." A number of the Kashmiri Pandit notables of Baramulla, were arrested, then humiliated and ultimately put in prison and later on drowned in Vitasta river.

Rise of Nand Ram Tiku. Zaman Khan deputed Mirza Khan, Mir Hazar's father to Kas'mira to bring the latter round by peaceful methods. Mirza Khan tried his best to wean away his son but failed and was imprisoned by his son Mir Hazar. Zaman Khan, ruler of Kabul, sent a huge army under Ahmad Khan. Mir Hazar Khan also started with a huge force and the two armies met at Baramulla. Before the battle between the two sides began, Mir Hazar Khan brought out of prison all the Pandit notables who were suffering imprisonment at Baramulla and drowned them in river Jhelum (Vitasta). During the battle, which ensued, Mir Hazar was defeated and fled to take shelter inside Shah-e-Hamdan mosque at Srinagar but was arrested and put in prison. Rahmatullah Khan became the Subedar but was not destined to remain long in Kas'mira on being recalled by Kabul king. He went to Kabul with a Kashmiri Pandit by name Nand Ram Tiku, who in course of time rose to the eminent place of Diwan at Kabul and changed the course of Kas'mira history; more than once. Kifayat Khan was the next Subedar; just, humane and kind, but he too was recalled after three months and Arsala Khan succeeded him as Subedar in 1795 AD. During the last two years, there had been frequent changes of Subedars, who were mostly indifferent to the plight of the people. Intrigues, loot and murder expeditions of Bombas, quarrels between rival factions of power had taken dominant place in the daily life in Kas'mira. Factional fights were the main noteworthy events of these two fateful years, which created a veritable hell in the country. It is amidst this situation Abdullah Khan Alkozai took over as Subedar in 1796 AD.

Recognition to Pandit Sahaj Ram Dhar: Abdullah Khan Alkozai had most difficult task to accomplish; control lawlessness, bring to book bands of robbers and thieves and stop the menance of Bomba and Khoka tribals. Being a man of courage and organising skills appointed Pandit Sahaj Ram Dhar as his *Sahibekar*, in preference to other Muslim notables and delegated to him all the administrative powers as necessary. Pandit Sahaj Ram Dhar possessed great talent, was statesman of high order, a man of great talent and marked statesmanship. He had all the good qualities to hold the exalted office of *Sahibekar*. The Pandit engaged himself in right earnest upon the task of the rehabilitation of the country

Pandit Nand Ram Tiku as Diwan of Kabul: Pandit Nand Ram Tiku who went to Kabul and settled there was a man of great sagacity and tact. He came to the notice of Wazir Wafadar Khan, who then was the Chief Minister of Zaman Khan, the king of Kabul. Wazir took Nand Ram in his service. Gradually Nand Ram rose to the exalted position of Diwan at Kabul. He is credited at one time with having struck coin in his own name with the inscription (Persian) '*Sim az mabud wa zarb az Nand Ram*'. This rupee was known as *Nand Rami Rupiah* and was in circulation in the Tribal areas of Kas'mira till about 1910 AD. A number of Kashmiri Pandits had settled in

Kabul, chief amongst them being Pandit Daya Ram Kachru *'Khushdil'*, whose son Birbal Kachru became a noted poet.

Pandit Nand Ram had a brother, Pandit Har Das Tiku, who was residing in Kas'mira and was considered important person due to his brother being in the court of Kabul King. However, due to his proximity to the Kabul Court, differences arose with Subedar Abdullah Khan Alkozai. Pandit Nand Ram got an order issued from the king calling Abdullah Khan to Kabul, where he was imprisoned on the suggestion of Nand Ram. Atta Mohammad Khan Alkozai, brother of Abdullah Khan Alkozai. had been made officiating Subedar by his elder brother Abdullah. However, another brother, Vakil Khan Alkozai. secured an appointment order from Kabul King and accompanied by a huge force went to take over reins of Kas'mira. Atta Mohammad Khan Alkozai gave battle to Vakil Khan, defeated and killed him and put Pandit Har Das Tiku in prison.

Unrest and Rebellion in Kabul and Effects in Kas'mira: During this time there was rebellion in Kabul Court by Mohammad Shah. Abdullah Khan Alkozai took advantage of this situation in Kabul and secured his release from the prison and returned to Kas'mira and pronounced himself as an independent ruler. In Kabul, the battle of succession went in favour of Shah Shuja, who had wrested the throne of Kabul from Mohammad Shah. Efforts by Kabul court to bring Abdullah Khan Alkozai back under Kabul suzerainty failed. One tribal leader Sher Mohammad Khan with a huge army was sent to Kas'mira to regain the territory from Abdullah Khan Alkozai. In the ensuing battle Abdullah Khan Alkozai was defeated and killed. During the later years of Abdullah Khan Alkozai's rule, a severe earthquake rocked Kas'mira resulting in great deal of damage to life and property. Devastating high floods followed which rendered thousands homeless. This was not all; the winter was the most severe known in history. Even Vitasta (Jhelum) and all the water bodies had frozen. After regaining Kas'mira for Kabul King, Abdullah Khan Alkozai having been defeated, Sher Mohammed Khan remained in Kas'mira for about five months; restoring order and setting other matters right. In 1807 AD he got his son Atta Mohammad Khan appointed as Subedar and himself left for Kabul.

Pandit Sahaj Ram Dhar as Diwan: Pandit Sahaj Ram Dhar had been appointed *Saihbekar* by Abdullah Khan Alkozai. The new Subedar Atta Mohammad Khan retained him in the post of *Sahibekar*, even though Sahaj Ram Dhar had sided with Abdullah Khan Alkozai. This was because of high administrative skills of the Pandit. The relations between Kas'mira and Kabul were basically that of token suzerainty and regular payment of annual tribute, which was sent through Sahaj Ram Dhar, who looked after the revenue accounts of Kas'mira also. During this time Pandit Sahaj Ram Dhar was sent to Kabul with the accounts which were to be presented to the king.

While crossing Indus in a ferry, pony which carried the accounts took fright and jumped into the river and was drowned along with the accounts. Sahaj Ram Dhar continued his journey and on reaching Kabul sought audience with the king. He then related the incident but within four days presented a graphic duplicate account of the revenue accounts, from his memory, to the King. These presented accounts were found to tally with the accounts copy lying in Kas'mira and sent to the King later.

This Kabul King was pleased and bestowed a Khillat, hereditary title of Diwan and *Jagir* of two villages in Kas'mira (Dachhan Para and Marhama) were bestowed upon him as *Jagir* in perpetuity. Sahaj Ram's brother was given charge of Kamraj division of Kas'mira. In addition village of Deosar was given to his cousin Pandit Birbal Dhar. Atta Mohammad Khan as Subedar held great promise. Man of simple habits, deep religious convictions, his attention was concentrated on raising prosperity of the people. In his quest for better administration he got full support from Pandit Sahaj Ram Dhar. During this time agriculture output increased, trade was revived and law and order brought under control. However, there was unrest in Kabul; Mohammad Shah's rebellion against Shah Shuja King of Kabul was successful. Shah Shuja escaped and took asylum in Punjab under Maharaja Ranjit Singh. Seeing the change in Kabul, Atta Mohammad Khan, like his many predecessors declared independence. Mohammad Shah King of Kabul deputed a huge force under the command of General Akram Khan Bamezai for the conquest of Kas'mira. Kabul expedition met with defeat and with this Atta Mohammad Khan became stronger and assertive.

Ranjit Singh of Punjab Enters the Scene: The importance to hold Kas'mira was not lost in the eyes of Mohammad Shah at Kabul, An expedition under Wazir Fateh Mohommad Khan was mounted to regain Kas'mira. Cunning Atta Mohammad Khan opened negotiations with Shah Shuja, the deposed Kabul King, to come to Kas'mira. Diwan Nand Ram Tiku was deputed to approach Shah Shuja, who finally came to Kas'mira, but was virtually kept as a prisoner. Atta Mohammad Khan deputed his brother Jahandar Khan to seize the Attock Fort, which was literal gateway for entry to Kas'mira. Wazir Fateh Mohammad Khan the Afghan General dared not attack the fort and opened negotiations with Ranjit Singh for help, who agreed to help provided annual tribute of eight lakh rupees was paid to him from the Kas'mira revenues. This term was accepted and Ranjit Singh deputed Diwan Mohkam Chand with a sizeable force to help Wazir Fateh Mohammad's forces. In the battle that ensued, Atta Mohammad Khan was defeated as some of his close followers deserted at the crucial moment. Atta Mohammad Khan opened negotiations with Diwan Mohkam Chand and sought a safe passage to return to Kabul. Diwan Mohkam Chand took a Hundi (Promissory Note) also for eight lakh rupees.

Sikh Army's Second Foray Into Kas'mira: Wazir Fateh Mohammad Khan did not stay in for more than a few months and accompanied by Diwan Nand Ram Tiku left for Kabul (1813 AD) leaving the administration of the country in the hands of his brother Azim Khan. Azim Khan appointed Sahaj Ram Dhar as his Diwan, and Pandit Har Das Tiku as his *Sahibkar.* Appointment of Har Das Tiku was to take care of any reservation and ward off opposition on behalf of his brother, Diwan Nand Ram Tiku. For the first time during Afghan Rule complete administrative machinery was in the hand of Pandits, though selected few. Having obtained safe passage to Kabul, Atta Mohammad Khan handed over the Attock Fort to Ranjit Singh in lieu of one lakh rupees. Azim Khan interpreted this action of the Ranjit Singh as a breach of faith on his part and refused to pay the annual tribute of eight lakhs, as agreed. Maharaja Ranjit Singh was incensed and ordered an expedition to conquer Kas'mira but met with a complete disaster. Sikh forces were routed and with very great difficulty that the main force under direct command of Ranjit Singh was saved from total disaster. Sikhs were driven out of the country and victorious Azim Khan returned back to Kas'mira.

Pandit Mission to Maharaja Ranjit Singh: Drunk with power Azim Khan blamed Pandit notables for failed Sikh incursion. Pandit Har Das Tiku was killed but appointed Mirza Pandit, Birbal Dhar and Sukh Ram Safaya as the revenue collectors. After some time Birbal Dhar was accused of shortfall of revenue and asked to pay the deficit amount. Under Birbal Dhar a meeting of Pandit Notables decided that Pandit Birbal Dhar should quietly slip away to meet Ranjit Singh on behalf of Kashmiri Pandits to request him for conquest of Kas'mira. Some more Pandits secretly followed him. After sometime Birbal Dhar's escape, his wife and daughter-in-law were traced and taken in custody by Azim Khan. At Jammu Dogra rulers of Jammu received them well. In the meanwhile Azim Khan left Kas'mira and appointed his brother Jabbar Khan in his place.

Pandit Birbal through the kind offices of Dhian Singh, younger brother of Gulab Singh of Jammu, help from Kashmiri Pandit notables at the Sikh Ruler's Court, got an audience with the Ranjit Singh and laid before him the request of Kashmiri Pandits. Ranjit Singh, smarting under earlier defeat, ordered an organised and fully equipped force to mount an expedition. As a surety he held back Birbal Dhar's son in the Sikh Durbar's custody. It was not that Ranjit Singh was waiting for Kashmiri Pandits to invite him to conquest Kas'mira. After capturing Lahore in 1799 AD, he shifted his Capital to Lahore in 1802 AD and spent following years fighting the Afghans, driving them out of the Punjab. He captured Pashtun territory including Peshawar (now referred to as North West Frontier Province and the Tribal Areas). In 1813 AD, Ranjit Singh's general Dewan Mokham Chand led the Sikh forces against the Afghan forces of Mohammad Shah led by Fateh Khan Barakzai. Following this encounter, duly helped by Kas'mira Subedar Atta Mohammad Khan, Afghans lost their stronghold at Attock, gateway to Kas'mira as well as frontier provinces. Subsequently he also captured the Pothohar plateau, Sindh Sagar Doab and hill states North of Anandpur Sahib, the largest of which was Kangra. Now taking his expeditions deep into Afghan territory, he captured Multan which encompassed the southern parts of Punjab and finally Peshawar in 1818 AD. This was the first time that Peshawari Pashtuns were ruled by Punjabis and Sikhs. In this arc only a speck remained in the form of Kas'mira. Jammu was already held by his colleagues in arms Jamwal Dogras.

Kas'mira Passes to Sikh Kingdom: Ranjit Singh's force consisted of 30,000 strong army under the command of Gulab Singh of Jammu, Hari Singh Nalwa, Diwan Mokham Chand, Sardars Jwala Singh, Hukum Singh and Sham Singh. Jabbar Khan also collected a strong army to meet Sikh Army. Sikh army encamped near Shopian while Jabbar Khan with his force went via Chrar-e-Shariff. In the multi pronged battle around Shopian, Gulab Singh's forces made a pincer movement from the East and isolated Jabbar Khan's forces from that direction. Hari Singh Nalwa's force was in front facing Jabbar Khan's force. The remainder force had moved due west and put pressure on Afghan Forces from that direction. In the ensuing battle Jabbar Khan was identified and wounded and Afghan army fell back in a melee. In this battle Jabbar Khan had tied many pieces of cloth of different colours around his turban. Even before this battle he used to be dressed up shabbily with similar pieces of cloth. For being shabbily dressed he was called Jabbar *Jhanda* (Shabbily dressed Jabbar). This acronym found its way into Kashmiri way of life; anyone shabbily dressed was called Jabbar Jhanda in disdain. In fact it is said that Jabbar Khan was identified by Sikh Forces from the dress and pieces of cloth around his turban during the battle. The retreating Afghan forces took away injured Jabbar Khan, who died at Baramulla, while others went into hiding and many more were killed. Sikh Army was also able to get Shah Shuja freed from Jabbar Khan's custody. Shah Shuja's wife Wafa Begum had promised Kohinoor Diamond held by Shuja for Maharaja Ranjit Singh, if her husband was freed from Kas'mira prison. Sikhs had won, had annexed Kas'mira, freed Shah Shuja, who gave Kohinoor Diamond as present for Maharaja Ranjit Singh. From that day on till his death Ranjit Singh wore that diamond on his right shoulder; it was his pride. With the annexation of Kas'mira, *Sarkar Khalsaji's*, as reign of Ranjit Singh, was called, put an end to nearly five hundred years of Muslim rule in Kas'mira. Annexation of Kas'mira was followed by subduing the Kas'mira mountains territory west of the river Jhelum; todays, Hazara in Pakistan and Pakistan Administered Kashmir.

Late 19th Century Photograph of Muslim Paper Machie Artisans on Work

Under Afghans: After Sukh Jiwan *'Zamanai Sukhju'* had ended and replaced by feudal Afghan rule, significant for intrigues and nepotism by well placed Pandits prevalent and brutal killing of Kailash Dhar in 1770 AD, then Bhatta *Madhurmilan.* vitiating the general environment. In 1766 AD services of a large number of *Bombas* were enlisted by Afghans from the neighbouring hilly districts with the sole purpose of teasing, tormenting and tyrannising Bhattas. Thereafter a systematic process was adopted for the extermination of Pandits with various methods adopted for their killing. "Thousands of them were killed, many more were put in sacks and drowned in the Dal Lake, and those who survived were harassed. Pandits were strictly forbidden to read Persian and the penalty for the infringement was certain death. Consequences of this order can well be understood when we bear in mind that the Persian was the court language." Whatever comforts or standing community had been hard to come by and they had to work in a hostile environment. Amply the situation was what Lalitaditya Muktapira (697–733 AD) had impressed upon; "when the villagers have clothes; wives eatables, ornaments, elephants, horses and houses like the citizens. When soldiers are raised from one district only when Government officials establish marriage alliances with each other, then you should know that the lot of the people turns worse." A terrible famine also occurred in Kas'mira during those very days.

Sikh Rule (Jun 1819-June 1846)

Sikh Rule and Hari Singh Nalwa: On 20th of June 1819 AD Sikh army of Maharaja Ranjit Singh made a triumphant entry into the Srinagar city.

After the conquest of the country by the Sikhs, Diwan Mokham Chand remained in charge of Kas'mira for a few months. He was succeeded by Diwan Moti Ram, a soft and peace loving man. It was during his regime an attempt was made by some Sikh Generals to destroy *Khanqah-e-Maullah* (Shah-e-Hamdan Mosque), but Pandit's persuaded the Sikhs not to resort to such a measure.

After a brief period of a year Diwan Moti Ram was replaced by Hari Singh Nalwa in 1820 AD. Hari Singh Nalwa abolished *Jaziya* and the other taxes, which Pandits and Sikh population had to pay to Muslim rulers. For these reasons, several Muslim historians have labelled Hari Singh Nalwa as a tyrant and called his rule as '*Sikha Shahi*' or 'Rule of Sikhs'. It was a matter of pride for Sikh Army that they did not destroy any Muslim religious place nor abducted Muslim women. Hari Singh Nalwa restored order in the turbulent areas, subdued *Bomba* and *Khoka* Tribals, controlled *Lavanias* (Lones) and Tantray's and reorganized civil administration. Under his *Subedarship* Kas'mira was divided into Parganas, each under a collector. The habitual criminals were bound down and robbers infesting the forests were suppressed. Construction of forts at Uri and Muzaffarabad and gurudwaras at Mattan and Baramulla were undertaken. To alleviate the misery of the people, in the wake of the unprecedented floods of 1821 AD, he took measures to provide prompt relief. For all his exemplary services to Sikh Durbar, Hari Singh received a special favour from Maharaja Ranjit Singh; he was allowed to strike a coin in his own name. This coin, known as the *Hari Singhi Rupee*, remained in circulation in the valley till the closing years of the nineteenth century. During Hari Singh's time Birbal Dhar started showing indifferent attitude towards his colleagues and even to the Sikh Subedar. The rumour was the Birbal Dhar's ambition of becoming ruler made him to conspire with Muslim Hill Chieftans against Sikh Rule. Though this charge was proved false, Birbal Dhar fell from grace and lost his positions as well as prestige. He was called to Sikh Durbar at Lahore and kept there.

In 1822 AD Hari Singh Nalwa was assigned the task of annexing Pathan territory of Hazara on the Northwest of the Sikh kingdom, where he remained for fifteen years and settled the disturbed area. Diwan Moti Ram was appointed as Subedar for second time. In the meantime Birbal Dar secured permission to return to Kas'mira but his relations even with Moti Ram were no good. All his movable property was confiscated and he was sent to prison. After sometime Birbal Dhar died in custody. There was hardly any sympathy for him during his last days, in spite of the fact that he had done lot of good for Kas'mira to rid them from Afghan rule. It was apparent that his ambition and his pride had overtaken his faculty of saner judgement.

Diwan Moti Ram did not remain as Subedar for long due to untimely death of his son. His successor Chuni Lal committed suicide, when he was summoned to Lahore to explain his inability to collect revenues. Diwan Kripa Ram, who followed, did not have an easy time either and during his time Kas'mira had series of misfortunes; severe earthquakes and cholera. To cap it all Raja Zabardast Khan Chieftan of Muzaffarabad, backed by almost all the hill chieftains, rebelled against the Sikh rule. Bhiman Singh Ardali now became Subedar in 1831 AD, for about a year. He appointed Pandit Ganesh Dhar as his Chief Minister. Even this one year witnessed no better days and in particular there broke out terrible Shia-Sunni riots. The main cause of riots was the shawl industry as majority of the Shawl factory owners were Shias and their ruin would have been the precursor of a greater ruin to the Sunni's, who were workers.

In 1832 AD Shahzada Sher Singh, second son of Ranjit Singh, succeeded Bhiman Singh Ardali as Subedar of Kas'mira. The general policy of the Sikhs was to keep the Kashmiri Muslims fully and completely subdued so as to eliminate any chance of their rising. Some of the principal mosques which afforded a meeting ground for the people were either confiscated or closed for prayers. Even *Azan*, call to prayers, was stopped. Shahzada Sher Singh was recalled and Colonel Mehan Singh, a man of a humane and just temperament appointed in his place in 1834 AD.

Sikh Rule on Downslide: Ranjit Singh died in the year 1839 AD. After his death pandemonium reigned supreme in Punjab and annexed territories. Chieftans and Rajas started exerting themselves. Sikh Army now freed from the iron grip of the late Maharaja, became all powerful. Rival factions sought the help of the army for their self advance, and made lavish promises to the troops and their commanders. Lawlessness at Lahore had greatly weakened the military might of the Sikhs and Sikh Army had become unpopular in Punjab. Sikh army in Kas'mira also showed signs of restiveness, which in course of time broke into open rebellion. Irrespective of the situation around him, Colonel Mehan Singh turned a new leaf in the administered areas. During his time a crushing defeat upon the Raja of Skardu was inflicted by General Zorawar Singh of Dogra Army and Skardu Raja became a tributory to the Sikh ruler through Dogra Kings of Jammu. On the administrative side he devised plans for the rehabilitation of the uprooted people and imported food grains from Punjab and sold at cheap rates. Many European, English, French, and German travellers visited Kas'mira. They took shawls as gifts and by this a fresh impetus was given to the shawl trade in the European market. However, the rot in the Sikh Army in Kas'mira had set in with the result Colonel Mehan Singh was murdered by the insurgent soldiers, though Pandit Ganesh Dhar his Chief Minister succeeded in saving his son.

With the murder of Colonel Mehan Singh, Kas'mira fell into a complete grip of lawlessness and misrule. Sheikh Ghulam Mohi-ud-Din, a trusted servant of the Sikh State was appointed as Subedar in 1841 AD. It was hoped that with a Muslim as Subedar, goodwill of Kashmiri Muslims might secure stability of Sikh rule. A Pandit, Pandit Tilak Chand Munshi, was appointed as his Chief Minister. Jama Masjid which was kept closed for public prayers from the time of Diwan Moti Ram was now left open for prayers. This act went a long way in winning the goodwill of Muslims. On the death of Sheikh Ghulam Mohi-ud-Din in the end of 1845 AD, he was succeeded by his son, Sheikh Imam-ud-Din, who too was in Kas'mira.

Sheikh Imam-ud-Din along with Ranjur Singh and Dewan Dina Nath–1847 (Courtesy James Duffield Harding). Sheikh Imam-ud-din was the governor of Kashmir under the Sikhs, and fought on the side of the English in the battle of Multan during the Second Anglo-Sikh War (1848-49)

Sheikh Imam-ud-Din will be remembered for long for his tactfulness with which he tackled the problems relating to shawl weavers. Imam-ud-Din freed them from the virtual slavery of their masters and further ordered an increment in their wages. Besides that it was ordered that State paddy be supplied to shawl weavers from State granaries at a price, which was less by two annas in a rupee. Shawl manufacturers, mostly Shias, were ordered to give bonus of three per cent from their profits to the weavers. But in spite of his good intentions he was not destined to remain long in Kas'mira. Things were changing fast. *Raja Gulab Singh* of Jammu had in the meantime expanded his territory and the Anglo Sikh War was on. Within six months Sheikh Imam-ud-Din had to hand over Kas'mira to Raja Gulab Singh as a result of the treaty between the defeated Sikhs and the British, but not without a fight.

Assesment of Sikh Rule: While the Sikhs under Maharaja Ranjit Singh were active in erstwhile Punjab and annexing nearby principalities, Jamwal Rajput Clan ruled Jammu Region. This clan, known later as Dogra Kings, were to establish a reign of 103 Years in Jammu and Kashmir State. After the annexation of Kas'mira in 1819 AD, the rule of Lahore Durbar was implemented through Administrators called Subedars, deputed from Lahore. The tenure of many was brief and very few like Hari Singh Nalwa or Colonel Mehan Singh could make a deep impression. The local bureaucracy was mainly manned by the Pandits; mostly restricted to few families of Dhars. Though they did contribute a lot in the general administration, their ambitions, and intrigues were constant threat to other community members. These Pandits had powerful supporters in the Lahore Court, where a number of Kashmiri Pandits held very prominent places of trust and honour. Ranjit Singh tried on more than one occasion to set the matters right by punishing the delinquents, but as he himself shared the belief that the stability of the rule in Kas'mira depended upon the spirit of the people of Kas'mira being in complete subjugation, even he could achieve no tangible results. The Sikh policy it seems was not to allow the growth of a rich class in Kashmir. In this they made no exception between the Pandit and the Muslim. Wherever a suspicion arose about the possession of wealth by some person, it was taken from him in the shape of *Nazarana* (Presents). During Shahzada Sher Singh's Subedarship, *Nazaranas* were recovered from the high class Pandits also. Sikh rule lasted for nearly 27 years with calamities, premature snowfalls, which destroyed ripe rice crop leading to famines followed by diseases. Thousands migrated again to Bharatvarasha during these hard days and the population of the valley came down. There is no doubt that atrocities committed on people, be they be Pandit's or Muslims, were nowhere near the scale of Afghan rulers, immediate predecessor rulers of Sikhs. However, Sikh General Akali Phula Singh, who too had a short stint as the head of the Sikh Army in Kas'mira, left an impression by reversing certain tyrannical trends of the Afghan Rule.

5

Dogra Rule

We are shaped by our thoughts; we become what we think. When the mind is pure, joy follows like a shadow that never leaves.

Gautama Buddha

Raja Gulab Singh of Jammu

***Surya Vanshi* Jamwal Rajput Ruling Clan:** The Ruling Jamwal Rajput Clan of Jammu trace their descent from the ancient *Kshatriyas* mentioned frequently in *Mahabharata* and are *Surya Vanshis*. Their earliest known ancestor was Agnivarna of Parol, brother or kinsman of Raja of Ayodhya. Seven generations later, their ancestor Rai Jambu-Lochana, founded Jammu. The clan then descended from Rai Suraj Dev (850-920 AD), who had ousted Bajar Dhar dynasty and established himself as ruler of Jammu. The dynasty maintained its principality of Jammu except few times; in 1423 AD Jasrath Khokhar of Khokhar Dynasty of Sialkot killed Rai Hamir Dev (Rai Bhim-1400-1423) and occupied Jammu. Till end of 16th Century the head was called as Rai but from 1594 AD onwards the head was called Raja; Raja Sangram Dev, being the first Raja of Jammu (1594-1624 AD), during the reign of Akbar and Jehangir). During the Moghul Rule, they maintained their principality but from Akbar's time onwards remained vassals of the Moghuls until early eighteenth century. It was during Dhruv Dev's time (1703 – 1725 AD), Moghuls were driven out and independent rule re-established. In 1725, on the death of his father Dhruv Dev, Ranjit Dev became the ruler of Jammu. His forces joined Ahmad Shah Abdali's (Durrani) (1722–1773 AD) for invasion of India in 1752 and was rewarded with substantial *Jagir*. By this alignment with Afghan Ruler, the territory of Jammu Kingdom was greatly increased. However, his attempt to conquer Kas'mira from Afghans in 1779 AD, during the Afghan Subedar Haji Karim Dad's time failed, which infuriated Afghan Rulers, who imprisoned Ranjit Dev at Lahore but later released him on payment of ransom of Two Lakh Rupees. During the reign of his son, Brijraj

Dev Sahib (Bajai Deo) (1782 – 1787 AD) Sikhs invaded Jammu in 1787 AD. During the battle with the Sikhs, Raja Brijraj Dev Sahib (Bajai Deo) was killed at Rumal and Jammu became vassal of then Sikh Durbar (*Sarkar Khalsaji*). On the death of Brijraj Dev Sahib, his eldest son, Mian Chet Singh, renounced his claims to the principality in favour of Gulab Singh clan. However, Sampuran Singh, his younger brother, ascended as the ruler and reigned from 1787 to 1797 AD as boy king under the guardianship of Mian Mota, the *Madar-ul-Maham*. On the death of Sampuran Singh in 1797, at the age of twelve years, his cousin Jit Singh son of Dalal Singh, younger brother of late Brijraj Dev Sahib (Bajai Deo) and grandson of Ranjit Dev, was made ruler of Jammu. Jammu remained independent, though a vassal of Sikh Durbar, till Maharaja Ranjit Singh invaded, conquered and annexed Jammu with Sikh Empire in 1808 AD. Jit Singh remained a figure head ruler for eight years, with internal autonomy of the principality under the suzerainty of Sikh Durbar.

In 1816 Jit Singh was deposed, expelled and exiled to British territory, where he was given Akhrcta Estate near Gurdaspur by British. Sikh Durbar appointed a governor to administer the annexed area of Jammu. In 1819 this conquered area got further expanded with the annexation of Kas'mira by Sikh Army, called Khalsa Army, under Hari Singh Nalwa and Diwan Mokham Chand, which also had force under Gulab Singh. During the period 1816 to 1820, there was nobody from Jamwal Rajput Clan in power, as it continued to be part of Sikh Durbar. In 1820 Kishore Singh son of Mian Zorawar Singh of Diyavan was installed as Raja of Jammu by Maharaja Ranjit Singh. Mian Zorawar Singh was grandson of Raja Dhruv Dev (1703 – 1725) and his son Kishore Singh was preferred to erstwhile Jit Singh, his deposed cousin. In fact other than the sons of deposed Jit Singh, Kishore Singh was the eldest of the claimants to the *Gaddi* (Throne). This bestowment of Jammu region as a hereditary fief upon Raja Kishore Singh was in appreciation of sterling services rendered by the family to Sikh Durbar; Gulab Singh in particular. In fact Gulab Singh had come into limelight during the Punjab Durbar expedition to re-annex Jammu in 1808 and possibly his standing in the Sikh Durbar put the dice in favour of his aging father Kishore Singh. With this descendants of Raja Kishore Singh came in the direct line of future claimants of Jammu throne. Kishore Singh had three sons; eldest Gulab Singh, Dhian Singh and youngest Suchet Singh.

Rise of Gulab Singh: Gulab Singh was born on 18 October 1792 AD at Diyavan and grew up in the care of his grandfather, Mian Zorawar Singh, from whom he learned the arts of horse riding and warfare. When Sikh army of Maharaja Ranjit Singh under Bhai Hukma Singh (Chimni) invaded Jammu in 1808, a brave Gulab Singh, without informing his grandfather, joined the battle for the defence of Jammu. Due to resistance put forward by him and his group against the Sikh forces, Sikh forces were forced to withdraw to Saidgarh. However, Jammu became a tributary of the Sikh Empire. In the year 1809 AD Ranjit Singh, impressed by the account of Gulab Singh's bravery, invited him (Gulab Singh) to Kot Daska, a village situated a few miles from Sialkot and offered him to get enrolled in Khalsa Army (Sikh Army), which Gulab Singh did and was made commander of Dogra Cavalry contingent. While in the service of Maharaja Ranjit Singh, Gulab Singh was assigned many campaigns including the conquest of Multan in 1816. On return from victorious campaign in Multan, he led an independent and successful campaign, in the same year, to Reasi, a hill town close to Jammu. During the period 1816-1819 Gulab Singh continued in the service of Ranjit Singh's Army. In 1819 he was particularly selected by Ranjit Singh to be part of 30000 force to annex Kas'mira. This force had three main commanders; Gulab Singh with his Dogra Force, Hari Singh Nalwa with the Khalsa Army assisted by Diwan Mokham Chand with third force. In the battle, which ensued near Kas'mira town of Shopian, Gulab Singh's force made an eastwardly pincer movement and took on the Kas'mira's Subedar Jabbar Khan's force from the East. It was a combined operation and the force triumphantly entered Kas'mira on 20th of June 1819, though Hari Singh Nalwa got more kudos. This campaign and role of Gulab Singh did not go without notice in the Sikh Durbar. In 1820 Maharaja Ranjit Singh restored the Dogra rule by installing Raja Kishore Singh, father of Gulab Singh, as the Raja of Jammu.

In 1821, under the rule of his father, Gulab Singh further extended the Jammu Kingdom by conquering Rajauri from Aghar Khan and Kishtwar from Tegh Muhammad Singh. In the same year Gulab Singh, as part of Sikh Force, conquered Dera Ghazi Khan. Since Sikh Durbar had shown special interest in the family line of Kishore Singh, Gulab Singh did all he could in the interest of Sikh Durbar. He even executed his own clansman and relative, Mian Dido Jamwal, who had been leading a rebellion against the Sikhs. Raja Kishore Singh died in 1822 and Gulab Singh was installed as ruler of Jammu on 4th May 1822 AD. Maharaja Ranjit Singh personally performed the *Raj Tilak* Ceremony of Gulab Singh at Jia Pota on the bank of River Chenab near Akhnoor (Jammu). Even after this Gulab Singh strived for acceptability of his rule by all his clansmen and relatives, made reconciliation efforts with deposed Jit Singh and obtained a formal declaration of renunciation from him. This declaration by Raja Jit Singh, translated from Persian, reads (Translated):

> "I, Raja Jit Singh, grandson of Raja Sahib Ranjit Devji, on this occasion and out of internal inclination and dignified favours, in my own lifetime, and as a token of intrinsic love and heartfelt affection, hereby renounce proprietorship to all the protected

territories of my ancestors, and my own inheritance, in favour of my prosperous *barkhurdar*, Raja-i-Rajgan Raja Gulab Singhji, and Raja Sahib Dhian Singhji and Raja Suchet Singhji, by way of *dharam* and *niyam*, mutual agreement and on oaths of my predecessors and Thakurs and Gurus".

With this master stroke Gulab Singh obtained loyalty of all his clansmen, which made him more determined, assertive and with a quest to add more territory to his domain. In 1824 Gulab Singh captured fort of Samartah, near holy Mansar Lake. In 1827 he accompanied Sikh Commander-In-Chief Hari Singh Nalwa, fought and defeated a horde of Afghan rebels led by Sayyid Ahmed at the Battle of Shaidu. Gulab Singh had conquered Reasi in 1816 and had employed Zorawar Singh Kahluria of Bilaspur (Himachal Pradesh) under the commandant of Reasi Fort (Bhimgarh Fort). He later made him in-charge of the fort. Zorawar Singh, under the name of General Zorawar Singh, mounted many expeditions in Trans-Himalayan Region during the period 1835- December 1841, under the directions of Gulab Singh. Pleased with Gulab Singh's efforts as the ruler of Jammu and larger cause of Sikh Durbar, Maharaja Ranjit Singh, between 1831-39 bestowed nearby Punjabi towns like Bhera, Jhelum, Rohtas, and Gujaat to the Raja of Jammu.

Expeditions of General Zorawar Singh-Paddar and Ladakh: After his successful stint at Reasi, Gulab Singh appointed Zorawar Singh in-charge of all forts North of Jammu and later appointed him as Governor of Kishtwar. Though the population of Kishtwar, conquered in 1821, was divided by different faiths, Zorawar Singh maintained peace and even recruited many local Rajputs into his Army. In 1834 one of the principalities of Ladakh Region of Raja of Timbus, sought Zorawar's help against the Gyalpo Tsepal Namgyal (King of Ladakh), which fell within the ambition of Zorawar Singh to expand territory for Gulab Singh. Zorawar entered Ladakh with a force of 5000 and defeated an army of local *Bots*, as Ladakhis are called, moved further to Kargil, subduing minor principalities en-route and received submission of the Ladakhis. However, a force of Gyalpo Tsepal Namgyal, under Banko Kahlon, tried to cut off Zorawars rear route of maintenance. Zorwar's force swiftly moved back to Kartse, where he sheltered through the winter. In the spring of 1835 he defeated the large Ladakhi army of Banko Kahlon and marched his victorious troops towards Leh. The Gyalpo now agreed to pay 50,000 rupees as war-indemnity and 20,000 rupees as an annual tribute. In 1835 Zorawar also conquered Paddar of Chamba Division, which literally was a minor campaign in comparison to one he had launched a year earlier (1834 AD) in the Ladakh Region, which consisted of several petty principalities, which were tributary to King of Ladakh.

Alarmed at the victory of Gulab Singh's Forces, Sikh Durbar Subedar of Kas'mira, Colonel Mehan Singh, in 1836 incited the Ladakhi Gyalpo to rebel. Zorawar Singh force-marched his army for ten days and surprised Ladakhis and forced them to surrender. A fort was built outside Leh for 300 men garrison of Zorawar Singh's Force, to keep Ladakh under control. Gyalpo Tsepal Namgyal was deposed and a Ladakhi General, Ngorub Stanzin, was made King. However, as the imposed King proved to be disloyal, Tsepal Namgyal was restored to the throne in 1838 AD. In this campaign he forced the Raja of Zanskar also to pay a separate tribute to Jammu.

An 1877 AD Sketch Painting of Skardu Fort Captured by Dogra Troops in 1840

Zorawar Conquers Baltistan for Gulab Singh: North of Kashmir and Northwest of Ladakh, lies the region of Baltistan. In 1840 AD Muhammad Shah, son of the ruler of Skardu (Also spelled Askardu), Ahmad Shah, fled to Leh and sought the aid of the Zorawar and Gyalpo against his father. Taking advantage, Ladakhis allowed Muhammad Shah to be imprisoned by his father Ahmad Shah and sought his aid in a general rebellion against the Dogras. Zorawar Singh quelled the rebellion and as punishment decided to mount an expedition to conquer Baltistan, in the winter of 1840 AD, adding a large contingent of Ladakhis to his force. The forces of Skardu were defeated, forced to flee and chased to the fort of Skardu. Zorawar's force invested the fort for few days and one night Dogra Forces scaled the steep mountain behind the fort, captured the fort on its crest and next day forced Ahmad Shah to surrender. After this victory Ahmad Shah's son Mohammad Shah was made the ruler under the suzerainty of Gulab Singh, ostensibly for Sikh Durbar. A fort was built on the banks of Indus River and occupied by

Dogra Forces. Zorawar's force after conquering Skardu, moved westwards and conquered strategic fort of Astor and took its Dard Chieftain as prisoner. This Dard territory was direct tributary to Kas'mira, which was under Sikh Durbar at that time. Subedar of Kas'mira Colonel Mehan Singh was alarmed, as the expedition expanded the territory of Gulab Singh at the cost of Sikh Durbar at Lahore. He complained to then Sikh Maharaja Sher Singh at Lahore, which was forwarded to Gulab Singh at Jammu, who merely ordered Dard Chieftain to be released. These achievements of Raja Gulab Singh through the medium of his trusted general Zorawar Singh were akin to what King Lalitaditya (724-761 AD) had achieved 1100 years back.

Death of Maharaja Ranjit Singh and Turmoil in Sikh Durbar: Ranjit Singh's health had started deteriorating from 1837 AD onwards. Various Chieftains and Sikh Misl (Clan) Heads had starting exerting themselves in the Sikh Durbar. Rajas of territories conquered and under suzerainty of Sikh Durbar had undertaken their own expansions and in many cases attitudes bordered on diffidence. Within the Sikh royal family there were many claimants to the throne, duly supported by one group or the other. Ranjit Singh had eight known sons from different wives. Each wing of the royal family had their cliques and many of the princes were minors at the time of his death. On 20th June 1839 Prince Kharak Singh was appointed as heir apparent by his dying father with the title of *Tika Sahib Bahadur*. On 27 June 1839 Ranjit Singh, who ruled over Punjab (Sikh Empire) for forty years from 1799 to 1839, breathed his last. Ranjit Singh's fifth wife Maharani Mahtab Devi Sahiba and some other wives committed Sati, but there were few other wives who continued to protect the interests of their sons; tenth wife of Late Maharaja, Maharani Jindan Kaur, Mother of Prince Duleep Singh, being one of them. Shahzada Kharak Singh, eldest son, succeeded Maharaja Ranjit Singh. On the death of Ranjit Singh Lahore became a centre of conspiracies and intrigues, within the royal family, Sikh nobles and even the Khalsa Army. To add to it, within matter of days of taking over, it became evident that Kharak Singh was not mentally fit enough and prepared for ruling such a vast Sikh empire, a fit successor may have possibly made efforts for a durable and powerful empire. Immediately after the death of Ranjit Singh, British East India Company had begun increasing its military strength, particularly in the regions adjacent to the Punjab and in 1844 AD annexed Sindh, South of Punjab. They had also established a military cantonment at Ferozepur, few miles from the Sutlej River, which marked the frontier between British-ruled India and the Punjab. On 8 October 1839 AD Kharak Singh was deposed and put into prison and was succeeded by his son, Prince Nau Nihal Singh, who became Maharaja (Defacto Ruler) of the Sikh Empire. Rani Chand Kaur, wife of Kharak Singh acted briefly as Regent as Nau Nihal Singh, born in 1821 AD, had not attained the age of 18 years on the date of his accession. He had been married at the age of sixteen to the daughter of Sham Singh Attariwala, a known figure in the Sikh Durbar and Khalsa Army. Though Rani Chand Kaur, his mother, was Regent for a brief period, she played her cards well and many nobles, including her father Sham Singh Attariwala, Misl chiefs aligned with her. On 5 November Kharak Singh, the deposed ruler died of suspected poisoning due to excess use of opium and alcohol. On the same day Maharaja Nau Nihal Singh, while returning from the cremation of his father, was injured when falling masonry from the *Roshnai Darwaza*, gateway of the Lahore Fort, fell on him. He died of wounds on the next day (6 November). Ironically Mian Udham Singh, eldest Son of Raja Gulab Singh, was also killed in the same accident. Dhian Singh Prime Minister of Sikh Durbar, brother of Gulab Singh, who was moving close to Maharaja Nau-Nihal Singh was lucky to escape with bruises. Some chroniclers/ historians have averred that Nau Nihal Singh was killed in captivity on 6 November by Dhian Singh, Prime Minister Sikh Durbar. The incident of 5 November, about the crash of gateway of the fort is well chronicled, which also resulted in the death of Mian Udham Singh, nephew of Dhian Singh. Dr. John Honisberger, who was the court physician of the Sikh Durbar during that period and who was also a witness to the accident, was certain that the collapse of the structure due to which Nau Nihal Singh died was a pure accident. Shahzada Sher Singh, second son of late Maharaja Ranjit Singh, with the support of many Misl Chiefs and part of Khalsa Army, acceded to the throne on 9 November 1840 AD. His reign lasted 23 days only, as Rani Chand Kaur, widow of Late Kharak Singh and mother of Nau Nihal Singh, was proclaimed as *Malika Mukkadas* (Queen Empress-actually *Mukkadas* means sacred) on 2nd December. In the meantime deposed Sher Singh sought the help of various Misl Chiefs and Khalsa Army. Elevation of Rani Chand Kaur was a combined decision of the nobles, including Gulab Singh. Deposed Sher Singh's Forces even attacked Lahore Fort, which was then under Gulab Singh and was defeated. Alexander Gardner European artillery commander of Raja Gulab Singh recounts this engagement between the two forces thus: *"The Dogras on the walls began to look over and were jeered at by Sher Singh's troops, the little fort was surrounded by a sea of human heads. Gulab Singh made contemptuous replies, and roared out to Sher Singh, demanding that he should surrender... With a wild yell some 300 Akalis swept up the Hazuri Bagh and crowded into the gate. Just at that moment, when the crowd was rushing in on us, their swords high in the air, I managed to fire the ten guns, and literally blew them into the air... Then Sher Singh fled and grievous carnage ensued. The Dogras, always excellent marksmen, seemed that day not to miss a man from the walls... we counted the bodies of no less than 2800 soldiers, 200 artillerymen, and 180 horses."* The two sides then made peace and agreed that Sher Singh being the deserving claimant to the throne of Sikh Durbar and on 18 January 1841 Sher Singh again ascended the throne. Raja Gulab Singh with his force left Lahore and on his way back to Jammu conquered Mangla, near the present Mangla Dam on Jhelum River.

Dogra Expedition to Tibet and Treaty of Chushul: Since he took over in 1822 AD, Gulab Singh had expanded Dogra Empire considerably and his able General Zorawar Singh had conquered adjacent areas of Paddar, Kishtwar, Ladakh and Baltistan including Skardu as part of Jammu Kingdom. Gulab Singh would have loved to expand towards West but it would have clashed with the interest of Sikh Durbar at Lahore. He therefore, turned his eyes eastwards towards Tibet and he had General Zorawar Singh to accomplish this task. Zorawar in the meantime had recruited Baltis, men from Baltistan, in his force. The force had groups of men from Jammu hills, Kishtwar and Ladakhis. The force of about six thousand soldiers were divided into three columns and in May 1841 marched parallel to each other towards unknown land of Tibet. Ladakhi troops column under Ladakhi prince, Nono Sungnam, followed the course of the Indus River to its source in Tibet. Another column of 300 Baltis under Ghulam Khan, marched along the mountains South of Indus to Mount Kailash range. General Zorawar with the remainder of the force of about 3000 troops moved along the plateau region along Pangong Lake. Overcoming opposition enroute, column passed sacred Mansarovar Lake and captured Gartok, defeating the small Tibetan force stationed there. The Tibetan commander fled to Taklakot but Zorawar stormed that fort on 6th September 1841. The daring Zorawar's force had extended communication and supply line over 450 miles of inhospitable terrain by building small forts and pickets along the way. The fort Chi-T'ang was built near Taklakot under command of Bast Ram Mehta with 500 men and 8-9 Canons. In spite of meticulous preparations and planning, inhospitable terrain and extended communications affected the chain of supplies to the force. With the onset of winter many soldiers lost their fingers and toes due to frost bite, some starved to death and even wood of the muskets was burnt to keep themselves warm. Weather had put its stop to the bravery of the men. Taking advantage of the cold weather, Tibetan force reinforced by Chinese regrouped themselves, bypassed Dogra Fort of Chi-T'ang and took on the force at To-yo on 12 December 1841. General Zorawar was injured in his right shoulder but grabbed a sword in his left hand. A Tibetan horseman then charged the Dogra position and one of them thrust his lance in Zorawar Singh's chest and killed him. Gulab Singh, who was then in Peshawar, leading the Anglo-Sikh campaign in Afghanistan, was informed of this disaster by Henry Lawrence. Thereafter Tibetan-Chinese force cleared other Dogra garrisons and advanced to Ladakh and laid seize of Leh. Reinforcements to Dogra Force at Leh under Diwan Hari Chand and Wazir Ratnu were sent from Jammu and Tibetan-Chinese Force repulsed. The

Dogra Force then chased them to Chushul, where battle was fought in August 1842 AD and Tibetan-Chinese Force defeated. The boundary between Ladakh and Tibet was finally settled by the **Treaty of Chushul**, which was signed on behalf of Raja Gulab Singh by Diwan Hari Chand and Wazir Ratnu on 16th/17th September 1842. This boundary remained so till it was violated by Chinese in 1950's and Sino-India War 1962.

Sikh Durbar- Killings, Intrigues, Reprisals and on way to Subjugation: Maharaja Sher Singh could barely control the affairs of Sikh Empire, as many Misl Chieftains pursued policy of self interest. Even within the royal family, there were groups and each group had a supporter amongst the ministers, Khalsa Army and various Misl (Clan) Sardars. The first casualty in this war of attrition in Sikh Durbar was killing of Rani Chand Kaur on 9 June 1842, who was thought to be a threat to Maharaja Sher Singh. During this time Sandhanwalia Misl Sardars, Ajit Singh Sandhanwalia and Lehna Singh raised their head. On 15 September 1843, Sher Singh along with his son Prince Partap Singh were killed at the Shah Bilaal gardens, by his cousin, Sardar Ajit Singh Sandhanwalia. They also killed Dhian Singh, younger brother of Gulab Singh, who had been Prime Minister in Sikh Durbar since 1828. On the death of Maharaja Sher Singh, 5 year old Prince Duleep Singh son of Maharani Jindan Kaur ascended the throne on the same day. Next day (16th September) Sandhanwalia Sardars Ajit Singh and Lehna Singh were murdered at the instigation of Hira Singh, son of Dhian Singh, nephew of Gulab Singh. Maharani Jindan Kaur, mother of the boy king Prince Duleep Singh, was acting as regent to her minor son. Hira Singh was appointed Prime Minister of Sikh Durbar in place of his father Raja Dhian Singh. On 26th March 1844, General Suchet Singh, youngest brother of Gulab Singh, Commander-in-Chief of Khalsa Army was killed by Sikh troops, allegedly loyal to his nephew Hira Singh. It was suspected that Suchet Singh had hand in the killing of Sher Singh and Dhian Singh. On 7th May Prince Kashmira Singh, son of Maharaja Ranjit Singh along with two Misl Chieftains of Naurangabad and Sandhanwalia were put to death by Khalsa Army, alleged to be at the behest of Hira Singh, the Prime Minister of Sikh Durbar, nephew of Gulab Singh. On 21 December Hira Singh, Prime Minister along with Mian Randhir (Sohan) Singh, second son of Gulab Singh and Pandit Jalla, one of the advisors, were put to death at Buddha-ka-Ava (Shahadra – Lahore) by Khalsa Army at the behest of Sardar Shyam Singh Attariwala (Father in law of late Nau Nihal Singh and father of slain Rani Chand Kaur), Sardar Mewa Singh Majithia and Sardar Jawahar Singh, brother of Maharani Jindan Kaur. Tacit approval of the killings by Maharani Jindan Kaur cannot be ruled out. As a result of this killing Sardar Jawahar Singh, brother of Maharani Jindan

Kaur, was appointed Prime Minister of the Sikh Empire on 14 May 1845 AD. Many chroniclers/historians have erroneously attributed this killing of Hira Singh to Jawahar Singh, his younger brother, possibly due to similarity in the name; Sardar Jawahar Singh. Similarly Jawahar Singh is also mentioned as the Prime Minister of Sikh Empire, due to similar mistaken identity. By now the administration by Sikh Durbar had nearly collapsed; Khalsa Army Soldiers had not been paid their wages and corruption was galore in the Durbar. The corrupt Sikh Durbar decided on invasion of Jammu to extract money from Gulab Singh, reputed to be richest Raja North of Sutlej River. The Sikh Soldiers failed to capture Jammu Forts and made peace with Gulab Singh and agreed to negotiate with Sikh Durbar on his behalf. On 30 August Prince Peshaura Singh son of Maharaja Ranjit Singh was slain (strangled) at Attock Fort by Fateh Khan Tiwana and Sardar Chattar Singh Attariwala. It was suspected that there was hand of Sardar Jawahar Singh in the killing of the prince. Sardar Jawahar Singh, Prime Minister, was condemned for instigating the murder of Prince Peshaura Singh at Attock and was shot dead on 21 September in the presence of his sister Maharani Jindan Kaur and infant Maharaja Duleep Singh. On 8 November Misser Lal Singh took over as the Prime Minister and Misser Tej Singh as the Commander-in-Chief of the Sikh Army. Both were originally high-caste Hindus from outside the Punjab and like the majority of the Sikhs in Punjab at that time, had converted to Sikhism in 1818 AD.

Events to Anglo Sikh War and Treaties of Amritsar/Lahore: Ever since the accession of Duleep Singh to the throne, Maharani Jind Kaur, duly aided by inner coterie of relatives and some Sikh Misl Chieftains, had been exercising her control over all the affairs of the Sikh Empire. Assassinations of Princes, Ministers, Advisors and relations were rampant. Intrigue and rumours further fuelled the deteriorating situation, as the central control of the Sikh Durbar from Lahore diminished, starting from the death of Kharak Singh. Rumours abounded that Kharak Singh was poisoned, while Nau Nihal Singh was supposedly killed by a well planned accident by Dhian Singh! All these stories were totally fabricated to break Sikh-Dogra Rajput alliance. Though himself injured, Prime Minister Raja Dhian Singh, brother of Gulab Singh, demonstrated political acumen, loyalty and initiative. Unfortunately, as time passed, rift between the Rajputs and Sikhs widened. British rumours started that assassinations of Maharaja Sher Singh and his son Prince Pratap Singh were planned by Dhian Singh with help of Sandhanwalia Chiefs (Ajit Singh and Lehna Singh) and Sandhanwalia's later killed Dhian Singh, to put a lid on the plot. This rumour further fuelled the rift between the Sikhs and Dogra Rajputs and became irreversible. It is well established that Dhian Singh was loyal to Sikh Durbar and had nothing to do with the murder of Sher Singh. Reprisals by Dogra Rajputs was swift and Sandhanwalia culprits

Ajit Singh, Lehna Singh with about 600 of their followers were put to the sword. British who were looking for an opportunity to seize the territories of the late Maharaja Ranjit Singh, were delighted and Lord Ellenborough, Governor General of India wrote on 20 October 1843 AD to Queen Victoria; "..it is impossible not to perceive that the ultimate tendency of the late events at Lahore is without, any effort on our part, to bring the plains first, and at somewhat later period the hills, under our protection or control." These lines clearly gave out the British plan to grab the Sikh territory duly aided by the dissentions and misrule within Sikh Durbar.

Unfortunately further intrigues, struggles and assassinations continued and the Sikh Durbar became weaker day by day. Hira Singh who was made the Prime Minister, was killed on 21 December 1844 AD, along with his relatives. Following this Sardar Jawahar Singh, brother of Maharani Jindan Kaur, was appointed as Prime Minister and all efforts made to beleaguer Gulab Singh. Eventually a conflict developed between the Sikh Durbar and Gulab Singh. Many more unfortunate events followed with severe strain in the trust for each other. Sikh Forces even invaded Jammu and battle took place on the plain of the Satwari. Gulab Singh's Forces under Diwan Hari Chand defeated the Sikhs.

After this victory Gulab Singh boldly marched into the Sikh camp, where he had many Sikh followers. However, some inimical element literally made him a prisoner. Many Sikh soldiers made it clear to Sikh Durbar that they would not spare Sikh Durbar, if anything untoward happened to Gulab Singh. Gulab Singh was later released and his assets and lands restored after he paid of 27 lakh rupees. However, intrigue and assassinations in the Sikh Durbar continued and Sardar Jawahar Singh, brother of Maharani Jindan Kaur, was killed on the orders of the *Panch* (Military Council) for his role in the killing of Prince Peshaura Singh. The *Panchs* had now become effective and exerted themselves, as Maharani Jindan Kaur could hardly control warring groups. Relations between the British and the Sikhs already were severely strained because of the refusal by Sikh Durbar to allow passage of British troops through their territory during the first Afghan War of the 1838-1842 AD. In order to regain their pre eminent position, Sikh Durbar now headed by Maharani Jindan Kaur, Regent of Maharaja Duleep Singh, tried to salvage the situation by declaring war on British on 17 November 1845 AD.

First Anglo-Sikh War: Gulab Singh had suffered extensively during the intrigues, bloodthirsty turn of events which had resulted in the death of his brothers, nephew and two elder sons, within a period of 15 months in 1843 and 1844 AD. He still tried to convince Maharani Jindan Kaur to avoid a conflict with the British. After mutual accusations between the Sikh Durbar and the British, diplomatic relations were broken and East India Company army began marching towards Ferozepur, where a division was already stationed. In response to the British move, the Sikh army began crossing the Sutlej River on 11 December 1845 AD. In retaliation Lord Henry Hardinge, British Governor General issued a 'Proclamation of War' on the Sikhs on 13 December declaring that all Sikh territory left of River Sutlej be annexed to British dominion.

Gulab Singh during this conflict took no sides but still had sympathy for the Sikhs and sent them food and animals. He, however, still was not sure of Sikh Durbar support to him. The First Anglo Sikh War started on 18 December with the Battle of Mudki, where British won an untidy encounter battle. Result of battle of Ferozeshah, 21 December, tilted in favour of British due to Lal Singh, Prime Minister, making no effort to rally his army and force under Tej Singh, Commander-in-Chief, appeared briefly and inexplicably withdrew. Battle of Buddowal was fought on 21 January 1846 though British had upper hand, they were barely able to repulse the Sikhs. During this time Gulab Singh left for a pilgrimage to Vaishno Devi and Purmandel. Following this alarming situation Maharani Jindan Kaur summoned Raja Gulab Singh. In the meantime in the battle of Aliwal on 28 January, British won a model victory, eliminating the Sikh bridgehead. By now Maharani Jindan Kaur, inexperienced in matters of the state, became panicky.

Raja Gulab Singh and Peace Negotiations: On being summoned by Maharani Jindan Kaur, Gulab Singh, his son Ranbir Singh, nephew Jawahar Singh along with four thousand horsemen and about five thousand Rajputs left for Sikh Durbar in Lahore. On arriving in Sikh Durbar, Gulab Singh was informed by Maharani Jindan Kaur that she had lost all control of the affairs of the State. Gulab Singh clarified that due to circumstances and the happenings in the Sikh Durbar he himself felt powerless. Finally in the Sikh Durbar, held on January 31, 1846, Maharani Jindan Kaur was cursed by the *Panchas* for pushing the Sikh kingdom towards destruction by moving the army across the Sutlej River, resulting in their destruction. The *Panchas* made it clear to Maharani Jindan Kaur that she could be killed if she did not make Gulab Singh the Prime Minister and effort should be made to buy peace with British in order to save Sikh Empire. Accepting the Prime Ministership, Gulab Singh made it clear he would only continue in this position only if the Sikh Durbar committed in writing that they would not interfere with his peace efforts with the British. The battles between the Sikhs and the British had not initially been decisive except at Aliwal, but with time British started to make gains. Eventually on February 10, 1846 AD, Sir Hugh Gough attacked the Sikhs at Sobraon with heavy artillery and Sikhs suffered reverses. Commander-in-Chief of Khalsa Army, Tej Singh is said to have deserted the Sikh army early in the battle.

In pursuance of the directive by *Panchas*, Raja Gulab Singh accompanied by many Sikh Chiefs met Lord Henry Hardinge, Governor General of India on 15 February 1846. No agreements were reached. Thereafter, Henry Lawrence, agent of the Governor-General and Frederick Currie British Chief Secretary had a lengthy discussion with Gulab Singh and his group. Initially the British demanded two Crore rupees from the Sikh Durbar as a fine and also wanted the valuable region of Jullundur Doab, between Beas and Sutlej River to be handed over to the British. Gulab Singh made it clear to the British that these terms were rather harsh and cautioned British that the Sikh power was still formidable. As anticipated the British, as a part of the standard strategy, tried to create a rift between the Dogra Rajputs and the Sikhs by mentioning to Gulab Singh that in the past he and his family had been badly treated by the Sikh Durbar. British also made attempts to tempt Gulab Singh by offering him territory of Kohistan and accept him as a Maharaja, which Gulab Singh declined. British then put forward fresh proposals; Duleep Singh would continue as the Maharaja and accepted as the Sovereign of Sikh Empire, Doab and territories; hill and plain, situated between the Rivers Beas and Sutlej to be handed over to British and one and half Crore of rupees as indemnity to the British as war expenses. In addition to this there were several clauses set up by the British; ceding of territories, situated between the Rivers Beas and Indus, positioning of British troops at Lahore till December 1846 AD, ostensibly for the protection of Maharaja Duleep Singh and many more. In short, the British wanted to subjugate the Sikhs. who were their rivals. Lord Hardinge also suggested that Maharaja Duleep Singh must submit to the British, at Luliani, a place between the Sutlej and the Ravi rivers and whole party should then move to Lahore. Gulab Singh being a perceptive person immediately understood the British game-plan and suggested to the British that Maharaja Duleep Singh would meet the British at Kasur on 18th February, 1846 AD. However, the meeting took place, when Raja Gulab Singh and Lal Singh took infant Maharaja Duleep Singh to the British camp at village Lulliani in the Lahore district for his submission to Sir Henry Hardinge, the Governor General of the British East India Company.

Intrigue and Lahore/Amritsar Treaties: Maharaja Duleep Singh was bought to Lahore where Governor General restored the title of Maharaja on him. Gulab Singh continued to be the Prime Minister. However, Lal Singh a confidant of Maharani Jindan Kaur aspired to be back into Prime Ministers post. Gulab Singh too was not happy with the affairs, however, Maharani Jindan Kaur dismissed him on 26 February 1846, suspecting him to be in league with British and Lal Singh was again made the Prime Minister. As per negotiations with the British, in which Lal Singh was also included, bankrupt Sikh Durbar could not come up with the money to be paid to British. Sikh

Durbar Prime Minister Lal Singh made an offer to the British to offer all the hill territory between Rivers Indus (Sindh) and Beas (Kashmir, Hazara including the territory of Jammu) in lieu of rupees one Crore. Raja Gulab Singh somehow got information of this move and felt double crossed by Sikh Durbar. Raja Gulab Singh met Governor General Sir Henry Hardinge, who was sympathetic and had realised that Gulab Singh with his fighting capabilities would make a good ally. Later Gulab Singh sent Diwan Jwala Sahai, his confidant, to the British suggesting territory of Jammu be handed over to his dependents, while he would himself lead a retired life in the holy city of Varanasi.

Hardinge had his own plans and informed Diwan Jwala Sahai, that British would be willing to hand over the territories lying between the source of Beas including the areas of Kas'mira and Hazara to Gulab Singh for rupees one Crore. Since Gulab Singh could not come up with this kind of money, hence, he decided to trade some territory on the right side of the Beas River for less money. On receiving this proposal from Gulab Singh, Hardinge wrote the following to a secret committee; "that the trans Beas portion of Kulu and Mandi with the fertile district and strong position of Nurpur and the celebrated fort of Kangra and the key to the Himalayas in native estimation with its districts and its dependencies should be in our possession."

It was finally accepted that Gulab Singh would pay rupees 75 lakhs to the British for the smaller territory. Lal Singh and Maharani Jindan Kaur dispatched the loyal Kashmiri Brahmin Diwan Dina Nath to Sir Henry Lawrence and Frederic Currie, with a request to cancel their deal with Raja Gulab Singh, as Sikh Durbar was willing to pay all the money in order to retain their territory. As the British were keen to get rid of the Sikh threat to their Empire, they stuck with Raja Gulab Singh. Following this a treaty was signed on March 9, 1846 AD between the Sikhs and the British, referred to as the **Treaty of Lahore**, under which the British were able to further their political interests and also get some territory from the Sikh Durbar. As per the treaty Sikh Durbar was to; renounce all claims pertaining to territories South of the River Sutlej, cede Doab territory, hills and plains, between Rivers Beas and Sutlej, and territories between River Beas and Indus including Kashmir (Cashmere) and Hazara provinces in lieu of fine of Rupees one Crore. Also pay a sum of rupees 60 Lakhs as war indemnity, disband part of Khalsa Army and limit their numbers and British troops to be stationed at Lahore till December 1846 AD. The treaty was specific about independent sovereign rights of territories of Jammu held under Raja Gulab Singh, which was to be recognised by both sides; Sikh Durbar and British. This may also include any additional hill territory given to Gulab Singh as per agreement between Gulab Singh and the British. Maharaja Duleep Singh under the

Regency of Maharani Jindan Kaur was recognised as the head of the Sikh Empire.

Treaty of Amritsar: Following the signing of the treaty of Lahore, Raja Gulab Singh was invited by the British Governor General at a camp on 15 March 1846. Following this Gulab Singh was bestowed with the title of a Maharaja and the **Treaty of Amritsar** was signed between the British and Maharaja Gulab Singh on 16 March, 1846 AD. Sir Henry Hardinge in a letter to a near relative termed transfer of Jammu and Kashmir to Gulab Singh as 'necessary to weaken the Sikhs by depriving them of Kashmir'. The treaty envisaged:

- Transfers in independent possession all the hilly or mountainous country situated to East of the River Indus and West of River Ravi including **Chamba** and excluding Lahul, which were earlier part of Sikh Empire. Initially Chamba came under Sikh control in 1770 AD and in 1786 came under the control of Raja Sansar Chand of Chamba, but was brought again under Sikh Durbar in 1809. As per the Treaty of Amritsar, the territory (Chamba State) was to be part of area under Maharaja Gulab Singh of Jammu. On the other hand, Raja of Chamba claimed back Bhadarwah, which had been conquered by Dogra Rulers earlier. In 1847 as a compromise settlement with the Raja of Chamba, who claimed Bhadarwah as a part of his possessions, British and Gulab Singh arrived at a tripartite agreement; Chamba to come under British suzerainty instead of Gulab Singh. In return State of Chamba renounced claim on Bhadarwah.
- Eastern boundary of transferred area to Gulab Singh to be laid down by both sides separately.
- Maharaja Gulab Singh to pay sum of seventy-five lakh of rupees (Nanak Shahi); fifty lakhs to be paid on or before the 1st October of 1846 AD.
- Gulab Singh acknowledged supremacy of the British Government and as a token of such supremacy was to present annually to the British Government, one horse, twelve shawl goats of approved breed (six male and six female) and three pairs of Cashmere (Kashmiri) shawls. The three items represented the three territorial segments of the new territories of Jammu and Kashmir under Gulab Singh. Pony representing Jammu and hilly terrain, shawl goats (*Pashmina* Goats) representing the mountainous areas of Ladakh and Gilgit, while shawls represented the Kashmir valley.

Raja Gulab Singh and Sikh Durbar – 1809 to 26 February 1946: Lot has been said and written about Gulab Singh and his dealings with Sikh Durbar, from the time of his enrolment into Khalsa Army (1809) to the time when Treaty of Amritsar was signed on 16 March 1946 AD. Gulab Singh was accused of fomenting split in the Sikh Durbar, pursuing his own goals and hobnobbing with British before and during the Anglo Sikh War. He has even been accused of passing on sensitive information about Khalsa Army and their movements to British during the crucial phases of the Anglo Sikh War.

The Dogra brothers by dint of their services had won the loyalty of Maharaja Ranjit Singh and they rose to positions of power in the Sikh Durbar. Gulab Singh was allowed to expand his territory, which had the approval of Ranjit Singh. After all these expeditions, apart from expanding the territories of Jammu King, enhanced the reputation and limits of the Sikh Empire. Jealousy impelled the Misl Chiefs and other inimical Sikh Sardars to dislodge Dogra brothers from power and position. Intrigues and counter-intrigues were then set afoot, which took the lives of Maharaja Sher Singh, Dhian Singh, Suchet Singh, Hira Singh, Princes Kashmira Singh and Peshaura Singh. Even two elder sons of Gulab Singh, Mian Udham Singh and Mian Randhir (Sohan) Singh, died/killed in the cause of Sikh Durbar. The men in power in Lahore even dispatched rebellious Khalsa Army against Gulab Singh in March 1845. After the death of Ranjit Singh, his successors made frequent overtures to British, which had almost become routine. There were many Sikh Sardars, who covertly were in communication with British. It was known that loyalty of Gulab Singh to Sikh Durbar was unquestionable. He had not forgotten the way his father Raja Kishore Singh was put on the Jammu throne, nor had he forgotten his own *Raj Tilak* done personally by Maharaja Ranjit Singh. But friendly overtures to Sikh Durbar by Gulab Singh were not responded to favourably. His bravery and leadership had made deep impression in the minds of Khalsa Army, who wanted him to lead them in the war. Since he was opposed to war with the British, due to state of Sikh Empire and inner conflicts, he politely declined. He also had not forgotten the events of invasion of Jammu in March 1845, his being held briefly by Khalsa Army and that many of his dear ones had been killed on the orders of the Sikh Durbar, executed by Sikh Army. Sikh Durbar, because of his popularity with a number of Chiefs of the Army, wanted to keep him away from the battlefield. The state of affairs of Sikh Durbar under Maharani Jindan Kaur had deteriorated to such an extent that he was even forbidden to leave Jammu for Lahore without her prior permission. By the end January 1946 AD, when Raja Gulab Singh was summoned to Lahore, Khalsa Army had fought and lost three battles. He still along with his son Ranbir Singh, nephew Jawahar Singh, 4000 horsemen and 5000 troops left for Lahore to help the beleaguered Sikh Durbar. His appointment as Prime Minister on the suggestion of Sikh Durbar *Panchas*, was indicative of the trust reposed on him to bail out Sikh Durbar at a critical stage. Gulab Singh knew from his statesmanship and knowledge that buying peace on favourable terms, even at this critical stage, could save Sikh Empire. Even this was negated by whimsical Maharani Jindan Kaur by dismissing him from the appointment of Prime Minister. From his dismissal it was evident that many Sikh Chiefs were working against the Sikh Durbar as well as Gulab Singh. By this time the last gamble of Sikh Durbar, battle at Sabraon, had also failed with implicit victory for British.

The British had their strategy for determining the peace terms with Sikh Durbar and pursued it with all their might, divide and rule, buying the loyalty of Sikh Sardars and skilful negotiations and terms. Their top priority was to clip the wings of the Sikh Durbar, so that it could not challenge them again. British had also to make arrangements by which the Northwest Frontier could be defended against the Afghans. Earlier, Sikh Empire had become a useful buffer state between the British and Afghans. Things were different now as Sikh Durbar being against the British could no longer be trusted or depended upon in the future. This put an idea in the minds of British to utilise Raja Gulab Singh in furtherance of their plan. They evolved a plan which could kill two birds with one stone. Clip the wings and territory of Sikh Empire and create a fresh amenable buffer in the North. Even during the peace negotiations, which Gulab Singh attended along with many Sikh Chiefs, he was unyielding in-spite of the critical state of affairs in Sikh Durbar. However, his position in the Sikh Durbar was such that the inimical elements in Sikh Durbar could trade or sacrifice his or Jammu's interest for furtherance of their own interest. That is what happened, when the wily Sardar Lal Singh, the Sikh Prime Minister, offered territory of Jammu and Kashmir to British. In this situation it was natural for Gulab Singh to protect the interest of his domain and even volunteered to retire leaving Jammu for his heir. Agreeably things turned to his advantage by sheer luck, statesmanship and negotiation skills. Of course miscalculation and mismanagement by Sikh Durbar added to these factors. After all from the time he fought for the defence of Jammu in 1808 to the events leading to Treaty of Lahore (9 March 1846) and Treaty of Amritsar (16 March 1846) Raja Gulab Singh proved to be a brave warrior and a statesman. Naturally he deserved to be a Maharaja of such a vast and diverse kingdom. A year plus later he traded Chamba for peace with its neighbour and renunciation of claim on Bhaderwah by State of Chamba. Gulab Singh was still sympathetic to the Sikh soldiers, even though he was antagonized from the Sikh Durbar. During the second Sikh War of 1849, he allowed his Sikh soldiers to desert and go to fight alongside their brethren in Khalsa Army.

The achievements of Gulab Singh can best be summed by words of Dr Soft, whose words used to be measured with harsh comments; "Gulab Singh was unquestionably a remarkable figure in the history of Northern India during the first half of the 19th Century. He was a distinguished soldier and diplomat and knew the state craft of his own days exceedingly well."

Gulab Singh (1846–56)

Maharaja Gulab Singh's Reign: Raja Gulab Singh was bestowed with the title of Maharaja and independent sovereign of the areas East of the River Indus and the West of the River Ravi including Chamba and excluding Lahul, being part of the territories ceded to the British Government by the Sikh Durbar, which included Kas'mira and conquered areas by Jammu Kings. Within the existing domain of Jammu, prior to the signing of Treaty of Amritsar, Gulab Singh had conquered different places and regions of the state; Poonch, Ram Nagar, Bhasoli, Bhaderwah, Kishtwar, Bhimber, Rajauri, Reasi, Skardu, Kharmang, Kiris, Khaplu, Sheghar, Astor Gilgit, Chitral, Yasin, Hunza, Nagar, and Punial. Added to this, vale of Kas'mira made it as one of the biggest domains in the Northern India.

The newly formed Dogra Kingdom, called Princely State of Kashmir and Jammu, as it was first called, combined disparate regions, religions, and ethnicities. The Treaties of Chushul (1842) and Amritsar (1846) had defined the borders of the Kingdom of Jammu in the East, South and West but the Northern border was still undefined. To the East, Ladakh with Buddhism as predominant religion and ethnically and culturally closer to Tibet. Jammu in the South had a mixed population of Hindus, Muslims and Sikhs. In the heavily populated central Kas'mira valley, population was overwhelmingly Sunni Muslims, with a small but influential Hindu minority; the Kashmiri Brahmans (Pandits). In the Northeast was the sparsely populated Baltistan, ethnically related to Ladakh, but were Muslims of Shia faith. To the North was sparsely populated Gilgit, of diverse faith though mostly Shia Muslims. In the West were the Muslims of Poonch, but of different ethnicity than the Kas'mira valley. Though Dard territory was tributary of Kas'mira under Sikh Rule, the conditions were rebellious towards Dogra Rule and it was in 1850 the fort of Chilas in the Dard country was conquered. However, Gilgit was lost to rebellion in 1852, but was recovered ten years later by Ranbir Singh. In the words of eminent historian K.M. Panikar; 'an area of more than eighty thousand square miles including parts of Tibet, as well as part of Pamir, besides the genuine kingdoms of Jammu and Kashmir came into Maharaja Gulab Singh's possession. This area had never been effectively united under one ruler and much of it with of course, the exception of the valley of Kashmir had never known any settled government'. Another writer P N Kaul Bamzai writes; "Maharaja Gulab Singh is the only Indian ruler to have carved out a state during the 19th century out of the wreckage of the great kingdom of Sikhs. Moreover he is the only Indian ruler to have extended the frontiers of India to their natural boundary".

The first task of Gulab Singh, after the Treaty of Amritsar, after having obtained de- jure possession of Kas'mira and its surrounding territories, was to physically take over the territories, consolidate and give them an efficient and effective administration. A force under Wazir Lakhpat was despatched to take over Kas'mira from the Sikh Army. Sheikh Imam-ud-Din, the Sikh Governor, incited by the Sikh Durbar specially Lal Singh and aided by the restless Bombas, Khokas and Dards from the Jhelum valley, contested the force at the foot of Shankracharya Hill. In the battle that ensued, Wazir Lakhpat was killed and Dogra Force defeated. Maharaja Gulab Singh approached British, who sent Sir Henry Lawrence to mediate. Imam-ud-Din thereafter desisted from opposition and Kashmir passed without further disturbance to the new ruler. In fact, Sheikh Imam-ud-Din joined British side in the battle of Multan, during the Second Anglo-Sikh War (1848-49). At Astor and Gilgit Dogra troops relieved Sikhs, Nathu Shah, the Sikh commander of Gilgit, taking service under Maharaja Gulab Singh.

A Group of Dard Warriors – 1877 AD

Gulab Singh entered Srinagar on 9th November 1846 AD at 8 in the morning and Kashmir was made the summer capital of the kingdom. The task of consolidation being uppermost in his mind, he divided the State into two provinces, each under a Governor (*Nazim*) and two frontier areas, each under a *'Thanedar'*. Jammu Province covered the entire territory from the Ravi to the Jhelum, South of the Pir Panchal range, which included whole of Dugar region, Poonch together with Mirpur area of the western Punjabi speaking belt. Jawahar Singh the son of Dhian Singh was made Raja of

Poonch. Kas'mira province included Kas'mira valley and the Western district of Muzaffarabad. The valley was divided into two districts; Anantnag, which included the city of Srinagar and the strategic roads linking the valley. Second Baramulla, covering Northwestern parts of the valley adjoining Muzaffarabad and Poonch. The two frontier regions were Ladakh and Baltistan, each under a *'Thanedar'*. A number of efficient and capable persons like Magna, Mehta Basti Ram and Mehta Mangal were made *Thanedars* of Ladakh, who for the first time gave modern administration to the frontier region. They built Leh Fort and bazzar, laid plantations for a perennial supply of fuel, built and repaired bridle roads linking Leh with Srinagar, Lahaul, Yarkand and Gartok. The traditional Ladakh-Tibet frontier was surveyed and land settlement made for the first time. Baltistan with its main town of Skardu was put under the charge of another *Thanedar*. Later, both Ladakh and Baltistan were joined together and put under the charge of one administrator, who had his headquarters at Leh in summer and Skardu in winter. Mian Hatthu Singh, son of Gulab Singh from a concubine was made *Nazim* of Kashmir from 1848-1849 AD, while his only son Ranbir Singh was made *Nazim* of Kashmir from 1849 onwards till Ranbir Singh ascended the throne in 1956 AD.

From the point of view of consolidation, Gilgit was the only area over which grip of Dogra Kingdom was not very firm. In 1840 one Gaur Rahman, Raja of Yasin of the *Khushwakhte* Dynasty, took Gilgit and killed the ruler Shah Sakandar. In 1842 Shah Sakandar's brother, Karim Khan, expelled Gaur Rahman, with the support of a Sikh army from Kas'mira. The Sikh General, Nathu Shah, left behind Sikh garrison troops and Karim Khan ruled until Gilgit was ceded to Gulab Singh in 1846. Dogra troops replaced the Sikh troops in Gilgit, while Nathu Shah and Karim Khan both transferred their allegiance to Gulab Singh, continuing local administration. In 1848 Hunza and their Yasin and Punial allies attacked and captured Gilgit. Gilgit was soon re-conquered by Dogra Forces. A serious uprising in Gilgit in 1852, with the help of the Rajas of Yasin, Hunza and Nagar took place. The entire Dogra garrison was cut to pieces and only a Gorkha woman swam across the Indus to tell the story of this disaster. It was a great blow to the prestige of Maharaja Gulab Singh, who had to accept Indus River as frontier between his kingdom and Gilgit proper and could not recapture Gilgit in his lifetime.

While reorganisation of the state was going on, there was trouble in the Sikh Durbar but British were proactive. On 3rd December 1946 Lal Singh, Prime Minister of Sikh Durbar, opposed the transfer of Kas'mira to Gulab Singh. He was tried by British and exiled from Punjab to live in Dehradun and Mussoorie till his death in 1867. On 16 December 1846 Anglo-Sikh treaty of Bharowal was signed by the Governor General, Hardinge and ratified on 26 December 1846. The treaty provided British controlled regency of Maharaja Duleep Singh till he attained majority on 4th September 1854, or till such period as the Governor General and the Sikh Durbar thought necessary.

Sir Henry Lawrence was appointed British Resident of Lahore. Maharani Jindan Kaur was deprived of all powers and pensioned off with an annuity.

British Efforts to Have British Resident. British, handed over Kas'mira to Gulab Singh because for clipping the wings of Sikh Empire they had no other alternative at that time. After the annexation of Punjab in 1849, after the Second Anglo Sikh War, a number of British officials began to have second thoughts.

An Old Basoli Painting Showing Maharaja Gulab Singh being Blessed by Lord Rama

In August 1847, Henry Lawrence and George Taylor had written to Gulab Singh suggesting the deputation of a British Resident in the state, which was refused. British, while conceding to the Maharaja's request not to have a British resident, placed in his court, services of a local Kas'miri, Mirza Saifuddin, to spy on behalf of the British on the policies of his administration and the general conditions in the state. Pressure began to be put again on Gulab Singh to accept a British Resident, like other Indian States and give some concessions to the British. Gulab Singh firmly refused though British continued to look for another opportunity. Nevertheless, in the beginning of 1852 Gulab Singh agreed to the posting of their one representative at Srinagar, to look after the European visitors to Kashmir, who could stay in Kas'mira for six summer months only.

Maharaja's Welfare Measures: In the year 1846, Gulab Singh created an endowment known as Dharmarth Trust with a personal donation of Rupees 5 Lakhs. The interest of this amount was to be utilised for the conduct of Muslim holy day of *Shabe Barat* and repairs and renovation of old temples. The foundation stone of Shri Raghunath Temple, Jammu, biggest temple complex in Northern India, was laid by Maharaja Gulab Singh in the year 1851, though the inauguration of the temple was done by Ranbir Singh in 1857. The main temple is of Lord Ram, *Kul Devta* of the Dogra Dynasty. The outer *Parikrama* consists of 14 temples dedicated to Vishnu, Ganesh and other gods.

During Gulab Singh's rule there was no distinctions between the Hindus and Muslims. Disorderly elements were ruthlessly suppressed and peace and order established. The troublesome Bombas, Dards and Khokas were controlled with a strong hand. In the matters of local administration efforts were made to rationalise the *jagir* system, regularise the forced labour and introduce rationing of rice. The shawl industry, the mainstay of the people of Kas'mira, was also reformed. Kashmiri Pandits enjoyed comparative peace and respite and barbaric treatment during the Muslim Rule was a history. However, some fanatical elements were lying in wait for an opportune moment to harass, intimidate, loot and plunder them. Dogra rulers subscribing to the faith of Hinduism proved a blessing for such fanatical elements to cause trouble, but such elements could not raise their head to make even a slight difference.

An Old Portrait of Maharaja Gulab Singh

Abdication: By early fifties Maharaja's health was failing and he had already appointed his only son Ranbir Singh as *Nizam* of Kashmir in 1849. On 20th February 1856 AD, he abdicated in favour of his only surviving son, whom he formally installed as the ruler at Purani Mandi, Jammu. He himself functioned as Governor of Kashmir province during the last two years of his life. Maharaja Gulab Singh died from dropsy, at Srinagar on 30th June 1857, leaving behind a vast Kingdom of Jammu and Kashmir with a sound and stable administration.

Maharaja Ranbir Singh (1856–1885)

Maharaja Ranbir Singh: Born in August 1830 at Ramgarh, third son of Gulab Singh, Ranbir Singh was adopted by his childless youngest uncle Suchet Singh. On the death of Suchet Singh and since Gulab Singh's two eldest sons had died/killed, Ranbir Singh was made heir apparent by his biological father Maharaja Gulab Singh. Ranbir Singh was a great patron of learning, a great Persian scholar, knowledgeable of Sanskrit, English and Pushtu. He contributed funds for the establishment of the Punjab University and became its first Fellow in 1882 and established Research and Translation Department for the collection and publication of important Sanskrit works on Hindu Law and Rituals, as well as for the translation of Sanskrit and Persian manuscripts into Hindi. Services of scores of scholars from the state, even from outside the state, were enlisted and large number of Sanskrit, Persian and Bodhi manuscripts collected. Collection of old Sanskrit manuscripts, now housed in the Raghunath temple library, is most prized in the whole of India. Many other manuscripts have been preserved and displayed in the SPS Museum. It was during his reign Dogri was introduced for official communications and even *firmans* (Edicts) issued in Dogri.

During the First War of Independence 1857 AD, called Mutiny by British, Jammu and Kashmir did not take sides. However, there was a small uprising within the Royal Family. Mian Jamiat Singh son of Gulab Singh from a slave, together with some troops, rebelled against his brother and Jamiat Singh was immediately put to death.

Re-conquest of Gilgit: A serious uprising in Gilgit with the support of Gaur Rahman had taken place in 1852. Gilgit had been lost, temporarily though, to Jammu and Kashmir State. Ranbir Singh, considered to be the greatest of the Dogra rulers, outstanding achievement, was the re-conquest of Gilgit and subjugation of the frontier states of Hunza and Nagar. In 1860, under his orders, a big expedition to which almost every Dogra family contributed a soldier, under the command of Colonel Devi Singh, was tasked to conquer Gilgit. Just before the arrival of Dogra Force, Gaur Rahman died. Dogra forces inflicted a crushing defeat on his forces and avenged the earlier defeat. The rule of Jammu and Kashmir over Gilgit was restored. In 1876 Gilgit was briefly held by Mehtar Aman-ul-Mulk of Chitral for a few months. Later, in the same year, Mehtar agreed to leave Gilgit, after Ranbir Singh agreed to pay him an annual subsidy and he as ruler of Chitral accepted Dogra sovereignty over Chitral also. Gilgit was thereafter connected to Srinagar by a telegraphic line.

British as part of governance of India endeavoured to strengthen its defence against any aggression from the North through Jammu and Kashmir. The developments in late sixties, wherein Russians conquered Tashkent, Khokand, Khojand and Samarkand had created a threat to British dominion. In this threat assessment Gilgit occupied an important strategic position, by virtue of its covering almost all the passes over Hindukush. British negotiated and in 1877 AD an agreement was reached with Ranbir Singh for establishment of a Political Agency, Gilgit Agency at Gilgit, under control of the British Agent. The areas of the agency comprised of Gilgit Wazarat, states of Hunza and Nagar; Punial Jagir; Governorships of Yasin, Kuh-Ghizr, Ishkoman, and Chilas. In 1880 Afghan Amir (Ruler) claimed Chitral as part of Afghan territory. Due to these unfavourable circumstances Gilgit Agency was withdrawn in 1881, but was re-established eight years later in 1889, when it came under British Agent after being unified with neighbouring Nagar and Hunza.

While the Kingdom was celebrating the conquest of Gilgit in 1860, there was inner feud within the Royal Family. Jawahar Singh, Raja of Poonch, cousin of Ranbir Singh, conspired with Mian Hatthu Singh (*Nazim* of Kashmir (1848-1849), *Nazim* Rajauri (1856-1860), step brother of the Maharaja, to overthrow/kill Ranbir Singh. Jawahar Singh was deposed and exiled to Ambala on a pension from the British government. In his place his younger brother Moti Singh was made Raja of Poonch. Mian Hatthu Singh was imprisoned at Doda Fort for his part in a plot to kill Ranbir Singh.

Ranbir Penal Code and Other Measures: With re-conquest of Gilgit, Jammu and Kashmir Force had re-established its prestige. It was now time for streamlining the systems in the state. Almost all the laws, civil and criminal, introduced in India were, with modifications, made applicable to the state. The Ranbir 'Dand-Vidhi' (Ranbir Penal Code), both civil and criminal, code of law which is operative till this day, was prepared and adopted by a decree. This code established his reputation as a law-giver. He reorganised state administration, establishing three separate departments dealing with revenue, civil and military affairs, on the pattern of departments as they existed in India. The state army was organised on the European model but with Sanskrit terms of Command. Two additional measures taken by him gave a further fillip to the trade. First, the posting of a British agent at Leh in 1867, regulated the flow of trade from and to Ladakh from the state and India. Second, a commercial treaty was concluded in 1870 between the Maharaja and the Government of India, resulting in the abolition of all the duties on the trade between the state and British India. British also succeeded in persuading Ranbir Singh to appoint Mr Drew in 1870 and Mr Jhonson in 1871 respectively, both Englishmen, as the Commissioner of Ladakh. This was for the first time Englishmen were given direct administrative responsibility in the state.

A Sketch Painting of Pravarpura (Srinagar-Shahr-e-Khas)-1877 AD With Jhelum (Wyeth-Vitasta) Flowing in Between (Original Photograph by Frith)

Ranbir Singh's initiative in the organization of his civil and military administration were not to the liking of the British. In 1873 another attempt to force a British Resident on Jammu and Kashmir was made. But like his father, Ranbir Singh declined on the ground that there was no provision in the Treaty of Amritsar to effect a change and appoint a British Resident. The British felt very much chagrined and looked for opportune moment to force a British Resident.

Proposal to Reconvert Muslims: During his time Muslims of Kashmir collectively approached him to be allowed to re-embrace their old faith, Brahmanism, as they had been forcibly converted to Islam against their will. The Pandits vehemently opposed the idea on the plea that re-conversion was not allowed. Pandit's had conveniently forgotten that after Buddhism was on wane in Kas'mira in 300-400 AD, Buddhists were re-converted to Brahmanism and in fact some Buddhists rituals were adopted in their day to day life. It is learnt that some influential Brahmans of Kashi, when consulted, also opposed the suggestion of re-conversion. Maharaja even sought guidance from Swami Dayanand Saraswati, founder of Arya Samaj, who advised him that re-conversion could take place after performing certain rites. With continued strong opposition from Pandit's, even threats, plan of re-conversion of Kashmiri Muslims fell through. It was Pandits who had obstructed Rinchen's adoption of Brahmanism in 1324 AD, which led to Muslim rule for nearly 500 years. The History never forgets blunders but these get magnified as the time passes by!

Ranbir Singh must have had lot of dreams for his kingdom, but they were cut short by his death on 12th September 1885 at Jammu, at relatively young age of 55 years. He was cremated on the banks of the River Tawi and was succeeded by his eldest son Pratap Singh, though Maharaja Ranbir Singh was inclined towards his third son, Raja Amar Singh (Raja Ram Singh was the second son). This inclination is confirmed by a despatch dated 5 March 1888 by British Resident to Viceroy; " ......and the well-known fact that the Late Maharaja would have liked to supersede Partap Singh in favour of his youngest brother......."

Kashmiri Pandits Writing Religious Papers in Sharda-1870's

Kashmiri Pandits 1877 AD

Pandits under Dogra Rule: Maharaja Gulab Singh's 11 years may have sounded less but he was on the scene ever since Sikhs had defeated

Afghans in 1819 AD. Ranbir Singh, who ruled from 1856 to 1885, succeeded him. The scholarship of the Pandits in Persian, Sanskrit, Sharda reached its high watermark during this period. They wrote exquisite poetry and were master writers in prose. The knowledge of Persian had stood them in good stead even in the early days of the British presence in the form of agent. All of a sudden Kas'mira became active for British adventurers, explorers, historians and even few missionaries. These visitors had to deal with records maintained in Persian language. The result of all this was that Pandits came to be employed in large numbers, where knowledge of Persian was necessary for the interpretation of documents, written mainly in Persian.

Kashmiri Houses Near a Graveyard (Photograph Courtesy Cole–1869 AD)

Over Hundred Year Old Photograph (1895 AD) of a Combined Group of Bhattas and Musalmans

Pratap Singh (1885–1925)

Pratap Singh and British Resident: Even before Pratap Singh had acceded to the throne, British had been active with the late Maharaja to have a British Resident in the state, like other states in British India. During the last few years of Ranbir Singh rule, his ill health had created a feeling amongst British that he had lost control over the state, suspecting problems of accession to the throne, even division of the state amongst his three sons. Ranbir Singh in his own wisdom and the circumstances, had constituted a State Council for general administration of the state. Apart from three princes, the other prominent members of the council were Wazir Punnu, Babu Nilamber Mukerji and Dewan Anant Ram. As was anticipated the council was divided along power lines, till Wazir Punnu died on 6 September 1885 AD, just six days before the death of Ranbir Singh. A combination of events, including a discussion in the British and British-Indian press during the famine of 1877 and Afghans claiming Chitral as part of Afghan territory, made the British moves in the Durbar with intentions of bringing the state under the ambit of British Resident. In 1884, Lord Ripon, then Viceroy, came to the conclusion that there was no alternative but to appoint a permanent British Resident. So far the representation of the British in the state was done by an Agent, who had limited advisory powers. It is also learnt that British, during the last year of Ranbir Singh's rule, made acceptance of a British Resident a pre-condition for giving recognition to his successor after his death. On 1 August 1884, Secretary to the Government of India wrote to the then British Political Agent in the State; "In case of Maharaja Ranbir Singh's death, his eldest son, Mian Pertab Singh (Pratap Singh), will succeed to the undivided Chiefship. The new Maharaja will be called upon to introduce such reforms as many seem to be necessary; and a Resident Political Officer will be stationed in Kashmir........ You should then announce that, with the view of aiding His Highness in the introduction and maintenance of those reforms, the Viceroy has decided to give His Highness the assistance of a Resident English Officer, and that for the future the British representative in Kashmir will have the same status and duties as the Political Residents in other Indian States in subordinate alliance with the British Government." However, in a communication by Viceroy to Pratap Singh on 14 September 1985 it was somewhat mellowed tone; 'recognise and confirm your succession to the Chiefship of Jammu and Kashmir' and 'But my agent, Sir Oliver St. John, will remain with you and help you to the utmost of his ability'. Last line of this communication was indicative of things to come; 'I hope that your Highness will not fail to consult him freely at all times and to be guided by his advice in carrying those views into execution'. During Pratap Singh's *Dastarbandi* (Coronation) on 25 September 1885, Maharaja was informed by Sir Oliver St. John, that a British Resident would be placed at the Kashmir

Durbar. In another British communication dated 19 October 1885; 'The position of political officer in Kashmir has been placed on the same footing with that of Residents in other Indian States in subordinate alliance with the Government.' British had played their cards well, taking the advantage of ill health of Ranbir Singh, his inclination either to partition the state or supersede Pratap Singh. Once Ranbir Singh was dead, British took the advantage of the vacuum created and got Dewan Lachman Das appointed as Prime Minister and President of the State Council, which was formed on the advice of Viceroy.

In spite of their known position on British Resident, the powers which British Government in India wanted British Resident to exercise were absent. British, therefore, toyed with different plans to have amiable power structure in the State. In a communication from Resident to Viceroy dated 5 March 1888, three plans were suggested to Viceroy. One; appoint Amar Singh as Prime Minister, on condition of his undertaking to carry out in all respects the policy of the British Government of India. Two; bring Prime Minister for the State from one of the outside states under British Rule. A third plan was to continue the existing Council with Resident as its head for a period of three years. In the meantime Pratap Singh dismissed Diwan Lachman Das, the Prime Minister and President of the State Council. In a communication dated 13 April 1888 to Viceroy, Maharaja informed him of the dismissal of Diwan Lachman Das and also suggesting a reorganised State Council of five members; Maharaja as the President, Vice-President (Amar Singh) and three members (Ram Singh, Babu Nilamber Mukerji and Diwan Janki Prasad as member cum Secretary). In reply Viceroy doubted if the dignity of the Maharaja allowed him to be a mere President of the Council and doubting success of such council. In a communication from British Government of India to Secretary of State Government of India dated 18 August 1888; 'it was essential to erect some reduction of the Maharaja's authority.' By end of 1888, Pratap Singh was de facto deposed and the control of the administration passed into the hands of the British Resident through State Council.

On 17 February 1889 a communication from Secretary of State to Government of India stated; 'a batch of letters thirty-four letters in the Maharaja's own handwriting ... no course open save his removal from the state... these treasonable letters ......any steps Government may take short of annexation will be right and necessary'. Under the garb of so called 'treasonable letters', which were actually personal letters by the Maharaja, he was charged with conspiring with Russia against the British and was forced to abdicate on 8 March 1889. This, after due diligence, was shaped in the form of an **'Edict of Abdication'** from the Maharaja to his brother Amar Singh, recommending constituting a five member council, for a period of five years, under Amar Singh, with Ram Singh, a British Officer, Rai Bahadur Suraj Kaul and Rai Bahadur Bhag Ram as members. The Maharaja was not to interfere and would have no voice in the administration of the public affairs of the State. The edict cum abdication letter was sent by British Resident to Viceroy, who on 1 April 88 generally confirmed the constitution of the council; 'but full powers of government will be vested in a Council consisting of the Maharaja's brothers and three or four officials selected by the Government of India. Council will have full powers of administration, they will be expected to exercise those powers under the guidance of the Resident. They will take no steps of importance without consulting him (British Resident), and they will follow his advice whenever it may be offered'. '.... and such other members as may be added from time to time by the Government of India Subject to the general control of the Resident The Resident shall be the final referee in all matters and may veto any resolution passed by the Council or suspend action thereon pending further explanation.'

British Resident Frederick Currie and the State Council of five members was constituted on 17th April 1889 by the Government of India on the instructions of Viceroy Lord Henry Lansdowne (1888-1894 AD). The State Council almost immediately assumed all powers of governance and the Maharaja was reduced to giving his approval to all measures enacted by the Council. Furthermore, the Council members Rai Bahadur Suraj Kaul and Rai Bahadur Bhag Ram were imported from British India States; literally there being no one from within the state, except the two brothers of the royal family. In partial modification, Pratap Singh was made as President of the State Council from 1891 to 1905 AD.

Control of Chitral and Gilgit by British: With the expansion in Central Asia by Russia, British interest in the Pamirs and states of Chitral, Hunza was aroused. The claim of Afghans on troublesome Chitral in 1880, vacillating attitudes of Chitral Rulers, British decided to have a more effective control over the Mehtar of Chitral. Between 1889 and 1895, various military expeditions were launched by the State forces but under the command of British officers. The expeditions were successful and Chitral passed under direct control of the British in practice, in theory it continued to be a feudatory of Maharaja of Jammu and Kashmir. These expeditions brought the strategic importance of Gilgit region to the notice of the British. The result was a concerted effort on the part of the British Government to bring the whole of Gilgit area under its direct control. A British political agent was stationed at Gilgit to watch British interests, though administrative control remained in the hands of the State Government.

Pratap Singh Restored to the Throne: Pratap Singh was restored to his *Gaddi* in 1905, after an attempt to completely oust him had been foiled by the timely revelation by the Indian Press of the machinations by the Political Department of the British Government of India. The issue had also been raised in the British House of Commons by opposition members. The speech by Viceroy, Lord Curzon, announcing the restoration of powers states thus; 'Hence forward the State Council which for the last sixteen years has administered the affairs of the State will cease to exist, and its power will be transferred under proper guarantees to your self. You will be assisted in the discharge of these duties by your brother Raja Sir Amar Singh, who has already occupied so prominent a position in the administration and who will be your chief minister and right-hand man. ....In all important matters you will be able to rely upon the counsel and support of the British Resident, who, owing to the peculiar conditions of Kashmir, has played so important a part........'. This not only was restoration order but also reaffirmation of the strong role of the British Resident, in running the affairs of the State. A council of Ministers under a Chief Minister was constituted to run the affairs of the State, who was to seek approval of the Maharaja for the proposals forwarded by the Council of Ministers. The role of the Resident remained unchanged.

Modernisation of the State Infrastructure and Systems: In spite of the constraints imposed by the British, it was during Pratap Singh's time that the real modernisation of the state took place and several progressive reforms were carried out. In 1887 A Wingate was appointed to carry out the first assessment of land revenue system on scientific lines in the state. In 1890 Sir Walter Lawrence took over from Wingate as Settlement Commissioner and followed the principles introduced by his predecessor in the land settlement. The first major step of improvement of road infrastructure was taken in 1889 when Jhelum Valley cart road from Kohala to Baramulla was completed and in 1897 extended to Srinagar. This road called as Jhelum Valley Road connected the state to Rawalpindi, Abbotabad and Sialkot. Banihal Cart Road, which connected Srinagar with Jammu, was thrown open to the public in 1922. Besides these, many feeder roads in the state including those connecting Srinagar to Gilgit and Leh were also constructed.

A water reservoir was constructed at Harwan for the supply of potable water to Srinagar City. For the first time electric generating plant at Mohra, near Uri, was commissioned, which provided electricity to Srinagar City and few big towns. Two colleges in the state, besides large number of education institutions were also established on the orders of the Maharaja. By 1915 Durbar had brought all religious educational institutions of the Valley, none of which could survive without the annual state grants-in-aid, under its direct control. Urdu replaced Persian as the court language in 1889, and subsequently became the language of administration.

A Group of Kashmiri Musalman Boatmen–1877 AD

There was development in the means of communication and telegraphs, telephones and post offices were opened in many places. The isolation of Kashmir from the rest of India was now a thing of the past. Large number of people, mostly Europeans, began to visit the valley. The fame of the valley, its climate and beauty spread in all parts of the world and it can truly be said that an era of tourist traffic started in right earnest in the state. Many efforts were made by Englishmen to obtain the right of purchasing land in the valley, which would have turned Kashmir into a British Colony. Maharaja stoutly refused to approve such a proposal and as an alternative led to the construction of House Boats. A bridge over Tawi River was constructed and Jammu linked to Sialkot by train, which significantly improved the communication system in the state. Two major irrigation canals Ranbir Canal and Pratap Canal were constructed, which increased the irrigation facilities leading to further progress in agriculture. It is during his time that the two world famous resorts of Pahalgam and Gulmarg were developed in the valley as tourist resorts. During the course of his reign, he clashed few times even with the British Resident, for the cause in betterment for the people of the state.

Assessment of Pratap Singh's Reign: The rule of Pratap Singh lasted 40 years, out of which for 16 years (1889-1905 AD) he was kept as notional head of the state. While his Grandfather established the State of Jammu and Kashmir in 1846, his father Ranbir Singh gave dynamic effect to the kingdom in the form of consolidation and expansion. Maharaja Pratap Singh's rule gave impetus to reforms, education and infrastructure. During his reign state government carried out the first land settlement, as a result of which the rights of the agriculturists were clearly defined and the states demand was fixed for ten years. '*Begar*' or forced labour, in its most objectionable form, was abolished. Admittedly the years of his reign were not without hiccups. Even during the period of his forced abdication, State Council under his brother Amar Singh worked for overall better results and reforms. There is no doubt that his brothers; Ram Singh and Amar Singh, executed reforms which did bring in sea change in the state. Machinations of the British, before Pratap Singh ascended the throne, forced presence of British Resident in the State during his time. During the period 1889 to 1905, the role of British Resident became more proactive, with active interference in the affairs of the state. British wanted Jammu and Kashmir, short of annexation, to be just like another state of British Dominion. With these constraints it is difficult to fully scale achievements of Pratap Singh, which otherwise would be termed as good. Comparisons with the rule of his grandfather or father, who carved a niche for themselves, who functioned in a different environment, may not be correct.

Hari Singh's Reign (1925–1949)

Hari Singh: Hari Singh born on 23 September 1895 was the only son of Amar Singh, brother of Pratap Singh. Since Maharaja Pratap Singh died issue less, Hari Singh succeeded him. He was the first Dogra King to be formally educated, having studied in Mayo College Ajmer. By the time he finished his education at Mayo College, he as Ruler-in-Waiting, being heir apparent to Maharaja Pratap Singh, went to Imperial Cadet College at Dehradun for military training. He was one of the rulers of the princely states, who had got world wide exposure, as he had spent many years of his early life in England. He was made Commander-in-Chief of the State Forces in 1915, till he ascended the throne and was also granted title of Raja on 20th January 1916.

The development around the world had created a strong urge of state development in his mind and in particular was aware of the backwardness of the Kas'mira Valley. He was the first Dogra King to ascend the throne first at Srinagar in Kas'mira Valley, for he knew the importance of the valley to his kingdom. He was later installed at Jammu, 24th February 1926. When he took over the reigns of his Kingdom, India was going through a period of freedom struggle. The Princely states were divided in support to the freedom struggle and within the Princes Conclave, ideas ranged from a larger combined India to Confederation of Princely States, of those not willing to join free India.

Views on Indian Independence: From the very beginning Hari Singh had greater interest of Indian Nation in heart, rather than carving a state of his own. He attended many meetings of Chambers of Princes and also Round Table Conferences. While his view was to continue to maintain relations with United Kingdom, he too advocated a free India. He was proud to be Indian and said; "As Indians and loyal to the land of our birth, we stand as solidly as the rest of our countrymen for our land's enjoyment of a position of honour and equality in the British Commonwealth. Our desire to cooperate to the best of our ability with all sections of the Conference is genuine, as also is our determination to base our cooperation upon the realities of the present situation." His misunderstanding with the British Resident began from the very day of his coronation and continued to grow in the succeeding years due to his spirit of independence. The breaking point, however, was brought by his speech at the first Round Table Conference in London in 1930 in the course of which he said; "While Indian Princes value British connection, they have full sympathy for the aspirations of their motherland for an equal and honourable place in the comity of nations." His patriotism is testified by the way he supported total independence for India as a representative of the Chamber of Princes in the roundtable conference in London in 1931. The Maharaja said candidly; "It is the first occasion when the Indian princes have come to discuss the political future of India with the representatives of the British Government and the British India. As Indians we want our motherland to enjoy a place of honour and equality in the British Union." However, there were vested interests within the Princely States duly supported by British Government. The latter wanted the treaties entered into individually with the Princely States to remain and this was possible only if these Princely States maintained their individual status. The British actions were to encourage such dissentions of Princes as is evident from Broadcast of Sir Stafford Cripps on 30 March, 1942; "... a constitution-making body should be set up consisting of elected representative from British India and if the Indian States wish, as we hope they will to become part of the new Indian Union, they too will be invited to send their representatives to this constitution-making body, though, if they do, that will not, of itself, bind them to become members of the Union. That is the broad outline of the future." The reaction of Hari Singh to this broadcast was in contrast to what Chamber of Princes advocated. "In any case, it is the duty of the Princes to show themselves the equals of nationals anywhere in the world......the proposals entrusted in Sir Stafford Cripps are fundamentally adverse to the interests of the Indian States and this is unthinkable there is no reason why there should not be ample common ground between the States and the rest of India." And "Freedom must be our watchword...freedom from crippling restrictions and strangling control, freedom from the subordination of India's interests to the interests of other parts of the Commonwealth." Compare this with the remarks of Jam Saheb of Nawanagar to Sir H Craik on 1 June 1942, advocating Princely States non opting for the Union and to have their own union of states; "the non-adhering States should be accorded the option of having a union of their own with full sovereign status in accordance with a suitable and agreed procedure devised for the purpose."

Lot has been commented on for his vacillation in 1947. One has to understand and compare these with the situations, as they arose; in Junagarh and Hyderabad. In both cases the rulers were Muslims and majority of the subjects Hindus. In case of Junagarh accession to Pakistan was not acceptable, so was the independent state as propagated by Nizam. Hari Singh ruled over a state with clear majority of Muslims. From 1940 onwards Jinnah had been trying his best to woo Hari Singh as well as the people, but had got a cold shoulder. Nehru had many times come to Kas'mira, in one case was turned back from Kohala Bridge under the orders of Maharaja. But his visits were not asking for accession but for more rights to the people of the state. Definitely Maharaja needed time and he sought stand still arrangements both with Pakistan as well as India. Even Sheikh Abdullah, then main political leader had not expressed his views for accession to India, though he was not for Pakistan. In 1946 Sheikh Abdullah said: "Take the instance of the cry of Pakistan. It was born of distress. Now it is stripped of all reasons. The question before the Muslims will be whether the realization of Pakistan is a blessing to them. I personally think that Pakistan will not help the Muslim masses but hinder them in their struggle for political and economic emancipation. In our State this question however, does not arise, because an overwhelming majority of the people are Muslims and there is no need to fear Hindu domination." Time proved Hari Singh correct in his assessment of the situation. 65 years on the problem of Jammu and Kashmir remains as hot as ever in the world and possibly a solution on the lines of his then thought process even being touted as only solution.

Democratic/Electoral Reforms: Hari Singh had been brought up in an environment, which had given him exposure of more freedom to the subjects, more so in Princely States. The first such measure taken by him was State Subject Notification on 20 April 1927, which granted State Subject ship to persons born and residing within the State before the commencement of the reign of Maharaja Gulab Singh and also persons who settled before 1995. The right also extended to wife or a widow of a State Subject. In his address to his subjects on 9 July 1931, he clearly enunciated his desire to be part of the people, ensure freedom of religion, cater for the aspirations of the people, participation in the development of the state and ensure maintenance of law and order.

To give representation to the people he formed a Constitutional Reforms Conference under B J Glancy to suggest functions, franchise basis and composition of a Legislative Assembly. The conference in its recommendations, duly accepted in May 1932, entailed establishment of Legislative Assembly of 60 members; 33 elected, 22 nominated and 5 Ministers. 33 elected members, based on area and province representation (Jammu, Kashmir and Frontier Province) (Muslims 19, Hindus 12, Sikhs 1 and Buddhists 1). A franchise committee was appointed and in March 1933, Sir Ivo Elliott, I.C.S. (Retd) appointed Franchise Officer (Present day Election Commissioner). By end of 1933, Franchise Committee recommended to raise the strength to 75 including 33 elected, 30 nominated members and 12 officials. The nominated members were to be notified based on area wise representation and catered for Muslims as well. The composition of elected members was fair and balanced with 21 Muslims, 10 Hindus, 2 Sikhs and total minimum number of Muslim members out of 75 was to be 32 excluding officials, while Hindu members strength was capped at maximum of 25. The first session of the Legislative Assembly (Praja Sabha) was held on 17th October 1934 at Rajgarh Palace, Srinagar. Four days before the meeting of the Praja Sabha, four Ministers under the Prime Minister Colonel E.J.D. Colvin, were nominated, which included one Muslim. On the same day six members were nominated, which included two Muslims. In the first elections Muslim Conference bagged 14 seats out of 21 reserved for the Muslims. In his inaugural address to the Assembly, Maharaja said: " .... Cultivate sobriety of thought and expression, shunning all that is disruptive, and devote all your energies to creative and constructive work which alone can help to ameliorate the lot, and conduce to the happiness of those whose spokesmen you have undertaken to be." In 1936 elections, Muslim Conference was able to raise its strength to 19 and established its claim to be called as a major political party. In June 1939, however, Sheikh Abdullah broke away from the Muslim Conference and established a new party; National Conference. Hari Singh acceding to popular demand for more powers, Praja Sabha was authorised to nominate a panel of 6 members (3 Muslims), out of which two were to be ministers, one of whom had to be a Muslim. This step was welcomed by all sections of the Assembly and led to the appointment of Mirza Afzal Baig, a close associate of Sheikh Abdullah, and Ganga Ram as the Ministers. The former belonged to the National Conference, while the latter was a Dogra politician. The strength of elected members was also raised to forty. By virtue of these reforms, Jammu and Kashmir State has the rare distinction of having the first Legislative Assembly in early thirties.

Hari Singh was much ahead in the electoral and democratic reforms and amongst the first few Princely States to have an elected assembly. This was also much before the Indian National Congress Working Committee resolution of 29 July - 1 August 1935; "...declared itself in favour of establishment of representative responsible government in the States and has in that behalf not only appealed to the Princes to establish such responsible government in their States and to guarantee fundamental rights of citizenship." However, he has been accused by Politicians as well as Historians for communalising electoral system in favour of Muslims. On the contrary Muslims allege that the electoral system was dominated by nominated members and they did not get fair representation. It was a first effort based on an estimated population data and amends made after it was realised that there were some flaws. Admittedly number of nominated members was rather high, but it also included officials and ministers. Other nominated members were evenly distributed amongst all the constituencies and religions. The overall maximum and minimum members stood at the ratio of over 60 per cent for Muslims and around 33 per cent for Hindus. Even this was corrected by accepting Praja Sabha to nominate 6 members two of whom were nominated as ministers. The sound basis of the composition of the Legislative Assembly can well be judged by the fact that the strength of Jammu and Kashmir Assembly remained at 75 for many decades and it is only later that 25 more seats were symbolically added for Pakistan Occupied Kashmir and kept vacant. As far as the nominated members are concerned, even British Parliament (House of Lords), our own Rajya Sabha and many State Councils have this system based on representation of people from various walks of life.

Ceding of Gilgit: Right from the time Maharaja Ranbir Singh had retaken Gilgit and adjoining areas, British were keen to have direct control of this area. British negotiated and an agreement was reached with Ranbir Singh in 1880 for establishment of a Political Agency at Gilgit, Gilgit Agency, under control of the British Agent. Eight years later in 1889, it came under British Agent after being unified with neighbouring Nagar and Hunza. During the period 1889 – 1895 AD British made many efforts to gain the territory under its direct control for importance of the area in view of the expansions by Russians in Central Asia. British did not succeed till about 1934 AD. During this period various agitations for electoral reforms were taking place in which Hari Singh was closely involved in evolving a democratic electoral system. British in the meantime had convinced him that dangers of expansionist Russia would also endanger the state and asked for 99 years lease of Gilgit Wazarat and Gilgit region was ceded in 1935 to the British on a sixty year lease. This brought the whole of Gilgit including the frontier States of Hunza and Nagar directly under the control of the British Political Agent stationed at Gilgit. In April 1947, British decided to formally retrocede the leased areas to Jammu and Kashmir State as on August 15, 1947 and transfer was to formally take place on 1 August. In 1947 British Officer incharge of the Wazarat, duly aided by some elements, raised flag of independence and joined Pakistan.

Social and Welfare Measures: Hari Singh has drawn flak for his political handling and his dilly dallying the accession process by Indian Politicians and Historians. On the other hand, Pakistanis blame him for spoiling their chances of gaining the Muslim majority state. But he is forgotten for the electoral reforms and the welfare measures he took during his reign. He formulated a realistic social policy in 1928 to suppress infant marriages, prevalent during those days and thus State became one of the earliest princely states of the country to pass a legislation under which girls were not allowed to marry before they attain the age of 14 years and boys 18 years. Primary and secondary education was made free throughout the state. A drive against adult literacy was launched with considerable success. Simple Urdu was made the medium of instruction in schools but students had the option of choosing either the Devanagri or Persian script. Timber was made available on concessional rates to the people living in the periphery of forests. As far as state jobs are concerned he proclaimed; "Justice is my religion and merit alone will be considered deciding factor for all types of employments and caste, creed, religion or sex will receive no consideration."

On 26th March 1928, High Court of Judicature was constituted, consisting of a Chief Justice and two or more Judges. In 1932, Hari Singh threw open the doors of temples to Harijans and ensured that people of all sections of societies drew water from the same well and made concerted efforts to discourage untouchability. He also left his family jewellery, shawls, carpets and regalia worth crores of rupees with the state treasury (*Toshakhana*). Number of hospitals and medical dispensaries with qualified doctors and nurses were increased. In 1945 Hari Singh Hospital was opened at Srinagar and a separate tuberculosis department was set up, being among the first in India. The Jammu & Kashmir Bank was established in 1938 and took over the government treasury both at Srinagar and Jammu. It is a common belief that Jammu and Kashmir Bank was established after 1947; which is not so.

Quit Kashmir Movement: In rest of India Muslim League had been demanding a set up which gave shape to aspirations of Muslims in India. Presidential Address of Dr. Sir Muhammad Iqbal delivered at the Allahabad Session of the All India Muslim League in December 1930 gave some indications. He said; "....would like to see the Punjab, North-West Frontier Province, Sind and Baluchistan amalgamated into a single state. Self-Government within the British Empire, or without the British Empire, the formation of a consolidated North-West Indian Muslim State appears to me to be the final destiny of the Muslim, at least of North West India. The proposal was put forward before the Nehru Committee." In Kas'mira Muslim Conference organised itself as the main political party of Kashmir. Sheikh Mohammad Abdullah, one of the leaders of the party, over the period felt that in the interest of the state, there should be participation of people from other religions also, as Muslim Conference in its present form was representative of Muslims only. On 26 March 1938, in his Presidential address Sheikh Abdullah felt the requirement of 're-christening our organization as a non-communal political body and introducing certain amendments in its constitution and its rules'. It also opened its doors for people to become members of the Conference irrespective of their caste, creed or religion. It succeeded in a way that a joint National Demand was put up to the Maharaja, which was signed by a mixed group of Muslims as well as Pandits. In June 1939, Sheikh Abdullah broke away from the Muslim Conference and established a new party the National Conference, which soon secured a large following.

While Indian National Congress struggled for a united free India, Muslim League under Mohammed Ali Jinnah, worked for the partition of the country and creation of Pakistan on the basis of religion. In its Lahore resolution of 4 March 1940 'emphatically reiterated that the scheme of federation is totally unsuited, unworkable and altogether unacceptable to Muslim India' and on 22 March 1940 emphatically demanded a separate home land for Muslims. In the meantime Nehru, who had Kashmiri roots, visited Kas'mira, established close rapport with Sheikh Abdullah and aroused great enthusiasm among the people. The National Conference believing in secularism, gradually came closer to the view of Indian National Congress. In 1944 Jinnah also visited Kas'mira and tried to patch up the differences between the leaders of the National Conference, which had become active since 1941 under Ghulam Abbas. He failed in his mission and returned bitter, which is best explained by his address to Muslims of Kashmir; "when I, after careful consideration, suggested that the Mussalmans should organize themselves under one flag and on one platform, not only my advice was not acceptable to Sheikh Abdullah but, as is his habit, which has become a second nature with him, he indulged in all sorts of language of a most offensive and vituperative character in attacking me." Thereafter, events moved swiftly both in India and Kashmir. In March 1946, Cabinet Mission of British Government proposed a federal union of India. On 26 May 1946 National Conference launched, on the pattern of 1942 Quit India Movement, a 'Quit Kashmir' movement against Maharaja Hari Singh. The state government arrested Sheikh Abdullah. Thereupon, Nehru came to Kas'mira in support of the movement, but had to return soon.

Pakistani Invasion and Accession to India: On 3rd June 1947 British announced their intention to quit India and envisaged partitioning of the country into two dominions of India and Pakistan. As far as the Princely States were concerned, they were to decide either to join India or Pakistan. Unlike other states Hari Singh was in a peculiar situation and could not come to a decision. The role of his then advisors further deepened the dilemma in-spite of a visit by Lord Mountbatten, the last British Viceroy, on 19 June 1947. With independence slated for night of 14/15 August, Maharaja Hari Singh, to gain time for his decision making process, tried to enter into a 'standstill agreement' with both India and Pakistan. While the former hesitated, the latter accepted this arrangement two days later.

Independence and partition of India took place and Maharaja had yet to make up his mind. On the face of it Hari Singh gaining some time for coming to a final decision came to a naught when Pakistan revoked 'Stand Still' agreement on 18 September 1947 and suspended supplies of all essential commodities to the state. Apparently this was part of a larger plan by Pakistan. On 22 October 1947, large number of tribesmen, equipped with modern weapons by Pakistan invaded Kas'mira from the side of Abbotabad. Within days these tribal bands had reached Baramulla and Maharaja had no option but to ask for Military help from India, for which formal accession was necessary. Accordingly on 26 October 1947 Instrument of Accession was signed by Maharaja and sent to Lord Mountbatten Governor General of India through Mr V P Menon. The letter from Maharaja accompanying the instrument mentioned that; 'I may also inform your Excellency's Government that it is my intention at once to set up an interim government and to ask Sheikh Abdullah to carry the responsibilities in this emergency with my Prime Minister'. The instrument was accepted very next day, 27th October, and a battalion of Indian Army was flown to Srinagar. This was followed by induction of more troops for operations against the tribal's. By 7 November Indian Army had evicted the tribals from key towns and by March 1948 these invaders, called *Kabailis* by locals, were pushed back from major portion of the state territory. As promised Maharaja issued an order on 30 October 1947 appointing Sheikh Abdullah as the Head of the Emergency Administration, replacing it, on March 5, 1948, with Interim Government with Sheikh as Prime Minister. The emergency administration was enjoined to convene a National Assembly 'to frame a Constitution' for the State. Sheikh Abdullah had since been freed and Interim Government under him had since started functioning. With a popular nominated Government functioning under a Prime Minister, it was question of time when the state would have been freed from the invaders, when Pakistan's regular army was also employed along with these tribals in May 1948. In the meantime the dispute and aggression by Pakistan was taken to UN Security Council by India, while operations against the invaders continued. In the last days of 1948, a ceasefire was agreed under UN auspices and operations came to halt. This left Muzaffarabad, Gilgit, Mirpur and part of Poonch with the invaders under overall control of Pakistan. While occupied parts were promptly called Azad Kashmir by Pakistan, Pakistan Occupied Kashmir by India, erstwhile Gilgit Wazarat came directly under the control of Pakistan.

End of Dogra Rule: While the Kashmir question lay before the world body, on June 9, 1949 Hari Singh signed a decree designating Yuvraj Karan Singh as Regent of the state and went into exile. From the memoirs of Late Hari Singh and other details, his son Doctor Karan Singh and his wife Maharani Tara Devi was somewhat responsible for his decision. It is also a known fact that Pandit Nehru, who did not see eye to eye with Hari Singh, had separate channels opened with young Yuvraj and his mother. On 1st May 1951 Yuvraj Karan Singh, as the Regent, issued proclamation for elections for constituting Constituent Assembly for the purpose of framing a Constitution for the State of Jammu and Kashmir, which were to be held forthwith. National Conference under Sheikh Abdullah won all the 75 seats and in its very first session in October 1951, Constituent Assembly abolished the Monarchy and with this Dogra rule of 103 Years came to an end. During the process of formalising separate constitution of Jammu and Kashmir, Dr Karan Singh, only son of Hari Singh, continued to be the Head of the State as Regent with the title of *Yuvraj* from 20th June 1949 to 31st October 1956. In 1952 the Constituent Assembly passed a resolution to designate the head of the State as *Sadar-i-Riyasat* and also the Head of the Government as Prime Minister. Dr Karan Singh assumed the appointment of *Sadar-i-Riyasat* from 1st November 1956 to 9th April 1965. On the change of designation of the Head of the State, to be appointed by Government of India. Dr Karan Singh took over as Governor of the State of Jammu and Kashmir from 10th April 1965 to 15th March 1967. Maharaja Hari Singh breathed his last at Bombay on April 26, 1961.

Assessment of Dogra Rule: When Gulab Singh entered Srinagar on 9 November 1846, no body had imagined that this Chieftain from Dogra clan would be the ruler of a state, which would have an area of more than eighty thousand square miles including parts of Tibet, part of Pamir, besides the genuine kingdoms of Jammu and Kashmir. This area had never been effectively united under one ruler and much of it with of course, the exception of the valley of Kashmir, had any known settled government. The borders of the State touched the Central Asian Region, Tibet albeit China, British India and Afghanistan. His rule was relatively short, but he had spent his life time, beginning in 1808 as a sixteen year old warrior till 1846, carving a niche for himself and creating a State which stood to be counted in the sub continent. 'Gulab Singh was unquestionably a remarkable figure in the history of Northern India during the first half of the 19th Century. He was a distinguished soldier and diplomat and knew the state craft of his own days exceedingly well'. If one studies the history of Kas'mira, from ancient days, very few rulers of Kas'mira can be compared to Dogra Rule. King Ashoka ruled a vast empire including Northern India, of which Kas'mira was a part. The rule perforce was not intimate, so was it during Kanishka's rule. It is during Karkota Dynasty (631- 855 AD) which flourished further during the rule of Lalitaditya (724-761 AD), third son of the Karkota King Partapaditya II, who is equated to Samudra Gupta of India.

Ranbir Singh took the threads left by Gulab Singh. He re-conquered Gilgit for the state and then diverted his attention to the measures which improved the lot of the citizens. Lawlessness on the borders of the State by Dards and Khokas, which had been there for centuries, was curbed with strong hand. For the first time laws were enforced for civil and criminal justice under Ranbir 'Dand-Vidhi' (Ranbir Penal Code), code of law which is operative till this day. Establishment of Research and Translation Department for preserving old manuscripts and translating them in other languages was established during his time.

During Pratap Singh's time impetus was given to building of communication and health infrastructure. By now signs of awakening of the people towards their democratic rights, unheard of earlier, was palpable and it fell on Hari Singh to address these aspirations, who can be called a reformist ruler who tried his best to give his citizens democratic and election rights. From 1930's onwards there was general awakening, of higher order, towards independence of British India, which also had effects on Princely States. The position of the State in the sub continent, demand for separate land for Muslims, made the situation challenging for him. He sought to draw a fine line, but had to yield to popular demand. One can debate his views of stand still agreements and quest for a peculiar status for the state between the two emerging countries. Jammu and Kashmir, worlds top most dispute, remains as hot as ever even today.

Kas'mira had history of Kings, barring few, who had self interest upper most in their minds. Advent of Islam, which followed Hindu Rule, had a different hue; forcible conversions, assassinations, repressions, Shia-Sunni conflicts, forcible conversions even within Muslim factions and anarchy of highest order. The State for centuries had been controlled mostly by feudal lords and peasantry had to bear the brunt of their tyranny. Royal Coups and holding for ransom were order of the day and later Afghan rule was so tyrannical that even Muslims migrated to other parts of neighbouring countries. Dogra Rule of 103 years will be remembered for a lot of benevolent things. There were no forcible conversions, nor communal riots or killings. There was absolute freedom to practices and preach your faith. People were not held to ransom and welfare measures from land to education to infrastructure implemented. There were no Royal Coups, to give uncertainty to the State. Just four rulers in 103 years, when it was the time of general awakening of the rights of the people around the world and India. Citizens could no longer be herded like cattle but had to be treated as humans with a need and governance of their liking. Compare this with earlier times and one gets the answer.

6

Religious Worship Era's

"The place is more beautiful than the heaven and is the benefactor of supreme bliss and happiness. It seems to me that I am taking a bath in the lake of nectar here."

–Sanskrit Poet Kalidasa

Kas'mira - Abode of Gods, Evolution and Dating Inhabitants

The Abode of Gods: Ancient Greeks called Kas'mira '**Kasperia**' and the Chinese pilgrim Huen-Tsang, who visited the valley around 631 AD, called it "**KaShi-Mi-Lo.**" Kalhan pays tribute to Kas'mira in Rajatarangini (Verse 36 Book I) (Rajatarangini was written by the chronicler between 1148-50 AD) and associates *Nandikshetra*, area of snow-clad mountains of Dras, Mahadev, Baltal and Amarkanth as abode of Shiva in Kas'mira. He wrote Rajatarangini when Shaivism, more so in Shakta Worship form, was at its peak and immediately after Abhinav Gupta had left an indelible mark on the religious inclination of Aryan Saraswat Brahmins of Kas'mira. Abhinav Gupta born around 940 AD and might have lived even beyond 1015 AD, when he is believed to have entered Birwa caves reciting *Bhairavastava*.. He, during his life and after had been extolled as "*Mahamahesvara*" by Kashmiri scholars, which precisely means the "great devotee of Shiva", or the "Supreme-Self" in Shaivistic parlance. Rajatarangini basically being history of the Kings of Kas'mira, Kalhan very briefly mentions religious aspects and the religion practised in Kas'mira from the time of Nagas upto his time. He, however, does narrate various Gods, religious activities of the Kings or construction of important temples or installation of idols. From the study of various scriptures and Rajatarangini it may be construed that Shaivism had been the prime wing of the Brahmin religion in Kas'mira. Not so, as the Kas'mira Brahmin built upon the native inhabitants, Nagas and other races i.e. *Daitaya's*, *Pis'acas*.

Original Inhabitants of Bharatvarsha and Aryans: Civilised human inhabitation in the Indian subcontinent (Bharatvarasha) is traced to the Palaeolithic and Neolithic period dating from about 3000 BC ±. This civilization is considered to be at par with the other civilizations of the world. Traces of Indus Valley Civilisation were first discovered in 1921-22 and archaeologists, keeping in view the already well-established Vedic chronology, concluded that the Indus Valley Civilisation belonged to the period between 3250 BC and 2750 BC and was pre-Vedic. These excavations also pointed to a highly complex civilization that first developed some 4,000-4,500 years ago. There are some more indications from excavations and finds, mostly in present Gujarat Coastal areas; that this civilisation could be earlier than the currently concluded Indus Valley Civilisation and indications of human "civilisation" in Bharatvarasha being earlier than 3000 BC; roughly in the band of 4000-4500 BC. However, arrival of *Homosapiens* (Human Beings) in, from the African Continent, Bharatvarasha is attributed to much earlier period; before 4000-4500 BC. In this "indefinable period- 4500 to 2750 BC", historians feel that Bharatvarasha was peopled by men with dark skin: known as Dravidians and Moundases. Initially humans in Bharatvarasha were restricted to specific areas and there were little or no major movements from one place to another. Excavations at Harappa and many other places have thrown up that Harappan Civilization (Indus Valley Civilization) were at their height between 2600-2500 BC, also part of Neolithic period, which collapsed around 2000-1800 BC. Traces of the Indus valley civilization discovered at Ropar in Punjab and Rangpur and Lothal in Saurashtra, Bharatpur in Rajasthan, Banawali, Kalibangan are proof of the existence of the Indus valley civilization.(Harappa is a site on the west bank of Ravi; Kalibangan is a site on the right bank of Sutlej; Amri is a site on the west bank of Indus (close to the Arabian Sea); Banawali is located 15 kilometers Northwest of Fatehbad (Haryana), near the mythical Saraswati River and about 120 km east of Kalibangan; Lothal and Rangpur are sites below the Rann of Kutch). Harappa being the main source of knowledge of Indian civilization, historians call this civilization as the Harappan culture. Harappan like sites have also been located in Northern Portion of Western India, North India and even in Jammu areas. Recently another site of later Harappan Civilization has been unearthed at Sanauli (Near Meerut- Uttar Pradesh). These sites, later capped with Aryan settlements, were basically that of indigenous inhabitants of Bharatvarasha, called Dasayus (Dark Skinned) by Aryans. However, Kalhan uses this term differently in his Rajatarangini; Dasayus is reference to small time warlords equated to robbers of Kas'mira.

The place of origin of the Aryans has been variously sought in Europe and Asia. Aryan race is presumed to have branched off at different periods; Northwest and Westward into Europe and Southward into Persia and

Bharatvarasha. They entered Bharatvarasha through the fabled Khyber Pass, after initial hostile attitude, as the time passed, intermingled with the local populace (Dravidians and Moundases) and assimilated into the amalgamated social framework. They adopted the settled agricultural lifestyle of their predecessors and established small agrarian communities. During this period many original inhabitants of Bharatvarasha migrated from one part to other and not all original inhabitants of the areas having Aryan settlements moved out or were pushed out. Some stayed and served the Aryans, others moved to live in the forests and the jungles of Northern portions of Bharatvarasha. However, it is well known that Aryans kept the Dravidians and Moundases at lower pedestal than their own. Before the arrival of the Aryans, there were other communities in extended Bharatvarsha; Sino-Mongoloids and Austroloids. There were also other foreign immigrations and invaders from East/North, who arrived in Bharatvarsha, from time to time. With the passage of time, the most basic division of Bharatvarasha society is that of Aryans and Dravidians. According to this division, nearly 65 per cent are Aryans, 25–27 per cent Dravidians and rest others. North Indians, mostly, are the descendants of Aryans and the South Indians are Dravidians. However, there is no clear-cut line, as the original inhabitant stock is also found all across Bharatvarasha; North, Central, Southern and Western Bharatvarasha. There is not much material or indications available about the religion of the original inhabitants of Bharatvarasha. In fact, no such common denominator has been established that could be termed as religion of ancient Bharatvarasha. As in other parts of world, day-to-day essentials; water, fire, air, food etc, became the objects of veneration, not worship.

Development of Aryan Scriptures: With passage of time Aryans and amalgamated people of Bharatvarasha developed language and made significant progress to have basis of a religion. Admittedly Aryans had a major role in this development. These development factors were to play a fundamental role in the shaping of Bharatvarasha culture and religion. Cavalry warfare, introduced with the introduction of horse in the subcontinent by the Aryans, facilitated the rapid spread of Aryan culture and religion across North India and allowed the emergence of large empires. Language and religion became the basis and the unifying factor of the vast majority. The religion, that now took root during this era, with its rich pantheon of Gods and Goddesses and its storehouse of myths and legends, became the foundation of the Hindu religion, as the time passed, which arguably became single most important common denominator of Bharatvarasha culture. Hinduism and the caste system are believed to have been established as a result of close co-existence of Aryans and original residents of Bharatvarasha; the Dravidians. The Aryans did not have a script, but they developed a rich tradition. They composed hymns of the Vedas, the great philosophic poems that are at the heart of Hindu thought. As the Nobel Laureate, Rabindranath Tagore expressed it, "The hymns (of Vedas) are a poetic testament of a people's collective reaction to the wonder and awe of existence....A people of vigorous and unsophisticated imagination awakened at the very dawn of civilisation to a sense of inexhaustible mystery that is implicit in life." These (Vedas) were composed orally, sung and preserved as *Shruti* (voice heard by generations) and *Smriti* (remembered; again by generations) and finally compiled, as language/ scripts developed. As regards when Vedic Hymns were composed Max Muller opines: "Whether the Vedic hymns were composed 1000 or 1500 or 2000 or 3000 years BC, no power on earth will ever determine."

Dating Earliest Inhabitants of Kas'mira: To analyse the original inhabitants, religion and its development since *Satisar* or Kas'mira was inhabited, there is need to date the original inhabitants and their arrival in Kas'mira, in this case Nagas, and later induction of other races and *Manus* (Aryans). Appearance of humans in Kas'mira is 'attributed', mostly 'claimed' as Aryans, to about 5000 to 6000 years ago, correlating with *Sapatrishi Samvat* (Era) (5088 (2012). Survey, Archaeological evidence, carbon dating of many ancient human dwelling sites in Kas'mira has, however, found that Neolithic people settlements scientifically attributed to that of Nagas (Aborigines) and not Aryans, who came to the valley around 2600 ± 200 BC. They came in a trickle and this settlement process continued for nearly thousand years. The settlements found in the survey were either abandoned ones or destroyed by the vagaries of nature. There would have been many more Neolithic (Naga) settlements, which continued to develop for further centuries but have not been located or traced as yet. Many of these settlements were capped with or developed along with Megalithic people, attributed to *Manus* (Aryans), dating 1600 ± 200 BC.

Aryan Arrival in Kas'mira: The height of the Harappan Civilization in Bharatvarasha also coincides with the appearance of Neolithic man in Kas'mira and firmly indicates that Neolithic culture was evolved in the valley around 2600 ± 200 BC. These dates however do not correlate to Gonanda Dynasty (Gonanda I (2448 BC - date disputed. This is an Era aberration by Kalhan. Read Chapter 9), which is the beginning of Rajatarangini by Kalhan and termed as the arrival of Aryans in the valley (More of it later). Apparently there is discrepancy in the chronicled history compiled later, folk lore and matching with archaeological and geological finds.

In the process of migration an enterprising batch of Aryans went to the mountains in the North and to Kas'mir Valley of whose beauty and salubrious climate they had heard from their forefathers, who used to go there during summer. They sought the protection of Nila; the Lord of the Nagas and begged his permission to settle permanently in the Valley as his subjects. Thus, immigration of this initial group of *Manus* (Aryans) kept pace with their movements in other parts of Bharatvarasha and to Kas'mira; roughly around 1600 BC±.

What was being adopted before Arya Bhatta's calculation has connection with the present Laukika or *Saptarishi* era as well and a remarkable coincidence of 60 years cycle for 60 years that is 3600 years. That is *Saptarishi Samvat* was a repetitive one after expiry of 60 years cycle for 60 years i.e. 6676 BC less 3076 BC = 3600 years, commencement of current *Saptarishi* Era. Around 500 AD, a major review of the Indian calendar was attempted. Varahamihir, a Kas'mira Aryan Saraswat Brahmin (560 AD) and others used the *Nakshatra* references that the *Saptarishi's* (Ursa Major) were in *Magha Nakshatra* at the time of the Mahabharata War. While Arya Bhatta declared the War to have occurred in 3137 BC, Varahamihir assigned it 2449 BC. This discrepancy arose perhaps from the different assumptions regarding the *Nakshatras* (27 or 28; actually 27 with overlap) in the calculations of the two astronomers. Commencement of the current *Laukika Era* or *Saptarishi Era* is thus placed on *Chaitra Shudi* 1 (First day of Bright Half of *Chaitra,* also the New Year (*Navreh*) of Aryan Saraswat Brahmins of Kas'mira) of the, of Kali *Samvat* 25 (expired) or the year 3076-75 BC. Laukika Era or *Saptarishi*, is 25 years less than commencement of Kali *Yuga* (3102 BC + 2012 = 5114), while current *Saptarish*i Era is 5089, a difference of 25 years). It was essential to dwell on genesis of Laukika Era, to derive the date of entry of Aryans into the valley.

It is apparent that the Bharatvarasha inhabitants of later centuries and Aryans adopted this *Samvat* for their lunar calculations, which was so essential for their day to day worship, rituals and routine. While migration of Aryans in earlier and later centuries took place before the time of Arya Bhatta (5th Century BC), Aryans too used this *samvat* for their record, calculations, worship etc, after it had been introduced in Bharatvarasha in 5th Century BC. Laukika or *Sapatrishi* Era thus calculated in Bharatvarasha by Arya Bhatta and has no co-relation with the entry of *Manu's* (Aryans) in Kas'mira or even Bharatvarasha. It may be that this *Samvat* relates to calculation of the era when the first inhabitants moved into Kas'mira; in this case Nagas, which is estimated to be between 3000 to 1500 BC ±. In any case the *Samvat* was calculated in 5th Century BC and could have earliest been applied or used from 5th Century BC onwards and it would have been difficult to calculate and connect it with the entry of Aryans, which would have happened at least a millennium back from this date (5th Century BC). By this time (5th Century BC) both Nagas as well as Aryans were inhabiting Kas'mira and had amalgamated with each other.

Laukika or *Sapatrishi Samvat* reckoning calculated around 500 BC is to be found in all handbooks of Indian chronology and thus this *Samvat* was adopted by Aryans as well as Nagas in Kas'mira approximately from that time onwards. Kashmir Brahmin community may feel that required antiquity to Aryan entry to Kas'mira has not been given by not connecting *Sapatrishi Samvat* to entry of the community into the valley. One must understand that all the indications, surveys, archaeological excavations in Bharatvarasha and Kas'mira point out that the Aryan entry into Bharatvarasha dates to megalithic period (1600 ± 200 BC) and any effort to try to give more antiquity to our entry in the valley may as well be counter productive; that we are not from the Aryan race. However, we must feel proud that this *samvat* may as well be the era of entry of original inhabitants in Kas'mira; that of Nagas. We do accept and acknowledge their existence and as *marg darshaks* to Aryans in Kas'mira. In any case even the Aryans entry to Kas'mira is around 3612 ± years earlier. Dwelling upon the era's connected with the entry of Aryans into Kas'mira was essential so as to bring home the religion and practices Aryans brought with them when they migrated to Kas'mira.

Vedic Religion and Vedic Gods/Goddesses

Rig Vedic, Brahmanic and Later Vedic Period: The earliest history of the Aryans in Bharatvarasha, is called the Rig Vedic Period (1600 ± BC), named after the religious praise poems, oldest pieces of literature in Bharatvarasha. In mid of Rig Vedic Period and early centuries of Later Vedic Period or Brahmanic Period (1000 BC), Aryans migrated across the Doab, which is a larger plain separating Yamuna River from the Ganges, even to River Sarayu in present day Uttar Pradesh, as mentioned in this Rig Veda Hymn; "Let the great Streams come hither with their mighty help, Sindhu, Saraswati, and Sarayu with waves; Book 10; 64-9)." This civilisation thrived in these areas what is now called Indo-Gangetic Civilisation, encompassing most of the present day North India. While the Rig Veda represents primitive religion of the Aryans during the Rig Vedic period, the religion of the Later Vedic period is dominated by the Brahmins or priestly book, composed sometime between 1000 and 850 BC. The Brahmins dominated later Vedic society and every aspect of Aryan life came under the control of priestly rituals and spells. In history, as we understand it, the Later Vedic Period is the Epic Age. Epics, great literary heroic epics of Bharatvarasha culture, the *Mahabharata* and the *Ramayana*, were composed in the Later Vedic Period, between 500 and 200 BC respectively, kept as *Shruti* (voice heard by generations) and *Smriti* (remembered; again by generations). Both these epics deal with heroes from this period and demonstrate how Aryan cultural values, as we can understand them from the Rig Veda, were transformed by mixing with Indus Valley Civilisation cultures.

The hymns of Rig Veda, epics and later scriptures are a period of mixing in that the culture of Aryans gradually mixed with indigenous cultures, the war-religion of the Aryans still preserved in parts of Rig Veda, slowly became more ritualised and more meditative. This was also the beginning of [Brahmanic

Period (1000 BC)], when religion started taking firm roots. Aryan Gods and Goddesses mixed with a new pantheon of local deities and forms started taking roots during the next few centuries, specific religious scriptures in praise of these Gods and Goddesses composed and written. A new line of Gods and Goddesses came up for a religion, which was to follow; Hinduism. By 500 BC, this process of mixing and transformation was more or less complete and the culture we now call "Indian" was fully formed.

Vedas: Aryan beliefs, rituals and daily life are described in the four Vedas, collection of poems and sacred hymns and have become most ancient sacred literature of Hinduism with direct effect on the development of religion. This collection of hymns, poems and ceremonial formulas represent the beliefs of several Aryan tribes. Initially the Vedas were considered so sacred that they were only transmitted orally from one generation of Brahmans to other. The passages of the Vedas were 'eventually' written in Sanskrit, we believe, near the end of the third century BC and consist of four collections called the Rig Veda, Sam Veda, Yajur Veda, and Atharv Veda. Collectively, these are referred to as the *Samhitas*. The first three *Samhitas* were used in the *Vedic* period by the priestly class as ritual handbooks. The Rig Veda, the oldest of the four Vedas, started being composed around 1800-1600 BC and codified around 600 + BC. It is not known when it was finally committed to writing, but this probably was at some point around 500 BC. Rig Veda was originally written in *Khartoshi.* Sam Veda consisted of various portions taken from the Rig Veda and were utilized by the *udgatri* chanters (Priests who sang the verses in rhythm). Yajur Veda was used by the *adhvaryu* priests (Priests who specialised in specific sacrificial *yajnas*). This work contains specific sacrificial formulas which were recited during that form of ceremony. Atharv Veda, is attributed to a sage (*Rishi*) Atharvan and consists of number of hymns and magical incantations. To my mind probably after the composition of first three Vedas, Atharv Veda is the outcome of amalgamated ethos of Aryans and Dasayus and Atharv *Rishi* himself had imbibed the rituals of Dasayus/Dravidians.

Vedic Literature: Although the Rig Veda is still considered the most important of these ancient texts, it was still never very popular. Much of this comes from the fact of its composition by and for religious aristocracy. In contrast, the Atharv Veda, composed around 1000 BC compiled and written perhaps as late as 500 BC, much later than the rest of the Vedas, was very popular. This can be attributed to varied contents of magical incantations, thus getting major following amongst the Dravidians and Aryans. Atharv Veda frequently refers to many lesser functional gods considered useful in the daily lives and simple rituals of the ordinary Aryan that did not need the mediation of priests. How far back the national and religious Vedic period, so called, extends; "It is impossible to tell" confesses Prof. Max Muller; nevertheless, he traces it 'to a period anterior to 1,000 BC,' and brings us 'to 1,100 or 1,200 BC', as the earliest time when we may suppose the collection of the Vedic hymns to have been finished.' The Vedas were followed by *Upanishads*, a continuation of the Vedic philosophy and were composed between 800 and 400 BC. They elaborate on how the soul (*Atman*) can be united with the ultimate truth (Brahman) through 'contemplation and mediation, as well as the doctrine of *Karma*— the cumulative effects of a person's actions'. This was followed by other *Granthas*, *Puranas, Greh Sutras* and other scriptures. The epic *Mahabharata,* attributed to the sage Vyasa, was written somewhere 540 - 300 BC. *Mahabharata* tells the legends of the *Bharatas*, a Vedic Aryan group. The *Ramayana*, attributed to the poet Valmiki, was written somewhere during the first century AD, although it is based on oral traditions that go back six or seven centuries earlier (700 – 800 BC).

Vedic Religion: Initial Vedic Religion is concerned mainly with the worship of gods that are largely personifications of the powers of nature. The hymns are mainly invocations of these gods, meant to accompany the oblation of *Soma* juice and fire sacrifice of melted butter. It was thus essentially a polytheistic religion, which assumes a pantheistic colouring only in a few of its latest hymns. The gods mainly stated in the Rig Veda; thirty-three in number, divided into three groups of eleven and further distributed in Earth, Air, and Heaven; the three divisions of the Universe. That they (Aryans) were considered to have been originally mortal is implied in the statement that they acquired immortality by drinking *Soma* or by receiving it as a gift from Agni (Fire) and Savitr (Another God of Rig Veda. Savitr also finds mention in basic Hinduism *mantra*; *Gayatri Mantra*). The gods were conceived as human in appearance, some appear equipped as warriors, especially Indra and others described as priests; especially Agni and Brhaspati (Guru; Jupiter). The most important *mantra* of the Vedas, which is considered the 'root' or all Vedas, is the *Gayatri Mantra.*

Goddesses play an insignificant part in the Rig Veda. The only one of importance is Usas (Usha; Dawn). Next comes Saraswati, named fter Saraswati River or could be vice versa, celebrated in two whole hymns as well as parts of others, and *Vak* (*Vakh*; Speech). One hymn each is addressed to Prthivi (Earth), Ratri (Night) and Aranyani (Goddess of the Forest). Others are only sporadically mentioned. The wives of the great gods are still more insignificant, being mere names formed from those of their consorts, and altogether lacking in individuality: such are Agnayi, Indrani, Varunani, spouses of Agni, Indra, and Varuna respectively.

Some scholars have misunderstood Vedic Religion, which emanated from Vedas and later transited to Brahmanic period and during later centuries into various other schools of thoughts and Godhood. It is given to understand that present Hindu religion is in toto that of Vedas; not so. It is in the later centuries and when other religious scriptures appeared during Brahmanic period (*Upanishads, Granthas, Puranas* etc.) that current day Hindu religion emerged with Gods, deities, ranging from the Trinity, Mahadevis, to local deities Kul Devi/Devas etc. With passage of time, Aryans had amalgamated people of Bharatvarasha, developed language and made significant progress to have basis of a religion. Admittedly Vedas and Aryans had a major role in this development. These development factors were to play a fundamental role in the shaping of Bharatvarasha religion and culture. All said and done Bharatvarasha was inhabited by various races, located in many parts of current Bharatvarasha and all these amalgamated over millenniums. Even today whole of Bharatvarasha does not claim to be Aryans or Dravidians alone. The religion, that took root starting from Vedic Period, with its rich pantheon of Gods and Goddesses and its storehouse of myths and legends, became the foundation of the Hindu religion, as the time passed, which arguably became single most important common denominator of Bharatvarasha religion and culture. Hinduism and the caste system are believed to have been established as a result of close co-existence of Aryans and the Dravidians.

Importance of Some Vedic Gods: Vishnu (Visnu) occupies a subordinate position in the Rig Veda, being celebrated in only five or six hymns. The only anthropomorphic traits mentioned about him are the strides he takes and the description of him as a youth vast in body, who is no longer a child. Vishnu (Visnu) is also mentioned in Sam Veda and a hymn in his praise is in Book 8; 4 of Sam Veda. In comparison today Vishnu (Visnu) is one of the Gods of Trinity and has considerable standing amongst the Trinity Gods, next to Shiva. The Vishnu of today's Hinduism is so different from what has been described of him in the Veda. Indra alone is invoked in about one-fourth of the hymns of the Rig Veda, far more than addressed to any other deity; for he is the favourite national god of the Vedic people. Indra is praised as the protector, helper, and friend of his worshippers. He is described as bestowing on them wealth, which is considered the result of victories. In todays Brahmanic religion Indra has literally no role to play.

Origin of Saraswats: Many Aryans accepted the Great Sage Saraswat Muni (son of *Rishi* Daḍichi), living on the banks of Saraswati, as their Guru. There were about 60,000 (*Shatsahasara*) Brahmins who were his disciples, later called Saraswats or Saraswat Brahmins. When a severe famine, which lasted for about 12 years, hit the region and the crops were not enough to feed everyone, the survival of the Saraswats was at stake. When they could find no apparent solution to their vexing problem, at the advice of their Guru, who was pragmatic, they started to feed on fish from the Saraswati River for survival. Thus, they became the only fish-eating Brahmins ever known. This settlement was in the land between the Saraswati and *Drishadvati* rivers- Ghaggar River which reaches the Hakra branch in Bahawalpur (Pakistan), is traditionally identified with the Saraswati river (Sir Auriel Stein's explorations in the Valley: Ancient India by Sir M A Stein 1949); 25 Harappan sites were discovered in the 'region beginning right from the Pakistan border (Eastwards) up to midway between Hanumangarh (called *Bhatner* or *Bhattinagara*) and Suratgarh in the Saraswati valley and about 25 kilometers east of Bhadra (All in Rajashtan) called *Drishadvati* valley'. The migration to various other parts happened not overnight but spread over centuries. The last of the exodus, as described above, was due to a widespread famine, which again lasted for 12 years. These Saraswats migrated in three directions, mostly followed the river routes and migrated to the Southwest (Sind), North (Kas'mira), East (Bihar). This also caters for the fish eating habits of Aryan Saraswat Brahmins not only of Kas'mira but of other places too.

Religion and philosophy in the later Vedic period became more confirmed with elaborate sacrifices and amalgamation with philosophy, rituals of original inhabitants of Bharatvarasha. The doctrines of *Karma, Maya, Atma,* and *Mukti* were established. Brahma, Vishnu and Maheswara (Shiva) became the important gods who were worshipped. In Bharatvarasha, a thousand years would pass before there was a noticeable change in the religious thinking. A new kind of spirituality and with it a new way of looking at the gods came due to the teachings of the Brahmans (the priests and monks of Bharatvarasha). These men who refused to commit any act of violence, demonstrated by the example of their saintly life that; 'the gods were not there to kill all living things, but instead to help the weak and to inspire the human race to live in a new spirit of conciliation and a search for perfection'.

This new faith found one of its principal tenants in the theory of the reincarnation cycles of the lives of souls, which are sent back to earth until they are judged to be worthy of going up to heaven and becoming immortal, like the Gods. From this evolution of spirituality was born successively; Hinduism with a pantheon of Gods and Goddesses, Buddhism and Jainism, which replaced the Vedic religion. As the time passed many differing forms of Gods and Goddesses, mostly pertaining to geographic areas in Bharatvarasha manifested. This stage came not with the Aryan scriptures alone but new scriptures in praise of Gods and Goddesses being composed. Gods and Goddesses started taking a definite shape and sculptures made for their worship. Many remained as cosmic deities and even the same God or Goddess being venerated in many forms (*Roop*). These forms differed and so also their religious veneration, depending upon a particular demographic area. These forms first in thought process and refined further took sculptured forms on rocks, then idols and replaced by metal idols; surprisingly mostly black. Was it availability of black coloured metal or the new Gods/Goddesses being 'created' by indigenous Brahmins (Dasayus, Dravidians)? Answer is both. Gods/Goddesses took the indigenous hues of the inhabitants and transformed into reality with the available metal. Enterprising as they were, they even found the alloys and mix which gave black hue, like *Ashtadattu* (Black alloy made from eight metals).

Nilamat Puranam and Religion in Kas'mira

Nilamat Puranam: The Aryans settled alongside the Indus Valley, mythical river Saraswati migrated to other areas including present day Punjab (India and as well as Pakistan) and further to the plains of Yamuna-Ganga-Saryu Rivers. An enterprising batch went to the mountains in the North to reside in the Kas'mira Valley of whose beauty and salubrious climate they had heard from their forefathers, who used to go there during summer. They sought the protection of Nila; the King of the Nagas who then ruled over Kas'mira and sought his permission to settle in the Valley permanently as his subjects. Nila listened to their tale of woe sympathetically, but promised to grant permission on condition that they conformed to the social usages, rituals and customs of the Nagas. They agreed to these conditions and Naga chief permitted them to reside in the Valley. Initially the period was about six months in a year, as Aryans moved out during cold and snow period. Their permanent move into the valley connected with Naga rituals to be adopted by them is best narrated by the following passage (edited) from Nilamat Puranam. "After the passing away of the four ages, the *Manavas* (Aryans), as usual, had gone out for six months. An old Brahman, Candradeva did not accompany them. Troubled by the Pis'acas, he approached the Naga King Nila and begged of him to ordain that *Manavas* (*Manus*; Aryans) might henceforth inhabit Kas'mira without the fear of emigration. Nila complied with this request on the condition that the *Manavas* (*Manus* : Aryans) should follow his instructions revealed to him (Nila) by God Kesava (Shiva). Candradeva lived for six months in the palace of Nila and was initiated into the mysteries of rites or ceremonies prescribed by Nila. In Chaitra (March), when the emigrant population of Kas'mira (*Manus*: Aryans) came back, he related the whole incident to Virodaya - King of *Manavas* (*Manus*: Aryans)." The lengthy dialogue held between Nila and Candradeva, later narrated to Aryan King describes sixty-five rites, ceremonies and festivals many of which are similar to those mentioned in other *Puranic* works and observed in many parts of Bharatvarasha, while a few are peculiar to Kas'mira only. Nilamat Puranam, is one of the famous *Puranas* that deals with the Valley of Kas'mira in respect of its ancient history, evolution, the style of living of

Nagas and Manus, their religion, customs, festivals and topography, sacred rivers and lots more.

Veda Connection of Nilamat Puranam: The Nilamat Puranam is not Naga centric. Admittedly there are certain places, rivers and few Naga Kings who are to be venerated, but Nilamat is full of mention of various Gods and Goddesses, who manifested specifically in Bharatvarasha. Naga King Nila is equated with Indra, wherein Indra holds the prime position of God of Gods. Hymn (Nilamat Puranam) "O Nila, the Vedas have sung about you - the eternal one - as the essence of the Vedas, the object of worship in the fire, the fulfiller of the desires of those who seek salvation and those who are ambitious (of material gain)." He (Nila) is compared to God Indra (Protector) of the Aryans (Verse 369 Nilamat Puranam. Translated); "You are the refuge of the Nagas as Indra is of the gods. O pious one, know that I am full of devotion for you." This indicates that when *Manus* (Aryans) entered Kas'mira, Nila headed the Neolithic people. It also indicates the origin of the Nagas as the tribes of Northern India and that the Naga Kings where from the stock of original inhabitants of Bharatvarasha.

A close study of Nilamat Puranam will show that certain days/*tithis* have been specifically been mentioned for certain rituals. Use of Brahmincal calendar (Bright Moon and Dark Moon fortnight), which started in Bharatvarasha, also indicates this umbilical cord to pre Vedic era, Vedic period and Vedic Aryans.

Vitasta (River Wyeth, Jhelum), the main source of water of the valley is mentioned in detail, including its origin, role as goddess and equation with Yamuna, mentioned in the *mantras* of the Vedas and its degree of sacredness gets equated with Ganga and Yamuna.

Rituals of Nilamat Puranam: All indicators and contents make it apparent that Nilamat Puranam was written during the later Vaishnavite period (4–6th Century AD), when Vaishnavite philosophy had just re-started taking roots. Many of the rituals, amounting to religious customs, mentioned in the Puranam started with Naga inhabitants but after Vedas had been composed, these rituals and way of living firmed up and got modified as the Aryans settled down in Kas'mira, adopted Naga culture and created a conducive atmosphere with Nagas to make them incorporate and accept parts of their (Aryan) way of life, rituals and forms of worship. The Gods and Goddesses quoted in Nilamat are not from Vedas, but a new line which developed with the mixed civilisation of original inhabitants of Bharatvarasha and Aryans; somewhere around 500 - 400 BC. This is the period when major portion of the way of life, rituals and forms of worship, as mentioned in Nilamat manifested in Bharatvarasha as well as in Kas'mira. Many changes and additions in these crept in during later centuries (300 BC – 400 AD) and found their way in the written Nilamat Puranam, which by now represented compendium of way of life, rituals and forms of worship encompassing a broad band of 500 BC to 400 AD.

Religious Philosophy Contents: Concerning religious life Puranam shows not only the other cults adopting the Naga deities but also the Naga cult bringing the deities of other cults into its fold. *Bhava Mahadeva* and *Sambhu* which are names of Shiva; Guha and Kumara which are names of Shiva's son; Narayana and the four yuhas; Vasudeva, Sankarsana, Anirudha and Pradyumna; the epic heroes Rama, Lakshmana and Yudhisthira all appear in the Naga list of the Nilamat. On the whole the Nilamat reveals the spirit of compromise and synthesis in the field of religion. The Brahmanic deities, the Nagas, the *Pis'acas* and the Buddha, all receive their due share of worship from 'inhabitants of Kas'mira'. It would be going too far to suggest that it contains the tenets of the Monistic Shaiva philosophy of Kas'mira only. It is clear that the cult of Vishnu, Brahma, Shiva, Surya, Durga, Bhadrakali, Nagas, Buddha, etc. flourished side by side in the time of the Nilamat. Vaishnavism no doubt occupies a prominent place in this work but there is no indication of the creator of the creator; Brahma. Uma, the Goddess is the mother having antagonistic attitude towards other cults.

Gods and Goddesses of Nilamat: The theology of the Nilamat is replete with numerous Gods and Goddesses. The trinity of Brahma, Vishnu and Shiva play due role but there are others like Indra, Varuna, Yama, Kartikeya, Baladeva; Asvina, Visvedevas, Vasus, Yaksas, Nagas, Gandharvas, Prthivi, Surabhi, Sita, Saci (Sati – after whom the lake was named), Laksmi, Durga, Bhadrakali, Uma, Syama, Bharati, Prajna, Mati etc. The tendency of describing one deity as the highest among others at one time and transferring the same epithet to the other at another time is clearly perceptible in the praises of Brahma, Vishnu, Shiva, Nila and the Goddesses Bhadrakali, Uma and Laksmi. At some places, Vishnu is praised as the best amongst the gods; unfathomable, the highest, the eternal, the refuge of all gods, the lord of the gods, cause of the causes of the world, the lord of three worlds, worshipped by Shiva, praised by Brahma. Later the focus suddenly shifts to Shiva. In fact there is lot of mention of Shiva and his consort but few rituals connected with Shiv-Parvati *Pujan.*

Earliest Religion of Kas'mira

Aboriginal (Neolithic) Religious Beliefs: The earliest inhabitants of Kas'mira cherished some aboriginal beliefs, the details of which are not traceable now. The snake-cult or Naga-worship seems to have been established in the valley from a remote period and undoubtedly had been one of the earliest religions of the land. In the third century BC, Buddhism seems to have made some headway, converted a large number of people and overshadowed the Naga cult, which ultimately sunk into oblivion. Among

Hindu Gods, Shiva either originated or entered the valley sometime before Buddhism made its entrance around 3rd Century BC, followed by Vishnu, Surya and other Brahmincal gods and Goddesses from Bharatvarasha. A brief history of the different types of religious cults and beliefs of early Kas'mira, may be sketched as follows. Kas'mira was one of the principal centres of serpent-worship in India. Though detailed evidence is lacking, there is no doubt that snake-worship prevailed in the valley from a very early period; possibly from later Neolithic period and beginning of Megalithic period. Regarding the exact date when the snake-cult was prevalent in the land, no direct testimony is available. But there are reasons to believe that in the 6th and 5th Centuries BC, it might have been the principal religion of Kas'mira. In the *Mahavamsa*, it is said that Ashoka's adviser Moggaliputta Tissa sent Majjhantika, his disciple, to preach Buddhism in Kas'mira (3rd Century BC). When he reached the valley, he found that Aravala, the king of the Nagas, was ruling over it. Aravala was destroying the corns of the country by hailstorm. Majjhantika, however, due to his powers remained unaffected from rains and storms. This made the Naga king furious who sent lightning and struck rocks against the Buddhist monk in order to kill him; all in vain. Convinced of the great powers of Majjhantika, Naga king Aravala, together with his followers, submitted before the monk and accepted Buddhism. This was followed by the conversion of large number of Naga worshippers of Kas'mira and Gandhara (Northwest Frontier and Afghanistan) to Buddhism. Huen Tsang, who visited Kas'mira in 631 AD, also writes that Kas'mira was originally a 'dragon' lake. In his detailed and vivid account of how the *Arhat* (Buddhist Monk) Madhyantika (apparently Majjhantika) rescued the valley of Kas'mira from the Nagas, established the religion of Buddha and settled 500 *Arhats* in the country, has been preserved in the Chinese *Vinaya* of the *Mula-Sarvasti-Vadin* sect. The Tibetan scholar Buston, who composed his famous history of Buddhism in the 14th century AD, points out that; "when Madhyanti (Buddhist Monk Madhyantika apparently Majjhantika) went to Kas'mira to preach Buddhism, he found the Nagas 'presiding' in the valley. They at first gave a tough opposition to Madhyantika (Majjhantika), but at the end, the Buddhist monk succeeded in subduing the Nagas." That Naga-worship prevailed in early Kas'mira receives confirmation not only from the accounts of Ceylon, China and Tibet but also from literatures and scriptures found in Bharatvarasha. It may not be true that the entire inhabitants of Kas'mira then were Nagas only. Aryans had since moved in and had mixed well, culturally and socially, with Nagas. Any mention of merely Nagas, therefore, is construed as the mixed society of Nagas and Aryans. Motivated by the breadth of cultural ethos, the Aryans having come into contact with the aboriginal Naga worshippers were not ruthless in extirpating and decimating the contents and contours of their Naga faith. Instead they assimilated their (Naga) faith and modes of worship without resorting to religious persecution. It goes to the credit of Aryans that, as promised to Naga King Nila, they stood by their undertaking of adopting Naga way of life in Kas'mira.

Naga Worship Rituals: The Nagas were 'supposed', according to the Nilamat Puranam, to reside in and around lakes and springs of the valley. What is meant that the Naga settlements were closer to lakes and springs, the major source of water. With the draining of water from Satisar and formation of *Karewas* (*Uddars* in *Kas'miri*), the sources of perennial water had reduced to available lakes, small or big and springs. Naturally these springs also became the sites of veneration. Even now names of places like Verinag, Anantanag, etc; mostly in South Kas'mira, show traces of ancient Naga beliefs and '*Nag*' (Spring) fixed with their name. That the Nagas were eminently popular deities in the happy valley is also testified to by Kalhan's Chronicle Rajatarangini that Kas'mira was a 'land protected by Nila, the lord of all Nagas'. Verse 983 of Nilamat Puranam (Translated) says thus of Nagas; "All the Naga's are boon-givers, all are obedient to Nila and all are great favourites of the high-minded *Vasuki* (The serpent Deity)."

Even when Buddhism had undermined the Naga beliefs, one of its kings Gonanda III (3rd/4th Century AD?) is said to have reintroduced the pilgrimages, sacrifices and other worship in honour of the Nagas, as they had been earlier. Kalhan in Rajatarangini speaks of the annual festivals in honour of Naga Mahapadma, the tutelary serpent deity of the Wular lake and Great Serpent King Taksaka; 'Frequented by dances and strolling players and thronged by crowds of spectators' which was celebrated on the 12th day of the dark half of *Zyeshta*. Kshemendra (It is presumed that he was born during the period when King Ananta Raja (1028-1063 AD) ruled Kas'mira) also refers to this as '*Taksak Avatra*' festival in his *Samayamatrka* (*Samayamatrika*, ii, 88). Thus, the Naga-cult prevailed in the valley throughout the Hindu rule and even afterwards, somewhere upto 6th Century AD. It was not solely Naga Cult but mixed one, which by now had assimilated parts of Buddhist rituals and Aryan way of life. Abul Fazl, the chronicler during Moghul King Akbar's time, tells us that during the reign of Akbar (1556-1605 AD) there were 45 places dedicated to Shiva, 64 to Vishnu, 3 to Brahma and 22 to Durga, but there were 700 places in the valley where there were carved images of snakes in Kas'mira, which the inhabitants worshipped. Meat seems to have been a popular item of diet of that era, otherwise there would have been no necessity of 'strongly prohibiting' eating of meat for five days dedicated to the worship of Vishnu, as mentioned in one of the verses of Nilamat Puranam. Wine was also recommended as a drink on new snowfall day (*Iraman Jari Pujana*), which was a ritual in normal course with Aryans in the form of *Soma* Juice.

Even the Naga deity Nila is described as the lord of the Gods, the creator of the creator, illuminating Brahma. Uma is the mother of all Gods, higher than *Sarva*, and Laksmi is raised to the highest position by saying that all the Goddesses are her forms. The idea that the whole world is God or a manifestation of God is also present in the Nilamat. The whole earth is a form of the Goddess Sati. The earth, the water, the air, the sky, the fire, the sun, the moon, and the 'sacrificer', all these are regarded as eight forms of Shiva. Here we find that connection with Vedas is re-established. Aryans too venerated these elements and had elevated them to the pedestal of Aryan Gods and this includes the 'sacrificer', who forms the important element of Yajur Veda, containing sacrificial ceremony hymns.

Most of the rites prescribed by Nila are concerned with popular deities. There are some festivals, which are particularly connected with the worship of Naga or serpents. Nila was worshipped on the first snowfall. He and Nagas were 'propitiated' with drinking of wine on the *Iraman Jari Puja* (New Snow Fall Day; In Kas'miri *Navsheen*) festivity, which took place on first snow fall, generally during December. Another ceremony called *Varuna Panchami* was held on the fifth day of *Bhadra* and was connected with the worship of King Nila. A large number of temples, built near some of the famous springs and undoubtedly early origin of the pilgrimage centres, clearly point out the popularity of the Naga-cult in ancient Kas'mira. There is specific mention of Bhadrakali Puja in Nilamat Puranam (Verse 674, 675 Nilamat Puranam); which would have been included when **Bhadrakali Puja** had gained ground in Bharatvarasha; somewhere in 5th Century BC. It is, however, difficult to enumerate or deduce as to which Gods or Goddesses from the pantheon mentioned in Nilamat were exclusively worshiped either by Nagas or by Aryans. The list appears to be common, indicative of equal stress by both communities.

Religious Eras of Kas'mira

Eras: Aryan's laid foundation of Vedic Era, which laid initial foundation of a religion which was to develop in later centuries; Brahmanism, what is also now called Hinduism. Brahmanism did not come on its own but started in the later Vedic period or Brahmanic Period (1000 BC), with the amalgamation of Vedic and indigenous culture. During 800- 600 BC many religious codes were codified, composed and written later, new names of amalgamated Gods/ Goddesses firmed up and a distinct religion of Brahmanism took roots in Bharatvarasha. By 600 BC the *Triad* of Shiva, Vishnu and Brahma replaced Vedic Gods, with predominance of Vishnu as the supreme of Gods. With the passage of time priority within the triad, in Bharatvarasha, changed from one to another, Shiva also getting prominence. For Brahma, it was least, possibly due to his creation attributed from the naval of Vishnu, who at most of the times was also called the 'creator'. This era also percolated down to Kas'mira through immigrants; Aryans as well as Nagas. There are four different periods pertaining to variant eras of subsequent religion, in Kas'mira, which are important for purpose of this evaluation. First, when Aryan Saraswats settled in Kas'mira and Vaishnavite Brahmanism took shape mixed with Naga rituals; Second, advent of Buddhism; Third, Shaivism taking firm routes and finally changes that took place during the subsequent centuries.

Vaishnavite Brahmanism: The cult of Vishnu seems to have existed in Kas'mira from a very early period. Lack of material, suitable scriptures, however, prevents from tracing its origin and early character. Vaishnavite Brahmanism mixed and alongside with rituals of Nagas and not so strong Shaivite faith, formed the religion of mixed inhabitants of Kas'mira, till appearance of Emperor Ashoka along with 5000 Bhikshus (300 BC) to propagate Buddhism. In later centuries Vaishnavite faith, Buddhist and Shaivite thoughts co-existed with worshipping of Triad; Shiva, Vishnu and Brahma and their Consorts; Parvati or Uma (Consort of Shiva), Lakshmi (Consort of Vishnu) and Vagheswari or Saraswati (Consort of Brahma). Each manifestation of these Goddesses had a benedictory role; not mixed with roles of other Goddess Consorts. In the Vaishnavism of Kas'mira, we find a synthesis of different Vaishnava cults, which were current in ancient Bharatvarasha too. In it seems that the faith of Vedic Vishnu, the system of *Pancaratra* School, religion of the *Satvats* and faith in the cowherd god Gopala Krishna to have mingled. Rama was worshipped as an incarnation of Vishnu, but there is no definite evidence of the existence of Rama-cult in early Kas'mira. In *Mahabaharat*a a Kas'mira clan is named in and Nilamat Puranam, a Vaishnavite work, declares Kas'mira as the seat of *Cakradhara-Cakrin* (Vishnu).

Progress till 9th Century: Apart from Nilamat Puranam, which frequently mentions Vishnu and his worship, the other earliest historical reference to the worship of Vishnu occurs in the pages of the Rajatarangini, where it is said that an image of Vishnu, *'Jayasvamin'* was consecrated by King Pravarsena II (End of 6th Century AD). A flicker of renaissance of Brahmanism in Kas'mira started when Pravarsena II ruled the valley, an era of full revival of Brahmanism when the Buddhism had not fully waned. Pravarsena installed *Sri Chakra* at Chakreshwar, and established present city of Srinagar. Praversena ruled ably for 60 years and is supposed to have directly ascended to heaven while worshipping in his temple '*Pravesha*', now standing in ruins near Hari Parvat fort.

Once the Buddhism waned, it was the Karkota Dynasty (627 – 761 AD) founder, Durlabha Vardhana, who came from Kanoj, who brought fresh Vaishnavite philosophy to Kas'mira. The kings of the Karkota dynasty were followers of Vaishnavism and worshipped in general gods like Vishnu, Shiva and Surya; all belonging to the Hindu pantheon. Vishnu worship flourished further during the rule of Lalitaditya, a great devotee of Vishnu. At Huskapura (Uskar; Ushkar or Wushkur of Baramulla District) he built a splendid shrine of Vishnu *Muktasvamin* and made an offering of some villages to Vishnu (The name is a corruption of Huvishkapura, which, according to Kalhan, was the name of a city founded by Huvishka, Kushan king in the second century AD). In the town of Parihasapura (Close to Shadipur, the confluence of Lower Indus (Sindh) and Vitasta on the Karewas (*Udhars*) of Paraspore and Divar; situated at a distance of 23 kilometres from Srinagar on the Baramulla road), which the monarch constructed in honour of his adored deity, he built the glorious silver statue of Vishnu *Parihasakesava*. He also built four Vishnu temples and a Buddhist Vihara at other places. Kalhan gives their names as *Parihaskesava, Muktakesava, Mahavaraha, Govardhanadara* and *Raja Vihara*. His (Lalitaditya) queen Kamalavati also put up a large silver image of Vishnu in one of the temples built exclusively by her. Nonetheless, some of the monarchs of this dynasty (Karkota) also gave liberal patronage to Buddhism.

Some of the later Kings of Karkota and of Utpala dynasty (855- 939 AD) also adhered to the faith of Vishnu. Avanti Varman (855-883 AD), the first King from Utpala Dynasty is termed as the first Vaishnavite King of Kas'mira, who built the shrines of Vishnu *Avantisvamin*, even before he became a king. Lastly, Suya, the irrigation minister of Avanti Varman built Vishnu temple at the 'new' confluence of Sindhu and Vitasta (Shadipur-Prayag of Kas'mira) of *Hrsikesa Yogasayin*. The popularity of the cult of Vishnu in the valley during the 8th and 9th centuries is further attested to by a number of images discovered from various ancient ruins. These include Vijabror (Vijeshwara; Bijhbeara), three-faced Vishnu figures carved on the walls of the Martanda temple, relief sculptures of *Chaturbhuja* Vishnu and Vishnu seated from the ruins of Andarkot (Near Sumbal. At a distance of a mile from it is situated Andarkot, known originally by the name of Jayapura, the capital of King Jayapira) and four-headed Vishnu images of Avantipura and the surroundings. The development of Vaishnavism in Kas'mira, from the 10th Century onwards, continued at slower scale, which includes patronage and temple constructions by Queens Sugandha (904-906 AD) and Didda (958-980- as regent for Abhimanyu II and later as ruler 980 AD to 1003 AD) who founded a series of Vishnu shrines. The iconoclast King Harsha (1089-1101 AD) destroyed a large number of temples including famous *Parihasakesava,* but his successor Uccala (1101- 1111 AD) put up a new image. Amongst the later Hindu kings who professed Vaishnavism, historian Jonaraja (1389-1459 AD) mentions Rama Deva (1252-1273 AD) who renovated the Vishnu temple at Utpalapura and Udayan Deva (1321-1323 and 1326-41 AD) who gave all golden armaments in his treasury to Vishnu. Abul Fazl, the chronicler during Moghul King Akbar's time, tells us that during the reign of Akbar (1556-1605 AD) there were 64 major places dedicated to the worship of Vishnu, in Kas'mira.

Payar Temple

Minature Temple at Pattan

Spread of Buddhism: Buddhism made initial inroads in Bharatvarasha as well as Kas'mira, during the period 300 BC to about 200 AD. Buddhism started in Kas'mira from the time when Ashoka (273 – 232 BC) extended full control over Kas'mira, which continued till end of 100 AD with Kushan Dynasty (Kanishka, Huska, Juska, Abhimanyu, Vibhisana I, Indrajit, Ravana, Vibhisana II). In Kas'mira it can be said that it reached its peak during Kanishka's time. It did not 'materially' alter the religion of the inhabitants of Kas'mira. Verses 709-710a of Nilamat Puranam hold Buddha as the incarnation of Vishnu.

Accounts of Chinese travellers/scholars to this region, however, claim Buddhism had spread in Kas'mira just fifty years after Gautam Buddha (623–547 BC) i.e. around 500 BC. Chinese scholars believe that Madhyantika (Majjhantika) disciple of famous Buddhist scholar Anant was the first man to preach Buddhism in Kas'mira. (Anant, famous Buddhist scholar and a monk who lived in Ayodhya. It is after him the important fast of *Anant Chaturdeshi* (*Bhadra Shukla Paksh*- Full Moon Fortnight) is undertaken by women throughout Bharatvarasha and Kas'mira). When Anant visited his disciple in Kas'mira, spring where he meditated, was named after him; the present day Anantnag. This very Buddhist preacher, Madhyantika (Majjhantika), is supposed to have introduced the farming and cultivation of world famous saffron in the valley and not the Iranians, as we are made to believe.

Old Temple at Pandrethan- 2nd Century AD

Buddhism continued for a while in Kas'mira, till about 300 AD. One thing is noteworthy that the Buddhism in Kas'mira propelled a new wave of Buddhist Scholars of Kas'mira, who propagated Buddhism in far off places like Gandhara (Afghanistan), Tibet, China. It is said that because of Nagarjuna's tremendous scholarship and preaching, Kas'mira's traditional Naga cult of Naga's was almost wiped out, though it partially revived later. Buddhism in Kas'mira brought changes in composite culture of the Kas'mira inhabitants; Nagas and Aryans. Animal sacrifices became lesser and eating of meat was looked down upon. It is also believed that human sacrifices, which were still carried out by Nagas were stopped. In spite of this customs, traditions and form of worship did not radically change. Admittedly there were conversions to Buddhism, but few centuries later there were re-conversions. By this time composite religion of Aryans and Nagas had not materially changed and they willingly imbibed some good parameters of Buddhism. There are Kas'miri Buddhist missionaries such as Shakyashri Badhra (405 AD), Ratnavera, Shama Bhatta (5th Century AD) etc., who went to China and Tibet to preach Buddhism there in the later period, but this did not mean that Buddhism was flourishing in Kas'mira during their time. They appear to be continued followers of Buddhism or even trying to evade persecution of Buddhists during the 5th Century. The first organized crusade against Buddhists in Kas'mira was made by Raja 'Nara', who is said to have harassed and terrorised Buddhists to such an extent that famous Buddhist Scholar Nagarjuna had to run away from Kas'mira. Buddhism thereafter was on a downslide till about 515 AD, when Mihir Kula (515-550 AD), a Hun General also called terrorist king, ascended the throne. He devastated *Viharas, Chaityas* and *Mutts* and killed Buddhists ruthlessly. But even under such terrorism Buddhism in Kas'mira remained alive, in small pockets. In seventh-eight century AD Buddhism got official 'protection', during the time of Lalitaditya (724-761AD). A huge Buddhist monastery was built during his reign. He gifted 84,000 *tolas* (*Tola* is nearly 12 Grams) of gold for its construction, which was named as '*Raja Vihara*'. He served both Brahmins as well as Buddhists in Kas'mira. In fact the revival of Naga cult was the result of tremendous hard work by a Brahmin named 'Chandadeva' during this time (Chander Dev. Not to be misunderstood with Brahman Candradeva, who was instrumental in getting King Nila's permission to allow Aryans to settle down in Kas'mira throughout the year).

Buddhism on Wane: After this, Buddhism, because of its inherent weaknesses, started decaying morally, however, there was selective adhering to their customs/rituals by others in Kas'mira; Aryans, Nagas. Kalhan writes that Shankar Varman's (883–902 AD) wife Sugandha was nurtured in the Nishpalaka *Vihara*. But soon Kshema Gupta (950-958 A D), a Shaivite King, razed the *Jainendra Vihara* and with its stones he built a massive temple dedicated to lord Shiva (Acharya Abhinav Gupta (933–1015 AD), the famous Shaivite scholar and literary of Kas'mira was most important Shaivite scholars of this time). During the reign of Lohara dynasty (1003–1273 AD), there was brief attempt to revive Buddhism in Kas'mira. One can have ample references about this fact in the literary writings of Kshemendra and Somadeva. *Vaishakha Purnima,* the day Buddha was born or attained '*Bodhi*' and '*Mahanirvana*' used to be celebrated and Buddha's statues and *Chaityas-Stupas* used to be decorated with flowers and paintings. This tradition continued almost till eleventh century AD. Kshemendra (10 -11th Century AD) started writing of his famous treatise '*Avdhankalaplataon*' on the auspicious day of *Buddha Purnima* (Kshemendra's work on Buddha's philosophy *Budhavandana Kalpalata* written in 1052 AD is well known). Scholar Somdeva (1027 AD) brought out this fact (Quote); "*Samvatsare Saptavinshe Vaishikhasya Sitodaye Kriteyam Kalpalatiki Jinjanmotsave*" (Translation: This writing of treatise *Kalpalata* was started by the author on auspicious day of *Vaishakha Purnima*). By the time of King Harsha (1089-1101 AD) the Buddhism in Kas'mira had set and had come under the influence of Kas'miri *Shakatmata* and slowly was breathing last. There are well-chronicled descriptions of Buddhists monuments established in the valley from 300 BC onwards. Some of these Buddhist monuments, which are generally talked about are: Kanishka's city Kanishkapur known as Kanispur (Baramulla); 3rd Century Hushkapura (The name is a corruption of Huvishkapura a city founded by Huska (Huvishka), Kushan king in the 2nd Century AD; Harvan – Srinagar; Pandrethan near Srinagar. *Vihars*; Jalora *Vihara* (Zainageer; Sopore); *Stupas* in Malangpura (3 kilometres from Avantipur), Parihaspura, Anderkot (Anderkot; Near Manasbal Lake), Ahen (Sumbal) and Raithan.

Bodhisattva Discovered at Pandrethan (Puranadishtan)

Shiva Worship in Kas'mira: Though Nilamat Puranam is basically a Vaishnavite work, *Bhava Mahadeva* and *Sambhu* (names of Shiva and *Guha* and *Kumara* (names of Shiva's sons) find mention in the Puranam. Verse 184 of the Puranam (Translated) speaks thus; "See, O King, these are those peaks - Brahma, Vishnu, and Maheswar (Shiva): That which is Naubandhana peak is Shankara (Shiva)." It would be going too far to suggest that Puranam contains tenets of the Monistic Shaiva philosophy of Kas'mira. It is clear that the cult of Vishnu, Brahma, Shiva, Surya, Durga, Nagas, and Buddha, etc. flourished side by side during the time of the Nilamat. Shiva worship can be attributed to the later era of later Brahmanic Period (1000 BC), with the amalgamation of Vedic and indigenous culture. It came to Kas'mira around 500 BC, but could not overtake the worship of Vishnu, which had stronger following. Worship of Shiva, his abode thought and perceived to be in Himalayas/Kailash, took stronger roots in mountainous and hilly areas before spreading in Yamuna – Ganga Basin. In the course of its spread it had to compete with the emerging Buddhism. For next few centuries it was the Vaishnavite worship, which remained predominant. With waning of Buddhism and before arrival of Adi Shankara (May/June 788 – May/June 820 AD) there was a sort of resurgence of Shaivite Philosophy in Bharatvarasha. Once Adi Shankara was on the scene; with his teachings, constructions of *Mutts/Peeths* (Puri-Orissa), Srinegri (Tamil Nadu), Jyotirmath (Badrinath), Dwarka (Gujarat)) and Kamakothi Peeth, Shiva worship increased and started in Bharatvarasha and started spreading towards North including Kas'mira and Gandhara (Northwest Frontier and Afghanistan).

The Shaivite religious philosophy of later Kas'mira is rooted in Kas'miri Shaivism, a school that originated around 400 AD near *Kailash* in Himalayas. The first teacher of this school was Tryambak Aditya, a disciple of sage Durvasa. Around 800 AD Sangam Aditya, the sixteenth descendent in the line of Tryambak Aditya, settled in Kas'mira and started propagating Shaivism with earnest. Many centuries after Tryambak Aditya, Somananda (8th Century AD), fourth descendent of Sangam Aditya, extracted the principles of monistic Shaiva philosophy from the scriptures and incorporated them in his own work, *Shivadrishti*, which gives the origin and is first philosophical treatise on Kas'miri Shaivism. The other scholars were; Eraka Natha, Sumati Natha and Vasu Gupta. Around last part of 8th Century, Vasu Gupta found seventy-seven terse sutras etched on stone near Mahadev Peak, as revealed to him in a dream, which he named the Shiv *Sutras*. These teachers (Somananda, Eraka Natha, Sumati Natha and Vasu Gupta) established four different schools named; *Pratyabhijna* School, *Krama* School, *Kula* School and *Spanda* School respectively. Over the centuries and with the influence of different Shaivite scholars, certain other deviations and *agams* (Doctrines) took place and shape Shiva worship in Kas'mira which includes the combined worship of Shiva and his consort called Shakti. These, as discussed below, are;

Shakta Worship, Trika Shastra, Tantra Shastra. Aim is to give brief insight into these variations in Shavism of Kas'mira.

Shakta Worship: In *Shaiva Sidhanta* Shiva is All, and His divine energy, Shakti, is inseparable from Him. The religious practices of Aryan Saraswat Brahmins of Kas'mira (Popularly known as Bhatta or Kashmiri Pandits) revolved around the worship of Shiva and Shakti. All other deities (Gods and Goddesses) of the traditional Brahmanical pantheon were worshipped as various manifestations of Shiva and Shakti. Shakti is represented as female and Shiva as male. This depiction has its source in the folk-narrative sections of the Puranas, Shakti personified in many forms as the consorts of the Gods. Shakti is the Divine Mother of manifest creation, visualized as a female form and Shiva is specifically the unmanifest *'Absolute'*. The forms of the Goddess include, Durga, Bhadrakali, Uma, Gauri, Ambika, Parvati and Bhairavi. As *Rajarajeshwari* (divine queen of kings) she is the presiding Deity of *Sri Chakra Yantra*. She is also worshiped as *Mahavidyas*, manifestation of highest knowledge. Some Shakta's (followers of Shakti) view these as individual beings; most revere them as manifestations of the singular *Devi*. There are also numerous minor forms of Goddess, in the category of *Gram Devi* (Village Deity). Kas'mira, Shaivism was preceded by *Shaktism*, and if we say that Kas'mira is more the land of Shakti than Shiva, we are within our proper bounds; because even now wherever you go you find the shrines of *Devi* (Shakti)) spread over, worshipped and maintained more than the temples of Shiva. There are two broad forms of Shakta worship viz the *Shri Kul* and *Kali Kul*. *Kularnava Tantra* (Defining *Shri Kul* worship) is the authoritative *Agam* (Doctrine) for *Shri Kul* and the *Mahanirvana Tantra* for *Kali Kul* (Defining *Kali Kul* worship). It is well known that Abhinav Gupta and Sidha Natha (alias Shambu Natha) eulogized *'deities of Karmanya'* (Gods and Goddesses who shape destiny) mentioned in *Kularnava Tantra*. The practitioner and *Sadhaks* (Preachers) of this doctrine reach top of spiritual climb and becomes a *Kauli* or *Kaulas* or *Kaul*; an *Aghoreshwara* (Enlightened), who cuts off all *Karmic* bonds (Worldly duties); there is no death or rebirth; neither *Mangal* or *Amangal* (Good or bad); no pain or pleasure for him. In his mortal body he is Shiva and when he dies he remains on the *'astral plane'* and carries on his wishes from this plane through the medium of other persons. *Shastras* (Scriptures) are full of praise for *Kaulas* (Enlightened) and line of such *Kaulas* continued in Kas'mira, with few advanced *Sadhaks* (Preachers/Scholars) directing the *Karma* (Worldly duties), while people in general carried on general *Kulapuja* (Worship of *Kul Devi's* (Family Deities)). One of the Yoga systems popular and propounded in Kas'mira is also called *Kaula Yoga*; other being *Trika Yoga*. In the process of transition and refinement of Shaivism in Kas'mira, *Kali Bhakti* and *Shakta* worship followed, after initial burst of devotion, with admixture *Tantra*. Basically *Tantra* theology is 8-fold; "Right view,

Right aspiration, Right speech, Right behaviour, Right livelihood, Right effort, Right thought and Right contemplation." With advent of Islam *Sufi-Rishi* order also took roots making a strange combination of Shaivism, Tantra, Shakta Worship with admix of *Sufi-Rishi* cult. In the process of transition and refinement of Shaivism in Kas'mira, Kali/Bhadrakali Bhakti and Shakta worship followed, after initial burst of devotion, with admixture of Tantra. Once Shaivism took roots, Shakta and Kali/Bhadrakali worship (more so in her form of Bhadrakali), started upwards during the time of Abhinav Gupta, an ardent Shakta worshipper and Kali Bhakta. Bhairavas and Ganas are also divine companions and they are also worshipped with Shiva *or* Shakti on important festivals, such as Shivaratri. The shrines dedicated to Shakti in Kas'mira are Tripurasundari, Jwala, Shailaputri, Sharika, Sharda, Raghyna and Bhadrakali.

Abhinav Gupta's ancestor Atri Gupta, a scholarly Brahmin, was brought by Laltaditya (697 AD to 733 AD) to Kas'mira. One of the best authorities on Shaiva philosophy and various branches of Sanskrit literature e.g., rhetoric and poetic; Abhinav Gupta wrote some forty works, including *Tantraloka* (Light on Tantra) a comprehensive text on *Agamic Shaiva* Philosophy and rituals. Abhinav Gupta's literary period extended from 990-1015 AD. Some of his other works are; *Para - Trimshika Vivarna, Prataybhijna Vimarshini* (expurgated), *Pratyabhijna Vivriti Vimarshini* (full), *Tantrasara, Parmarthasara* and Commentary on *Bhagvadgita* called *Gitartha-Sangraha.*

Trika: The philosophy of Kas'miri Shaivism is generally called *Trika Shastra,* since it is a philosophy of the Triad: Shiva, Shakti, and *Nara* (the bound individual self). The literature of the *Trika* System of Kas'mira comprises of three categories; *Agama Shastra, Spanda Shastra,* and *Pratyabhijna Shastra.* This comparatively younger philosophy has tried to explain ambiguities which the ancient scholars have failed to resolve. Like *Advaita Vedanta* it is monistic, like Vaishnavism it is theistic, like *Yoga* it is practical, like *Nayaya* it is logical and appeasing like Buddhism. Kas'mira Shaivism is, therefore, idealistic and realistic in essence, strongly advocating a pragmatic approach to life. Thus, the *Trika* philosophy of Kas'mira Shaivism advocates how a human being, engrossed in the inferior objective energy of Shiva, can be taken upwards viz. towards the supreme energy through his cognitive energy. A galaxy of many scholars, such as Bhatta Kallata (9th Century), Utppal Deva ((10th Century) Also known as Utppal Acharaya) and Abhinav Gupta refined this philosophy. Abhinav Gupta wrote accounts of monistic Kas'mira Shaivism in his extraordinary work '*Tantraloka*'. He says that three *Siddhas* (masters of perfection) namely *'tryambak', 'aamardak'* and *'srinaatha'* came to this mortal world under the control of *'Srikanth Natha'*. These three *Siddhas,* who were proficient in the monistic, the dualistic and the monistic cum dualistic Shaiva philosophy respectively, established three separate schools of Shaivism, as discussed above. On this scriptural foundation arose the school known as Kas'mir Shaivism *Trikashasana* (*Trika* System).

Tantra: A further modification to Kas'mira Shaivism took place in the form of Tantra *Shastra*. Tantras are taken as to be revealed by Shiva through his five mouths namely *Ishana, Tatpurusha, Sadyojata, Vamadeva*, and *Aghora*. These very five mouths represent his five energies namely *Chit Shakti* (consciousness), *Ananda Shakti* (Bliss), *Ichha Shakti* (will) *Jnana Shakti* (knowledge) and *Kriya Shakti* (Action) respectively. When these aforesaid five energies of Shiva unite in such a way that each of these takes hold of the rest simultaneously, they reveal sixty four *Bhairava Tantras* which are purely monistic. This very approach explained in these *Tantras* is also part of *Trika* philosophy. *Veda, Shaiva, Vama, Dakshina, Kaula, Matta,* and *Trika* are the seven *Acharas* (systems) recognised by Kas'mira Shaivism. The most popular among the seven *Acharas* is the *Trika* system. *Trika* means trinity of *Nara,* Shakti and Shiva as is given in *Tantras*. *Nara* means an individual, *Shakti* means the Universal Energy and Shiva means the 'Transcendental Being'. Thus, a soul recognizes himself as Shiva by means of the realisation of his *Shakti* - the powers of God-head. *Trika* system advocates the practical path towards complete self-realisation of three energies of Shiva namely *Para, Parapara* and *Apara. Para* energy is subjective energy and regarded as the supreme. *Parapara* energy is cognitive energy and is called as intermediate. *Apara* energy is objective energy and it is known as inferior energy.

Patronage by Rulers During Later Centuries: Shankar Varman (883-902 AD), with famous scholars like Vasu Gupta during his time, gave impetus to their Shaivite Philosophy by constructing temples dedicated to Shiva. Perhaps it would be well to remark here that vandalism of a serious kind had already begun in pre-Muslim times, as some of the materials used in the construction of Brahmanic temples, built by Lalitaditya, were removed from his erstwhile capital site of Parihasapura. The three temples named by Rajatarangini constructed during Shankar Varman's time and dedicated to Shiva are; *Shankara Gaurishvara* (temple near Pattan, built by Shankar Varman), *Sugandhesa* (near Srinagar; named after Sugandha, his queen) and *Ratnavardhanesa* (Built by Ratnavardhana, his minister of which no credible trace has so far been found). During the reign of Akbar (1556-1605 AD) it has been recorded by his biographer Abul Fazl that there were 45 major places dedicated to the worship of Shiva, in Kas'mira. There are numerous important Shiva Shrines like *Amareshvara* (*Amaresvara* shrine of the same name i.e. present-day *Amburher* near Srinagar and not Amarnath), *Vardhamanesa* (Ganpatyar), *Vijayeshvara* (Vijebror), *Someshwara* (Somyar Mandir: Habba Kadal-Srinagar), *Harsheshvara* (Khonmoh), *Mahadeva*

(Harvan near Srinagar), *Bhuteshvara* (Naran Nag-Wangat Temples near Kangan), *Haramukheshvara* (The top of Harmukh Range, above Gangabal Lake; worshipped as abode of Shiva) and many more.

Transitions in Religious Worship

Priests and Rituals in Kas'mira: Not much can be construed as to the conduct of priestly duties in Kas'mira from earliest known period. During Naga era, it appears that cermonies like that of Pagans were conducted with no set rituals. Nagas had their own system of rituals, conducted under the aegis of group or clan head, who presided over these ceremonies; mostly action oriented with no *mantras* or scriptures on which these were based. These were primitive, staggered with no fixed dates, days or rituals There is some indication that places like Ashrams existed closer to places revered but not similar to those of Sarswati Ashrams. From study of Nilamat Puranam it is noticed that *Rishis* are mentioned but connected with immigrated Aryans. This does not mean that *Rishism* was Aryan centeric only. There are indications in the scripture to indicate *Rishis* of indigenous origin were even *Gotra* heads. Reference to Kashyapa, father of Nila, also indicates Nagas had their own *Rishis* or religious heads. It is difficult to assess the magnitude of their influence on the day to day life of Nagas. It is, however, evident that Naga Kings in their own right commanded more respect in that era. Like head of any family, Naga Kings or Chieftains presided over functions duly assisted by nominated Nagas, who could be described as Naga Priests. Around 600-700 BC Nagas had a parallel system with Aryans, that of Priests. Aryans after immigration had brought *varna* system along with them from Saraswati Ashrams and they had Aryan bards, called *Arthvan.* In fact, Nagas refined their system in accordance with that of Aryans, except their rituals were initially different. As the time elapsed there was hardly any difference between the two types of priests; of Nagas and *Manus* (Aryans). With the arrival of *Arthvan,* Naga rituals were now mixed with hymns and in the later Brahmanic period with *Mantras*. Around 5th Century BC Kashmiri King Gopaditya founded *agraharas* (jagirs) and built temples of Jyestheswara and Gopadiri (Shankaracharya); 'Having founded Jyestheswara on the Gopa Hill, the Brahmans born in the land of 'Aryans' were induced to accept Gopa *Agraharas* (jagirs) by that pious King (Verse 341 Book I Rajataragini)'. This King is given date of 417-357 BC. It is around this time and thereafter, when Buddhism had just manifested, that Brahmins or priests were given separate means of their living; income from *Agraharas* (Jagirs) so that they could concentrate only on priestly duties. Similar set ups took shape in subsequent centuries.

Sakayas of Buddhism: With spread of Buddhism in Kas'mira, place of Naga/Aryan priests were taken over by Sakayas (Buddhist Monks). In fact majority of these were convertee priests of Nagas/Aryans, who converted their *agraharas* for the spread of Buddhism. The rituals and *mantras* underwent change, more so sacrifical rituals, which were deleted or abandoned. They (Sakayas) had imported many rituals from Bharatvarasha. Since Buddhist religion had started few centuries earlier, the rituals and *mantras* were under development. The system of Aryans/Nagas of priestly worship at *Gram*, *Kul* and *Sthaney* (Local) level took back stage, as Buddhist worship was restricted and took place only in *Viharas* or within the confines of home. Their worship rituals started taking shape in Kas'mira during First Century BC/AD, more so during the reign of King Kanishka, when the fourth Buddhist Council took place. By this time Buddhist scholars had manifested and they took the role of monks, both at *Viharas* as well as to take newly manifested religion to far off places. By and large the methodology of functioning was different; demonstrative by Naga/Aryan priests, subtle by Buddhist Sakayas. With the spread of Buddhism priests who did not convert to Buddhism either lost their importance or had reduced utility. With this phase decline of Naga/Aryan priests, moral as well as spiritual, took place and reached lowest level. With Buddhist scholar Nagarjuna's tremendous scholarship and preaching, Kas'mira's traditional Naga cult of Nagas was almost wiped out and there was general degradation of Naga and Aryan Priests. These Priests with forced circumstances, decline in clientele, adopted shameless methods, which even forced Gopaditya (6th Century) to expel them and bring in Brahmins from outside. Even the *agraharas* had been converted for their personal use of comfort and even debauchery. Things started looking up after the Buddhism started effectively waning in 6th Century and the rule of King Pravarsena II (End of 6th Century AD). From this period the Brahmins started to exercise clout in the administration and conduct of Kings; not without bias towards their own betterment.

Role of *Agraharas*, *Sadaks* (Preachers): Around 800 AD Sangam Aditya, Shaivite Scholar gave a new dimension to the priestly cult in Kas'miris his scholarly work for the rituals to take shape. This was followed by Vasu Gupta, Somananda, Eraka Natha, Sumati Natha at the end of the 8th Century. Between the reigns of King Pravarsena and Lalitaditya many temples were constructed together with *agraharas* (*Jagirs*) to finance their activities and provide living to the Priestly class looking after these. They like the priests of Tulla Mulya *Agrahara* became a force to reckon with. During the reign of Jayapira (764-95 AD), cursed by these priests for levying taxes for the construction of new capital at Anderkot called Jayapura and coincidently Jayapira died due to an accident, immediately after the curse. This incident had some effect on the psyche of the ruler Kings, who now on gave considerable importance to the priestly class. Avanti Varman (Utpal Dynasty; 855-June 883 AD) famous for construction of Avantipura temples and Martand and his successor Shankar Varman (883-902 AD) rule and his wife's benevolence saw their stock rise. In fact majority of these Priests got involved in intrigue and there was little or no contribution from their side in the development of religion. In the meantime different types of religious preachers were taking shape. Abhinav Gupta (940-1015 AD), Sidha Natha (alias Shambu Natha; 11th Century) and scores came up as religious scholars known as *Sadaks*. They became the highest rung of the religious hierarchy, giving new dimensions to the religion in Kas'mira; Shiva-Shakti of Shakta worship. These scholars wrote religious scriptures, laid down fresh set of rituals and worship parameters. They were revered by all; priests as well as common man. The priestly flock now restricted themselves to the temples, festivals and rituals of common man. Thus, three sets of Aryan Saraswat Brahmins emerged during this period; *Sadaks*, Priests and common man. With the passing phase of scholars, priests roles got restricted, while common man restricted himself to the simplistic normal daily *Puja* of deities.

Intrigue by Priests: Kas'mir Shaivism, reached its peak in 10th to 11th Century AD and continued to be so till the next century (12th Century). During the reign of Gopa Deva (1171 to 1180 A D) priests gained a great deal of supremacy, but were thwarted by the *Lavanyas* who sided with the king. During the reign of Ram Dev (1252-1273 AD) some of them who had helped in his investiture as king, having been insulted by him, conspired to install somebody from amongst *Khasas* on the throne of Kas'mira. But their conspiracy did not long remain a secret and an orgy of destruction and plunder was let loose upon them. This was the turning point of the forms of worship of common man in Kas'mira. With the passing phase of scholars, common man slowly moved away from the *Sadhak* (Preacher) type of worship, away from intrigues of priests and restricted himself to the normal daily *Puja* of the deities. This is the time worship of local deities in the form of Shaktis named as *Kul Devis*; mostly on geographical locations, took roots. This was the time (12th /13th Century) various *Stotras* (*Shlokas* in praise of deity) and *Bhavani Sahasranama* (Thousand Names of the Goddess, Bhavani) were composed.

Bhasha Bhatta or Bhacha Bhatta: The role of priests during Muslim rule was negligible; due to dwindling numbers of Brahmins and atrocities by Muslim rulers. However, during the reign of Zain-ul-Abidin (Shahi Khan) (1420 -1470 AD) many religious and devotional scriptures and philosophies of 10th to 14th Century AD were retrieved, rewritten and few translated into Persian. This was mostly done by limited number of *Sadaks* and Priests. After death of Zain-ul-Abidin, with indifferent short rule of a year of Haider Shah followed by his son Hassan Khan (1475-1487 AD) environment was not conducive to continue with the efforts at the level of what was done during Zain-ul-Abidin's rule. In 15th and 16th Century when Islam continued to make sizeable inroads into the community, essential measures were taken to preserve their entity and religion to the extent they could. At this stage there were hardly any Priestly class; either they had been first target for conversion or killed or many had migrated to Bharatvarasha. They separated spiritual and temporal seats and were divided into two sub-castes, the *Karkuns* (Derived from word *Karinda* (Persian- literally meaning white collar workers who studied Persian and entered Government service) and the *Bhasha Bhatta* or *Bhacha Bhatta* (Those who studied *Bhasha*- Religious Language i.e., Sanskrit/Sharda) who took charge of the religious affairs of the community. Daughter's son was made to study *Bhasha* (*Language/ scriptures*) to administer religious needs of his maternal family. Since grandchildren were very young to learn *Bhasha*, they were called *Bhacha* (Kids) thus *Bhacha Bhatta*. Some of these Gurujis combined their religious responsibility with development of scriptures, astronomy and teaching of Sharda language. Some took to exclusive duties of religious worship and rituals in Temples. Yet some, after achieving mastery over their religious knowledge, turned into *Sadak* type of role; saintly and revered Brahmins. Many eminent Gurujis were gainfully utilised by the state to trace old religious manuscripts, scriptures and translate them into Sanskrit or in Sharda. Many of these also found their employment in Schools and Research and Translation Department, exclusively established for religious functions and preservance of scriptures by Dogra Rulers, more so by Maharaja Ranbir Singh.

7

Goddess Bhadrakali Worship

> They are forever free who renounce all selfish desires and break away from the ego cage of I, me and mine-in order to be united with God. Attain to this, and pass from death to immorality.
>
> *Bhagavad Gita 2.71*

Goddesses as Devi, Durga and Bhadrakali

Manifestation of Goddesses in Bharatvarasha and Kas'mira: The Great Goddess, known as *Devi* (Goddess), has many guises. She is '*Ma*' (Mother); the gentle and approachable mother. As *Jagatmata*, or Mother of the Universe, She assumes cosmic proportions, destroying evil and addressing herself to the creation and dissolution of the world. *Devi* is all-important in the Brahmanic tradition and all Goddesses are different manifestations of *Devi*. Today millions of Brahmans; men and women, conduct regular *pujas* of *Devi* through one of her many forms. For some **She** is their primary deity, for others **She** is part of a greater pantheon. The most talked Goddess in Kas'mira was Uma; a form of *Devi*. The very land of Kas'mira was mother Goddess Kas'mira, a form of Uma; mother antagonistic attitude towards other cults. The other Goddesses revered were; Sita, Saci, Lakshmi, Bhadrakali, Durga. In Kas'mira the tendency of describing one deity as the highest among others, at one time or the other, and transferring the same epithet to the other at another time, was clearly perceptible in the praises of Brahma, Vishnu, Shiva, Nila and Goddesses Uma, Lakshmi, Bhadrakali and Durga. Lakshmi was also raised to the high position by saying that all the Goddesses are **Her** forms. The earth too was a form of goddess Sati. Earth, Water, Air, Sky, Fire, Sun, and Moon were regarded as forms of Shiva; while Shiva's consort Parvati was also called *Shakti*; power or strength (*Shakti*) of Shiva.

Goddess Durga: Durga, in fact, is the goddess widely worshipped in Bharatvarasha, in various ways and under various names. Durga name does not figure in any of the Vedas. Goddess Durga has nine important forms including **Bhadrakali** (Also named *Siddhidhatri*). Each has a different form; two to ten hands, two or three eyes, lotus to rosary or trident or pitcher or weapon in hand, riding bull or tiger and black, marble white or black complexion. During the *Navaratri* festival (October), each of these Goddesses is to be worshipped on a particular night for the destruction of evil and for the preservation of *Dharma* (Religion). In the form of Chamundi, Durga killed two demons; Chanda and Munda. The narration of the killing of these two demons is typical of a warrior's assault, associating her from time immemorial with warrior class. In Nilamat Puranam her worship is mentioned on three days. First on 15th of the Bright Half of Chaitra (Chaitra Puranmashi- Full Moon–March), when Durga and other Gods and Goddesses are to be worshipped; 'when Nikumba goes for fighting the Pisacas (Verses: 683,702 Nilamat Puranam)'. Second on 14th day of the *Pitra Paksh* (Asuj – September/ October), prescribed for *shraddha* of those who were killed by means of weapons (Verse 761a Nilamat Puranam). Third on Durga Ashtami (8th of the Bright Half of Kartik- October) (Verse 819-20a Translated); "O twice-born, the books should be worshipped in the temple of Durga and the artisans should also worship their tools." In addition specific worship of Durga is in Verse 767-69; 'the weapons should be worshipped at night in the temple of Durga'; apart from mentioning worship by artisans, astronomers and stage performers in these verses. On all these days, rituals and events, weapons, warriors and the artisans are the focus of her worship. From Nilamat Puranam and other scriptures it is evident that in the initial period of the settlement of Aryan Saraswat Brahmins in Kas'mira, the pantheon of Goddesses did not include Durga. The increasing worship of Durga in Bharatvarasha, as well as Kas'mira, is attributed to the fact that most of the ruling Kings came from warrior class and worshipped Durga as their Mother Goddess; invocation of whom before setting out for a campaign was a must. Not many temples of Durga, in particular, were constructed or exist, yet basic form of other Goddesses was assumed that of Durga. Even in *Shakta* and *Tantric* worship, Durga finds prominent place in her own or other forms. Goddess Durga thus became 'somewhat' Mother Goddess, mentioned many times, not displayed in physical terms, yet giving direct space for the worship of other Goddesses, in their own and separate form.

Goddess Bhadrakali: Worship of Bhadrakali is indigenous to Bharatvarasha, with obscure place of origin. Its manifestation can be attributed to the areas closer to Himalayas during the Later Vedic Period, also called **Brahmanic Period** (Around 1000 BC). This is the time Aryans migrated across the Doab; large plain that separates the Yamuna River from the Ganges, including Kas'mira, where they came into contact with the indigenous inhabitants in these areas. Goddess Bhadrakali or for that matter other Gods and Goddesse's of present day Brahmanism have not been mentioned in

Vedas except Visnu (Vishnu) and that too in a different form than perceived in present incarnation. None of the Goddesses of the later Brahmanic pantheon are talked about in Rig Veda. This Brahmanic period passed smoothly and was flourishing by 700 to 600 BC. At this time two more forms of Goddesses manifested; Durga and Bhadrakali; more or less simultaneously. It is difficult to pin point the areas where their worship started first. Artisans and warriors were required to worship their tools and weapons in the temples of Durga; connoting that Durga manifested for certain class; warriors and artisans. This is also reinforced by the fact that Aryans had since established their class system of four groups: *Brahmin* (Priests; *Arthvan*), *Kshatriya* (Warriors; *Ratheshwar* (Charioteer), *Vaishya* (traders and agriculturists and their workers and herders; *Vastrayosh*), and *Shudra* (Workers, camp followers; *Hatoksha*). Thus, deities for specific class like *Kshatriyas* took separate shape. These Goddesses, Durga and Bhadrakali, held fort for a considerable time, adopted equally by original inhabitants of Bharatvarasha and Aryans and accompanied Aryans wherever they migrated to, including Kas'mira. The manifestation and acceptance of these Goddesses is mentioned in Brahman Purana. By the time of Buddha (May 623-547 BC), Bhadrakali and Durga worship had taken strong roots. Even when Buddhism flourished, the worship of these Goddesses did not diminish, as they represented the benign form of the pantheon, not against the teaching of Buddha. One good thing in Buddhism, during its initial stages, was that it had Buddha's teachings complimenting then existing religious beliefs, except those of sacrifices. Admittedly the followers of these Goddesses, during Buddhist period, could not increase as the Buddhist *Sakyas* (Preachers) added further *agams* (Doctrines, Philosophy) to their teachings, which considerably increased during the 100 AD.

Goddess Bhadrakali is also mentioned in *Devi Mahatmaya* and another account of the origins of Bhadrakali is found in the *Matsaya Purana*, which states that She manifested in the North-Central part of Bharatvarasha, in the region of Mount Kalanjara (now known as Kalinjar). Bhadrakali, is an auspicious form of *Devi* and the legend states that She came into being by *Devi's* wrath, when Daksha insulted Shiva and assimilated into the mainstream Brahmanism, particularly into Shaiva mythology of Shiva. She (Bhadrakali) is the consort of Virabhadra. In the central regions of Kerala lie hundreds of temples dedicated to Bhadrakali called *Bhadrakalikavus.* Rituals, bordering on art performances and other artistic manifestations of worship have, for centuries, been performed here to appease Bhadrakali. Bhadrakali worship is also predominant in the hilly tracts and plains closer to the Himalayas (Himachal Pradesh, Garhwal, and Kumaon), many places in South Tamil Nadu, parts of Karnataka and Andhra, Central India, Gujarat and Nepal. In Kas'mira Bhadrakali and Durga worship came simultaneously, as in

Bharatvarasha. People mistake Bhadrakali and Kali being same form, which is erroneous. They are two different manifestations of the *Devi*; Bhadrakali being ante Kali; the roles also being different.

Bhadrakali Worship in Kas'mira: Apart from Uma and various rivers of Kas'mira, Vitasta (Wyeth, Jhelum) in particular, Goddess Bhadrakali finds mention in Nilamat Puranam and days fixed for her specific worship. As the legend goes, when the Aryans migrated to Kas'mira, they were allowed by Naga King Nila to remain in the valley, initially for six months and this process continued for a long long time. Naga King Nila then narrates a list of practices to be followed by the Aryans while in Kas'mira, which included Bhadrakali worship. This is best explained in Verse 607 of Nilamat Puranam (Translated); "Rddhi, Vrddhi, Nidra, Dhanesa and Nadakubara (should be worshipped). The treasures *Sankha* and *Padma* should be worshipped and so also Bhadrakali and Saraswati." The reference is unambiguous and refers to Goddess Bhadrakali and Saraswati (Consort of Brahma). This verse also connotes that Bhadrakali had manifested amongst the original inhabitants of Kas'mira and was required to be adhered to by immigrant Aryans and equated with Saraswati; latter having been adopted from Aryans. It also implies that Brahmanic rituals and worship, in initial form, had already manifested amongst the Nagas and Aryans more or less at the same time.

Bhadrakali Worship Days: Nilamat Puranam specifically mentions Bhadrakali worship on certain specific days of the year. Firstly worship during *Chaitra Shukla Paksh* (Bright Half of the Moon-March) Verses 674 and 675 thus (Translated); "On that very 9th (*Chaitra Navami*), the purified man, observing fast, should worship Bhadrakali with plenty of flowers, incense and grains. Bhadrakali who rules over the gods, should be worshipped on all the 9 days, (but) he who worships her on that (9th), obtains success in his undertakings." The importance of these days for the *Puja* of the deity is significant. Kashmiri *Navreh* (New Year) on the first day of the bright half of *Chaitra* has to start with worship of Bhadrakali, to be continued on all nine days. Flowers, incense and grains are to be used for the worship, which implies all the ingredients of the faith and living; flowers denoting devotion, incense purifying *Yavu* (Air) and grains depict gratefulness for providing means of living. If the contents of *Thal* (Plate) kept by Kashmiris for *Navreh* are analysed; it has flower and grain (Rice) associated with the worship of Bhadrakali. This degree of veneration (Bhadrakali who rules over the gods) gave her place next to Goddess Uma in the Kas'mira pantheon. Secondly, it calls for similar worship ritual during *Asuj Navratras* (October-Dussehra) on 8th day. Verse 816-19a of the Nilamat speaks thus (Translated); "Then, on the 8th (Asuj), the artisans, having undergone fast, should worship Bhadrakali in proper manner, with valuable incenses, garlands, clothes, lamps, jewels, eatables, fruits, herb-roots, meat and various sorts of vegetables, and by gratifying the fire and the Brahmanas. (Bhadrakali should be worshipped) also with leaves of Bilva, Sandalwood, purified butter, drinks of various types and grains and by decoration of the earth, dancing and singing and the observation of vigil at night." The sacrificial ritual, so different from partaking meat, is absent in Bhadrakali worship in Kas'mira, though meat could be offered. There is an erroneous impression that meat eating was forbidden in Nilamat Puranam; it is not true, as many rituals are connected with meat eating and drinking wine (Also read verse above). Eating meat, fish, drinking wine (in the form of *Soma*, brew mentioned in Vedas) has been part of rituals of Aryans and original inhabitants of both Kas'mira as well as Bharatvarasha. Another impression that Buddhists did not or do not take meat is also erroneous. Buddhists abhor killings but take meat and other non-vegetarian items including wine. It was and is more common amongst the Buddhists living in hilly and mountainous areas. No wonder Bhadrakali worship continued during the Buddhist period in Kas'mira. Had it been otherwise including sacrifices, the worship of Bhadrakali would have stopped or been on a downward trend during and after Buddhist period (300 BC to about 200 AD). In fact, none of the religious rituals of Aryan Saraswat Brahmins, even today, calls for sacrifices of animals, which is a practice for Bhadrakali Worship in Nepal and most of our hilly areas of Himachal and Uttaraanchal. Meat was and can, however, be offered to deities in Kas'mira and religious worships like *Herath* (Shivratri), birthdays and many other festivals. Centuries back meat was even offered at Tulla Mulya (Tul Mul) (Kheer Bhawani).

This day in Chaitra (March-*Navreh*) apart from Kas'mira is also celebrated as New Year in most parts of the Bharatvarasha as Brahmanic New Year, under various names. In Nepal it is also New Year and throughout these nine days Bhairav and Bhadrakali's chariots are pulled to celebrate the festival. First nine days of Bright Half of *Chaitra* (March-*Navreh*) and *Asuj* (October-Dussehra) are also associated with *Nav Durga* and each day dedicated to a particular form of the Goddess; like *Shailaputri, Brahmakumari (Brahmaputri), Chandraghanta, Kushmanda, Skandamata, Katyayani, Kalaratri, Mahagauri* and **Bhadrakali** (Also named *Siddhidhatri*); in ascending order. In Kas'mira except for *Shailputri* worship at *Devi Bal* temple at Varhamulla (Baramulla), on the ninth day, no separate worship of these Goddesses is carried out now. Actually *Shailputri* Worship is to be carried out on first day but with the passage of time *Shailputri* took place as one of the regional *Kul Devis* and her specific worship in the areas around Varhamulla (Baramulla) was carried out on ninth day. In certain parts of the Bharatvarasha nine different forms, other than mentioned above, with different aspects of *Nav Durga* are worshipped over these nine days. These are: **Durga**: goddess beyond reach; **Bhadrakali** the auspicious power of time; **Amba** or Jagdamba: mother of the world; **Annapurna**: giver of food and plenty; **Sarvamangala**: auspicious goddess; **Bhairavi**: terrible, fearful, power of death; Chandika or Chandi: violent, wrathful, furious; **Lalita**: playful; and **Bhavani**: giver of existence. Aryan Saraswat Brahmins of Kas'mira specifically celebrate Jyeshta Ekadashi as Bhadrakali Ekadashi (Eleventh of the Dark Half of the month of Jyeshta); her birthday. This amply points out Universal as well as Goddess Bhadrakali's role and specific role for Goddess Durga in Kas'mira.

Kali (Maha Kali) Worship in Kas'mira: Kali is first described in *Devi Mahatmaya* written around 600 AD, where she is said to have emanated from the brow of the Goddess Durga (Slayer of Demons during one of the battles between the divine and anti-divine forces). In this context, Kali is considered the 'forceful' form of the Goddess Durga. Other Goddesses with less 'forceful' form, such as Parvati, Sita and Sati, are also said to emanate Kali, or even become her, to defeat enemies. These enemies are sometimes only susceptible to female assault, making the intervention of the male consort impossible. In some cases, the Kali is even able to destroy a far greater enemy than her consort, as when Sita becomes Kali to defeat Ravana. As her consort Rama is usually the warrior, but in this case freezes in fear, taken as a sign of great potential power of women, when their Shakti is not controlled by and gifted to a male consort. Another account of the origins of Kali; she originated as a mountain tribal goddess in the North-Central part of Bharatvarasha. Kali is known as Kali-Ma, the Black Goddess, Maha Kali, Nitya Kali, Smashana Kali, Raksha Kali, Shyama Kali, Kalikamata and Kalaratri. Maha Kali and Nitya Kali are mentioned in the Tantra philosophy. 'Kal' means Darkness; Kali takes away that Darkness. She takes away the darkness from every individual, who strives in the path of perfection by performing the spiritual disciplines of purifying austerities. The Vedas (which were written much before the Puranas), however, associate the name Kali with the most horrifying, black tongue of the seven flickering tongues of Agni, the god of fire.

Upto 600 Century AD there was no Kali worship in Kas'mira. With the advent of Shakta Worship and *tantric* nature of Shaivism taking roots from 8th Century onwards, Kali worship also took roots. At that time there was a distinct separation of Kali worship from other Goddesses, which slowly startrd getting mixed with Durga, Bhadrakali and even other Goddesses. Nilamat Puranam does not mention Goddess Kali or her worship. In fact, Verse 657-59 calls '*Mahasanti* as the destroyer of bad dreams of Kali' and in one verse (975) Kali is mentioned as a Naga Chief.

Aryan Saraswat Brahmins of Kas'mira celebrate her day (Mahakali Jayanti) on Pausa Krishna Paksh Navmi (Ninth day of dark moon in December/ January). Worship of Kali took more roots in Kas'mira from 9th Century onwards with Her worshipers like Shaivite philosophers Somananda, Abhinav

Gupta and Jayaratha. *Panchastavi*, a popular scripture, does mention Goddess Kali. There were few temples dedicated to Kali or Mahakali in Kas'mira. In recent times there were only two major Mahakali Temples in Kas'mira; Srinagar and Vadora. The former called as *Kalishri* temple, associated with Abhinav Gupta before he left the city, on persuasion by his disciple, to move to North Kas'mira for his *tapasya* (Meditation). *Kalishri* (Kali) temple was demolished and converted into an Estrada (Platform) on which Mir Ali Hamdani or Shah-e-Hamdan recited *Quran* and offered *namaz* five times a day in last quarter of 14th Century and where a *Masjid* (*Khanqah-e-Maula*) now stands. Without going into details the priest of the *Kalishri* temple got converted to Islam and was called Shyk Baba Wuli (Sheikh Baba Wali). The idol is reported to have been immersed in the deep spring, which remains covered even today and even cleaners of the area around it are blindfolded so as not to allow them to have a peep by mistake. As a young boy I slipped in Shah-e-Hamdan Mosque and saw, from a distance, enclosure covering the *kund* in the centre of the mosque. I believe this *kund* was venerated before Shah-e-Hamdan mosque came up. The water of this spring finds outlet on the bank of Vitasta (Jhelum), where a make shift temple of Kali has been made on the banks of Vitasta.

Kali worship was a must for Tantra puja, so much so even other *Kul Devis*, erroneously though, were presumed as forms of Kali by Tantra *Sadhaks* (Preachers). The reason was that Kali is manifested form of Durga and Durga's role in Kas'mira was mixed or combined with other Goddesses. With the advent of *Kul Devi* worship in Kas'mira from 12th Century, common people not going in for pure *tantric* worship, restricted Kali worship in the form of Maha Kali on some specific special days and seldom associated Kali worship with *Kul Devi's* worship. However, Kali was invoked during the ninth day of *Navratras*; possibly ritual imported from Bharatvarasha in later centuries.

Kul Devis: Plethora of forms of Gods and Goddesses were object of veneration in Kas'mira. Mostly they were geographically located near combined habitation areas (Villages). The spectrum of deities till about 8th Century became mixed; that of Nagas, Buddhists, Vaishnavite and Shaivism. Around 8th Century Somananda (8th Century AD) extracted the principles of monistic Shaiva philosophy and by the end of 9th Century, plethora of religious scholars had come to Kas'mira and the place became centre of religious learning for Bharatvarasha, mainly Monistic Shaivism. They also brought the concept of specific Shaivite *Pujan* with them, which initially did not find favour with common man. The *Sadhana* mentioned in the Tantra (*Malinivijayottara* Tantra, which lays down the *Trika Sadhana)* was different from worship by common man. With Kas'mira Shaivism reaching its peak during 11th – 12th Century AD, there had to be someone to carry out the

Karma (Day to day work) as common man found it difficult to adjust in the maze of religious doctrines (*Agams*). The common man slowly moved away from *Sadhak* (Preacher) type of worship and restricted himself to the simplistic normal daily *Shakta Puja* of the deities. This is the time worship of local deities in the form of Shaktis took strong roots; named as *Kul Devi's* (Deity of the clan), mostly on clan (*Gotra*), geographical locations, nearer to cluster of habitation and a new set of deities; *Kul Devis.*

Bhadrakali as Kul Devi: The worship of Bhadrakali in Kas'mira was neither sudden nor out of nowhere. The evolution of Bhadrakali worship in Kas'mira is nearly as old as the entry of Aryan Saraswat Brahmins in Kas'mira. Though Nilamat Puranam calls Uma higher than *Sarva* and the mother of all gods, Laksmi is raised to the highest position by saying that all the Goddesses are her forms. However, next to worship of Uma, Bhadrakali Worship gets prominence.

Again in *Asuj Ashtami* Verse 816-19a of the Nilamat Puranam speaks thus; "should worship Bhadrakali in proper manner" ; "(Bhadrakali should be worshipped) also with leaves of Bilva." No other Goddesse's worship has been described so elaborately, which also indicates that almost every family (Purified Man) would be having in-house Bhadrakali idol/image and many temples of Bhadrakali existed at that time. Analysis of the two sets of worship ritual of Bhadrakali in Chaitra (March) and Asuj (October) clearly indicates that apart from Uma, Bhadrakali took the role of principal deity of Nagas as well as Aryans. She was the *Kul Devi* of Kas'mira inhabitants. Bhadrakali was the benign and universal form of *Devi* in Kas'mira upto 7th Century AD, somewhat different from the role Goddess had gained in Bharatvarasha. The worship was all along the valley and not restricted to any particular pocket during this period. It is with the installation of *Sri Chakra* by King Pravarsena in 6th Century AD that *tantric* or *Shakti* tinge to the Goddesses was being given and certain other forms of Goddesses manifested, Kali being one of them. In the next few centuries' *Tantric* worship took roots in Kas'mira. Acharaya Abhinav Gupta was an ardent Bhadrakali devotee. He and other Shaivite scholars of that time also eulogised Kali, which had a specific role in the Tantra *Shastra*. With plethora of *Tantric* and Shakta philosophy coming during this time the common man assumed Bhadrakali and Kali being the same goddess. With the evolution of *Kul Devi* worship concept, the role of Bhadrakali, erroneously got mixed with that of Kali, diminished and many of her temples converted to the newly manifested Goddesses/*Kul Devis*. However, Bhadrakali worship remained strong in North Kas'mira, where majority of Aryan Saraswat Brahmins worshipped her as *Kul Devi*. This belt mainly consisted of areas around Handwara, Kupwara etc and continued to be so till the 20th Century. Areas of Baramulla (Varahamulla) ardent worshippers of Bhadrakali converted to

Shailputri worship, when her temple was established. Similarly areas of Sopore (Suyapur, Sopur) also fell of the Bhadrakali worship map, when Bhairava worship took roots and they had the *Nandkishwar Bhairav* of Seer Jagir as their deity.

Goddess Bhadrakali's Abodes in Kas'mira

Upto 12th Century AD*:* Bhadrakali worship, being one of the main points in Nilamat Puranam, continued extensively till about 2nd Century AD when it was disturbed by the advent of King Nagarjuna on the Kas'mira scene. He lived at *Shadarhatvana* (Harvan) and took preaching of Buddhism in right earnest. This provoked the 'orthodoxy' adhering to Nilamat Rituals. Insult was added to the injury by Nagarjuna (125-60 AD), who encouraged the propagation of the Buddhist teachings and gave it royal patronage. Kalhan in Rajatarangini, has this to say (Translated): "After defeating in disputations all learned opponents (Nagarjuna), these enemies of tradition brought to an end etc the observance of the rites prescribed in the Nilamata." This was a veritable revolt against the established faith of the land and the Aryan Saraswat Brahmins lost no opportunity in providing a more palatable alternative to Buddhist tenets, with worship of different type and pantheon of God's and Goddesse's sprouted. Upto this time the temples dedicated to Bhadrakali had been numerous, apart from worship within homes. Many of these worship places either were converted to Buddhist *Viharas* or went into disuse during the next few centuries. Firstly around 400 AD, religious philosophy of Kas'mira started rooting in Vaishnavism and Shaivism under Tryambak Aditya. Then Mihir Kula (515-550 AD) came on the scene and process continued till around 800 AD under Sangam Aditya, descendent in the line of Tryambak Aditya. Many centuries after evolution of Tantra *Shastra* in Kas'mira, the existing Goddesses transited into various forms and facets. A classical example of this is Goddess Kali being taken as manifestation of mother goddess and Goddess Bhadrakali. It was not so with religious scholars, who were quite clear of the role of either. In Tantra *Shastra* the role of Goddess in fierce and *tantric* manifestation was necessary, hence frequent mention of Goddess Kali in Tantra Worship as enumerated in Tantra *Shastra*. These scholars continued to worship Goddesses in their original form but it was the common worshipper who started combining Kali and Bhadrakali. Shaivite Scholar Abhinav Gupta (940-1015 AD?) appropriately quoted or utilised them in his *sadhna*, based on their respective roles. He in his celebrated work *Tantra Loka* refers to thirteen different forms of the Goddess including Bhadrakali and Kali. From ancient scriptures and various accounts, North Kas'mira retained the area of influence of Goddess Bhadrakali and temples in her form were many: Hanalwara (Handwara), Kotitirtha (Varhamulla), Bhadrakal (Near Wadipur) etc. It is at this time the idol of Bhadrakali, nearly

4 feet in height, carved of rock stone, was installed on the hilltop adjacent to a spring; just under the shadow of a Deodhar tree at Bhadrakal near Wadipur (Handwara). The idol in no way resembled the known shape of Goddess Kali; skull garland, stretched out tongue etc. It is the simple image of the Goddess in her form; a benevolent one and worshipped as such for two millenniums in Kas'mira. Recently some bronze idols of around 9th/10th Century have been excavated/found in general area of Kupwara. One idol with a crown, assumed as crown of skulls (It is a carved crown) is erroneously attributed to Goddess Kali. The idols sitting posture, position of hands and absence of features associated with Kali, clearly indicates the idol that of Bhadrakali. Kali, on the other hand has a garland of skulls but not crown. This find of ancient Bhadrakali idol, erroneously claimed as Kali idol, also indicates the continuance of Bhadrakali worship in 9th Century, amidst the newly found *agam* (doctrine) of Shaivism and later in Tantra Worship.

Religious Lore: The Goddess Bhadrakali lore based on a *Mahatmaya*, possibly written few centuries earlier (18th ?) by a religious scholar concerns the lore of her manifestation at Her present location; Bhadrakal. Interesting point in this lore is combination of Kali in the Bhadrakali role, the killing of *Mahishasura*, the buffalo demon and basically restricted to North Kas'mira Areas and around Handwara. The lore goes as under. *Mahishasura* had terrorised *Devtas* in the area of Hananlwara (Handwara) and the Goddess comes from Kolkatta (Calcutta). She makes her journey through Baramulla where *Devtas* gave her their power and She transforms into empowered Bhadrakali and becomes *Mahashakti*. She finally comes to Bhadrakal where she rests under a deodhar tree and *Devtas* led by Vishnu reach Bhadrakal for thanks giving to the Goddess. Some of the places associated with the lore still exist though with different names and many springs associated with her have dried up. The different forms taken by Goddess Bhadrakali in this lore are; Kali, Gauri, Jagatamba (Amba) and Durga. This gives the extent of her forms from these Goddesses. Basically this lore is localised to North Kas'mira, probably by an Aryan Saraswat Brahmin of that area(s). It however, does not touch her role from Nilamat/Naga era and, mistakenly or erroneously, links it up with the role of Kali. The writer cannot be blamed as there had been amalgamation of religious *agams*, thinking by this time, which can be softly called as misinterpretation of the forms and roles of different Goddesses that had manifested in Kas'mira.

Svayambhu, Abhinav Gupta Connection: Bhadrakal is about nine kilometres from Handwara and about eight kilometres from nearby Nichom. Suyam, close to Nichom/Tsakvaar (*Vaar* in Kashmiri means a grazing meadow; generally a flat piece of ground on a ridgeline) has its own significance in Kas'mira. Apart from Jwala (Khrew) it is the place of Svayambhu (Self created fire) emanating from a low hill top, which has been a sacred place of worship from time immemorial and even from the time of Nagas and ante Jwala (Khrew). Nilamat Verse 1057-1064 (Translated); "O great king, one is released from all the sins by seeing everyone of these viz., Sudarsana Hara near Cakrasvami, Svayambhu, (Hara's image) erected by the: Fire-god, (Hara's images called) Pidgalesvara .... O king, the god Hara-the lord of the Bhutas is always present (in all these images)." The reverence to this fire and place is evident.

In fact the area during medieval times has been centre of *sadhna* by *sadhaks*, saints and sages; Bhadrakal, close to Svayambhu, has similar history. Situated between two ridge lines with miles of plain strips of land in between, a small river flowing through, a largish lake close by, it was an ideal place for settlements. The river, now only with a trickle of water, is about 60-75 feet wide and bed being about 40-45 feet deep. The tell tale sedementation and water level marks on the sides indicates that water level would have been about 20-25 feet, indicating that it was deep with perennial source of water. This source of water widens as it moves downwards towards Wadipur and finally joins River Talar near Zachaldara. Traces of cleared terrace cultivation strips along the spurs on the ridges, on the sides and small valleys indicate old abandoned cultivated areas dating to medieval period. Interestingly faded alignments of old and sedement filled water channels, closer to the plain ground on the side of the river bed have also been observed in the area. This indicated that the area had water channels to take water from the river, for irrigation purposes. Certain other tell tales of these living settlements, have been observed in the forms of stone piles and pits in the area. The area generally has wild Walnut and Pine trees in abundance, but other varieties of trees, associated with earlier human settlements in the valley, have also been found in reasonable numbers in the area. Even today on the other side of Bhadrakal Hillock, barely a kilometre short of Bhadrakal, lands are cultivated with maize and have sparing settlements of *Gujjars*, who claim their settlements dating to medieval period. The other significant find is a deep well next to the main mandir of the Goddess, just below the hill top and called *Keshav Nag*. It is only in early nineteen fifties it was barricaded and a roof constructed over it. The crude digging and the non existence of a plinth then, indicates its construction to few centuries earlier, if not more. Probably this was the source of water for the *sadhaks* who resided close to the Goddess idol on top of the hill.

Connected with the possible installation of *shila* (Rock or stone) idol of the Goddess around 9th Century, Bhadrakal appears to have been a settlement from Naga times to medieval times and even later. Mention of Bhadrakali worship in Nilamat, further reinforces the point of settlements in the area. It was natural to have such settlements at venerated places of worship. While Vasu Gupta found *Shivsutra* on the Mahadev Peak in 8th

Century, other places in the valley were also centre of attention of many *sadhaks*. Places in the area like Gushi (Buddhist scholar Ava Gosha who lived in Ghushi (Kanishka's time 25-60 AD)) and who wrote "*Buddhacarita*" (A verse compendium of Buddha's teachings and first of Buddhist scriptures written in the valley), Tikar, Suyam (Svayambhu), complete belt between Varhamulla (Baramulla), Hananlwara (Handwara), Syamala (Kupwara District), Bumai /Saadamalyun, *Raja Ram Di Lari* (Kupwara District), Shardi (Sharda), Kishanganga River, etc. have been either places of worship or related to sages, saints and various Goddesses. Excavation of idols recently in Lolab Valley confirms this assertion. With the Bhadrakali worship revival from 8th Century onwards, 9th Century worshipers like Shaivite philosophers Somananda, Abhinav Gupta and Jayaratha could not have remained away from this place. In fact it has been chronicled in the first verse on the *Vartika* on "*Malini Vijaya*" that Abhinav Gupta initially resided in the East of Pravarpura (Srinagar). However, there is a reference in the *Tantraloka* of his having shifted to another city at the request of one of his disciples Mandra; "Mandra in order to save him (Abhinava Gupta) from distraction requested him to shift."

From the historical fact that he, Abhinav Gupta, finally entered Birwa Caves (Magam-Baramulla District), it is evident that his place of *sadhna*, after leaving Pravarpura (Srinagar) and before attaining *nirvana* was closer to Bhadrakal. How could he remain away from the famous shrine of Goddess Bhadrakali, of whom he was an ardent devotee? Sir M.A. Stein (Auriel Stein) who stayed in Kas'mira for nearly 55 years (1888- 1943) had visited many places of religious importance during 1888 to 1905. He records 'Bhadrakal *tirtha* as a small village about four miles Southeast of Krambhar, marked by a spring and old *lingas*.' This also confirms to the antiquity of *shila* idol and settlement at Bhadrakal. Even as late as beginning of 20th Century *sadhaks*, *sadhus* have been staying in the area. There was an incident during that time when Shriman Pandit Jee Maharaj (1899-1973; Sage of Bhadrakal Shriman Keshav Buoy, also called Kisha Kak but to his thousands of devotees he was Pandit Jee Maharaj) was a young boy of about twelve. On a daily visit to the *tirtha* from Wadipura, where he lived at that time, he was met by a *tantrik sadhu* near the *tirth*. It is evident that Bhadrakal was an important place of worship of Goddess Bhadrakali, possibly from ancient times pulsating with human settlements. The *tirtha* was also an important stop for *sadhaks* of Shaivism and devotees of Bhadrakali including Abhinav Gupta. The *shila* idol of the *tirtha* can also be placed to have been installed around 9th Century. It appears that the human settlements shifted elsewhere as the source of water of the Bhadrakal River diminished; possibly due to change in the course/blockade somewhere upstream. This appears to be a gradual process, leaving finally small settlements in the area. Just to the South and

North of the *tirath,* across the low hill range are the villages of Lachh, Kalam Chakla, Naugam to the South and Satkahuj to the South respectively. These villages date to medieval times and are indicative of a missing settlement belt of humans in the vicinity of Bhadrakal. Only extensive archealogical surveys will indicate the time of such settlements. As has been the results of such surveys in the area of North Kas'mira, definitely in these will probability pertain to Naga or early Aryan (*Manu*) era. Similar traces of ancient settlements have been found in nearby Karnah (Titwal) and Kupwara.

Ancient *Shila* (Rock) Idol dating to Medieval Times at the Bhadrakal Tirath

Bhadrakal Later Centuries: The shrine of the Goddess continued to flourish till 14th Century, even though *Kul Devis* had started manifesting in Kas'mira from 12th Century onwards. Certainly there was some decline in the number of worshippers but Goddess Bhadrakali worship continued and She continued to be most popular deity amongst the population of Handwara belt and in and around nerve centre of the *tirth;* Wadipura (Transited name of Wadipur; even now it is called Wadipur). The name Pura itself is old, dating to 6th Century when villages/hamlets were called Pur (pura) like Parihaspura/Pravarpura. Wadi is corrupted name of *Baed* meaning big and can be attributed to a place of *Baed*; literally meaning people of high stature (Religious; Enlightened). This must be true as Wadipur has by and large stood out in North Kas'mira as the centre place of learned Aryan Saraswat

Brahmin scholars of Kas'mira, associated with the importance of the place due to Bhadrakali *Tirtha*, who stayed there. Most probably Wadipur is the place where the settlements of Bhadrakal shifted to, after the drying up of Bhadrakal River. With the advent of Islam in Kas'mira from 14th Century, followed by Muslim rule till early 19th Century, conversions took large chunk of her devotees as also that of other Gods/Goddesses. The shrine was somewhat neglected during this period, though her worship as Goddess cum *Kul Devi* continued in the confines of home in the area. The things were better from the middle of 19th Century and with the Dogra King Gulab Singh's rule from 1846 onwards, when Aryan Saraswat Brahmin's religious worship freedom improved. Gulab Singh was known for his reverence to the Brahmanic shrines in the valley. Though Dogra rulers claimed to be descendants of Lord Rama and had constructed many temples of Lord Rama, their reverence to the temples of and the pantheon of Gods and Goddesses of Kas'mira remained equally strong.

Pilgrims from general areas Baramulla, Handwara and the belt around would visit Bhadrakal and then proceed to Sharda. During 19th Century the shrine was generally managed by father of Pandit Sarva Buoy (Pandit Sarvanand fondly called Sarva Buoy- 19th/20th Century) of Wadipura. There is also a local account of the idol of Bhadrakali having been brought from Mahakali Temple at Srinagar in later part of 19th Century. It is said that the Goddess directed Pandit Sarva Buoy, in a dream, to take her out from Khanyar Srinagar. The Goddess expressed her desire to be taken in a boat to Bhadrakal. About the identification of the spot, Goddess told him to look for a crow and opposite that She would be found embedded in a wall. The Goddess, as per the account, was finally taken to Kulangam (Close riverhead (River Mawar) to Handwara) and installed in the shrine of Bhadrakal. The account is not supported by historical evidence. Firstly, there is no evidence of a Bhadrakali Temple in or around Khanyar, which is closer to Rainawari of Srinagar. Secondly; the idol cannot even be from Khanqah, where the temple Mahakali (Kalishri) Temple existed. The idol at this *Khanqah* (Kalishri Temple) has presumably been buried inside the spring within the premises of the Masjid (Read Above). Thirdly; the *shila* idol of the Goddess Bhadrakali dates back to 9th Century, when presumably it was installed at Bhadrakal. Fourthly; the size and weight of the *shila* idol precluded it to be embedded in a wall. It would have been impossible for Pandit Sawa Buoy to have removed the idol and carried idol, single handed, by a boat. However, there is some merit in the account. In addition to Goddess Bhadrakali's *shila* idol, there were three smaller *shila* idols of other Gods including Ganapati, which were of later vintage. It may be that Pandit Sarva Buoy had brought these from Srinagar. Pandit Sarva Buoy in his religious beliefs was helped by his equally pious wife; fondly called Ded. The family lived in Wadipur and it was their daily ritual to go to Bhadrakal, as a group, for daily worship. Even during this time, there are accounts, that Bhadrakal had small settlements of Bhadrakali *Sadhaks* around the shrine.

Sage of Bhadrakal: In *Sapatrishi Samvat* 4974 (1899 AD; Vikrami Savant 1853) on *Asadh Shukla Paksh Navmi* a son was born to Sarva Buoy and Ded at Wadipur. The family named him Keshav Nath. Young Keshav Nath, from his childhood days, was deeply religious and an ardent worshiper of Bhadrakali and used to go to Bhadrakal shrine more or less every day. It is one of these days, he met a *tantrik sadhu* at the shrine, who possibly tried to bring him also on his own line of worship, which he declined. As the time passed, young Keshav Nath, under the guidance of his parents, Sarva Buoy and Ded, grew amongst the maze of *agams* and worship rituals. He would spend time in silent meditation, both at his house as well as the Bhadrakal. By the time he was in his late twenties, he had attained a high degree of spirituality. After the death of Sarva Buoy, he further went deep into the Goddesses worship, though a *grahasti* by this time. By late 1930's as he spent more time in *sadhna*, he had acquired spiritual standing amongst the population of the belt. An ardent worshipper of Bhadrakali, he worshipped other Gods and Goddesses too. By the beginning of 1940's his devotees had swelled and included many luminaries of the community. By this time he had achieved the goal a *sadhak* would aspire for; reaching the apical level of spirituality. He, I believe, used to spend time in meditation and *yajnas*, mostly in and around Handwara and Wadipur. He had his personal tragedy also, when in early 1930's, his wife Lilawati, died leaving behind three young children; Nath Jee, Jagar Nath and Shori (Youngest; barely three years old then). While Pandit Jee took the tragedy as God's will, his mother Ded and brother-in-law Gopi Nath (Gupa Kak) looked after the children. *Kabaili* Raid of 1947 affected the area of Handwara and Wadipur badly and a community member who then in his early teens remininsces; "Our village had substantial (250) Pandit population. Many Pandit employees from Handwara had shifted to Wadipur. They included Shridhar Joo Dhar, SHO, Sham Lal Handoo, Tehsildar etc. Wadipora gained 'notoriety' for raiders since the treasury from Handwara was also shifted here. ..... Back home in Wadipora, evening meet of the community became a routine for us. Keshav Bouy, the venerated head priest of the Bhadrakali Shrine passed a word to every family in and around Wadipur to observe special fast on *Shavchaturdashi* festival. He argued, "Since we had become *Brasht* and *Shavchaturdashi* was approaching, we should observe fast on 10th, 11th and 12th day of the fortnight". Pandit Jee did shift to Srinagar for some time, but returned to Wadipur, as soon as *Kabailis* were evicted. There were tell tales of destruction at Handwara, Wadipur and even Bhadrakal. Though many Muslims had stood by the community, there were many who had also been instrumental in ransacking houses of the community members. His devotees from Srinagar and other places would visit him at Wadipur and take his blessings. He was so deep in his meditation that his daughter Shori's *Kanyadan* in 1949 was done by a devotee; Late Ved Lal Vazir, Director J & K Animal Husbandry. His place of meditation was a small room on the first floor of out house, next to his house. He never claimed to be a miracle man but sitting in his presence gave abundant solace to his devotees. He never claimed to have stopped marching enemy armies on our borders either in 1947, 62 or 65, by his divine powers. He simply believed in peace of mind and one could get it by just sitting in his presence or hearing his brief *parvachan, artis* or reciting of *Shloka's* and partaking *Prasad* he would offer. To some he would offer *vibhuti* or *dhoop*.

Shriman Pandit Jee

In Early fifties he ensured that Bhadrakal shrine gets a facelift, renovation of the *mandir*, getting approach road to the Bhadrakal repaired for vehicular traffic, regular assembly of thousands of devotees at Bhadrakal in Chaitra and Asuj *Ram Navmi* days, construction of *Dharamshala* and *Yajna Shala* at Bhadrakal. He also made it a point to have a yajna at Tul Mul on Asadh Saptmi and move next day to *Chakreshwar* for another *yajna* on *Haar Navmi.* Many attribute many miracles to him, like when a disabled young boy when asked by him to get up just stood up, to the disbelief of all those present. But never did the Sage claim to be a miracle man. Man of few words, he spoke in monosyllables. His greatness was in his compassion, respect for other holy people and concern for everyone of his devotees. He would remember them by their first or pet name. He attained *nirvana* in March 1973, *Chaitra Krishna Paksh Navmi*. He was cremated at the foothills of Bhadrakal, to be around the shrine for ever. *Navmi*, the day of Goddess Bhadrakali had special significance for the sage. He was born on *Navmi*, Goddesse's day is *Navmi* and he attained Nirvana on a *Navmi*; truly the sage was a messenger from the Goddess. It was at his behest that his devotees Sat Pal Mehra and Prabhu Dayal got an *Ashtdatu* image of Goddess, though in a different *roop* of Kali, installed at the shrine in 1966. Things were not same after he left. The *ashtdatu* image was stolen and then recovered. Pandit Jee Maharaj never really passed on his mantle to anyone of his family members. It was left to them or devotees to take up the unfinished job. Shori, his daughter did try but her effort was cut short by her death. Post 1991 shrine was vandalized, temple destroyed, ancient idols stolen, his *Samadhi* razed, *Dharamshala* and *Yag Shala* burnt. It was the Army who reconstructed the shrine (7 Sector Rashtriya Rifles Handwara) and for the first time a gathering was held after 14 years in 2004 under their arrangements. Sadly many of his devotees forgot about the ancient antique *shila* (Rock) idols and clamoured to give antiquity to the *ashtdatu* idol of recent years, which remain untraced to date.

Ashtdatu Idol of Bhadrakali Installed in Mid Sixties at Bhadrakal Temple (Wadipora)

Pandit Jee Conducting a Yajna at the foothills of Bhadrakal in 1949

As I knew Sage of Bhadrakal: He did not grieve when inert body of my two year old elder sister, who had died on that day at *Veta Vain* (Between Sopore and Handwara) in early 1940's, lay in front of him; with a grieving mother and a brother of the child being consoled by his mother; *Ded.* He finally, I believe, gave up his *mudra* and termed it as God's will, consoled them and said that the family will be blessed with a '*Ratna*'. My first impression of the Sage and Ded, as a few year old was when a '*Tejasvi*' man in a white *pheran* (Cloak), white *safa* (Turban) with round *chandan tilak* accompanied by his mother and young daughter arrived at our house, with his few possessions due to *Kabali* raid in his Wadipur village. I saw, I vividly remember, a Sage with aura around him and involuntarily I prostrated and touched his feet. A day or two with us, with stream of disciples, he shifted to another disciple's place. This was beginning of my privilege to have known the Sage of Wadipur. He was Pandit Jee Maharaj, for I never took his name. Our family, dedicated to *Sharika,* had singled me out to be dedicated to Bhadrakali. It was, me as 'Ratna' (named Rattan), as I learnt, he had talked about. As I grew, so did my trips to Wadipur and to Bhadrakal. Whenever I touched his lotus feet, I watched radiance around his face and felt absolute peace within. I watched with awe; his *pujas* for hours; his tête-à-tête while moving on horseback with Lambardar (Village Head) Zoon Ded of Wadipur, his talk with his mother or discussions with his daughter Shori, who after death of Ded looked after him.

His day would start with his special attention to *Nanaji* and his brother, both deaf and dumb; a big *tilak*, blessings and *prasad*. His evening discourses in the log cabin or at the foot of Bhadrakal hill were purely enchanting and sacred, with a log fire completing the mystique environment. An *aarti*, the glowing ambers and yet one day spent in the company of the Sage. That is how I grew, oblivious to the miracles he performed. In me the miracle was a growing boy completely independent. My trips to Bhadrakal, as I grew, did reduce but he was always with me. When I decided to join the Army, his blessing was with me. During 1965 War he was with me and in 1971 War, literally on a suicide mission, I just closed my eyes and flew to Bhadrakal and the Sage, to seek their blessings. We cleared our opposition with ease, though outnumbered. In 1978, I was a few Kilometres away from Bhadrakal, as crow flies, on a high mountain pass inspecting a freshly made *kutcha* road, when my jeep with me on the wheel slipped and started rolling down to the *Nallah*, 1000 feet deep below. I closed my eyes, took leave of my wife and children and final *namaskar* to Bhadrakali and the Sage. He was sitting beneath the giant Deodhar tree at the temple; blessing me. Lo behold I was thrown out of the jeep with bruises only, while jeep rolled down.

Pandit Jee Maharaj had single handedly established Bhadrakal temple and infrastructure around Bhadrakal. *Keshav Nag, Keshav Kutir, Keshav Sar* are testimony to the devotion of this Sage and his disciples. At the start of the climb, a young walnut tree stood out amongst other bigger trees, tree planted as a token of my arrival in this world by the Sage. It still stands and is called "Papa's Walnut Tree" by my children. Even my 12 year old granddaughter, Praharishta, who has never been to Kas'mira, will narrate, in typical school story narration, story of the Sage of Bhadrakal and the walnut tree having been planted as a token of arrival of a big man. It is only at the end she will round up the story that ; 'That Walnut Tree is my Nana's Tree'. I believe when a close disciple of the Sage wanted to adopt me, he is reported to have told the other family and my mother; 'Tulsi *Benji* , this boy will flower in your house. He is destined to do well in his family'. Bhadrakal, during my tenure in mid 70's at close by Naugam, became a frequent visiting place of my colleagues, seniors, troops and a place for military exercises. We just needed an excuse to visit the *tirath* as frequently as possible. This ritual was continued later by my cousin Brigadier PK Kaul (Aima), who was posted there in the 80's. So deep is the association that the *Zarkasai* hair of my Grandson Atharv was specially sent to Bhadrakal to be sown together with a walnut, so that another walnut tree comes up to replace the older walnut tree!!!

Hundreds of miles away, every morning I trudge to Bhadrakal, climb along the track, pass *Keshav Nag, Keshav Kutir*, The Walnut tree, *Keshav Sar* and at the Lotus feet of Bhadrakali; suddenly Pandit Jee Maharaj seated in front of the giant Deodhar tree, adored with *sindoor, moli dhaga* (*narevand*) and Silver foil, smiles and puts *tilak* on my forehead with this hymn to Bhadrakali "*Jayanti Managala* Kali *Bhadrakali Kripa Leni-Jeevata Sharada Shatam*"; for Sage is sitting there in the company of mother divine Bhadrakali.

Ruins of Ancient Temple at Avantipur Constructed by Avanti Varman (855-883 AD) (Photograph Courtesy Rohit Kaul – June 2012)

Old Painting Showing Shaivite Philosopher Abhinav Gupta (10th Century) with his Disciples

Hari Singh Nalwa as Governor of Kashmir Comforting a Local Kashmiri

Muslim Shawl Makers at Work-1867 Courtesy William Simpson

An Ancient Embossed Painting of Goddess Sharika (Sarika, Chakreshwari)

Idols of Raghnya at Tulla Mulla (Photograph Courtesy Rohit Kaul-June 2012)

Current Tul Mul Temple

Temple at Khrew

8

Manifestation of Kul Devis

From oneness, He has brought forth the countless multitudes.
Nanak, they shall merge into the One once again......

Guru Gran]th Sahib

Manifestation of Gods/Goddesses in Bharatvarasha and Kas'mira

Gods and Goddesses: Religion of original inhabitants of Kas'mira, Nagas, basically revolved around the worship of springs, rivers, important Naga Chieftains and had predominance of snake-cult. With the immigration of *Manus* (Aryans) to Kas'mira, whose religious beliefs had amalgamated with those of original inhabitants of Bharatvarasha at the time of immigration, their worship had incorporated God/Goddesses forms, which had manifested in Bharatvarasha. These beliefs also took roots in Kas'mira. In Bharatvarasha, it was somewhat different as the Gods and Goddesses manifested from two directions. Firstly, from the original inhabitants. These were mostly unspecific or those who effected daily life of the people and were on geographical location basis. These included mountains like Kailash, Lakes, Springs even Banyan trees, carved stones etc. There are, however, no specific details of graves or burial sites being revered enblock. Yet some of specific ones drew attention like *Samadhis* of saints or holy men. The number of such worshipped Gods and Goddesses was minimal. In comparison to female deities, male deities scored over the former for a number of centuries. In case of female deities they got names from the gender of the places revered like a river was given a feminine name and later worshipped as Goddess; Ganga, Yamuna, Satutri etc. Secondly, from Aryans/Vedas. Till Brahmanic religion took roots on the Banks of Saraswati River, basic elements of universe were taken as strong contenders in shaping the life cycle; nearing to the role of Gods. While such Gods were many, there were few of female entities of such elements to be revered. It is during later stages names of Gods and Goddesses were evolved and specific shape or roles attributed to them. It thus helped evolving the basic Trinity of the Brahmanic religion; Brahma, Vishnu and Mahesh (Shiva). In Bharatvarsha after Brahmanic religion had taken roots, Trinity Gods were given high importance, which generally revolved around Vishnu and Shiva, while Brahma was somewhat relegated. Their spouses also manifested and were given benign roles, within the parameters of the role of their spouses; the Gods. Down the period Shiva's spouse seems to have got prominence as did her spouse Shiva. It is interesting to analyse the reasons for giving Shiva more prominence. It has something to do with the shapes of the Gods. Shiva clad in minimum clothes, atop a snow clad mountain was more in line with the inhabitants than the Vishnu resting on the Serpent in an ocean or Brahma perched atop of the extension of Vishnu's umbical chord. Similarly for their spouses different individual forms were evolved and worshipped. These forms of Goddesses were more in the case of Shiva's spouse Parvati, who initially got scores of names, based on her other forms. It was not so with Vishnu's spouse Lakshmi or Brahma's spouse Saraswati. The same percolated down to combined elements of Nagas, Aryans in Kas'mira over the centuries after the immigration of Aryans (*Manu's*). Over the period, some of the forms, mostly of Parvati, manifested in Bharatvarsha as well as Kas'mira. The most talked Goddess in Kas'mira was Uma. In Kas'mira other Goddesses revered were; Sita, Saci, Lakshmi, Bhadrakali, Durga.

In Kas'mira there was clear perceptible praises of Brahma, Vishnu, Shiva, Nila and Goddesse's Uma, Lakshmi, Bhadrakali and Durga. From Nilamat Puranam and other scriptures it is evident that in the initial period of the settlement of Aryan Saraswat Brahmins in Kas'mira, the pantheon of Goddesses did not include Durga, however, worship of Bhadrakali was indigenous to Bharatvarasha, with obscure place of origin. Overall during the BC period of late Brahmanic period (500 BC to 200 AD), Vishnu was the main diety amongst the Trinity and it is during this period Buddhism spread and even incorporated Vaishnavite worship; that of Vishnu. During AD period, both in Kas'mira as well as Bharatvarasha, Shiva emerged as more important than other two of the Trinity, while his spouse Parvati's importance also grew many fold, more than that of her spouse Shiva. From various scriptures, chronicles, accounts of travellers, temples one can specifically find worship restricted to the Trinity and spouses including some of their forms. Few centuries later some more specific forms of Mother Goddess were evolved and deep within it was the form of Parvati; may it be in form of Rivers, Shakti or connected with day to day life. Strangely as this was happening, common people evolved different forms of Goddesses at geographical level, called as *Kul Devis*, who were worshiped and revered more than the Gods. This phenomenon was not restricted to Kas'mira only but took shape in selected areas of Bharatvarsha also. It is also interesting to note that during the first millennium AD, in Kas'mira the worship was mainly of the male deities and suddenly during the later period of the millennium, the names changed from male to female deities; like *Chakraeshwar* became *Chakreshwari* etc. Surprisingly both in Bharatvarasha as well as Kas'mira there was rarely used terminology like *Kul Devta*, apparently like a mother Devi was to be benefactor of the family. However, there were *Gram Devta/ Gram Devi,* the defenders of the *Gram* (Village), who took on the role of invisible leader, defender of the village inhabitants.

Manifestation of *Kul Devis*: From the days of Nagas and later Aryan culture, plethora of forms of Gods and Goddesses were object of veneration in Kas'mira. Mostly they were geographically located near combined habitation areas (Villages); which became wider range of local area objects of worship or deities (*Gram Devta/Devi),* with least commonality with other habitation areas (Villages). Each household had a specific place, object or a deity of worship, unspecific in most cases, no fixed form or shape, worshiped at the level of household; *Greh Devi/Devta*. Over the centuries much did not change in Kas'mira, except, many such deities, places became extinct and numbers reduced. However, a function in honour of *Greh Devta,* called *Gar Devta* in Kashmiri, Gada Bhatta (Feast of Fish and Rice), during the dark fortnight *Pausha* (December/January) remained and became an annual ritual. Even the form or shape of *Gar Devta* was not specific; he came in the dead of the night and went away in the hours of darkness after nibbling the food offerings placed at a secluded place of the house. The spectrum of deities till about 8th Century became mixed; that of Nagas, Buddhists, Vaishnavite and Shaivism. Around the end of 8th Century the religious practices revolved around the worship of Shiva and Shakti. *Shakti* the Divine Mother, presiding Deity of *Sri Chakra Yantra* and also worshiped as *Mahavidyas*, manifestations the highest knowledge. Scholars and worshippers of Shakti consider *Sri Chakra* as the holiest and most significant of divine symbols, conceived as Shiva-Shakti. This has led to devotees of different forms of *Devi* to consider the '*Bindu*' of the *Yantra* representing only their particular goddess, as the great mother. By the end of 9th Century, plethora of religious scholars had come to Kas'mira and the place became centre of religious learning for Bharatvarasha, mainly Monistic Shaivism. They also brought the concept of specific Shaivite *Gram Devta/Devi Pujan* with them, which initially did not find favour with common man, as it was different from their normal way of worship over the centuries. With the advent of monistic Shaivism, with a mix of Tantra, in Kas'mira there had to be someone to carry out the *Karma* (Day to day work) as common man found it difficult to adjust in the maze of religious doctrines (*Agams*). This is the time worship of local deities took strong roots; named as *Kul Devis* (Deity of the clan), mostly on clan (*Gotra*), geographical locations, nearer to cluster of habitation and a new set of deities emerged; *Kul Devis.*

In Bharatvarsha, Parvati was regarded as a representation of *Shakti*; albeit the gentle aspect of that goddess. This form of Parvati in *Shakti Roop* (Form of Power or Strength) became stronger in Kas'mira and even *Kul Devis* were taken, directly or indirectly, as the form of Parvati (*Shakti*) as Durga and *stotras*, scriptures invariably made mention of it. Even the physical appearance of many hands (*Bujas*), complexion, articles carried in the hands, number of eyes and riding mode etc found way in the appearance/form of other Goddesses and *Kul Devis*.

***Kul Devi* Forms**. The mother Goddess of all worship of *Shakti* in Kas'mira was Uma or Parvati and various forms/names of the Goddess were formulated for *Kul Devi* Worship; mostly forms of Gauri/Durga. There also seems to be conflict of the forms of *Kul Devis*, based on black complexion of idols, while *Mahatmayas, Stotras, Bhija Mantras* attribute their form, in some cases fair complexion. In a query raised by a Kas'mira Shaivite Scholar (Shri Laxman Joo) with one of our great Shaivite Scholars (Justice S N Katju) of recent times as to whether the *Kul Devis* being of *Krishna Yoni* (dark) complexion indicated that they were manifestation of Goddess Kali, the answer by the great scholar was in affirmative. This impression is erroneous and it can be attributed to the thinking of the Kas'mira Shaivite Scholars, who adhered to *tantric agams* and not plain *Shakta or Shakti Puja,* with Kali as the main deity. Kali is one of the forms of the Mother Goddess and manifested for a particular cause. New names for the *Kul Devis*, like Sharika, Raghnya etc., mostly new to Brahmanic pantheon manifested; unique and peculiar to Kas'mira. Since the *Kul Devi*'s main shrines were limited and catered for local populace, shrines of deities with other or similar names came up in other areas and became more or less *Gram Devis*. Their manifestation, festivals or dedicated days were either overlapping or common, which continues till today. This new dispensation enabled common man to carry out his normal duties (*Karma*) with routine of *Kulapuja* (Worship of Family Deities) within his place and *Kul Devis* closer to their locations. In this process of transition and refinement, *Bhairavas* and *Ganas* also became divine companions to be worshipped with Shiva and/or *Shakti* (in the form of *Kul Devis*) on important festivals and days.

Firming of *Kul Devi* Worship: While Shaivite religious doctrine given by Shaivite Scholars was reaching epical level, King Harsha (1089-1101 AD), whom Kalhan calls a '*Rakshasa*', indulged in plunder and destruction of the shrines and desecration of *Murtis*, a setback to the process of further development of Shaivitic Brahmanism in Kas'mira. Jai Simha (1128–55 AD), after the religious terror of Harsha, gave Vedic renaissance programme in the form of '*Shakti-Upasana*' (Worship of Shakti) to Kas'mira and many shrines were built or rebuilt. As continuation of Jai Simha's rule, during the reign of Bopa Deva (1171-81 AD) the Brahmans (*Sadhaks*) gained a great deal of supremacy but during the reigns of Raja Deva (1213-36 AD) an orgy of destruction and plunder was let loose. This was another turning point reinforcing revised form of worship of *Kul Devis* by common man in Kas'mira. This was the time (12th / beginning 13th century) various *Stotras* (*Shlokas*), *Bhija Mantras* (Seed or Basic *Mantras* in Verse Form) and *Mahatmayas* in praise of deities; mostly *Kul Devis* were composed. *Mahatmayas* (Eulogising of deities in verse form) generally set forth the different legends connected with various places of pilgrimage, the merit to be appeared by their visits and the rites to be performed in each of the sites. They contain lores, legends and local traditions. Composed *Stotras* (*Shlokas*) are the verses invoking the Gods/Goddesses and *Bhija Mantras* (Seed or Basic *Mantras* in Verse Form) in their praise in musical mode. Many manuscripts of these scriptures have been found; mostly in 19th Century. A compendium of *Mahatmayas* named *Bringesh Samhita* was composed by one Brahmin scholar Bringesh Bhatta of a South Kas'mira village containing mythological, spiritual, religious and tantric backgrounds regarding different *tirthas* of Kas'mira (Bringee village and Bringee Nallah is known after his name). Whether it contained contents of extant *Mahatmayas* also is not known but *Samhita* covered most of the *tirthas* of Kas'mira. Many of the manuscripts have been recovered; though many are either lost or had been recomposed by later scholars. From the analysis of recovered manuscripts *Bringesh Samhita* seems to be work of the later part of 18th Century, whose contents spread around beginning of 19th Century in Kas'mira, as it also contains details of *Amarnath Yatra*, which had been found around 1750-75 AD. It was in the last quarter of nineteenth century that Dr Buhler's collected some 16 *Mahatmayas* and later M A Stein collected some more. 51 *Mahatmayas* have been traced in Kas'mira; most of them are from *Bringesh Samhita* pertaining to shrines, which had come up during beginning of 2nd millennium AD, till date of composition of *Samhita*.

Kul Devis: Major shrines dedicated to Shakti (*Kul Devis*) in Kas'mira are; Chakreshwari (Sharika), Raghnya, Tripursundari, Jwala, Shailputri and Bhadrakali. In fact there are many more *Kul Devis* of smaller hamlets, villages in the valley, basically connected with the Goddesses of yore or of that particular geographical location. Some of these are Uma, *Baed Brari* of Bheda Devi, Vijaya of Bijebehara, and Bala Devi, etc. However, there are no worship places in honour of Gods termed as *Kul Devtas*, as the Trinity took place of being the supreme of Gods. Their shape and form was fixed and unlike other Goddesses their forms and role did not change as in the case of Goddesses. With advent of Islam, *Sufi-Rishi* order also took roots making a strange combination of Shaivism, Tantra, Shakta and *Kul Devi* worship with admix of *Sufi-Rishi* cult.

Devi Rahasya: Manuscripts of an old compendium, *Udharkosa Grantha* for *mantrodhara* (Recital of *mantras*), were found whose contents are in the form of a dialogue between Dakshinamurti and his disciple Akshyaya. The first half includes 25 *patalas* (paragraphs) and has been composed in the form of *adhyayas* (chapters), which deal mainly with the *Bhija Mantra's* (Seed or basic *Mantra's* in verse form) of Gods and Goddesses etc. The other half known as *Rahasyayiya* contains 35 *adhyayas* (chapters). Goddesses mentioned therein and the *Bhija Mantras* related to these Goddesses are: Jawala, Sharika, Raghnya, Bala Tripursundari, Lakshmi, Saraswati, Tara, Bhuvaneswari, Matangi, and Bheda. It also contains *mantras* of other Goddesses; Bhadrakali, Turin, Chhinamasta, Dakshinamurti, Shyama, Kalaratri. In the third section Varahi, Vajra-yogini, Kameshwari, Gauri, Annapurna, Sharda etc. are included along with basic *mantras* and *Bhija Mantras*. The *mantras* of Ganesha, Vatuka Kumara, Mrtyunjaya, Kartaviryarjuna, Sugriva, Hanuman, and those of *Navagrehas* (Nine *Greh's* (Planets)) are also included. Similarly, the basic *mantras* of *Varnamala* and the *mantras* of *Navagrehas* as also those of *Bhavani* (*Bhawani*), *Baguemukhi, Indrakshi, Khechari* too find a place therein. The *dhyana-dharana* of these Goddesses and *Grehas* are also included. Though the date of its composition is not known, it is fair to assume that this *Grantha* (Compendium of Religious scriptures) was composed somewhere after 12th Century, after most of the *Kul Devi* worship had been formulated in Kas'mira. Based on manuscripts found, the *Grantha* compendium has been published by Kas'mira Research and Translation Department in 1941. From the contents of the manuscript of *Udharkosa Grantha (Devi Rahasya)* it will be seen that a number of Goddesses and few Gods have been mentioned. While the prominent Goddesses or Kul Devis get mentioned, other Goddesses who have taken the role of *Gram Kul Devis* have also been mentioned like Tara, Bhuvaneswari, Matangi, and Bheda Varahi, Vajra-yogini.

Kul Devis

***Chakreshwari* (Sharika):** 9th of Ashad (Har- July) Shukla Paksh (Bright Half of Moon) is the special day for the worship of *Chakreshwari* (Sharika); the *Kul Devi* of most of the people living in the city of Srinagar (Pravarpura) and close by areas. Though She is *Kul Devi* in some pockets of rural areas also, separate and exclusive places of worship of the deity in Kas'mira are very few. She is one of the *Kul Devis*, specific to a geographical location; that of Srinagar and areas around it. The deity, *Chakreshwari* (Sharika), is not talked about in Kas'mira till about end of 6th Century, when *Sri Chakra*, worshipped in the cosmic form, engraved on a green, circular shaped stone of Sapphire, called *Sri Chakra Yantra*, also known as *Matra Chakra,* was installed at the site (Hari Parvat (*Sarika Parvat, Sharika Parvat*)) by King Pravarsena II (End of 6th Century AD; Gonanda Dynasty; son of the King

Megha Vaahana) who ruled Kas'mira. King Pravarsena II is credited with the establishment of five shrines of the goddess Lakshmi, Consort of Vishnu and established the new capital, naming it Pravarpura.

Sri Chakra, installed at *Sarika Parvat* (Hari Parvat), form of *Shakti* (Power) is depicted in the form of a diagram representing a *Chakra* (Circular wheel of life) and is associated with *Chakreshwari. Sri Chakra* originates from one central point (*Bindu*) that represents the core of the whole cosmos; 3 circles around it and 4 gates to enter, 43 triangles and lotuses vibrate from the very basic central point that represents the core (*Bindu*) depicting the form of *Mahadevi.* It has 6 triangles representing *Shat-Dal* (Six forms/ Goddesses; Saraswati, Lakshmi, Gauri, Ashtadashbujaye (Having ten arms), Ashtabujaye (Eight Arms), Dashannanaye (Ten pair of eyes)) and 18 angles representing *Ashtadash Bujas* (18 Arms) of *Devi* respectively. Adi Shankaracharya (788-820 AD) also installed *Sri Chakras* in many temples like Kamakshi temple of Kanchi, Nara Narayana temple of Badrinath and Guhyeshwari temple in Nepal; but not in Kas'mira, as some scholars claim. In fact there is no historical evidence or chronicle of that era that Adi Shankaracharya visited Kas'mira during his short span of his life.

Nilamat Puranam Verse 1051-53 refers to various deities including **Cakresvari** (*Cakre* (*Chakra*; Wheel); Svari (*Shewari*; Feminine, generally for goddess); closer to name of *Sri Chakra*) thus translated; "By a sight of the goddess Bhima, one gets the best wealth and by seeing the goddess Kapinjali, the goddess Suresvari. (The Goddesses) Bhadresvari, Gautamesi, the goddess Kalasila, (the goddess) named Udyogasri, (the Goddesses) Gavaksi, Candika, Durga, Gauri, Suvijaya, Sakuni Brahmacarini and Cakresvari, one gets one's desire fulfilled." This reference to Cakresvari (Chakreshwari) refers to Vishnu's, the bearer of *Chakra,* consort and her Vaishnavite form (Lakshmi), as Cakrin in the scripture refers to Vishnu. Next Verse 1054 of Nilamat Puranam refers to Cakrasvami (Vishnu) thus (Translated); "After seeing near Cakrasvami (Vishnu), the goddess sitting in the lap of Hara, one is freed from all the sins and is honoured in the world of Rudra." Kalhan in his Rajatarangini Verse 354 Book III mentions King Pravarsena II and *Sri Chakra* thus (Translated); "He (Pravarsena) founded the city of Pravarpura (Srinagar) on the outskirts of *Sarika Parvat"*, which means that till 1150 AD, when Rajatarangini writing was completed, this place was called *Cakresvari*, another name for goddess *Sri Chakra* and place called *Sarika Parvat.* The city itself was then called Pravarpura and not Srinagar or Shri Nagar. Around 9th Century, with the Shakta Worship and concept of Mother Goddess taking roots, the Goddess Cakresvari was worshipped in Shaivite form of Gauri/ Parvati. *Sarika Mahatmaya* tells us the story of the defeat and destruction of demon Jalodbhava, who lived in water logged Satisar. This *Mahatmaya* relates, in verse form, legend of Goddess assuming form of a Sarika (Sharika;

bird (*Haar – Maina* in Kashmiri) and taking a pebble in her beak dropped it at the spot and the pebble swelled into gigantic *shila* (Rock) killing demon Jalodbhava; giving the name of *Sarika* (*Sharika*) *Parvat* to the place. This legendry pebble survives under the name of *Hari Parvat* name is the Kashmiri equivalent of the Sanskrit *Sarika Parvata*, 'the hill of *Sarika*'- *Haar* in Kashmiri). A depression in the ground outside the *Sangin Darwaza* (*Sangin* - Strong; *Darwaza*-Gate) of the fort wall is pointed out as the spot where panting breath of the demon (Jalodbhava) forced its way out, as he struggled under the crushing weight of the *shila* (rock) over him. However, the same legend in our oldest scripture Nilamat Puranam (6th Century) Verse 173-80 relates to the killing of the demon (Jalodbhava) to the effort of Naga King Ananta, who breaks the mountains of Satisar (Kas'mira) with a plough and once the water was drained, Vishnu, after terrible fight with the demon cuts off, forcibly, the head of the demon (Jalodbhava). Translated; "Breaking forth Himalaya today with the plough, make soon this lake devoid of water." "There was a terrible fight between Visnu and the demon, with trees and peaks of mountains. All those hosts of gods ...... (Hari) cut off, forcibly, the head of the demon and then Brahma obtained gratification."

Later scriptures mention of an idol of *Devi*, made of glazed black stone, having been installed at *Sarika Parvat* and when the deity was also called as *Sarika Devi* (Sharika, later Sharika Bhagwati), possibly installed during the reign of Jai Simha (1128–55 AD). *Bhawani Sahasranama* was composed in praise of the *Devi's* one thousand pious names lucidly explains this **cosmic** form of the goddess. This *Sahasranama* is in the form of questions put forth by *Nandi* and the answers given by Mahadeva. This *Granth* also praises King Jai Simha and thus would have been composed either at the end of his reign (1128–55 AD) or only after him; possibly in late 12th Century after the installation of the idol. From the contents of *Bhawani Sahasranama* it is also apparent that it has been composed after composition of *Sarika Mahatmaya. Sri Chakra* continued to be worshipped as *Chakreshwari* (Cakresvari), called *Sarika* on *Sarika Parvat* and became the *Kul Devi* of the people around Srinagar (Pravarpura). With passage of time and development of Kashmiri language, *Sarika* transited to *Haari* and the place from *Sarika Parvat* to *Hari Parvat.* The *murti* of the Goddess, which had been installed at the site was taken away to Sarthal (Kishtwar) by Ugra Deva, a feudal lord of Kishtwar, in 1170 AD, during the reign of Vanti Dev (1164-71 AD). It is during the reign of Vanti Dev when *shila* (Rock), where the *Sri Chakra* was first installed, became the rock of veneration in the absence of the idol and continues to be so. Incidentally *Har* (*Ashad* - June) *Navmi* is also the special day for worship of Vijyeshawari (Vijaya Devi) presiding deity (*Gram Devi*) of Vijeshawar (Bijebehara) and this day is famous for laying *Hara-mandul* (*Rangoli*) in Kas'mira. Similarly many deities of smaller temples in Kas'mira are also worshiped on this day. No details or lore are available to validate *Har Navmi* as special date of her worship. It is probable that *Sarika Mahatmaya* has given this day as the day of her manifestation in Kas'mira, which also could be the day her *Murti* was installed at the place of *Sri Chakra Yantara. Horashtmi* (8th of *Phalgun Krishna Paksha* (Dark Half February)) is also devoted to the worship of the Goddess *Chakreshwari*. Actually this day is celebrated in most of the *Devi mandirs* for the worship of *Gram Devi*/Goddesses across the valley and in Nilamat Puranam the day is associated with worship by women, by no means by men, of Goddess Kas'mira (Nilamat Verse 552). The connection of *Chakreshwari* (*Sharika*) to Durga has been adopted during the 19th Century (Dogra rule), when the situation for the community was more peaceful and *Chakreshwari*, taken as a form of Durga, '*Ishta Devi*' i.e. personal goddess of many Kings, who ruled Kas'mira including Dogra Rulers, though their *Isht Devta* is Rama, as they claim to be *Suryavanshi's*, descendants of Rama.

An Early 20th Century Photograph of Chakreshwar Temple

***Bhairav of Chakreshwari* (*Sharika*) is *Vamadeva*:** In Kas'mira Bhairav's are held at lesser pedestal than their Goddesse's, more like *Dwarpals*, and are to be worshipped after the goddess. The *Bhairavs* of *Kul Devis* are; *Vamadeva* (Sharika), *Bhuteswara* (Raghnya), *Karneshwara* (Tripursundari) and *Mahadeva* (Jawala) are different from the above eight *Bhairavas*.

Shrivara's Rajatarangini, covering 1459-86 AD period, records that the rock shrine of 'Ganesha' at the foot *Chakreshwari* (*Sharika;* Hari Parvat) was built at public level during the reign of Sultan Hassan Khan (1475-87 AD) grandson of Zain-ul-Abidin. Under Akbar (1556-1605 AD) a fort was constructed around the hill and a town founded there; named Nogar Nagar. The place was also called as '*Nogar*' meaning 'new home'. According to chronicles the construction of the Hari Parvat, or, as Akbar named it,

Nogar-Nagar, rampart was started as a relief work, to alleviate the distress of the people during a famine. He (Akbar) sent One Crore and Ten Lakhs of rupees of that time from his treasury for this work (Read Chapter 4).

Raghnya (Tul Mul, Kheer Bhawani): 8th of Zeyshta (June) and Ashad (Har- July) Shukla Paksh (Bright Half Moon) are the special days for the worship of the Goddess. The holy spring (*Nag*) is believed to have been rediscovered on 7th (Saptami) Ashad (Har- June) Shukla Paksh (Bright Half Moon), which is also considered equally auspicious day. There is no mention of the days of worship of Raghnya in Nilamat Puranam and generally 8th of Bright Half's, as per Nilamat Puranam, are to be devoted to worship of Vinayak (Ganesh) (Verse 724-725) and Ashad Saptami is to be devoted to the worship of Sun (Verse 469-470). This also gives first indication that manifestation of this Goddess, Raghnya is post Nilamat Puranam. She is the *Kul Devi* of people living around Tul Mul (Wokur, Lar, Manigam, and Sumbal etc); worshipped as *Kul Devi* by majority of the denizens of Rainawari and many pockets in rural areas, where separate temples of Raghnya have been constructed. With the legend of water of *Nag* changing colours and after Partap Singh, Dogra King (1885-1925 AD) built a temple, Tul Mul, *tirath* attracted pilgrims from Srinagar and nearby places, though Raghnya was not their *Kul Devi*. Over the last century the veneration of the Goddess due to accessibility of the area has increased many fold. In fact irrespective of their Kul Devi, most of the Kashmiri Pandits visit and revere the shrine. Brahmins of many places in the valley have also constructed shrines dedicated to Raghnya and worshipped on *Zeyshta Ashtami* like *Lokit Pur (Lo-qraer-pur), Manzgam (Noorabad), Khana Barni* and *Tikar, Bhuvaneshvar, Bheda, Manigam, Raithan* and *Baedpur.*

Nags (springs) have been places of veneration for more than two millenniums, mostly associated as the abode of Nagas. There is no mention of Tul Mul or the goddess Raghnya in our oldest religious scripture Nilamat Puranam (6th Century). A look at the areas connecting Vitsar *Nag* (Vichar Nag), Harvan, Burzhom, Wokur (Vaskur), Lahara (Lar), Naran *Nag* (Wangat; near Kangan), Ganga Bal (Harmukh), Anderkot (Sumbal), Parihaspura and Prayag (Shadipur) reveals their location closer to hill slopes on the fringes of water bodies, places which have been closely associated with places of veneration for Nagas, Buddhists and Brahmins. These areas flourished amongst Neolithic settlements of original inhabitants of Kas'mira-Nagas, Megalithic (Aryan) settlements, Buddhists and during Lalitaditya Muktapira's reign (724-761 AD). Lalitaditya had constructed *Jyeshthega* temple at Naran *Nag* spring (Wangath near Kangan, approximately 20 kilometres from Tul Mul) and had given *Agraharas* (*Jagir*) at various places to Brahmins including at Tul Mul *Nag*, which was close to his new capital Parihaspura. There is no evidence of his having constructed temple at the site of the *Nag* and it remained place of veneration and *sadhana* within Tul Mul *Agrahara* (*Jagir*). Situated on the banks of Tul Mul Nar (Rivulet), this *Agrahara* extended right up to Duderhama, place where Tul Mul Nar eminated from Sindhu (Sindh, Lower Sindh; equated with sacred River Ganga) and was an ideal place for religious development and *sadhana* of Brahmins. Duderhama is repeatedly referred to by Shrivara (Rajatarangini, covering 1459-86 AD) under its old name of Dugdhasrama. He also talks of the religious activities of Tul Mul *Agrahara* as (Translated); "The worship of the 'Mothers', which is identical with that of the *Shaktis* at Tul Mul *Agrahara* plays a great part in the Tantra ritual flourishing in Kas'mira from ancient times."

The area in and around Tul Mul pulsated during Naga period, flourished with religious fervour and knowledge during Buddhism and when Vaishnavism came back in 6th Century. For last 1300 years the place has been known as Tul Mul, derived from Sanskrit word "Tul Muli - of great value" given during 7th Century after Nilamat had been written; apparently referring to value of the place in terms of religious development. The mention of *Nag* (spring) is found in Kalhan's Rajatarangini (written 1148-50 AD); 'The sacred spring (Tulamulya) is situated in a marshy ground and Brahmins of Tul Mul have been described as full with spiritual powers'. It is also chronicled that Tul Mul Brahmins had become vain and force by themselves. Around end of 8th Century, Brahmins of Tul Mul took offence to the employment of *Rakshasas* (artisans) by Jayapira (764-95 AD) from King Vibisana of Lanka (Not to be mistaken with Vibhishana of Ramayana), to construct a castle in his newly built capital at Anderkot (Near Sumbal, then named Jayapura). He confiscated *Jagir* lands of Tul Mul *Agrahara* and as per Kalhan's Rajatarangini ninety-nine Brahmins committed suicide by jumping in the river; but it had no effect on Jayapira. Actually during this period Jayapira needed financial resources, especially when he had undertaken construction of a new capital at Jayapura (Anderkot) and he re-appropriated many *Agraharas* to boost his resources, including part of Tul Mul *Agrahara*. These Brahmins went to Jayapira and one Brahmin named Diyannu Attal 'threatened' that 'their (Brahmins of Tul Mul's) supernatural powers could finish the King'. Challenged by Jayapira 'that he (Brahmin) was no Vishwamitra', Diyannu Attal cursed him thus (Translated); "O you unfortunate King! May goddess destroy you before my very eyes." As per Rajatarangini, heavy pole of the throne's canopy fell on Jayapira and a few days later he died. With this event Brahmins of Tul Mul gained more standing for their spiritual powers. During the next century during the reign of Avanti Varman (Utpal Dynasty; 855- June 883 AD) large rocks obstructed Vitasta (River Jhelum, Wyeth) near Yaksadara (Dyargul – near Varhamulla (Baramulla)). The water rose along the course of Vitasta and Sindhu Rivers and vast tracks of the valley were submerged including Manasbal, Wokur (Vaskur) and Tul

Mul. Though Suya cleared this obstruction and the level of rivers lowered, the area continued to be under water for more than a century. This calamity was regarded as revenge against Brahmins, who had adopted confrontationist attitudes towards the Kings, aggravated by the feuds of Kashmiri tribes; Tantrins (Tantres), Damaras and Ekangas. With partial development of Anderkot (Jayapura), Shaivism and *Kul Devis* concept taking roots, Tul Mul belt (Sumbal, Wokur (Vaskur), Lar and Tul Mul) had become centre of large chunk of Brahmanic population. As part of renaissance of Brahmanism during Jai Simha's reign (1128– 55 AD), a miniature temple, similar to miniature temple at Pattan (Shankar Varman 883-902 AD), on a small Estrada (Platform) inside the *Nag* was constructed and an idol installed. Few centuries back when the *Nag* was being cleaned, remnants of an Estrada construction were found. An old photograph of the temple (late 19th Century) shows remnants of an Estrada in the spring. Before the main spring came to be worshipped, there were many places of worship within Tul Mul *Agrahara.* At Solur, under a chinar tree a spring still exists and called *Devot Wol Boine* (Chinar)*;* a mile Northeast near Ladwun village *Ganesh Bal* or *Vodjen,* where Ganesh is worshipped. Many springs in the area which are still known are: *Ashta Rudhar* to the South; *Tsandar Nag* to the Southeast; *Machi Nag, Naga Rad* and *Gokhin Nag* to the East.

Late 19th Century Photograph of Tulla Mulya (Tul Mul)

As part of *Bringesh Samhita*, Canto II (Chapter) known as *'Raghnya Pradurbhava'*, in an enquiry dialogue between Bhairvi and Bhairava, records appearance of Raghnya in Kas'mira from Ravana's Lanka, where She was his

Isht Devi; As per *Raghnya Pradurbhava* Lord Rama ordered Hanuman to carry *Maha Raghnya* to Satisar (Kas'mira). Hanuman installed the goddess with all her satellites in the area and from then onwards, legend says, Ram and Sita undertook pilgrimage to Tul Mul on every *Puranmashi* of Asuj and Hanuman stands guard all the time. As per almanac (*Patra*) of Kas'mira, there is no specific festival, day on this day at Tul Mul or elsewhere in Kas'mira. In the case of Raghnya her consort is Bhuteswara (Shiva) and her Bhairav is also Bhuteswara. This combination of roles of Bhairava's, as consort and Bhairav may be intriguing but not so. At Tul Mul the idol of Bhuteswara (Shiva) is on the right of Raghnya and adjacent to her and not on a lower pedestal. *Vijnana Bhairava* Tantra commented partly by Kshemaraja (Disciple of Abhinav Gupta; late 11th Century) and partly by Shivopadbyaya, is text of the Tantra *Shastra* of *Agamic* (Doctrine), is a conversation between Shiva as Bhairva and Shakti as Bhairvi. This connection of Bhuteswara Bhairava as Shiva is also clear when we refer to *Sodaritirath* (Naran Nag), whose deity is Bhuteswara (Shiva) (Jai Simha (12th Century) consecrated a *linga* of Shiva called Bhuteswara here) and *tirath* quoted widely in Nilamat Puranam (Verses 1065-66, 1151-52. 1167- 1168). In fact the mountain range of Bhuteswara is called But Sher, an acronym for Buteswara. The proximity of these two *tirathas*, with commonality of Bhuteswara (Shiva) at both places, also confirms to the construction of temple on an Estrada during Jai Simha's time.

Tul Mul fell in the area of Lahara (Lar) fiefdom of warlord Ram Chand Renu (Raina) (Koteh Ren's father and commander of Suh Dev's army (1301-1320 AD) and was later killed by Rinchen who became the King of Kas'mira, in 1324 AD. According to Jonaraja Rajatarangini (1050 to 1459 AD) Sikander *But Shikan* (1389-1413 AD), the iconoclast who destroyed temples in Kas'mira, tried to target this temple also but failed. In 1460 AD all the rivers, namely Vitasta, Ladri (Lidar), Veshav, Sindh and Kuta Kol were again in spate due to torrential rains and vied with each other in recording the highest water-level. Lot of areas in the valley got submerged including Tul Mul. It appears that the temple was destroyed between 1496 – 1518 AD, when Malik Musa Raina (Soma Chandra before conversion) then Chief Vazir, destroyed eighteen big temples, scriptures, massacred 700 to 800 prominent Brahmins in 1518 AD and revived *Jazia*. (Sourced partly from Muslim Chronicles, accounts and some other papers as Prajya Bhatta's Rajatarangini covering 1487-1513 AD has been lost and no authentic account of this period is available).

Next mention of *Nag* (Spring), not that of temple, is by Abul Fazal, chronicler of Akbar (1556-1605 AD), in *Aine-e-Akbari;* (Translated from Persian) "Area of Tul Mul extended over hundred bighas of land, which got sunk in the summer season and formed into a marsh and *Nag* waters changed colour"; apparently area had shrunk due to appropriation of land by convertees to Islam and is much more than what the area is today. Krishna Pandit Kar, guru of Rishi Pir (b; 1637 AD) was a great devotee of the goddess. Legend says that during the reign of Shah Jehan (1627-1659 AD), Shyam Sunder Kaul, a devotee of *Shakti* and adviser to Shah Jehan's son Dara Shikoh, used to make offering of meat and wine to Goddesses but when he offered the same at Tul Mul, they changed into vegetables. This was probably during Moghul Subedar Ali Mardan Khan's time (1650-1657 AD), known for his attraction to philosophy of *Shaivism* and sublime eulogy of *Devi*. Apparently the shrine was accessible till about mid 17th Century but during Subedarship of Afsari Beg Khan (1747-52 AD) valley had floods and the shrine became inaccessible again to people from other places in the valley. It is around 1840 AD Krishna Taploo of Habba Kadal (2nd Bridge Srinagar) found inland water way route from Shadipur (Prayag) along Tul Mul Nar and reached the shrine on 7th Saptami of Ashad (Har) Shukla Paksh (Bright Half). The worship of Goddess at Tul Mul was done under Brahmanic as well as *Tantric mantras*. On the conclusion of his puja, it is said that a piece of birch bark was seen floating over the water of the spring and Krishna Pandit took it up and found a *shloka* (Verse) written on it. The verse described the divine form of the goddess Raghnya. V*erse* (Translated from Sharda); "I make obeisance to that one goddess who, having taken the position of the Supreme God is the Queen in reality, whose form is made of light and is adorned by (the luster of) twelve suns, who cannot be observed through senses, who is seated on a throne and is wrapped with serpents." He composed a poem of as many stanzas as there were letters in this *Shloka* and this poem is still extant.

The water of the *Nag* changes colour from time to time. It is also said that *Sri Chakra* has been installed here. The only place in Kas'mira where *Sri Chakra* has been installed is Chakreshwari during 6th Century AD. It appears that as the worship of the Goddess progressed, *Yantra* of her worship was devised by Priests but has not been installed at the shrine. This *Yantra* of Raghnya has 4 Gates (*Dwars* to enter); 4 Middle lines (*Mudras*); 4 innermost lines (*Shaktis;* (Brahmi, Maheshwari, Kumari and Vaishnaivi), *Ashta Dal* (Eight lotus leaves resting on the circle representing Eight Mothers (*Ashta-Matrikas*) (*Adhishtratri Devis)*-Chamunda Brahmani, Maheshwari, Kumari, Vaishnavi, Varahi, Narsinghi, and Indrani); 6 *Shat Kon* (Saraswati, Lakshmi, Ashtadashbujaye, Ashtabujaye, Dashannanaye, Goauri), *Trikon* (Mahakali, Mahasaraswati and Mahalakshmi), and the *Bindu* (Core; The Goddess). Many parts of this Y*antra* are similar to that of Sri Chakreshwari.

Swami Vivekanada visited the shrine in 1894 AD and made offerings of *Kheer* to the holy spring and since then the *Devi* is also known as *Kheer Bhawani*. *Bhawani* (*Bhavani*) is a form of address of Mother Goddess

(*Shakti*) and used by Adi Shankara (Adi Shankaracharya - May/June 788 – May/June 820 AD) in *Soundarya Lahiri* (Verse (Stanza) 22 of *Soundarya Lahiri*). Swami Vivekananda, an ardent devotee of Adi Shankara, used this form of address for Raghnya as devotion to the Goddess. He (Vivekananda) has also mentioned the destruction of the temple, for during his time only an 'Estrada' existed in the spring. The worship of the Goddess is done with milk, Mentha Sylvestris (*Vena*), Lotus and sweets. Remains of a construction were found around when Partap Singh (1885 –1925 AD) built a temple at the place of Estrada in 1912 AD and *Murtis* of Raghnya and her consort/ Bhairava Bhuteswar were installed. There is no authentic account that the present *Murti* of the *Devi* and her consort/Bhairava are the old ones. An Aryan Saraswat Brahmin, aged about 90 in 1948, has been quoted that he knew of the time when reeds were placed along swampy foot-path from *Hur Mengin Wor*, close to Duderhama, to enable the pilgrims to walk to the island (*Hur Mengan* was a Spirit, who sometimes possessed the bodies of the persons traveling during the night and he was a dread to the inhabitants of Tul Mul neighbourhood). Kalhan's Rajatarangini calls the place Tul Mul (Tulamulya), a Sanskrit form of "great value." The place name Tul Mul is also being associated with Mulberry (*Tul*) tree. In Kashmiri *Mul* is root (*Mool*) and it is made that a mulberry tree root has given this name to the *tirath*. Kashmiri masses, on the other hand, then (12th Century) spoke *Apabramsha*, which assumed the form of Kashmiri only in 13th and 14th Century. Later Persian, Arabic words and expressions entered its vocabulary. Thus Tul Mul is corrupted name of Tulamulya and has nothing to do with root of a mulberry tree. Also mulberry tree cannot last that many centuries that too in a marshy area inside water and no authentic details of existence of a Mulberry Tree have been chronicled or found on ground at any time at Tul Mul.

Tripursundari (Bala Tripursundari, Tripura): Also called Lalitha (Parvati) Tripursundari, Maha Tripursundari). The special day of her worship is *Tripur Chaturthi* (*Magh Shukul Paksh Chaturthi-Fourth Day of Bright Half Moon of Magha Month*-January). Tripura is the consort of Tripurari (Shiva) and her Bhairava is Karneshwar. She is the *Kul Devi* of Tikus (*Tikus*; a Kashmiri rendering of ***trik,*** a clan of Aryan Saraswat Brahmins of Kas'mira) and a cross section of the Aryan Saraswat Brahmins of Kas'mira. Goddess Tripura is also worshipped in Bharatvarasha, especially in Nepal, Maharashtra, Eastern parts of the country and many pockets in the South. In Kas'mira the main shrines of the goddess are Tripursundari Temple at foothills of Gopadiri (Durga Nag) and Devsar (Anantnag District). In fact she is the Goddess well known in Bharatvarasha, though in Kas'mira *Mahatmaya, Bhija Mantras* and *Stotras* are different and peculiar to Tripursundari of Kas'mira.

Goddess Tripursundari

Adi Shankara composed *Saundarya Lahiri* (Wave of Consciousness and Bliss); hundred *Shlokas* (actually 103) eulogising the grace and purity of Goddess Parvati/Dakshayani, consort of Shiva. (Researchers who have analysed Adi Shankara's works, while acknowledging commentary on *Brahmasutra, Bhagavad Gita* and *Upanishads* etc as his major works, term composition attribution of *Saundarya Lahiri* to him as 'doubtful'). Each *Shloka*; describes *tantric* ways of performing devotion connected to that *Shloka*. The verses start with benedictory invocation that Shiva, when enjoined with Shakti, is the real power; Shiv-Shakti. Verses 1-41 describe the mystical experience of this union of Shiva and Shakti. Verses 42 to 100 describe the physical beauty of the Goddess, whom he addresses as Bhavani (Bhawani), Sri Vidya, Bhagawati, Uma, Mother (*Maha Devi*), Daughter of the Mountains (*Parvat Putri*), *Devi*, Parvati, Candi (Chandi?) and Mahamaya. Few of the verses refer to the third eye; *Tri* of the Goddess. Stanza 47 of *Saundarya Lahiri* (Translated); "Your right eye being of the nature of the sun, begets the day, your left (eye) being of the nature of the moon creates the night. Your third eye with the lustre of a slightly blossomed golden lotus produces well the twilight, abiding in between the day and night."

The manifestation of Goddess Tripursundari in Kas'mira is attributed to *Panchastavi,* a collection of devotional hymns divided into five Cantos (chapters) sung in the praise of Mother Goddess, which personifies absolute Godhead and lays stress on the Mother's worship which it connotes. It alludes to several doctrines of *Tantric* worship of mother Goddess through the use of *Bhija Mantras* and has therefore attracted the attention of commentators, well versed in *Tantric Sadhana*. It is through *Panchastavi*, Goddess Tripursundari manifested in Kas'mira; first amongst the *Sadhaks* (Preachers) and then amongst the common man.

Before proceeding further it seems pertinent to explain Tripursundari personifying the 'Divine Energy' and repeatedly used by the poet in all the cantos of *Panchastavi*. Tripursundari is regarded as the manifestation of *Prakriti,* the feminine power, the vital energy of the universe. *Tri* denotes number three, *pura* means cities or three worlds and *Sundari* refers to beauty of the deity; 'The Beauty of the Three Worlds' or more precisely whole cosmos. Perhaps to facilitate the exact comprehension of this word, the poet (Author of *Panchastavi*), on his own, has advanced reasons for calling this 'Divine Energy' as Tripura, by enumerating triple form of gods, fire, energies, basic vowels, worlds, Vedas and other cosmic manifestations and tries to establish that this threefold division is actually an extension of the essence of the Divine Energy, consequently called Tripursundari. Shaivistic lore confirms this view of the poet. The poet feels that Tripursundari on being discerned by physical eyes or through mastering a *Mantra* (mentally) dispels sins and mitigates the fear of death. '*Prapanchasara*' asserts that 'Ambika' is named as Tripura, because of its accent on the three basic vowels. '*Tripurarnava*' lays down that the energy residing in '*Sushumna, Pingala* and *Ida*' (Blood Vessels, mind, intellect and soul) is called Tripura. '*Kalika Purana*' says everything is threefold, so she (Divine Energy) is called Tripura. '*Vamakeshvara-Tantra*' believes that Tripura is threefold in the form of Brahma, Vishnu and Shiva, and also personifies in herself the three powers of desire, perception and action. '*Varaha Purana*' also explains the name on those very lines and word Tripura is actually the manifestation of triple power of the super energy of Raudri, Jyeshtha and Amba.

Vidyarnava Tantra by Vidyarany Muni, a religious saint scholar, gives description of Tripursundari; as the three main activities of powers of desire, perception and creation. *Parmashiva* has been eulogized and this represents the energy of Brahma, Vishnu and Rudra and is manifested in Mahasaraswati, Mahalakshmi and Mahakali. In the form of a 'male-female', dialogue a very apt description is given of Shiva-Shakti worship. Tripursundari is not only the *Sundari* (Beauty) of three worlds but is also the sole directing force of the activities of the Trinity and of the five different kinds of forces to the East, West, South and North and the higher regions in the form of *Unmani, Bhogini, Kumbika, Kalika* and *Maha Tripursundari* of the upper regions. The said *Granth* is in the form of hymns in worship of Maha Tripursundari. It has two large sections dealing with the numerous *mantras* etc., in praise of Maha Tripursundari and her twenty different forms. The date of composition of *Vidyarnava Tantra* is fixed at 1130 of Vikrami Samvat corresponding to 1073 AD. In popular parlance *Tantriks* are supposed to be those who are worshippers of Shakti (*Devi*). "When we speak of Goddess worship, Mother Maha Tripurasundari is the Goddess to be worshiped as the Mother residing in our Crown Chakra. She is one of the Maha Vidyas. Maha Tripurasundari, the absolute, the all pervading, beyond speech and mind and even beyond time and space." Her *Yantra* is also the Sri Chakra.

The manifestation of Tripursundari in Kas'mira took place at the beginning of 10th Century, when *Sadhaks* knew contents of *Panchastavi*. Being under the *Tantric agam* (Doctrine); it remained a scripture for *Sadhaks* (Preachers), who would worship it under *Tantric* rituals. By the beginning of 11th Century teachings of *Shaiva Darshan* and *Trika* raised a conflict among the Kashmiris whether to go in for worship on elaborate *Tantrik* methods or adopt simplistic rituals, particularly in their *Sadhana.* Circumstances in 11th Century and then in 12th Century, as discussed in the evolution of *Kul Devi* concept above, a different form of worship of Tripursundari evolved. She was adopted and worshipped as *Kul Devi* by a section but the recital of *Panchastavi* became a ritual in temples or at home. By this time even the *Sadhaks* of Tantra chose Kali as their tutelary deity (*Isht Devi*). Around 12th Century for common Brahmin of Kas'mira, Tripursundari became a *Kul Devi* or a goddess of the pantheon with *Panchastavi* recital becoming a daily worship ritual.

Some scholars have argued on the basis of *Tantra Shastra* and *Panchastavi*, Tripursundari is mother goddess and other *Kul Devis* are the form of Tripursundari, a stand, which does not hold ground. The mother goddess of Kas'mira is Uma, also called Parvati and Gauri. Stanza 71 of *Saundarya Lahiri* refers to this as the form of Goddess (Translated with additional explanation in brackets); "Oh Uma! you tell (us), how will we speak of the beauty of your hands, which detract (your) nails which shine with the redness of the new lotus? Alas, let the lotus some how obtain a little similarity (for becoming an object of comparison). (This will be possible only) if it acquires the red dye from the sole of the foot of Lakshmi who plays (on it)."

All *Kul Devis* including Tripursundari are the forms of the mother goddess, who manifested at different places and in different eras and circumastances and are associated with religious relics of the past. Like Chakraeshwari (*Sarika*) with Sri Chakra/ Sarika Parvat, Raghnya (Shyama; a form of Parvati) with the *Nag* of Tul Mul and Jwala with the fire of Khrew. Tripursundari manifested in Tantra *Agams* and unlike other *Kul Devis* of Kas'mira did not have any religious relic in Kas'mira to be associated with, but away from her *Tantrik* form of worship by *Sadhaks*, a benign and simplistic form in line with other *Kul Devis* was adopted by the common man and remains so till today.

Oldest religious scripture Nilamat Puranam does not mention anything about Goddess Tripursundari. Her manifestation as *Kul Devi* time frame is more or less same as the other *Kul Devis,* as discussed above. Though details of *Tik Choram* (*Tripur Chaturthi*) being special day of her worship is not known, it could be the day of completion of composition of *Panchastavi* or the day her idol was installed at Tripursundari Temple at Gopadhiri (Shankaracharya) Foot Hills (Durga Nag) or Devsar.

Jwala: 14th of Har (July) Shukla Paksh (Bright Half Moon) is the special day of Jwala's worship at Khrew, about 20 kilometres from Srinagar. Fire was worshipped by humans from time immemorial and the God of Fire, Agni, finds mention in Rig Veda also. Agni is the second most prominently mentioned deity in Rig Veda but is described in masculine form. In Nilamat Puranam there is mention of the fire God (Not Goddess) Svayambhu, in the close vicinity of Bhadrakali Shrine at Bhadrakal at Suyam near Nichom and Tsakvaar (Handwara). Kalhan Rajatarangini mentions the place as such; "The self-created fire rising from the womb of the earth, receives with numerous arms of flame the offerings of the sacrificers." Again it is the masculine form. Both Nilamat Puranam and Rajatarangini of Kalhan do not mention Jwala of Khrew. In fact Nilamat Puranam refers to performance of *Dhanahotra* on 14th Day of Ashad Shukla Paksh, dedicated now to Jwala in Kas'mira, thus (Translated) Verse 730; "On the 11th and the 14th (Ashad) Dhanahotra should be performed and vigil should be observed for two nights. The Brahmanas and the Satvatas should be worshipped on the 12th and the 15th."

Stairs Leading to Jwala Devi Temple

Volcanic fires are considered cosmic by nature and at Jwala (Khrew) cosmic fire is worshipped as the form of the mother goddess. The present shrine at the site of volcanic fire, constructed by Dr. Bal Krishen in the 18th Century, is perched on the top of a 200 feet high hillock approachable by flight of 360 *Devri* stone steps with more than a dozen landings. The octagonal shaped temple rests on a high base with small squarish sanctum sanctorum, where a six feet high, black stone image is placed. It is said that the image turned black due to occasional flames, which sparked here from time to time. The flame at one time is said to have been 2 feet high and alight for about half an hour and was last seen in 1962. I recall having seen a small flickering volcanic flame in mid fifties as a young boy. Goddess Jwala shrines exist in Bharatvarasha also, though very few, and are the self-created fires from the earth; mostly on a hill top. Most of them are called Jwala (Fire) *Devis*. In Himachal Pradesh Jwala is worshipped in the Kangra valley. Jwala's are nature's phenomenon and no time frame of its manifestation can be made. In any case fire (Agni) has been worshipped from time immemorial. There is no mention of this phenomenon-taking place at Khrew in any historical or religious scriptures of Kas'mira. Mihir Kula (515-550 AD), a Hun General, who ascended the throne of Kas'mira account does not mention anything of this fire; closer to area where he hunted.

Between 6/7th Century and beginning of 9th Century, a natural calamity seems to have occurred in Kas'mira, though of what type is not known. During this calamity a geographical fault or an earthquake seems to have occurred near *Varahkshetra* (Varhamulla, Baramulla). This could have resulted in a minor manifestation of Jwala (volcanic eruption) at Khrew. This does not find mention in Kalhan's Rajatarangini and may be it occurred after 1150 AD or it existed but did not find mention. Around 12th Century when the concept of *Kul Devis* found roots in Kas'mira, Jwala at Khrew also started to be worshipped as *Kul Devi*. By far the goddess, is also form of mother Goddess (Uma, Parvati, Gauri) worshipped as *Kul Devi* by a cross section of Kashmiris, mostly closer to Khrew (Pampur, Avantipur, Tral etc.), though lesser following than other *Kul Devis*. Like other *Kul Devis* she also became part of the worshipped pantheon of Kas'mira. Various *Stotras, Shlokas, Bhija Mantaras* and *Mahatmaya* (*Bringesh Samhita* and in *Udharkosa*, grantha for *mantrodhara* (*Devi Rahasya*)) mention Jwala. Jwala's Bhairava is Mahadeva.

Shailputri (Devi Bal, Nag Bal): *Nags* (springs) have always been venerated from the time of Naga's and *Nag Bal* of Baramulla is one of them. Here is the shrine of Shailputri; *Shail* (*Shila*-Rock; *Putri*-Daughter; meaning daughter of mountains) and is the form of Uma/Parvati. Actually in the pantheon of Bharatvarasha she is one of the *Navdurgas*; *Shailputri, Brahmaputri, Chandraghanta, Kushmanda, Skandamaata, Kaatyayani, Kaalratri, Mahagauri, Siddhada*; who are to be worshipped, one by one, on nine days starting 1st with Shailputri. She is specially worshipped on the 9th of *Chaitra Shukla Paksh* (Bright Half), on the final day of *Navratras*, on *Navmi*. How and when this day has been adopted is not known but can be attributed to the time (12th Century), when the concept of *Kul Devis* took root. It is well understood that the *Kul Devi* concept took roots in the form of Shakti worship, represented by Durga and thus the place was named after one of the forms of *Navdurga*. Located little away from Baramulla (Varahamulla) town on the road to Uri, literally on the banks of Vitasta, she is the *Kul Devi* of most of the people from Baramulla, Sopore and close by areas. There is Shiv *Linga* within the premises of the temple, while Goddess Shailputri idol is placed inside a small temple built in the centre of the *Nag* (Spring), just like Raghnya. The worship is that of Mother Goddess and devotees recite *Panchastavi* at the shrine as part of the daily worship; common in most of the temples of Kas'mira. There is no mention of Goddess Shailputri in Nilamat Puranam, various other *Samhitas* and *Mahatmayas*. Apparently she was adopted as *Kul Devi* due to geographical reasons. It is unlikely that this shrine had been targeted by Sikandar *But Shikan*, who possibly targeted the shrine of Adi-Varaha in the vicinity of this temple, due to the form of the god in the form of Boar (Varaha) for obvious reasons. The idol which was worshipped till recently; Goddess riding an Ox but it was the *Nag* (spring) which was the object of worship and idol installed later. Unfortunately this idol was damaged in 90's.

Baramulla (Varahamulla, *Varhakshetra*). The home of Shilputri has aglorious and historical past and it is necessary to give some details of this temple town, home of one of the Kul Devi's. The town of Baramulla (Varahamulla, Varhakshetra), a corrupted name of Varahamulla, named after the Boar incarnation of Vishnu, was an important place in mediaeval times. The temple of *Adi-Varaha* (Primeval Boar), destroyed by Sikandar *But-Shikan* (1389-1413 AD), is said to have been one of the most splendid temples in Kas'mira. A few architectural stones are still seen lying about at this place. The only object of interest, which it now contains, is the large human-faced Shiva *Linga*. Varahamulla (Baramulla) is identified, on the strength of local tradition, with the *Kotitiratha* situated half a mile away from the old bridge. *Kotitirtha* as per legend was resident to one crore *Devtas* hence the name *Kotitiratha* or as locals call it *Karoditiratha* (Crore Pilgrimage Centre). In fact Varahamulla has been a strong foothold, first of Buddhism and later of Vaishnaivsm in Kas'mira. The village of Ushkar or Wushkur, situated at a distance of half a mile from Baramulla, is corruption of Huvishkapura, which, according to Kalhan, was the name of a city founded by Huvishka, the Kushan King in the second century AD. It was a flourishing town in mediaeval times owing to its position on the principal trade route between Kas'mira and Northwestern India. Lalitaditya (724-761AD) built here a shrine of Vishnu named *Muktasvamin* and a large Vihara with a Stupa built in the middle of the eighth century AD. Huen Tsang, the famous Chinese pilgrim who visited Kas'mira in 631 AD, entered the valley by Baramulla route, and spent his first night at one of the monasteries here. At Fathgarh, a small village at a distance of nearly three miles from Baramulla, are the ruins of a large temple with a massive platform on which was placed a colossal Shiva *Linga*, a large fragment of which is still lying there. Then again are the ruins of temples of *Naranthal* village, about two and a half miles below Baramulla on the right bank of the river. The temple is of the late mediaeval era, not earlier than twelfth century. The temple of Buniar situated on the Jhelum Valley road, two miles short of Rampur; by far the best preserved of all the larger Kas'mira temples. The original image, which seems to have been of Vishnu, is now replaced by small Shiva *Lingas* originally brought from the bed of the Narbada River in Madhya Pradesh. Then there is *Dhath Mandir* (Bandi Temple) situated on the Jhelum Valley cart road, midway between Rampur and Uri, about two miles below Mohura. On the hillside, a few yards to the South-east of the temple are remains of two smaller shrines, which, like the subsidiary temples in the courtyard, are replicas of the main temple. The aim of the above narration is to indicate that Varahamulla (Baramulla) had been focal point of Naga worship, followed by Vaishnavism and Buddhism. After the waning of the Buddhism it became a strong hold of Vaishnavism upto 8th Century and got the patronage of Karkota Dynasty (Lalitaditya (724-761 AD) and Jayapira (764-795 AD) followed by Avanti Varman (855-83 AD -Uptala Dynasty) the first Vaishnavite king of Kas'mira and it is during his reign that many temples were dedicated to Vishnu.

Bhadrakali as *Kul Devi*: The worship of Bhadrakali in Kas'mira was neither sudden nor out of nowhere. The evolution of Bhadrakali worship in Kas'mira is nearly as old as the entry of Aryan Saraswat Brahmins in Kas'mira. However, next to worship of Uma, Bhadrakali Worship gets prominence.

Analysis of the two sets of worship ritual of Bhadrakali in Chaitra and Asuj clearly indicates that apart from Uma, Bhadrakali took the role of principal deity of Nagas as well as Aryans. She was the *Kul Devi* of Kas'mira inhabitants. Even the manifestation of strong Kali worship in medieval period with advent of monistic Shaivism and Tantra Worship took away a chunk of her dedicated devotees and worshippers. There are many smaller *tiraths* dedicated to Bhadrakali. However, like other *Kul Devis*, she too has a single major *tirath* dedicated to her; at Bhadrakal, near Handwara.

Kali (Mahakali) Worship in Kas'mira: Upto 600 Century AD there was no Kali worship in Kas'mira. Nilamat Puranam does not mention Goddess Kali or her worship. There were few temples dedicated to Kali or Mahakali, but her worship was a must for *tantric* worship. So much so even other *Kul*

Devis, erroneously though, were presumed as forms of Kali. With the advent of *Kul Devi* worship from 12th Century, few common people going in for pure *tantric* worship, Kali in form of Mahakali worship started, though restricted to special days only and seldom associated with *Kul Devis*. However, Kali was invoked during the ninth day of *Navratras*; possibly ritual imported from Bharatvarasha in later centuries. In recent times there were only two major Mahakali Mandirs; at Srinagar and Vadora.

Other Goddesses: With the evolution of *Kul Devi* worship, the pantheon of Goddesses in Kas'mira reduced considerably. Only the main form of the consorts of the *Trinity*; Lakshmi, Parvati and Saraswati held fort. Even Goddess Uma got relegated to a minor role. Similarly Vitasta, the river given the pedestal of the benefactor of Kas'mira got restricted to single day worship. Amongst the Goddesses Parvati remained the basic form of all the Goddesses but not directly worshipped except on *Shivratri*. The Goddesses predominantly worshipped are directly not Goddesses but their form, which have manifested in Kas'mira only. These *Kul Devis* carved geographical area of devotion in many parts of the valley. Also local Gods, Goddesses, myths, lores and even saints took over. Goddesses mentioned briefly in Nilamat Puranam took their place and became *Kul Devis* in the garb of *Gram Devi/ Devtas* for these clusters, villages and settlements. Even *Nags* (Springs), sources of rivers, ancient rocks/*shilas* and caves became places of veneration. Where Aryan Saraswat Brahmin of Kas'mira did not hesitate to accept variants of Shaivism including Tantra, but finally common man realised that he was no scholar but a *karmic* man and had to draw a line between his responsibility towards worldly and scholarly duties. He proved that he was a learned man but not a scholar, a devotee but not a preacher. So what if he had to adopt a mix of religious worship of *Kul Devis* for his religious inclination.

9

Goddess Sharda of Kas'mira

There is no religion greater than truth
and a truthful person knows no fear.

Rig Veda

Mother's Grace (Mahima), Sharda Mahatmaya and Grandeur

Mahima (Grace) of Mother Sharda: As a young boy I got used to hearing folk tales of *Sone Kisli* and other tales from Granny Zapar Ded, but what interested me was her narration of travelogue of Pandit Bhawani Kaul of 18th Century (Descendant of Pandit Narain Kaul; who wrote *History of Kas'mira* during Akbar's time). His travels through dense forests in quest of spiritual and literary enlightenment kept me, an eight-year-old, gazing for her next lip movement, however, it was Bhawani Kaul's challenging pilgrimage to Gangabal and Sharda Temple which impressed me most. At *Matamal* (Mothers parents place) uncle would hold court at his *Rehbab Sahib* residence and amongst various discourses, Pandit Harjoo Fehrist's (Mid 19th Century; social reformer and staunch *Vedhist*) visits to Sharda Temple, till he lost his life at the temple, held us spell bound. Those days Goddess Sharda meant a lot to me, in my quest to do well in studies. The *Mahima* of Goddess Sharda also came from our Guruji *Lala Sab*, maternal Guruji's *Nityanand*, *Vassa* and *Jagga Boui's*, when on *Gortrai* (Called all over Bharatvarasha as Guru Tritya) hand painted image of Goddess Sharda (*Gortrais)* were handed over to me and my siblings. Having been specifically dedicated to *Bhadrakali*, family devoted to *Chakreshwari*, did not damper my mental affiliation to Goddess Sharda. But alas, unlike other places, which I could visit, I had to satisfy myself with imaginative details of Sharda Temple. Time flew; in 1976, I was literally crawling on my fours to reach a mountain top in Kupwara District called as *Raja Ram Di Lari* (See Map on p. 300). As I stood on top of over 14000 feet high mountain; Nanga Parvat and K2 peaks formed the magnificent backdrop on the Northern skyline of

Kishanganga Valley (Neelam Valley) across Line Of Control (LOC); now under Pakistan. In the process of admiration of this scenic beauty, my local guide, nudged and in halting Kashmiri asked me to view two other peaks in the middle distance. Sharda and Narda Peak to the East of *Raja Ram Di Lari* formed two twin peaks overlooking Kishanganga River and dense forests on Northern slopes. Along forward slopes of these twin-peaks I could see, through binoculars, two major structures with a narrow walled passage leading to it. Kishanganga River flowed few hundred feet below with many more rivulets, small and big, racing to merge with the river. He was pointing out Sharda temple to me and to its immediate West was a fort like structure, now in ruins, called the Sirhasila Castle. As I bowed in obeisance, the accounts ingrained in childhood kaleidoscopically came back. Months later I was over the area in a helicopter and my pilot colleagues made it point to remain hovering over the area to enable me to have more look of the Temple. As we did so, hymn to Sharda; "Sharda *Varda Devi Mookshidata Saraswati, Sharneyetrambike Gauri Narayani...Namostute, Namastasyey, Namastaseyey, Namastaseyey, Nammo Namahah"* (Salutations to Goddess Sharda, Saraswati and Gauri) came out loudly from my lips, much to the amazement of my pilot colleagues. During next two years stint in the valley, as a foot soldier, I trudged almost all the area notably those associated with Sharda Pilgrimage. Wangat Temples (Sodaritirath; Narannag); Bandipur, Wullar, (North of Wullar Lake), Gushi, Rangwar, Kralpura, Kupwara, Keran (All near to Sharda Temple) and finally Handwara, Bhadrakali, Kazinag, Nastachun Pass and Karnah (Titwal; Northwest of Kupwara). The dye had been cast; narrations of Bhawani and Harjoo's travelogue got translated into real landmarks and did not remain fiction. Study of our history, religious places, translated scriptures, over the decades and inclination brought me to a stage that I could understand these accounts better. With maze of accounts, folklore and myths; Sharda Temple had become epicentre of religious philosophy, *Avtars*, Sages, Kings, Visitors, Rivers, Chroniclers accounts; yet the antiquity and *Mahima* of the temple, deity, pilgrimage account and changes, over the centuries, remained obscure, mostly hazy, or attributed to different sages, scholars etc. Possibly truth and facts were casualty while draped fiction held sway.

Temple of Goddess Sharda: Kas'mira has been known as Sharda Desh (Abode of Goddess Sharda - named after presiding deity of learning and fine arts. However, chroniclers like Kalhan refer to it by 'The land of Aryans' (Kalhan's *Rajatarangini* Verse 341 Book I) and not Sharda Desh, though the Goddess is reverently referred to three Goddesses. Sharda not only is important as a temple, but in her triple form of Sharda, Narda or Saraswati and Vaghdevi; giving impetus and excellence to Kashmiri learning.

Temple of Sharda is located in Neelam Valley (Upper Kishanganga), few Kilometers from Line of Control (LOC), in Pakistan Occupied Kas'mira (POK) in a small village called Shardi; near the confluence of Kishanganga (Referred, wrongly though, as Maha Sindhu, Sindhu Ganga, Parvati Ganga), Saraswati (Referred also as Kalnotri) and Madhumati Rivers. Its location can be fixed Northwest of Gangabal and North of Lolab Valley/ Wular Lake. Shardi, a small village gets its name from Goddess Sharda and is connected by road running along the bank of Kishanganga River from Muzzafarabad, called Neelam Valley Road. Kishanganga River meets Vitasta (Jhelum) at Muzzafarabad. One has to cross Kishanganga to reach Shardi or Sharda Temple if travelling along this road. From the valley one has to cross Shamsabari Range and descend nearly to the level of Kishanganga River and then move East along a foot/pony track. The main temple rises prominently on the lower slopes of Sharda Peak (Point 3287 Metres also called Domel Baihik); Narda Peak (Point 3805 Metres also called Katsil) is just East of it, higher in height but on the same ridge line. The twin-peaks are magnificent and prominent, even though to the South of the temple. The view from the Temple towards North would be splendid with Nanga Parvat and K2 Range paying obeisance to the Goddess from their towering heights. There are pine clad mountain slope between the temple and twin peaks (Forest cover in the area, more so in the vicinity of the temple, has now diminished and is sparse above the line of temple). Madhumati and Saraswati Rivers, flowing on either side of Sharda Temple, join Kishanganga closer to the temple and pilgrims refer the confluence as Sharda Sangam. Kalhan; author of Rajatarangini, in his introductory part on the vale of Kas'mira (Verses 28 to 38 Book I) says thus **'Whereby visiting the Goddess of Sharda one gets in moment to the river Madhumati and the Saraswati adored by the poets' (Verse 37 Book I)**. The reference is to the *mahima* of Sharda but has not used River prefix with Saraswati and apparently refers to Goddess Saraswati; other form of Sharda.

Sir Auriel Stein, who translated Rajatarangini in English, however, prefixes Saraswati with River in brackets; connoting his 'own' interpretation of River and not Goddess Saraswati. Apparently he had missed nuances of Saraswati as Goddess. Kalhan in Rajatarangini gives the location of the shrine, with reference to the siege of Sirhasila Castle, which took place in his own time (12th Century); **'where a huge temple complex came up.'** His reference indicates location of the shrine in proximity to Sirhasila Castle/Fort (also called Sirhala) West of Sharda. Sirhasila Fort is close to temple, now in ruins, overlooking Kishanganga and, as per Kalhan, encircled by Kishanganga, Madhumati and Muktasri (Verse 2492 Book VIII). While Kishanganga and Madhumati River referred to is next to Sharda (not to be mistaken with Madhumati River of Bandipore); Muktasri River would be further West and only guess can be made of its location closer to Tejjan. This interpretation is because Kalhan specifically refers to encirclement / isolation of Sirhasila

Castle, which is possible only if these rivers are in a ring around it. He also refers to the flight of Bhoja, from the battle scene, towards the shrine, which he refers as 'Sanctuary of Goddess Sharda' (Verse 2706 Book VIII); which also indicates proximity of the two landmarks. Kalhan, in his account of King Lalitaditya's reign, refers to visit by certain followers of a King of Bengal under the pretence of visit to Sharda to avenge the murder of their king by Lalitaditya but enter Parihaskeshwa (Parihaspura) temple and get killed (Verse 325/326 Book IV Rajatarangini) (Lalitaditya had conquered Bengal (Gauda) during his reign). This indicates that *mahima* of the shrine had spread to far off regions and that the shrine existed prior to the reign of King Lalitaditya of Kas'mira. Famous chronicler Al-Beruni describes Sharda shrine's position in 'Inner Kas'mira 'about two to three days journey towards the mountains of Bolor'. Bolor referred by him in his chronicle has been interpreted towards Upper Indus between Gilgit and Ladakh, however, reference to Bolor to mean 'Wulor' or 'Wular Lake' is most likely, as Gilgit and Ladakh are far away from Sharda and the area was never known as Bolor. Also the phonetics of 'Wulor' in Arabic is somewhat closer to 'Bolor.' He, Al-Beruni, speaks of the shrine; 'much venerated and frequented by pilgrims as those of *Surya* at Multan (Pakistan), *Vishnu Chakraswamin* (Thaneswar-Kurukshetra) and the *Linga* of Somnath (Gujarat)'. Al-Beruni (996-1031 AD) visited Kas'mira in 1030 AD and this description is not that of his visit as there is no evidence of Al-Beruni having visited the shrine. Al-Beruni, an Arab scholar came to India with Mohammad Ghaznavi, in the beginning of 11th Century AD stayed in India for a number of years. He wrote a book, which gives account of social, political and economic conditions of then India. He was killed in a battle in 1031 AD; just a year after visiting Kas'mira. Another Kashmiri scholar, Bilhana, in his description of Pravarapura (Srinagar), while in Deccan, mentions Sharda *tirath* shrine (Not temple) and ascribes excellence of learning of the people to Sharda. Bilhana; Born 1041 AD at Khonmukh (Khonmoh); fellow-poet of Kalhan, left Kas'mira in 1066 AD during the reign of King Kalsa (1063 to 1089 AD) to become Chief Pandit of Karnata (Present Day Mysore). He, Bilhana, was unheard of after 1088 AD, wrote *Vikramanka Deva Caritam*, a historical compendium of poems narrating the expedition of King Vikramaditya VI of Kalyan (1076 AD to 1127 AD) (Verse 937 Book VII Rajatarangini). In 1877 AD an old palm-leaf edition of *Vikramanka Deva Caritam* was found in Jaisalmer (Rajasthan). Other known compositions to Bilhana's credit are; *Caur Panchasika,* a lyric of fifty stanzas and *Karna Sundari* a drama of four acts.

Another reference to Sharda's form is found in Jonaraja's chronicle wherein he mentions Zain-ul-Abidin (Badshah) visit to the shrine in 1422 AD, to witness the miraculous manifestations of the Goddess (Jonaraja; Chronicler and writer of 14th and 15th Century (1389 -1459 AD), updated Rajatarangini).

The Valley acquired pride of place in Sanskrit, Sharda language, literature, medicine, astronomy, astrology, religion, art and architecture; all attributed to the benediction of Sharda. The temple became a sacred shrine to which thousands of devotees from distant parts of India were attracted to seek blessings. In 16th Century, Abul Fazl (He wrote *Ain-e-Akbari*) writes; 'At two days distance from Hayahom is the river named Madhumati, which flows from the Darda Country (Dardesa, apparently referring to Dardistan area, which was controlled by defiant Dards). On its banks is a stone temple called Sharda, dedicated to *Durga* and regarded with great veneration. On every eighth *tithi* (*Ashtami*) of the bright moon, it begins to shake and produces the most extraordinary effect.' The reference to Madhumati is specific to a stream North of Hayahom.

Saraswati River Near Sharda Temple

Goddess Sharda is said to be perched on a swan, carrying glittering gold washed from the sand of river Madhumati as her diadem. Madhumati River is considered sacred stream and gets mentioned in Nilamat Puranam (1276- 1289). However, this stream is no other than Bandpore Nala, marked Bodh Kul on the maps and falls into Wulor (Wular) lake near village of Kolus. This river (Bandpore Nala) gets also mentioned in Rajatarangini Verse 1171 Book VII. However, River Madhumati of Sharda is different which is a small stream getting this name in later centuries. Description of Goddess in our Sharda *Vandana* reads like this (Not in full); *Kas'mira Purvasini, Vidhya Dieyinam Shawetambuj Viharinam, Chaturbuj Dharini... Shattantriveena Vadini... Mokshadayini, Papanashneemam ... Vitasta Rupenam ... Himachidit Girishshobinam ... Kalashamrit Dharayae*. Translated this means; 'Residing in Kas'mira from ancient times..giver of knowledge.. seated on a white bird (Swan)..having four arms, carries hundred stringed veena.. giver of *moksha* and forgiver of sins.. just like with grace of Vitasta (Jhelum River).. gracing a snow clad mountain..carrying a pot with holy nectar.' In South India, where worship of Sharda is equally high, Goddess Sharda represents matrix of the universe displaying in her hands; jar full of nectar, book signifying learning, rosary signifying subtle nuances of universe, source of *Upanishadic* knowledge and three *Shaktis* (*Trimurtis*) known as Saraswati, Lakshmi and Iswari. Even today orthodox Brahmins in South India, on rising from his bed in the morning, faces North and with folded hands offers salutations to Goddess Sharda; '*Namaste Sarada Devi, Kas'mira Mandala Vasini (Salutations to Goddess Sarada who resides in Kas'mira.'* In Kas'mira the hymn to Sharda is; '*Sharda Varda Devi Mookshidata Saraswati, Sharneyetrambike Gauri Narayani...Namostute, Namastasyey, Namastaseyey, Namastaseyey Nammo Namaha.*'

The number of pilgrims to Sharda was ever increasing during the rule of Hindu Kings. With advent of Islam (1324 AD), it lost royal patronage but flow of pilgrims was reasonable even during Sultan and Chak rule (15th and16th Century). Fortunately destructive hands of Sikandar *Butshikan* did not reach the shrine, because of its location, where perhaps his writ did not run. It was politically disturbed conditions during Mughal and Pathan rule in Upper Kishanganga Valley, that had much to do with the neglect into which the shrine had fallen. Things improved during Dogra rule, however, with 1947 War and subsequent ceasefire, Sharda remained on the other side of LOC, in Pakistan Occupied Kashmir.

Sharda Mahatmaya: *Mahatmayas* are scriptures pertaining to various pilgrimages. 51 *Mahatmayas* existed or have been traced in Kas'mira. Most of these have been extracted from *Puranas* but many are of medieval period more so pertaining to those shrines which came up during middle of first millennium BC and later. *Sharda Mahatmaya*, a similar scripture, narrates *tirtha* as seen by Muni Shandalya. In order to see Goddess Sharda, Muni Shandalya is advised to proceed to jungles of Syamala (Possibly Kupwara District). There at Ghusa (Gushi) *Mahadevi* (Sharda) appears and promises to show herself in her true form as *Shakti* in the Sharda *Van*. *Mahadevi* - Consort of Shiva; Parvati or Uma, also called Kali, Durga. Religious scholars, historians (not all) refer *Mahadevi* as one form of Parvati, Lakshmi and Saraswati. This form of address, *Mahadevi,* is more common in Shavitie variant and that too in South. The Muni then proceeds to a spring known as Krishna Nag (Marked as Mari Nag (Point 3601 Metres) on the maps, in which he bathes and his body becomes golden; representing symbolic liberation from darkness. This spring is situated above the village of Dranga, close to Hayahom. Many chronicles claim that Dranga is in the foothills of mountain-ridge known as Kakudar (Kashmiri); a corrupt form of *Kara Kuta*

Dhara above *Tosa Maidan* of present day; *Tausi* plain of *Tohi* as known in Poonch and Persian *Maidan;* thus *Tosa Maidan*, which was a watch station along the Pir Panchal Range (Verses 140, 1352 Book VII Rajatarangini*)* in those days. Scholars who refer it to Dranga of Sharda *Mahatmaya* may be because of similarity of names; both are widely separated. Actually Dranga of Sharda is called Sona-Drang after word '*Swararnardhanguka'; Swarn* meaning gold and *anguka* body; apparent reference to Shandalya's body becoming golden. Muni Shandalya then ascends the mountain range to the North and sees dance of Goddess in a mountain meadow, known as *Rangavatika* ; Rangwar Forest, which lies below the pass; Rangwar Gali. He, Shandalaya then arrives at *Tejavana,* present day Tejjan, a small jungle close to Dudnial, the residence of Sage Gautama, on the banks of Kishanganga. The sage (Muni Shandalya) after crossing hill sees God Ganesh on the East mountain behind the temple and Sirhasila has resemblance to Lord Ganesha's head and trunk and arrives in the Sharda *Van*; pine clad forest North of the temple. Sirhasila means the rock head; *Sirah* – head; *sila* (shila-rock) referring to Ganesha's rock head. Sirhasila Fort/Castle seems to have got name from Sharda Peak in the *Mahatmaya.* After reciting a hymn in praise of her triple form of Sharda, Narda or Saraswati and Vaghdevi, goddess revealed herself to the Muni at the 'sacred spot.' The sacred spot is reference to place where shrine exists and temple was constructed later. Legend says that She disappears inside a spring (*Kund*) at the site of present day temple, now inside the Sanctum Sanctorum covered by a stone slab and invites him to her residence at Sirhasila. It is said that *Pitras* then approached Muni Shandalya and requested him to perform their *Shradas.* On his taking water from the 'Maha Sindhu' (Kishanganga) for the purpose of the *Tarpana* (Religious method of giving water to dead), half of its water turns into honey and forms the stream now known as Madhumati. It is said that bath and *Shrada*, rites associated with dead, at Sharda *Sangam* (confluence of Madhumati and Kishanganga Rivers of Sharda) assures remission of sins. On the other side Sindhu Ganga or Maha Sindhu of Kas'mira eminates from Dras and is mentioned in Nilamat Puranam (257-59). This river is called lower Sindh and finally joins Vitasta (Jhelum) at Shadipur. Geographically Sindhu (Indus), Maha Sindhu and Sharda are far apart. In *Mahatmaya* the reference to Maha Sindhu is to Kishanganga River. This custom of *shrada* adopted for this temple pilgrimage is not religiously connected with the Goddess of learning and fine arts; Sharda. Specific places for such rites for the dead have been designated in different parts of the valley; Shopian, Mattan, Shadipur, Khonmukh, Gangabal etc. Most probable reason for this could be that *Pitra Paksh* (Annual fortnight for *Shradhas* for dead ancestors starts just seven days after the designated day of pilgrimage and by that time they, pilgrims, may not have returned to their homes). Sharda *Vandana* (Hymn) also attributes *Mokshadayini* and *Papnashneemam,* giving freedom to soul and forgives sins, which may have also been reason for including *tarpan* rites as part of the pilgrimage. Goddesses Aryan Saraswats Brahmins worshipped initially were the *trinity* of Lakshmi, Parvati and Saraswati. Manifestation of Goddess in the shape of Sharda, as goddess of learning would have been subsequent (*Mahadevi* in the form as *Shakti*, as given in *Mahatmaya*). A broad spectrum would thus indicate Sharda *Mahatmaya* account refers to 'already manifested form of Goddess Sharda'; around 1000 BC, Brahmanic period, when *Gotras* and Brahmanism took strong roots after absorbing local rituals and worship of Goddesses in other forms, other than the *trinity*, started. *Sharda Mahtmaya* infers Sharda Goddess had already manifested in the valley before existence of Sage Gautama and Muni Shandalya (Founders of their respective *gotras).*

There are certain indications from *Sharda Mahatmaya;* it confirms that temple had not been constructed then. Peculiar names of places like Hayasrama, Syamala have been used; place names, features given in the account can even be identified today but others like *Tejavana,* etc. are more scholarly names. Hymn recited by the *muni* generally indicates composition era of *Sharda Mahatmaya* between 9th and 13th Century AD, when most of religious accounts, philosophies, and scriptures started taking shape in the valley and many scholars from outside, with fresh strong Shaivite inclination of the South, visited the valley. A further confirmation of the era is visualisation of Sharda in the form of *Mahadevi* (Form of *Shakti*); this manifestation is associated with 12th and 13th Century AD, when Kas'mira had come under the influence of *Shakatmata.* Also Kalhan's reference to sacred river Madhumati (Near Bandipore) and not Madhumati of Sharda Shrine also gives indication of the vintage of *Sharda Mahatmaya* to the later era. Scriptures and chronicles indicate *Shakatmata* influence started during King Harsha's rule (1089-1101 AD) (Not to be mistaken with King Harshavardhan). Is it that the author of *Sharda Mahatmaya*, a Shaivite to the core, wanted to project Sharda in the role of *Mahadevi* (*Shakti*) as per his own beliefs? Or was it another step to give impetus to 'Dualistic' Shaivism in the valley or bring it at par with similar belief of the Goddess Sharda in South?

The needle of authorship of *Sharda Mahatmaya* points towards Madhvacharya (Madhavacharaya (1199- 1276 AD); Vidyaranya after becoming an ascetic, disciple of Sri Vidyateertha (1247 - 1297 A.D), 51st Acharya of Kamakothi). We find some indication of Madhavacharya, a staunch devotee of Adi-Shankara, being the author. Madhavacharya is attributed with many scholarly works, longer stay in the valley and his life period (1199-1276 AD) coinciding with the period of probable temple construction (not manifestation of Goddess). He is known to have moved around the valley, North of the valley as well and such works of poetic imagination, evident from various landmarks used, can safely be attributed to him. There is, however, no record of his visiting Sharda Shrine. It also looks certain that Madhavacharya wrote *Sharda Mahatmaya* after becoming an ascetic, taking the name of Vidhyaranya, kept the work anonymous, as per unwritten customs of ascetics. The hymn used in the *Mahatmaya* (Sharda, Narda or Saraswati, Vaghdevi) is in accordance with the hymn in praise of Sharda in the South, except that the local variant name Narda has been added; another strong pointing needle to his authorship; who found it necessary to include local form of address as well.

If he is the author then it could have well been composed in the later half of 12th Century; possibly when he had become ascetic and wanted account to remain anonymous. There are, however, certain other points which need to be noted; account of the places traversed by Muni Shandalya are generalised and not specific. Shandalya is post Gautama and could not have met Gautama at *Tejavana*. Is *Sharda Mahatmaya* just referring to Gautama's residence; *Tejavana*? These sanskritised names, with a tinge of Southern bias, are somewhat new to Kashmiri vocabulary. However, Kalhan's account in Rajatarangini just says; 'where a huge temple complex came up' but does not give detailed account of the shrine/ temple like Sirhasila (Rajatarangini account is pre Madhavacharaya by about fifty years plus). This becomes all the more interesting that had *Sharda Mahatmaya* been available during Kalhan's time, he may possibly have dwelled on it in more detail, including the temple. Or is there any other reason for him to refrain from such mention? It is also apparent that description of various landmarks is that of the ones closer to the valley like Madhumati (Bandpore Nala), Maha Sindhu (Lower Sindh) and its equivalent names have been created for this *Mahatmaya.* Kalhan also refers to Sindhu Ganga and Madhumati, but these are different from Kishanganga and Madhumati of Sharda.

Grandeur of the Sharda Temple: The temple is approached from West by an imposing stone staircase from the direction of Sirhasila Castle/Fort, now nearly decayed, which leads up in 63 steps to the main entrance of the quadrangular court enclosing the temple. The stairs are about 9/10 feet wide and rise rather steeply in six flights between two flanking walls of massive row of parapet coping (Balustrade), now in ruins. The view from the staircase is magnificent; you can see the valleys of Madhumati, Kishanganga gorge and also their *Sangam.* The quadrangular court, enclosing the temple, is an accurately oriented oblong; 142 feet long and 94 feet 6 inches wide, having proportion of 3:2 and is enclosed by a massive wall, six feet thick and eleven feet high from the level of the court to the projecting rim at the foot of the coping. The later rises in pyramidal form to a height of eight feet above the top of the wall, giving it a look like a fortress wall. From outside, the walls appear massive and imposing, as they are raised on basement walls to equalise different elevations of the ground. The entrance to the central court is through a gate, with a double porch of Kashmiri design (when referred as Kashmiri design, it connotes design as found in other temple structures of mediaeval period). This gate occupies middle of the West face, in line with the porch, leading to the sanctum sanctorum. The other three walls have blank archway, standing to height of about 20 feet from the base to the apex. In the centre of the Northern wall is a small recess 3 feet by 3 inches square, containing two ancient *lingas,* which opens by a terafoil arched door towards the interior of the court (in earlier accounts there is no mention of existence of these *lingas*).

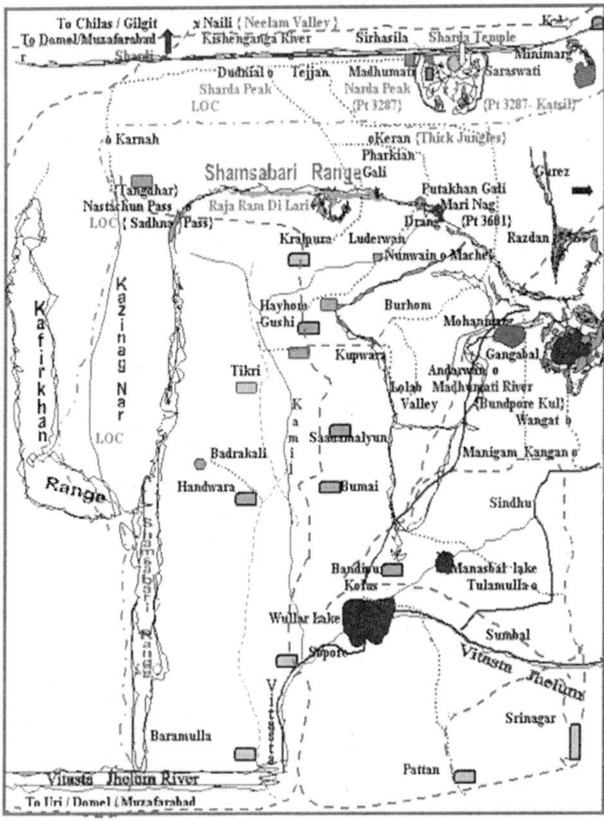

(Not to Scale)

Pilgrimage Routes to Sharda Temple in Kishenganga Valley from Pravarpura (Srinagar) where Pilgrim Groups Assembled

Sanctum Sanctorum: (The dimensions of the Sharda Temple Complex given hereunder are as they existed in late 19th Century. Since then due to vagaries of weather, neglect and major earthquake have changed the shape of stairs, arches and the main temple. The photographs are of 2004 vintage).

In the centre of the quadrangle is the temple raised on a basement of 24 feet square and 5 feet 3 inches high and is perfectly plane. The entrance to inner temple is from the West side and is approached by a flight of a few stairs, five and a half feet wide with flanking side walls. The cell of the main temple is 22 feet square. On each side of the porch way are two square pillars about 16 feet high and two feet six inches apart. The 'capital' of both the pillars seem to have been hewn from a single stone (This aspect is very important, as similar evidence can be found in temples constructed between 9th and 13th Centuries AD). The interior of the inner temple is a square of 12 feet and 3 inches and it has no decoration of any kind; perfectly plane and scarcely any traces of the usual pyramidal stone roof. The only conspicuous object inside is a large slab, which measures about 6 by 7 feet with a thickness of about six inches. This slab is believed to cover a *kund* or spring, from which Goddess Sharda appeared to the Sage Shandalya. This *kund* is the main object of special veneration of the pilgrims. In Kashmiri religious philosophy *Kund's* hold special reverence; like Kheer Bhawani, Devi Bal, Bhairav Temple Maisuma, Nandkeshwar Temple Seer (Sopore) and many more.

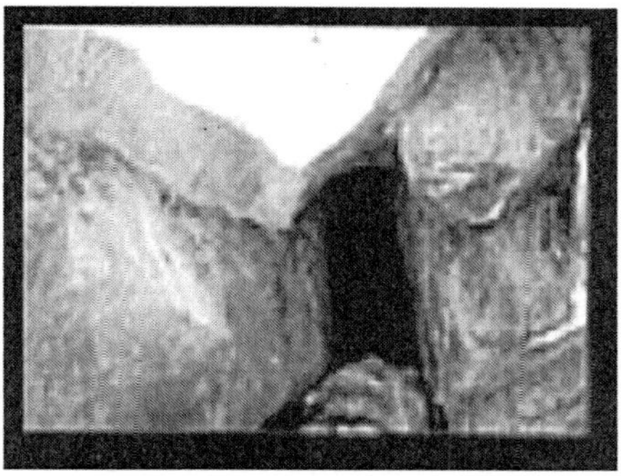

Cave in Ganesh Ghati

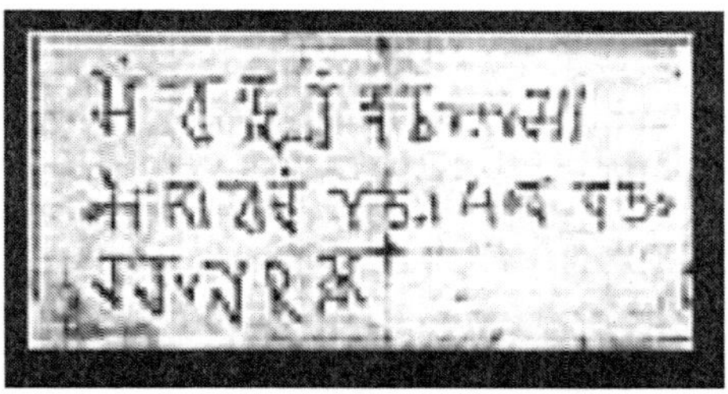

Sharda Inscription Outside the Cave

As the conditions deteriorated during medieval era around Sharda, a *kund* in the village of *Tsatsa*, 6-7 kilometres from the North edge of Dal Lake, West of Burzhom Village was named *Shardakund* and venerated at par with Sharda *kund* and as an alternative to the main Sharda Temple.

Some chronicles mention presence of an idol of Sharda, made of wood inside the temple. From Jonaraja's account of Zain-ul-Abidin's visit, it appears that the idol was there; "appearance of sweat on the face of the image of the goddess, shaking of the arm, and sensation of heat on touching the feet." Bilhana, Al-Beruni (Both 11th Century AD), Kalhan (12th Century AD) do not mention about this idol or two *lingas* but accounts of Jonaraja (15th Century AD) and Abul Fazl (16th Century) do mention this. This indicates that the idol and *lingas* had been installed somewhere after 12th Century (Kalhan) but before15th Century AD (Jonaraja); possibly before Muslim rule in 14th Century firmed in. Such installation of idols or *lingas* takes place at the time of *Kumbhabishekam* (Consecration) of a newly constructed or extensively renovated temple. The other factor is that representation of Gods and Goddesses in those days used to be of stone or *ashtdatu* (Metal alloys), not in man made form, which stood vagaries of weather and time; which is not so for wooden idols. The *kund* covered with stone slab was venerated as the form of the Goddess and no need was felt for an idol. In any case, during the medieval period, no firm shape was given to Gods and Goddesss and generally they were formless and if an idol was installed it would have been a temporary measure. It may be that custom of a wooden idol being installed, from year to year, by craftsmen, may have been adopted; Goddess Sharda being the deity for learning and fine crafts. Similar installation of Vishwa Karma, Durga or Ganesha idols on Vishwa Karma, Puja or Ganesh Chaturthi festivals respectively, has been followed throughout India. It, however, may not be an old custom but possibly imported in later centuries. A brief and latest account of the Temple comes from Justice Swaroop Nath Katju (Father of Retired Supreme Court Judge Justice Markandey Katju), who visited Sharda Temple in the summer of 1935. He narrates; 'The shrine is located on a hilltop like the shrine of *Jwalaji*. The steps leading to the top of the hill appeared to be twisted as if an earthquake had battered them. The question as to when did the University township cease to exist requires investigation.' The question remains, if, when and where!

Sri Chakra Inscription at Sharda Temple Sanctum Sanctorum: We are told of *Sri Chakra* inscription on the stone slab covering the *kund* at Sharda and Shankaracharaya (Called hereafter Adi-Shankara) having taken it from Sharda to other places in India for installation. No *Sri Chakra* ever existed or was installed for Goddess Sharda. Question of Adi – Shankara having taken it from Sharda for installation elsewhere is erroneous. In *Sri Chakra* form the Goddess, as *Shakti* (Power), is depicted in the form of a diagram representing a *Chakra* (Circular wheel of life; as understood philosophically). *Sharika,* the 'Cosmic Mother - *Sri Chakra*' is worshipped at *Hari Parvat* in the cosmic form of Divine Mother. It is engraved on a green, circular shaped stone of Sapphire. This diagram is also known as *Matra Chakra,* established here by King Pravarsena II at the end of the 6th century AD.

Descriptions in *Sharda Mahatmaya,* by Al-Beruni, Kalhan, Jonaraja describing Zain-ul-Abidin's visit, accounts of Abul Fazl's and MA Stein (1892) do not mention inscription of *Sri Chakra* on the slab covering *kund.* Admittedly Vermilion and *ghee* used to be pasted on this venerated slab, but these could not have fully covered engravings, if they existed. Chronicles only mention presence of an idol of Sharda (of wood ?); confirmed by Jonaraja's account (Zain-ul-Abidin's visit in 1422 AD). Abul Fazl (16th Century) writes; "On every eighth *tithi* (Ashtami) of the bright moon, it begins to shake and produces the most extraordinary effect." There is similarity in both accounts as far as extraordinary effects were observed, a phenomenon, which takes place when a worshipper, with full faith, goes to a shrine.

Sri Chakra form of Mother Goddess, in her form of *Shakti* and in Kas'mira is associated with *Chakrashwari* only. If Sharda was also to be *Mahadevi,* definitely she would have also been a Kul Devi. The ritual of marking a *Sri Chakra,* by priests, with lime or white powder or Vermilion is not new and this is what would have been happening in recent centuries and may have been introduced by Kashmiri Pandits, who were back to the valley, carrying certain rituals from plains of India; possibly after 15th Century (Badshah's visit) or during Moghul rule (16th and 17th Century). Abul Fazl's account, by reading between the lines, when he describes 'stone temple called Sharda, dedicated to *Durga'* is not indicator of any such markings of *Sri Chakra.*

Narda Linkage to Temple Construction: There are few facts, which remain to be unravelled as far as Sharda is concerned. First; reasons for another name of Narda, which is used apart from Sharda. Hymn to Sharda refers as '*Sharda Varda Devi'* and *Sharda Vandana* does not include Narda address but this is mentioned when Muni Shandalya recites hymn in praise of her triple form; '*Sharda, Narda* or *Saraswati* and *Vaghdevi*' (*Sharda Mahatmaya*). Second, all places of worship of Kashmiri's are within the valley; enclosed within mountain ranges of Pir Panchal, Shamsabari and lower ranges of Great Himalayan Range. At best we have Gangabal, Amarkanth (Amarnath) and Bhedagiri on the inward periphery of these ranges, but none across the major mountain range. This must be viewed in the context of majority, nearly 98 per cent, of then Kashmiris living within the valley. Thirdly, construction era and person (King, Feudal Chief, Religious Head, Group etc) who may have been instrumental in construction of the temple remains unknown. It is all the more intriguing when Sharda lends her name to this *Desh* (Country), proudly talked of from centuries.

Kalhan talks of siege of Sirhasila (Sirhala) Castle (Rajatarangini), which took place in his own time (12th Century) but is silent on details of Sharda. His statement is loaded with some indications by using words 'where a huge temple complex came up', not exists; using 'came up' expression with siege without giving reasons or any more details of the shrine. This siege took place in 12th Century, when Jai Simha (1128-55 AD) was the King. If it was constructed during his time, why his name is not mentioned, though he does figure closely in other facet of Sharda; the language/ *lipi.* Did it remain un-linked to him, as his other temples? Jai Simha's early days were critical, because of the preceding civil wars and political unrest. Sirhasila Castle siege indicates the area around Sharda Shrine to be part of then Kingdom, under the fiefdom of a local revolting feudal chief, who had to be reigned-in. From 958 AD (First Lohara Dynasty) till 1150 AD and even beyond, Hindu Shahi's reigned in Kabul, while Hindu Kings including Didda ruled in Kas'mira. Both these Kingdoms were contiguous with good relations; exchange of expertise, culture, religion, matrimonial relations and same language (*Upbrahmbasha*) and also shared Sharda *lipi*. In fact first artefacts in under-development Sharda *lipi* were found in the areas of Hindu Shahi's of Kabul.

Narda Peak During Summer

Let us go back to history of one group of Saraswat Aryans having strayed North of the valley, who had identical beliefs, rituals as that of the group who came directly to valley (The lost tribe of Jews is not being referred here). A variant of *Upbrahmbasha*, slightly influenced by the Northwestern *Upbrahmbasha,* was common in this area as well and the country(s) was called Darda or Drava. The spill over of changes in religion and beliefs from the valley covered this area as well. The valley of Kishanganga, part of a feudatory state, was also known as *Drava* derived from *Duranda* (Corrupted name of a local feudal lord) as per Kalhan and mentions that title of 'Shahi' was that of Dard and Kabul rulers. The tract of land known as Keran and Karnaha (Karnah) bordering Kishanganga Valley, though under local rule, was known to have paid tribute to Kas'mira Kings. Even Lohara Dynasty who were from the areas of Poonch, could have had influence in this area, as Poonch was easily connected to areas West of Pir Panchal and Shamsabari Range. All these factors may indicate Narda as another name for Sharda in that part of the country (in Darda). Sharda *Narda* form of combined address being used in *Sharda Mahatmaya* reinforces this point; as the shrine lay beyond geographical and controlled territory limits of Kas'mira valley and Narda being local form of address of the Goddess. Close similarity of phonetics of Sharda-Narda, in the respective variants of *Upbrahmbasha,* could be another reason of association. It is also certain that the people and material (Stones etc.) for the construction came from closeby area; rock examination points clearly to quarries of Ganesh Ghati along the mountain spur called Sharda Peak. In our history only works of Kings and Scholars have been chronicled and many works/constructions undertaken by local warlords/feudal lords or chieftains remain obscure; this has also been so with our great Chronicler Kalhan. It may be that King Jai Simha had to undertake reining in of this feudal lord of the area as its control was necessary since visitors from outside to the shrine first reached his court and the shrine was out of his jurisdiction.

The architecture of Sharda temple resembles that of Kapteshwar temple, located above the village of Kother (3 kilometres from Achabal); simple architecture and absence of any decoration; giving impression of King Mutskund (1040-1060 AD-also called Mucukund) being the builder of Sharda temple as well. He being an outsider could not have done so and that too so far away from Kapteshwar Temple. Rajatarangini identifies Mutskund, a *Gauda* warrior from Bengal, during reign of King Ananta (1028-1063 AD) who built Kapteshwar Temple. This king cursed with a pair of buffalo's ears, anxious to rid himself of this deformity, learnt about powers of Kapteshwar Spring. The King took a dip in the spring and got rid of his cursed ears. In gratitude, Mutskund built the Kapteshwar temple. Someway Mutskund has found way in Kashmiri way of taunt; *Mushtand* word commonly used for hefty/ugly specimen, in disdain. It may be that the design of Kapteshwar temple could have been taken back home by one of the pilgrims from this part of the Drava Country. Kapteshwar is also mentioned in Nilamat Puranam, when sage Bhadravasa narrates its *Mahatmaya* (Grace) to King Gonanda I (Pre *Mahabarata*); associating it with form of Shiva as a wooden log. In all probability, nearing certainty, the temple of Sharda in the form described, was constructed in 12th Century, during Jai Simha's (1128 - 1155 AD) reign; by a warlord of the Kishanganga Valley, a strong devotee of Sharda, whose ancestors too were Saraswat Brahmins and in fact de-facto Kashmiri Pandit. Though Sharda temple like Shankaracharaya Temple (Gopadiri), *Chakreshwari*, *Jwala* temples is on a low hill, its stairs, flanking walls, massive row of parapet coping indicates enormous effort to cater for vagaries of adverse weather and snow conditions and not really of great architecture design. This will also answer the question as to the simple but massive architecture of the temple, unlike temples which had royal patronage; like Sun Temple at Martand, Shankar Varman's temples at Pattan and many others.

Historical Evaluation, Shakti Roop, Lore and Pilgrimage Routes

Historical Evaluation of Sharda Temple: It is from various accounts, chronicles, events, and historical data that dating of the temple, its construction, changes and other major inferences can be made. There are four different periods, pertaining to religion variant eras, which are important for purpose of this evaluation. First, when Aryan Saraswats settled in Kas'mira and *Vaishnavite* Brahmanism took shape; Second, advent of Buddhism; Third, Shaivism taking firm routes and finally changes that took place during the subsequent centuries. There is an interesting twist to the group of Aryans, who entered Kas'mira; one group is reported to have entered the valley directly and another bifurcated while moving in the adjacent plains and moved Northeastwards and settled beyond the geographical limits of the valley. Another theory is that one group; albeit a smaller one, settled in areas North of the Shamsabari Range, as there was another valley, albeit smaller one (Now called Neelam Valley in Dardistan). This group is of interest to us, when we tried to answer the question as to reasons of the shrine coming up outside the geographical limits of the valley. There are well-chronicled descriptions of Buddhists monuments established in the valley from 300 BC onwards. Neither Sharda Shrine nor any area closer to Sharda/Shardi figures in these. Analysis of above periods leads to certain inferences with regard to Goddess Sharda and spot of her abode. First, around Sapatrishi Samvat 2000 $\pm$ (1000 BC-Brahmanic Period) crystallisation in the faith would have taken place for Goddess Sharda to manifest in Kas'mira and adequate time for firming in of faith and manifestations of other forms. This period also generally tallies with similar phenomenon in India; notably South. Some estimates are of 2600 BC, coinciding with entry of early settlers, Nagas, into the valley, is too early for manifestation of other forms *Roops* of Goddesses. Next thousand years plus must have seen settlement, development, deep rooting and spread of religious faith with evolutionary refinements during next few centuries; say up to 250 BC. At this time Buddhism started taking roots and attention would have been suddenly diverted to this new religion. The shrine where Sharda manifested in Kas'mira (assuming that it was the first spot) would have remained in that form, with certain neglect, up to around 700 AD; end of Buddhist period. Unlike Hindu rulers who maintained Buddhist *Vihara's*, there is no account of any of Buddhist Kings building temples for Hindus, also Sharda or close by locations do not figure in Buddhists scriptures and accounts. During this period Sharda shrine must have remained isolated, except that *Bauddhs* may have continued to pass through this area being on the gateway to Dardistan, Central Asia, Afghanistan, Ladakh and China (via Karakuram Pass) and was not under presence or influence of Buddhists. It is no longer possible to trace with certainty, dating of structures, temples based on ancient Hindu architecture in the valley which owed their existence to Lalitaditya Muktapira (697-733 AD). In any case if it had been constructed during his time it would have found specific mention in *Sharda Mahatamaya* or in chronicles of Kalhan, Al-Beruni, Bilhan, Jonaraja and Abul Fazl. The important phase of Kas'mira Brahminism came during the period 880 AD and 1320 AD, when prominent Hindu Kings (Avanti Varman 855-883 AD, founder of the Utpala dynasty; Shankara Varman 883-902 A D; Kalsa 1063-1089 AD; Jai Simha - 1128-55 AD) and many more ruled the valley. It is during this period that Brahminism got impetus; construction of temples on new architectural designs and styles, modifications, improvements and renovations to existing ones took place; historians and chroniclers like Kalhan, Al-Beruni, Bilhan and Jonaraja recorded events for posterity and foundation of religious philosophy laid, including composition of scores of scriptures by various scholars. This is also the period when Sharda, as language, had started taking definite regional shape and many religious scriptures, poems, *bhajans*, hymns were composed in praise of God and Goddesses.

Two identical pillars, possibly hewn from one stone, gate of Kashmiri design definitely points to an era, when other temples were constructed with similar or close resemblance to the pillars. Generally this period gets identified with 12th Century (After Kalhan), or 13th Century (Before Jonaraja); possibly during 12th. King Jai Simha (1128-55 AD) during his rule of 27 years repaired, restored many temples and shrines and laid numerous other foundations. Unfortunately they have not got prominence in various chronicles, even Kalhan concentrates on past than on the ones of Jai Simha's period. Surprisingly he (Kalhan) talks of Sirhasila Castle siege but not in detail of Sharda Temple. Subsequent period from Rinchen /Muslim rule (1324/1343 to 1819 AD) would not have seen much changes or improvements of the shrine, except during Zain-ul-Abidin (1420-1474 AD) and later Moghul rule (1586-1753 AD).

Thus, Goddess Sharda must have manifested in the valley around Sapatrishi Samvat 2600 (600 BC) and it is around this time that her shrine, not present day temple, was established. Somewhere in the 12th Century the temple was constructed over the shrine, when idol of the Goddess and two *lingas* must have also been installed. The two *lingas*, in all probability, are in the form of *pindis*, natural small rock formations depicting some *aakar* (Shape), depicting Goddess with her consort. *Lingas* would have been installed at the time of *Kumbhabishekam* (Consecration), as recess in the Northern wall of the temple would have been made, most probably, during temple construction.

Ram and Krishna Lore

There are scores of accounts and lores associated with Lord Ram and Lord Krishna, with specific reference to Sharda Temple. There is no scriptural, historical or archaeological indication of Lord Ram having been to Kas'mira. Lord Ram's (*Ramayana* is pre *Mahabarata* by about a millennium) birthplace and life was around Ajodhya (Ayodhya) in UP and areas in MP. For this reason and peculiar transition of our religious theology in earlier centuries, Lord Ram does not figure much in our worship, temples, *stotras* and *bhajans*. This is evident from the fact that there is hardly any temple of that period exclusively dedicated to Lord Ram in the valley. Some of the ones constructed in his or his other name *Raghunath*, are during the period of (1846-1947 AD) Dogra Rule. Irrespective of this, many places, men or women get associated with name of Ram. There is place called *Raja Ram Di Lari*, a rugged mountain top and close by few mountain outcrops called *Raja Ramun Lariyan*, all East of Kralpura, just on route to Sharda. *Raja Ram Di Lari* is not in Kashmiri or Sharda but is Takari (Dogri) origin. If one had interacted with local people, as I did few decades back, it would have been clear that the rugged mountaintop was named after the second son of Maharaja Ranbir Singh; Raja Ram Singh. Apparently the area was a Jagir of Raja Ram Singh.

Lord Krishna's association with Sharda temple is also talked about; Kishanganga being renamed after him. Same reasoning of attribution as in the case of Lord Ram holds good. Krishna's and lives of *Pandavas* revolves around *Brijbhumi* (Vrindavan, Mathura, Western UP and present day Haryana). Even for them, bestowed with super powers that be, they had neither the time nor cause to visit these parts of the valley. I recall old temples near Pattan called as *Pandav Lari* (Buildings of Pandavs) but constructed by Shankara Varman (Utpala Dynasty; during 883-902 AD) and had nothing to do with *Pandavas*. The only specific mention of Krishna in our chronicles is when Kalhan describes installation of Queen Yasomati on the throne of Kas'mira (Not dated) as the guardian of her son King Gonanda II by Lord Krishna. This should not be construed with physical visit of Lord Krishna to Sharda or areas close by. Absence of any significant temple of Krishna during medieval age is also a pointer. Kalhan while narrating the battle events around Sirhas'la Castle near Sharda Temple would have definitely mentioned about these places by their above names, as these areas came into prominence during the siege of Sirhasila Castle.

Sindhu Ganga, Kishanganga, Madhumati and Saraswati: *Sharda tirtha* sounds incomplete without the mention of three rivers deeply connected with it. They are Kishanganga, Madhumati and Saraswati. Present day Kishanganga is referred to as *Maha Sindhu* in *Mahatmaya*. Actual *Sindhu* or Indus emanates from Tibet, crosses Ladakh Range, flows through Skardu and Chilas (South of Gilgit) and any mention of Indus or Sindhu from the valley had to be with reference to any important landmarks close by in the valley and these were Gangabal (Harmukh) and Wullar Lake. Nilamat Puranam, however, mentions Sindhu Ganga (Verse 305-6) thus ; '*Ganga Sindhu tu*

Vijneya Vitasta Yamuna tatha'; (Translated) 'The Sindhu should be regarded as the Ganga and the Vitasta as the Yamuna.' *Harmukhganga* and *Nandishetra Mahatmaya's,* scriptures pertain to Gangabal and *Nandishetra* repectively. In *Harmukhganga Mahatmaya*, the stream flowing towards Naran Nag (Wangat near Kangan; Called Nund Kol) is referred as Sindhu Ganga, which joins Lower Sindh near Kangan. In *Nandishetra Mahatmaya* lower Sindh, emanating from Baltal area, is referred as Sindhu Ganga. Since Sindhu was referred North of these landmarks, the first such river in the region in that direction got referred to as Sindhu. The prefix of *Maha* has come to it because of the gorges and steep banks, which gives look of a big and swift (*Maha*) river. The snow-capped mountain peaks around the Valley and the river always-evoked image of Shiva with Ganga coming out of His locks.

Early chroniclers noticed traces of gold like particles being found in the river, which applies to Kishanganga too; coming through mountain region known as auriferous. Such rivers have shining particles of sand or clay like gold. This is more so in case of upper reaches of Indus (Sindh), Lower Sindh and other similar rivulets and streams in the region. Surprisingly this is also the case in the case of upper reaches of actual Ganga and another reason for Ganga suffix.

Kishanganga river starts from area between Dras and Gurez, just immediate North of Gangabal. Northern tributaries of Harmukh watershed (Gangabal) contribute waters to Kishanganga. Archaeological finds on the Southern side of Gangabal (Wangat, Naran Nag (*Sodaratirath*)) date back to first millennium and hence confirms this naming around 800 AD. Kalhan mentions the name of Kishanganga River at many places and it can be assumed that the naming of this river is pre 12th Century AD.

Sharda Temple, when seen from Shamsabari Range, has Sharda and Narda Peaks as the backdrop to the temple, which on the lower slopes of these twin-peaks. Two prominent and significant mountain streams flow in this area, on either flank. The one to the West of the temple ridge, generally emanates from Sharda Peak. This stream fits in with the description given as Madhumati. Al-Beruni and Jonaraja's accounts do not mention Madhumati by this name; it is Abul Fazl, the author of *Ain-e-Akbari*, who refers to Madhumati by name apart from *Sharda Mahatmaya*. Naming of the stream as Madhumati would have thus been somewhere between later part of 15th and 16th Century; adequate for Al-Beruni and Jonaraja not to mention it, but finding mention in Abul Fazl's account. The reason for other chroniclers not referring or associating this Madhumati stream with Sharda pilgrimage is due to the reason that actual Madhumati River, a sacred river in the valley in Bandipur area (Bandpore Nala: Bod Kol) was nowhere close to Sharda. It is also apparent that this name has been created to have a similar sacred stream next to Sharda pilgrim centre. The other rivulet, East of the temple, emanates from Narda Peak and finally all three join at a place referred as *Sharda Sangam.* In many chronicles this rivulet is referred as Kalnotri; along with Saraswati. There is no mention of *Kalnotri* in *Sharda Mahatmaya;* name alien to the valley but not in Central Himalayan area (Uttranchal); like Gangotri, Yamnotri. This name is linked with someone who must have been adherent of Shaivism, conversant with Central Himalayan region *tiraths* (Badrinath, Kedarnath) and then Sharda. All indicators thus generally refer to era between that of Adi-Shankara's followers (11th Century) and *Pravachandara* compositions (13th Century) which finds mention of these names. Around 13th Century seems to be more appropriate as Al-Beruni does not mention of any of these rivers. Kalnotri name also did not remain for long; Zain-ul-Abidin and Abul Fazal visits accounts do not mention Saraswati River, though Madhumati is talked about. In both cases of visits, eminent Kashmiri Saraswat Brahmin Scholars, would have accompanied them. There may have been some of those, whose or whose ancestors settlements in plains may have been in areas closer to legendary mythical Saraswati River, bringing Saraswati name to the River closer to their new place; somewhere between 15th and 16th Century (*Sharda Mahatmaya* also does not mention this name). Appropriately the name fitted well with Sharda; Saraswati being other form of the Goddess.

Single account of association of Lord Krishna with the valley is well chronicled, but no significant Radha Krishna temple existed anywhere in Kas'mira in early days, even though Nilamat Puranam describes the *Janam Ashtami* festival in Verses 716 to 722. Similar to renaming of Saraswati, prefix of Kishna can be traced to around Vasugupta's time, by then religious scholars would have found the flow actual route of Sindhu (Indus) and that these rivers were not connected with actual Sindhu (Indus). Ganga remained common suffix, Sindhu Ganga the sacred river mentioned in Nilamat Puranam existed, actual Sindhu far away and thus to have Kishanganga; albeit Ganga next to Sharda. Reason of Kishan prefix may be that since Nilamat Puranam quotes Sindhu Ganga as the sacred river, once this river was found, Kishan was one of the Avtars quoted therein and lend its name. One might get surprised on the nuances and phonetics of Kishanganga and Krishanganga (If it was to be named after Lord Krishna). With the development of Sharda Language and Script, subtle changes in intonations and phonetics peculiar to Kashmiri's pronunciation of 'Krishen' would have become 'Kishan.' Remember as to how Lord Krishna was pronounced, in Kashmiri; *Kishna Bagwan* or Krishan being called as Kishan and Krishna as Kishni). Thus, three rivers associated with Sharda got named to Kishanganga, Madhumati and Saraswati. We find all these names familiar; Madhumati River existed (Near Bandpore), Saraswati other name of the Goddess and Ganga now in the form of Kishanganga; all making a *Sangam* next to a pilgrimage centre. This also indicates, with other events, that Sharda pilgrimage took deeper roots around end of first millennium and effort was to concentrate all the ingredients of a *tirath* at one place. From the trail of events, religious developments and peculiarities it is between 13th and 16th Century when Madhumati and Saraswati names came about; may not be in one go but generally during this period.

Pilgrimage Later Centuries. Older and our generation do not know much about the places and pilgrimage routes to Sharda, as mentioned in many chronicles. Basically it is because of circumstances, lack of detailed, connected and accurate description of the places. Many accounts route it via or combine it with Gangabal. Pilgrims avoided difficult gorge route described in *Sharda Mahatmaya* and while selecting routes our ancestors kept some basics in view. These were; beaten tracks allowing use of ponies/ horses, halts so planned that movement in a day was from one to another villages having Pandit community for night halts and finally took routes, which led to existing crossings over River Kishanganga. Karnah and Drava, though in the domain of rulers of Kas'mira Valley were avoided, being away from the main routes and as Bomba's, inhabitants of these places, were inimical to the people of the valley. It is evident that during long period of anarchy, in last few centuries, pilgrimage to the shrine was less attractive for peaceful Brahmins of Kas'mira. (I have the privilege of being amongst very few of my generation, to have walked every foot of the area; Gangabal area, Shamsabari Range, Kazinag to close to Kishanganga, just opposite Sharda. It was constraints of LOC, which precluded foray across). Herewith routes and *modus operandi* of the *yatra*, used during last few centuries, with Srinagar as focal point, have been described for posterity. Graphic account of these routes and *yatra* by two noted Pandits of our community, who undertook frequent pilgrimages to Sharda in mid nineteen century (Somewhere between 1820 –1850 AD), has trickled down through few generations. The first one was Kas'mira's Philosopher, Historian, Writer, Artist and Intellectual Pandit Bhawani Koul (1790–1867 AD) of Gulshan Colony (Hariparbat/ Rainawari/Ram Kaul Mandir). Second, Pandit Harjoo Fehrist (Approximately 1870-1910 AD) of *Budhgair* (Near *Kawdore*); a staunch believer in Vedic rituals, who got drowned in Kishanganga while returning from Sharda pilgrimage.

Few months before the *Sharda Ashtami*, word went round about the basic planning of the *yatra;* dates and places for assembling were tentatively fixed and passed on. Places for assembling were; *Devi Angan* (Hari Parvat-Srinagar) for areas around and South of Srinagar; Sumbal and then Bandpore (Bandipur) for those in Northeast of Srinagar; Sopore/Bumai for those closer to Wullar/Sopore; Handwara for those from Baramulla /Handwara side.

Bumai/Saadamalyun for those South of Kupwara. Tikar (Tikri), Kupwara, Sogam (Lolab Valley) were also selected for assembling points. Approximate dates of arrival of *yatra jatha* (Pilgrim Party) at these places were also given and generally became places for night halts. Most of these places had important places of worship, small *tiraths* close to them, which were also briefly visited as part of *yatra*.

Sharda Pilgrimage Accounts

- Preparation would start immediately after *Janam Ashtami* and *yatris* (Pilgrims) would assemble at *Devi Angan* two or three days prior to *Bhadrapada Amavasa* [*Amavasa* of Bhadoon (Full dark night)] was considered inauspicious to start the *yatra*. Also journey to Sharda would take eight to nine days, on foot.
- On the designated day the caravan would move after early obeisance at *Chakrishwar* (Hari Parvat). The column used to be self contained in all respects with hired people for protection, guards of noblemen, younger ones carrying *lathis* and volunteers for cooking (I refrain to specifically call them anything other than volunteers). Generally at each halt the villagers looked after them. As the caravan moved towards the destination, strength swelled as *yatris* joined from different areas enroute.
- Columns taking different routes ultimately concentrated at Gushi (Gusha; Gosha) on 3rd *tithi* of Shudi Bhadrapada. On 4th Shudi of *Bhadrapada* they bathed in the rivulet which comes from Drang, instead of its source, when special holiness accumulates at the *tirtha*. They then visited walnut tree grove, on the banks of *Kamil* River, named Rangawar (Substitute for *Rangavatika*). Next day they moved towards Kishanganga River over Pharkian Gali (See Map).
- A parallel route, used by those from Lolab Valley, crosses over Burhom, Machel (both North of Lolab Valley) and meets main route East of *Tejavana* (Tejjan); the route thereafter is common. This route was not taken by many as they would miss bathing at Gushi and visit Rangwar (*Rangavatika*); considered part of the pilgrimage.
- People from plains, outside the valley, similarly moved via Muzzafarabad over Kafir Khan Range at Reshian Gali, cross Kazinag Nar at Karnah and cross over to other side of Kishanganaga near Karnah over the existing crossing place or move along the southern banks of Kishanganga river and join main route at Dudnial. The distance from Karnah to Shardi is over 30 kilometres.
- By the end of the day (6th Shudi) they reach general area of *Tejavana* (on the Northern slopes of the hill range, presumed to be the ashram of Gautama during Muni Shandalya's pilgrimage to Sharda). A night

halt, recitation of various *satotras* in praise of God and Goddesses in their various manifestations would end the day. On the 7th Shudi they, move Eastwards along the beaten track along Northern banks of Kishanganga and reach Sharda *tirath* by end of the day.

- Next day 8th Shudi of Bhadrapada also called *Sharda Ashtami* as well as *Ganga Ashtami. darshan* after bath, prayers, various rituals, etc followed by *Shradha* performed on the banks of Madhumati. An evening in the meditation around the temple rounded up the day. In plains of Northern India this day is called *Radha Ashtami.*
- Early next day, obeisance at the temple, return journey along same route would start and caravan strength would decrease at each night halt, when pilgrims detached enroute to return to their villages.
- During the reign of Hindu kings, such caravans used to be patronised by noblemen, visitors, scholars and protected by armed soldiers of that time. Even food and comforts were provided under the Kings decree. Chroniclers record such an arrangement during the reign of Zain-ul-Abidin (Who too had visited the shrine) and Akbar (His chronicler Abul Fazl also visited the shrine). During Muslim rule and later Afghan rule, number of pilgrims reduced and not many known organised caravans except few during the tenure of Pandit *Madhurmilans* (Chief Ministers) of Afghan rule. Things somewhat improved during Sikh rule and it is only after establishment of Dogra rule and the peaceful settlement of the Upper Kishanganga Valley that pilgrimage became once more open for regular visits. This is the time Pandits Harjoo Fehrist and Bhawani Kaul made many visits to the shrine. In case of Bhawani Kaul, he is reported to have accompanied Dogra King Gulab Singh for the pilgrimage, being a scholar of his regime.
- Narrations say that the pilgrimage ended at *Devi Angan* again after obeisance to *Chakrishwari.*

Gangabal and Sharda Tirath Together: Many of Sharda pilgrimage accounts talk of starting pilgrimage from Wangat (Naran Nag), then to Gangabal and culminate at Sharda on 8th (*Ashtami*) *Shudi of Bhadra*. Naran Nag, an important place of pilgrimage of ancient *Sodaratirth*, is the location of temples, which are commonly known as the Wangat temples. In ancient times, it was called *Sodaratirth* and the sanctity is derived from the existence of a large spring, *Sodaranag*. Gangabal (also referred as Harmukh) has lake surrounded by mountains all around and is a holy place for immersion of ashes of the dead; on *Ganga Ashtami* (8th *Shudi Bhadra*). After consigning ashes of their dead relatives in the Gangabal Lake, pilgrims made it a point to offer worship on return journey at Wangat (Naran Nag) and for religious beliefs *Ruch Kaam;* auspicious work cannot be part or combined with pilgrimage to temple like Sharda. A look at the map and terrain will also indicate that Gangabal Lake trek itself is tortuous and would take many days and it is humanly impossible to combine it with pilgrimage to Sharda along the difficult terrain, distances involved, more so day of pilgrimage being same. Few centuries back there was a catastrophe for Gangabal Pilgrims when hundreds of Pandits perished due to bad weather and difficult terrain. The later was undertaken in the year of additional month; *Mala Months.*

Sharda Temple Connection to Buddhism and Karnah Artefacts. Traces of civilisation and settlements have been excavated at a small hamlet Dildar (Karnah - Tanghdhar), which consists of Lance, Maze, Swords, stone pick-axe dating nearly 3000 years. A Buddha statue is reported to have been found in the area. These artefacts, local name of Mai Sharda, ruins of a fort have been associated with Sharda temple, Sharda Peeth (taken as University) and inadvertently associated with Buddhism also. These relics, crude as they are, are connected with Nagas civilisation but cannot be associated with Aryan settlers who had by that time moved beyond these primitive artefacts. These are also too earlier than Buddhists era, given their equal progress and abhorring weapons. Given the topography of the area, inhospitable terrain and weather conditions, it is more prudent to limit that Saraswat Aryans had mostly settled in the valley portion, Naga settlements and a stray group of Aryans continued in Kishanganga Valley. It may be that Buddha statue or relics found at Karnah, in all probability, being that of Buddhists staging camp while moving to Afghanistan and Dardistan and have to be of later vintage. These relics cannot be exclusively connected to Sharda temple of that period. Attributing location of Sharda Peeth at this location, during Buddhist era in Kas'mira, is out of question, as earliest records in under development Sharda script have been dated to about 800 AD over Northwest India (including Kas'mira). Karnah relics, Sharda Temple or Sharda Peeth do not find any mention in Buddhist scriptures, well chronicled travelogues of Buddhist scholars or visitors and Buddhist monuments of that period. The architectural design and construction of the temple, as discussed, precludes any Buddhist influence or hand in it. Even if they had, definitely it may have been named as *Sharda Vihara.* Reference to Sharda Mai in the area is interesting, which has nothing to do with Goddess Sharda. It is actually local lore of two sisters and brother, Muslims, who are believed to have had some Sufi powers. The lore is only few centuries old and possibly been brought up to have followers in the Muslim community.

Sharda Script, Myths, Adi - Shankara and Sharda Peeth

Sharda Language and Sharda Script: Sharda Script has been closely associated with Kas'mira, Goddess Sharda and bringing Sharda Desh

Temple Steps in Collapsed State

Entrance Dwar Sharda Temple (in Ruins)

Main Sharda Temple (in Ruins)

Rear View Main Sharda Temple

Massive Walls on the Northern Side of the Sharda Temple

Sirhasila with Sirhasila Castle in Ruins Jutting out over River Kishanganga

Kishanganga River and the Rope Bridge over it Near Shardi Village

Nanga Parvat also Called Mount Hari (Shiva) Parvat as Seen from Sharda Temple

designation to Kas'mira. In the evolution and assessment of history of a particular geographical area, spoken language and its script are important factors. While language evolves naturally, scripts adjust to spoken words of the speakers and get constantly modified to come up to appropriate medium, during which scripts get slowly altered till they get a distinct designation. Even in a uniform language, like Kashmiri, subtle variations in life-style, group behaviour, culture, geographic situation lead to changes in intonation from region to region. After passing through these stages, it is given a distinct name; like Sharda and the Goddess connected with literary achievements of Kas'mira lend her name to the language script of the valley. Unfortunately in our assessment and analysis of the Goddess, we allowed history of one of the best and expressive language scripts of the area to be diffused with attribution ranging from Vedic times to Buddhists and then to rulers of Kas'mira; measures which corrupt history. In this part aspects of language, scriptures and impact of personalities, having direct or indirect connection, have been discussed in sequential progression. The spoken language of ancient India (Brahmi) is generally attributed to era of 2500 BC. By about 7th and succeeding centuries AD gave way to new regional denominations. By around 9th Century AD Northwestern *Brahmi* language called *Upbrahmbasha* spoken language, a variant of Brahmi, began to evolve in different parts of this area including Kas'mira, Punjab, Himachal and the Northern parts of present day Pakistan. Brahmi was the script in which this *Upbrahmbasha* (and the earlier Sanskrit, Palli etc.) was written. Earliest Brahmi scripts are dated to 5-6th Century AD, but references to it in Rig Veda takes it to around 1000 BC. During 7th Century AD, *Upbrahmbasha* changed shape and gave rise to a slightly different and advanced form called *Siddha-Matrika*. Used in Kas'mira during Lalitaditya (697-735 AD) time, *Siddha-Matrika* was the *lipi* and called as such because alphabet starts with the benediction *Om Swasti Siddham*. Shankara Varman (883-902 AD) who conquered neighbouring principalities including Gujarat, refused to talk in Sanskrit and used the language used by the people; *Upbrahmbasha*. Al-Beruni (1030 AD) also refers to *Siddha-Matrika* as such. Sharda was this denomination of *Siddha-Matrika* and covered a vast region extending from Afghanistan to Delhi and its characters showed remarkable resemblance with earlier Brahmi characters and exhibited several positive developments to justify a new appellation by 1000 AD; including Gurumukhi. The earliest records in 'under development' Sharda script have been dated to about 800 AD in Northwestern India. Its characters appeared for the first time on the coins with inscriptions in the name of Avanti Varman (855-883 AD), the founder of the *Avantiswami* temple at Avantipur. Coins, copper plate, charter of Hindu Shahi's of Kabul and Gilgit (9th-10th Centuries); the fountain stone temple inscriptions (11th–13th Century) of this dynasty and other extant epigraphic and literary records of 14th Century represented the three stages of development of Sharda script. A birch bark manuscript of *Munimata Manimala,* which is 'earliest known Sharda manuscript' discovered in Kas'mira belongs to this third stage i.e. 14th Century. Kalhan wrote Rajatarangini in Sanskrit writing in Sharda script. Sharda remained par excellence language and script of Kas'mira till the present century and lend its name to the valley, which bore the alternative name of Sharda Desh and *Sharda Mandala,* owing it to deity Sharda. Some people wrongly believe that Sharda is a script of Sanskrit. Sharda was evolved when the language of Kas'mira was passing into Kashmiri, with its peculiar intonations, variations and sounds, as a result Sharda language, imprinted with vocal peculiarities, became unfit for Sanskrit but continued to be used for writing Sanskrit in Kas'mira. Sanskrit language lays emphasis on the sound of each alphabet; while Sanskrit writings in Sharda script could be understood but in speech it could not be deciphered. Kashmiris had difficulty in pronouncing Sanskrit correctly, because of lack of knowledge of Devnagri script and Sharda is so different from Devnagri.

Sharda script formed a vital link in the chain of communication of ideas, knowledge, and culture among the states comprised in the Northwestern Himalayan region; similar to the role of Brahmi and *Kharoshti* during that period. *Kharoshti* belongs to the same period as Brahmi. It had 37 letters of which 24 resembled Brahmi. Of the rest, a few (supposedly 3) seemed to resemble the Semitic script. In Kas'mira people irrespective of religion spoke Kashmiri and signed their names in Sharda; like 15th Century will of *Makhdoom Sahib.* Till 14th – 15th Century AD, even tombstones of Muslims in Kas'mira were inscribed in Sharda. By end of 16th Century, beginning of Moghul rule, *Kofi* and *Nasak* (Variants of Arabic script) were used for tombstone inscriptions, though Sharda side-by-side still existed. Sharda was thus pushed under, however, older generation of priests continued with Sharda till sixties/early seventies of 20th Century. I was sweetly surprised to see my horoscope, written in early sixties, in Sharda Script forcing me to learn Sharda alphabets. Sir Auriel Stein, who has chronicled his visit in 19th Century; unmistakably proves this fact, when he says, 'The continued popular use of Sanskrit (Read Sharda) even among Mohammedans is strikingly proved by the Sanskrit (Sharda) inscription on a tomb in the Cemetery of Bahau-Din-Sahib at Srinagar (AD 1484).'

Adi Shankara's Visit to Kas'mira, Sharda Temple and Authorship of Scriptures: Nothing has created ambiguity in attribution of our religious and scholarly works, worship places, etc. than the visit of Shankaracharaya and his being associated with Sharda, apart from other shrines and spread of Shaivism in Kas'mira. It is not only with us, the very institutions connected with Shankaracharaya are mired in differing dates, origin, and attribution of works and scriptures and life time events of Shankaracharaya. A brief explanation of institution of Shankaracharaya is, therefore, necessary. As per various accounts Great Adi Shankaracharaya (Also called Jagatguru, Great Adi Shankara), named Sankara (*San* means prosperity and *Kara* means the giver) was born 2500 years back at *Kaladi* (Kerala); son of Sivaguru and Aryambal. After him started the legend cum pontiffs seat called *Acharayas*. His descendant lineage has the *Acharyas* of four established *mutts* that exist even today; Puri (Est 484 BC), Srinegri (Est 483 BC), Jyotirmath (Badrinath) (Est 485 BC) and Dwarka (Est 490 BC). The fifth one at Kamakothi (Kanchi) is considered as the original seat of Great Adi Shankaracharaya. *Guhya-Sahasranama* (Sanskrit) refers to these five Shankaracharaya Peeths (*Mutts*); Kamakoti Peeth as presided over by Great Adi Shankaracharaya himself, others by his four disciples; Suresvara, Padmapada, Totaka and Hastamalaka. In fact lineage charts of these *mutts* start from these disciples; dated BC. However, researchers refer to Shankaracharaya being of later vintage (AD), though none of the *mutts* accept this, in-spite of strong and irrefutable evidence to prove it. There was and is only one Shankaracharaya for record; either Great Adi Shankaracharaya of BC or Shankaracharaya of AD era. Other heads of the *mutts* are actually *Acharayas* but are commonly referred to as Shankaracharayas in many scriptures, chronicles, visits etc. Thus discrepancies arose out of visits, scholarly works of these *Acharayas*, mistakenly referred as Shankaracharaya.

As per records of *Acharyas* of the medieval age of Kamakothi (Kanchi) *mutt*, Abhinava Sankara; a disciple of Sri Vidyaghana (37th *Acharya*), became 38th *Acharaya* of Kamakothi (Kanchi) and stands pre-eminent and his deeds are compared to that of Great Adi Shankaracharaya; hereafter he is called Adi-Shankara. Some refer to him as Adi Shankaracharaya; though none of the *mutts* call/called their *Acharayas* with prefix of the 'founder's prefix Adi.' As per succession records of the *mutt*, he is believed to have attained *samadhi* in Himalayas in 840 AD after 30 years of *achararyaship* (Actually 24 years). Notwithstanding various records of all the *mutts*, extensive research indicates Adi-Shankara was born in May/June 788 AD (Lunar month of *Vaishakha*, 26th year of the sixty year cycle) and attained *samadhi* in the month of May/June 820 AD (*Vaishaakha* or *Pausha* of 58th year of the sixty year cycle). Surprisingly the name of his father and mother, place of birth and various events in his life are same as in the case of Great Adi Shankaracharaya. Religious works of Adi-Shankara of AD era, who became monk at the age of eight (Commentary on *Brahmasutra*, *Bhagvad Gita*, *Upanishhads* etc.) fits into the personality of Abhinava Sankara, who as per records, as 38th Acharaya took name of Dhir-Shankarendra Saraswati. Many scholars and researchers are of the view that Adi-Shankara of 8th/9th Century is actual Great Adi Shankaracharaya. Government of India celebrated 1200th anniversary of Adi- Shankara's birth in 1988 indicating his birth in 788 AD. This in a way confirms AD status of Adi Shankaracharaya. However, all the *mutts* have lineage and succession charts from 5th Century BC, even Kamakothi (Kanchi) *Mutt* to which Abhinava Sankara belonged, dates lineage chart to 5th Century BC. If one ponders; both are *Acharayas,* their name Sankara, therefore in both cases they are *Sankara – Acharaya.* None of the other *Acharayas* of any of these Peeths had Shankaracharaya name, which remained restricted to these two only. Strange, though all the *mutts* talk of Great Adi Shankaracharaya, none of them other than Kamakothi (Kanchi) *mutt* talk much of Adi Shankara. Even in their case the references are guarded; all this to maintain antiquity of Shankaracharaya to BC era. Scholars have valid reasons for their dissent and most important of all that Gautam Buddha (May 623–547 BC) and Great Adi Shankaracharaya (409/414–516 BC) were around in the same era and operative in common areas. Gautam Buddha preceded and spread Buddhism, its spread would have been checked when Great Adi Shankaracharaya was operative and Hinduism revived. Facts, however, indicate Buddhism flourished till as late as 6/7th Century AD and it is after the revival efforts of Adi-Shankara (8th/9th Century) Hinduism bounced back. None of the five *mutts* accept existence of Abhinava Sankara as Adi-Shankara or as Shankaracharaya of 8th/9th Century. One can even notice this ambiguity in our Kas'mira chronicles also; Rajatarangini says that the Kashmiri King Gopaditya founded *agraharas* (jagirs) and built temples of Jyestheswara; 'Having founded Jyestheswara on the Gopa Hill, the Brahmans born in the land of 'Aryans' were induced to accept Gopa *Agraharas* (jagirs) by that pious King (Verse 341 Book I Rajatarangini).' This King is given date of 417–357 BC. An account says; 'Gopadri (*Gopadiri Tirath*) became known as Shankaracharaya after the visit in the 8th Century AD of 'Adi Shankaracharaya' to Kas'mira, when both Gopadri Hill and the Jyeshtheshwar temple (Present day Shankaracharaya Temple and *Zethyer* shrine) on it were given the new name in his honour.' Surely Kalhan would have mentioned this in his Rajatarangini instead of referring it to King Gopaditya.

Shankaracharaya word is not new to Kas'mira, which seems to have been used for defining even *Acharayas* of the *mutts*; it may also be of interest for us to know that two *Acharayas* of Kamakothi (Kanchi) are credited to be from Kas'mira; Sureswaracharya 2nd *Acharaya* (*Samadhi* in 407 BC); Sadasiva 17th Acharya (*Samadhi* in 375 AD). Also Ujvala Tapati 16th A*cahraya* is credited to have attained *samadhi* in Kas'mira in 367 AD. Another famous *Acharya* of the Kamakothi (Kanchi) Peeth was the 47th Sri Chandracuda Saraswati (1098-1166 AD). This *Acharaya* was held in great esteem by our scholars such as Mankha (*Srikanthacharita* composed between 1135 to 1145 AD), Jayadeva (*Prasanna Raghava, Chandraaloka and Bhakti Kalpa-Latika*). Jai Simha, then ruler of Kas'mira, was a staunch devotee of this *Acharya,* who too (47th *Acharaya*) is referred to as Shankaracharaya. He (Sri Chandracuda Saraswati) travelled widely all over the country, possibly including Kas'mira. Kalhan was also around at this time and wrote Rajatarangini but there is no mention of his visit. This period of 47th Acharaya fits in well, when Madhavacharaya (1199-1276 AD), who came to Kas'mira nearly a century later, would have known of his visit, in detail. Actually bias in Rajatarangini has been towards rulers and not godly men, who find very little or no mention in the chronicle.

Adi-Shankara's Visit: Facts and Fiction: As per one account of his visit; 'after he sat on the holy stone slab at the temple (Sharda), it gave him vision to compose *Saundriya Lahiri* in praise of Goddess Divine Mother (*Shakti*); considered excellent piece of poetic devotion after *Panchastavi.*' Further, 'he adopted *Sri Chakra* as reverence to Goddess Sharda and was conferred honour of Sharda Peeth.' Some accounts give us to understand that he ascended Temporal or Pontifical Seat at Sharda Temple and / or Sharda Peeth (Referred by some as university) during his visit to Sharda Mai (Not Sharda Temple. For Sharda Mai lore read above). Little known area near Karnah is referred as 'Sharda Mai' and being erroneously referred to as Goddess Sharda. Account of his (Shankaracharaya) visit has been composed by Madavacharya (1199-1276 AD), an erudite scholar, who after becoming ascetic is referred by the name of Vidhyaranya. His account was subsequently, apparently, suitably versioned by followers of Shankaracharaya, who had returned back to Kas'mira in the later part of the 15th Century during Zain-ul-Abidin reign. While in plains they had become Shankaracharaya devotees and generally followed *Shankaradivijya;* extensive poetic work on Adi-Shankara, composed by Madavacharya in 13th Century, five Centuries after Adi-Shankara. It may be of interest that during this Century (13th) Islam had taken roots, in pockets, in South and Khilji Armies were active for conversion to Islam. Many of then Hindu scholars of South could not continue their religious inclinations and found Kas'mira an ideal place and this was one of the reasons of extraordinary number of scholars of Shaivistic order of South, visiting Kas'mira during this period; even staying back for longer duration or till they attained *samadhi.* He (Madavacharya) did not adhere to his religious activities as given in *Sankaravi Jaya-Kavya* (Composed by Anantanandagiri; 10th Century AD) but adopted tradition of writing flourishing accounts based on *Puranic* mythology authors, poetic imagination, personal devotion containing stories and events, which in most of cases had no reality. His description of Sharda temple is also believed to be similar, interspersed with ground landmarks, duly assisted by our own little known scholars of that period.

Sharda Peeth Honours: Sharda or Sharda Peeth word or institutions are not new to Hinduism in India; followers of Great Adi Shankaracharaya (Adi-Shankara) started these institutions, which exist even today and are flourishing. Called Sharda Peethams or *Mutts* or Peethams of respective order etc., but Sharda is supreme in these institutions. In their religious philosophy; 'Sarada is *Guru Rupini;* she is of the form of the *guru.* Through the person of the *Jagadguru* (Shankaracharaya occupies *Sarvajna Pitha* or the Pontifical seat) she dispenses her grace.' The legends says; 'Great Adi Shankaracharaya (Adi-Shankara?) reached Srinegri in Karnataka, on the banks of Tungabhadra River. While Sri Sankara and Mandala Mishra (Another scholar) were walking, Sarasawani (wife of Mishra) did not move and stood fixed in the sands of Tungabhadra River. Great Adi Shankaracharaya (Adi-Shankara?) turned back and realised by his divine powers that Sarasawani did not want to proceed any further and created a seat for her for spreading *Advaita.* This seat is today called the Sharada Peetham or the Seat of Sharada (*Saradamba*)." This was the first *Mutt* installed by Great Adi Shankaracharaya (Adi-Shankara?), with the direction that all the heads of the *Mutts* will be called *Acharayas* and they will have a lineage of *Shishyas* (Disciples). Without going into many more details of the incident, similar event is recorded for Adi-Shankara; in which a variant tradition places the *Sarvajna Pitha* (the throne of transcendental wisdom) in Kamakothi (Kanchi). Adi-Shankara is the one credited with having made extensive tours in North India, even to Kas'mira (Sharda is not specifically referred) and between 788-820 AD; 'He defeated (in debate) the famous Vakpati Bhatta, a reputed scholar of the court of the King of Kas'mira. He ascended the *Sarvajna Pitha*, in Kas'mira (Srinagar) after winning over many great scholars.' 'History of Sanskrit Literature' refers to *Shankarendra Vilasa* by Vakpati Bhatta, a Kashmiri Pandit; biography of 38th *Acharya* Dhir-Shankarendra Saraswati (Abhinava Shankara), of Kamakothi (Kanchi) Peeth. Not much is known except that this biography pertains to same Adi-Shankara and is the only scholarly work mentioned in the name of Vakpati Bhatta; who has not been fully identified as per the *mutt* records. Kalhan in verse 144 Book IV Rajatarangini refers to one Vakhpatiraja who was around during Lalitaditya's time. Again there is no mention of Vakpati Bhatta being defeated in a debate by Great Adi Shankaracharaya (Adi-Shankara?). In Kas'mira Bhatta name is a generalised form and not specifically pinpointing to any scholar of that period. This is important as most of the scholars find place of honour in our records like; Vasugupta, Kayyatacharya and Somananda (Contemporary of Vasugupta), Muktakantha Swamin, Shiva Swamin, Ananda Vardhana and Kallata (Great Shaiva philosophers and authors) flourished during this period. Surely Kashmiri religious intelligentia would have fielded their best scholar, more so as the debate would have been on the shades of *Shaivism* and differing perception of the two debaters.

The only Kashmiri Scholar somewhat closer to this name during the period referred is Bhatta Kallatta (850-900 AD; Vasugupta's disciple), but he does not fit in the time period of Adi-Shankara. Biography writing of scholars cum religious heads on the move is not easy and may be that a Kashmiri

Scholar, named as such, was with Adi-Shankara and got into a debate and finally Adi-Shankara won in this debate at *Sarvajna Pitha* (Srinegri) and as is the custom ascended the place of honour after the debate. The visit and outcome should, if true, have also found place in the chronicles of King Jayapira (764-795 AD; a great conqueror and lover of learning. *Katayana's* commentary on *Panini* was re-compiled during his period) or his successors or that of Vasugupta. Vasugupta's *Shivsutra's* or any other scholars thinking would have also been influenced by the *advaita* or 'dualistic' Shaivite philosophy if Adi-Sankara had visited Kas'mira and defeated one of our representative scholars. A defeat would naturally mean that we accepted his philosophy, which was not so. No account/chronicle has used any word other than *Sarvajna Pitha* (Not Sharda Peeth), which has been commonly used in Shankaracharaya *Mutt,* taken as 'Pontifical Seat' and does not refer to a specific place.

Another significant event in the history of Adi-Shankara's, noted in his accounts, is his occupying the *Sarvajna Pitha* (Note the usage of *Sarvajna* which had been established at Kanchi; not Kas'mira). According to V. Raj Gopal Sharma, author of '*Acharya Sri Sankara's Advent*'; 'There have been several references to the visit of Shankara (Adi-Shankara) to Kas'mira. He did not establish a new Peeth there but ascended an existing Peeth.' As far as ascending an existing Peeth is concerned, it is unlike of Adi-Shankara, as wherever he went he 'established' a Peeth. Sharda Temple or Sharda Peeth is not specifically mentioned in this event and there was no 'pontifical seat' at Sharda Temple. Chronicles refer to debate in Kas'mira and when associated with dates, it may be one of the Buddhist *Vihara* turned into a *mutt* or Peeth, as at this time Buddhism in Kas'mira had started waning, not requiring his presence. In fact recently a scholar from South wrote to me to confirm about Adi-Shankara having ascended the *Sarvajna Pitha*. The event in the write up was described poetically that there are four doors to the temple as the door in the South was never opened as none from South had participated in the religious debate. As per the write up Adi-Shankara entered from the Southern door and defeated all the other scholars in the debate and ascended the *Pitha.* The assertion fell flat when I gave her the dimensions of the temple and that there is only one entry from the North.

Indicators of account being imaginative can also be gathered when Madhavacharya mentions that Abhinav Gupta, living in Assam (Kamrup) was a *Tantric* sorcerer who applied sorcery to Adi-Shankara with the result that the latter developed a dangerous disease (Same Madhvacharaya who in his '*Shankra Digvijaya*' makes this single reference to Abhinav Gupta being alleged sorcerer, wrote a *Shanker Bashya*, presumably on Badrayan's *Vedanta Sutras).* There is no evidence that can establish name Abhinav Gupta other than the great author of Kas'mira. The story is thus purely imaginary and also confirmed as there was a gap of nearly 150 years between the times of these two great teachers (788-820 AD - Adi-Shankara's and Abhinav Gupta 933-1015 AD). All the traditional tales about their meeting and associated accounts are mere fiction and do not establish any historical fact. Chroniclers confirm Adi-Shankara visited many places in South, Madhya Bharat and Himalayas, during his short life span, before he is supposed to have visited Kas'mira. His visits have been extensively chronicled in detail with dates/duration; but visit details to Kas'mira do not exist, uncorroborated, events devoid of facts and in many cases termed 'may have.' I respect religious sages and scholars like Adi-Shankara, but even he would not have liked to be part of an imaginative account, which would otherwise cover facts, more so of a civilisation that of Kashmiri Pandits. It is abundantly clear that had Adi-Shankara established a Peeth, this would have been named like other Peeths of Shankara and would have a line of *Acharayas* like other Muths or Peeths connected with Adi-Shankara. No muths of Adi-Shankara or their *acharayas* have claimed association with it. Recently there was one self styled Shankaracharaya claiming to be Shankaracharaya of Kas'mira *Sarvajna Pitha,* who was found to be a criminal rather than a religious man and is behind the bars. He made many efforts that I should meet him on Sharda Goddess but I flatly refused saying that there was and is no such peeth or Shankaracharaya.

Adoption of Sri Chakra: Adi-Shankara travelled around the land, refuting all objectionable practices in Hinduism, which had cropped up. There is no denial of his contribution and renaissance efforts, when Buddhism had started collapsing. Adi-Shankara founded the *Dasanami* (Ten) order; namely *Aranya, Ashrama, Bharati, Giri, Parvata, Puri, Saraswati, Sagara, Tirtha* and *Vana* (We have a wing of one of these orders in Srinagar-*Dasnami Akhara-Giri*) established during Dogra Rule. To spread his teaching evenly around the country, Adi-Shankara established m*utts* in four places; *Vimala* Peeth at Puri, *Kalika* Peeth in Dwarka, *Sarada* (Sharda) Peeth in *Srinegri* (Tamil Nadu), and the *Jyotirmath* in Badrinath. During these visits he installed *Sri Chakras* in many temples like Kamakshi temple of Kanchi, Nara Narayana temple of Badri and Guhyeshwari temple in Nepal. His visits and establishment of these *mutts* were all in the early parts of his life and pontification; before his purported visit to Kas'mira. It must be understood that Adi-Shankara and his predecessors were the back bone of revival of Hinduism, where Shakti and Shiva were given place of pride in their dualistic Shaivite theology and *Sri Chakra* was not new at that time, but had taken roots along with preaching of Hinduism. The theory of Adi-Shankara having adopted *Sri Chakra* during his purported visit, that too to Sharda, therefore, is not correct. In Kas'mira King Pravarsena II had established only *Sri Chakra* in Kas'mira at *Chakrashwar* in 6th Century AD.

Sharda Desh and Sharda Peeth: As far as university (Peeth) is concerned if it existed it would have been ideally next or closer to Sharda Temple or any other place closer to seats of power of then reigning Kings. The word 'Peeth' is a Sanskrit word used mostly with religious institutions in the South, meaning 'Pontiff's or exalted seat.' There are two major and many smaller Sharada Peetham (Peeth) in South associated with Shankaracharaya institutions and in most cases they claim to be of BC era. Sharda Goddess had manifested in other parts of India also, as presiding deity of learning and fine arts. We must not take it that Goddess Sharda in *Matri Rupen* (In the form of Mother Goddess) manifested in Kas'mira due to efforts of 'others' and not our own belief and divinity. Kas'mira got the name of Sharda Desh because the degree of worship to various deities in Kas'mira was always high, nearly complete, which included Sharda. The people being of Saraswat Aryan origin, travelled far and wide and were recognised as *Acharyas* (Scholars); all benediction of Sharda. The next reason is the naming of various smaller places in Kas'mira by Buddhists during the spread of their religion; for nearly a millennium (300 BC – 600 AD) Kas'mira did not get a single appropriate designation though geographical limits had got extended beyond Kas'mira valley. *Kashyapsar* connotation had got limited to restricted geographical limits of the valley but extended limits now met prerequisites of a Desh; developed religion (*Dharam*), language and Script (*Bhasha* and *Lipi*), reign (*Raja*), people (*Praja*) and intellectuality (*Budhjivita*). This appellation allowed people from outside to refer it by a single designation, Desh and not by small place name like Pravarpura (Srinagar). These smaller places could not represent Kas'mira as a whole. People from South had found another nomenclature for Kas'mira; *Kas'mira Mandala*; meaning Kas'mira State. It may well be argued that why such a peculiar name or dispensation did not come up in South or any other place in India. The reason is demographical, as these places were not purely composed of Brahmins but were conglomerates of various other castes, religions; segmented on different religious beliefs and caste lines were stronger to allow a single state to be named after any God or Goddess. For example, Nepal is a predominantly Hindu Desh (Presiding deity being *Durga* and her various forms), Buddhists flourish here but country is not named after the Goddess (Most popular derivation of the name is from *Ne* after an ascetic and *pala* meaning cherished or looked after. The word thus means country looked after by *Ne*). It was not so in Kas'mira as the valley was purely of *Brahmanical* order, after Buddhism waned and before Islam took roots. However, there are places known after *Avtars* like *Brijbhoomi* encompassing areas of Krishna lore, but this was due to a person and not the people. This appellation could have come about when visiting scholars, devotees of Goddess Sharda, finding high degree of scholarly inclination; attributed it to benevolence of Goddess Sharda in her Desh. On their return they started referring to Goddess as Kas'mira *Vasini,* area as *Mandala* and even composed a hymn for their morning prayer on getting out of bed. Subsequently *Mandala* shifted to Desh; a more Sanskritised word. It is not difficult to guess the origin, as many scriptures of 12th and 13th Century refer to it as such and most of these were from those who were associated with the institutions of Shankaracharaya.

The word Sharda Peeth has also been wrongly called as university and till today we just refer to it without having applied its actual meaning or found any historical proof of its location and if a Peeth; a 'particular single specific seat or institution of learning', ever existed. Some scholars suggest Karnah as its erstwhile location, based on the findings of relics, artefacts and Buddhist statues. This area most of the time, in both the AD millenniums (1st and 2nd) was hardly under effective control of rulers of Kas'mira, always taken as at a limb, away from the seat of governance and populace and had no religious or location advantage for a university. One must also remember that religious or scholarly institutions in Kas'mira were established next to temples or *tirath sthans,* as it was a must to pay obeisance to the ruling deity first and then enter the institution. Karnah, therefore, does not hold same position for Sharda temple; being miles away from the temple over a difficult terrain. Kas'mira had hundreds of renowned scholars on different facets of our religion, whose works have been well chronicled, institutions under their patronage well chronicled and mostly decentralised. These scholars had selected places closer to their place of worship and their operational field mostly their place of residence or worship; wisely they did not allow such places to prolifer. Scholars and pilgrims from all over India used to visit Kas'mira for discussions on religious topics and *Darshana Shastras* (Philosophy), especially during the regime of King Lalitaditya Muktapira, Varman's and Jai Simha, but not at a fixed place or venue. With tongue in cheek, I may add; Sages and Scholars had their own domain, intrusions from colleagues were rare, but works discussed, shared or disseminated during their visits to a centralised place or *yatras*, *samgamas* (Seminars), congregations and festivals. Even geographical location of Sharda Temple, cut off from the valley for nearly four to five months in a year, preclude a learning institution nearby. With the available details of the temple and temple complex, there is no place for so called Peeth. Like the temple, now in ruins, no ruins or remenants of a Peeth have been found. The only place close by is Sirhasila Castle, which was domain of the local warlord. It is that Dogra rulers had built up a place for the living of the Dogra soldiers, which used to look after the security of the area. In recent times someone has averred that convocation used to be held at Sharda Temple on Guru Tritya (*Gora Trai*) not knowing that this day falls in the middle of winter and the Temple area is cut off and covered with nearly 20 feet of snow.

Backside of the Fort Built 150 Years Ago by Dogra Kings

Close View of One of the Posts

In a more legendary light the temple of Sharda (Not Sharda Peeth) figures in a story related to scholar Hemachandra (1088-1172 AD) in *Prabhavakacarita;* a scholarly work on the influence of Kas'mira's progress in the sphere of religion and literature at that time. Commissioned by King Jayasimha of Gujarat (Now in West Pakistan) to compose a new grammar, he requested to be supplied with necessary material in the shape of older grammar. High officials were reportedly sent to Pravarapura to obtain the manuscripts (In Kas'mira the King was also Jai Simha (AD 1128-1155)). After arriving there, they proceeded to the temple of Sharda and offered prayers. The manuscripts were delivered to envoys and brought by them to Hemachandra, who, after perusing them, composed his own grammatical work the *Siddhahemachandra.* Let us collate other historical facts pertaining to this account.

Shankara Varman (883-902 AD) had conquered neighbouring principalities including Gujarat, which was then under the rule of one Alakhan. The language used at that time by the people was *Upbrahmbasha,* which further developed into *Siddha Matrika* (Sharda) and covered a vast region extending from Afghanistan to Delhi, which included Gujarat. During this period two Jai Simha's are being talked about; King Jai Simha (AD 1128-1155) of Kas'mira, and Jaisimha of Gujarat. The picture becomes more clear; Hemachandra's work *Siddhahemachandra* is his version of *Upbrahmbasha Lipi* (*Siddha Matrika*), duly adapted to the requirements of that area and instead of it being called *Siddha Matrika* was named after 'Hemchandra' and thus the name of *Siddhahemachandra*; a local variant. King Jai Simha may have tasked him for this assignment; there seems to be only one at that time and Gujarat had no King at that time. He, Jai Simha himself being a man of letters, must have pointed out mistakes and referred it to scholars of his kingdom for correction. Obeisance to Goddess of learning, Sharda, for such missions is normal way of life in our religion; when assigned a scholarly mission you start with a place of worship and on return obesiance again at a place of worship, as thanksgiving. Kalhan in Rajtarangini refers to Kas'mira as the land of 'Aryans' and not Sharda Desh. This is in line with the progress of *Siddhamatrika* to Sharda, which took deeper roots after Kalhan.

Panchastavi and Saundarya Lahiri: Stories have created many grey areas about inspiration, authorship and dates of composition of *Panchastavi* and *Saundarya Lahiri* (in this Adi-Shankara addresses *devi* as *Chidananda Lahiri* (Wave of consciousness and bliss) and this has been used as expression in *Saundarya Lahiri*). Some chronicles and accounts credit Adi-Shankara with the authorship of both (*Panchastavi* and *Saundarya Lahiri*), some talk of South Indian origin of both and some attribute authorship of both to Kashmiri Scholars. The resemblance between *Panchastavi* and *Saundarya Lahiri* is remarkable and is mainly responsible for creating such a dilemma. *Panchastavi,* however, does not resemble *Tattuagrabha-Stotra*, a hymn to Mother Goddess by Bhatta Pradyumana, a Kashmiri, chief disciple of Bhatta Kallata (during the reign of Shankar Varman 883-902 AD)). An oral tradition prevalent in Kas'mira is that *Panchastavi* was composed by Abhinav Gupta (11th Century) on the occasion of his discussions on *Shaktism* with Adi-Shankara. *Vedantist* teacher Sivopadhyaya, an 18th Century author and renowned teacher of Shaivism, refers to the meeting of the two in his *Srividya*, a small work aiming at reconciliation between *Tantric Shaivism* and *Upanishadic Vedanta*. He says that a boy disciple of Abhinav Gupta getting a nod from Abhinav Gupta, stood up and uttered *Laghustava* as a spontaneous flow of poetry. The account of *Laghustava*, as having been uttered by a boy disciple and composed by some *Laguacharya* (Child Scholar) is imaginary. Nityananda, an ancient commentator of some tantric works, says that *Laghustava* was composed by a poet named *Dharma*

Acharya (*Dharma* means Religious, *Acharya* meaning Scholar and could be a 'Religious Scholar' without giving his name). Vidhyaranya (Madhavacharya) in one of his works, *Srividyama Vatantra* referring to *'Maya Kundalini'* verse says that this theological doctrine had been indicated by *Dharma Acharya* in *Laghustava.* The author of *Maya Kundalini* was about one hundred years later from the time of Adi-Shankara and there is no evidence to prove correctness of any such attribution and further adds to imaginative accounts. Similarly, more imaginative accounts were heard from old Brahmins of Kas'mira, few decades ago.

Panchastavi, a collection of five chapters of hymns sung in the praise of Mother Goddess; personified absolute Godhead of the Lord and lays stress on the Mother's worship. *Panchastavi* appears to have been composed four centuries before *Bhavani Sahasranama* was revealed. *Panchastavi* and *Saundarya Lahiri* resemble in technique, with similar objective in view; to bring awareness of Mother's eminence. The composer of *Panchastavi* has maintained silence about his name, time or lineage throughout his versified composition. Ganapati Shastri, a noted Vedic scholar of last century brought out an edition of the first chapter of *Panchastavi* in 1917, naming it as *Laghustuti* with Sanskrit commentary by one Raghvananda, who attributed composition to a poet named as Laghu Bhattaraka. Bhattaraka or Bhatta was used as addendum to the names of learned Brahmins or Kings of Kas'mira, while its diminutive *Bhatta* is a generic name for Kashmiri Pandits; thus it means a small (*Laghu*) Bhatta, apparently refering to a boy scholar, which is not borne by facts. It is very well known that Shaivism of the South is predominantly 'Dualistic' in content while Kashmiri Shaivism is 'Monistic', which thrived only in Kas'mira and both are fundamentally at variance. Even if it is taken that *Panchastavi* is post *Saundarya Lahiri*, it could not have been composed after 1030-1040 AD as *Saraswati Kanthabharana* of King Bhoja, which has references to *Panchastavi* verses, was composed between 1030 and1040 AD. By this time *Panchastavi* must have attained sufficient fame and credence for being included in *Saraswati Kanthabharana*. Thus, composition date band of *Panchastavi* can be narrowed down between 800 and 1050 AD; may be second half of 9th Century. Culturally Kas'mira witnessed great advancement during 9th Century; Kayyatacharya, Somananda, Muktakantha Swamin, Shiva Swamin, Ananda Vardhana and Kallata; great Shiva philosophers and authors, flourished during this period. During 10th Century, which includes reign of Chakravarman (922-933 AD), though conditions were disturbed by political vicissitudes, Pradyumana Bhatta, Utpalacharya, Rama Kantha, Prajn Arjuna, Lachaman Gupta and Mahadeva Bhatta had made enormous contribution to Shaivite thoughts. Any of these scholars could be composer of this scripture, but then the work must have been completed very early, attained fame in a very short period but why the author should, if one of them, maintain anonymity while their other works were recognised under their proper name! The limited time to be accepted for inclusion in *Saraswati Kanthabharana,* if composed in 10th Century, throws the dice in favour of first option; 9th Century which had rulers like Ajitpira (813-850 AD), Avanti Varman (855-883 AD), his son Shankara Varman (883-902 AD). This option of 9th Century gave adequate time for *Panchastavi* verses to pick up accolades. This is not only possible but probable. Its verses have been quoted as examples by Mammata Acharya in his *Kavyaprakasa* composed during 12th Century.

Point requiring analysis; is *Panchastavi* work of one or a group of religious scholars (*Dharma Acharya*(s). Contents of the scripture, which is found in Kas'mira alone and recited even today, is based on monistic Shaivism founded and propagated in Kas'mira. Thus, author of *Panchastavi* could be Kashmiri by birth, who was also well versed with *Sabari* and *Kundalini Yoga* and had been long enough in the valley to be literally one of them. Kashmiri herb like *trupsi* is mentioned in *Panchastavi*; small but possible indication of author being a Kashmiri or the one who knew Kas'mira like palm of his hand.

The Southern Influence Indicators

But there are other indicators pointing towards Southern 'influence':

- *Panchastavi* resembles *Saundarya Lahiri* in technique, theology and philosophic contents. It, however, conveys importance of *Sabari,* favourite form of the Divine Mother; a Namboodhari (Keralite) tradition of *Tantric Sadhana* and not Kashmiri.
- *Panchastavi* does even mention *Kali*, popularly worshipped in Kas'mira especially by Somananda, Abhinav Gupta and Jayaratha, which rules out their authorship.
- *Yoga* system praised in *Panchastavi* is different from systems popular in Kas'mira (*Trika Yoga* and *Kaula Yoga*). The hymns also convey importance of *Kundalini Yoga*, again not popular in Kashmiri tradition, but highly popular in Tamilian and Canara (Kannad) (*Saundarya Lahiri* describes *Kundalini Yoga* as the main mean of unity with the 'Absolute').
- Abhinav Gupta and Siddha Natha (alias Sambbhu Natha) have eulogised deities of *Kramanya*, but such deities do not find any place either in *Panchastavi* or in other *stotras* like *Saundarya Lahiri*.
- The only important common element between the *Sadhana* of the *Trika* system and *Panchastavi* is the worship of *Tripura*; common factor of nearly all *Shaiva/Sakta* theology systems and traditions and cannot lead to any specific conclusion.

It is thus clear that *Panchastavi* does not follow Kashmiri tradition of *Sakta* theology but follows the one in South. Imagination has always been a strong element in the character of poetic brain, Madhavacharya alias Vidhyaranya is typical example of such poets. There is no unanimity about the authorship of *Panchastavi*, leading to that the author wanted to remain anonymous. To highlight his intentions to remain anonymous, the last verse of the first canto of *Panchastavi* gives his intentions. There is, however, no doubt in the fact that *Dharma Acharya* (Religious Scholar) who composed *Panchastavi*, was a master of *Shiva/Sakta* monism, a Hindu/Brahmin to the core hailing from area within four corners of Kas'mira-Dwaraka-Kanyakumari-Kamarup and whole of *Panchastavi* was composed by him alone; but he knew Kas'mira very well. May be a Kashmiri who had also imbibed Southern nuances also.

Epilogue: Our immortal Sanskrit poet Kalidasa writes about the valley being more beautiful than the heaven, benefactor of supreme bliss and happiness. Incidentally some historians and researchers are of the opinion of his, Kalidasa Kas'mira heritage. Reading about Goddess Sharda and understanding is easy but what is not easy are the diverse accounts, attributions and aspects associated with her great name, which have come about in her manifestation at Shardi. Typically many of our ancestor scholars and elders in their keenness allowed other accounts, lores, and myths to combine with the factual accounts and thus we find that many such attributions have diluted facts and *Mahima* (Importance) of Goddess Sharda.

- In all probability Sharda temple was constructed somewhere in mid 12th Century, during the reign of Jai Simha; may be by an Aryan Saraswat Brahmin warlord of Kishanganga Valley. Installations of idols and *lingas* seem to have taken place at the time of *Kumbhabhishekam* (Consecration).
- *Sharda Mahatmaya* was possibly composed between 9th and 13th Century AD, when religious accounts, philosophies, scriptures started taking shape in the valley and outside scholars visited the valley. It looks Madhavacharya composed it in later part of his life (after 1250 AD) after becoming ascetic, referred by the name of Vidhyaranya and not giving his name.
- Sharda being addressed as *Mahadevi* is an effort to show her in *Shakti* form, to convert Sharda too as Cosmic Divine Mother. This is a later addition and not as per the philosophy of *Shakti* worship.
- Adi-Shankara had installed *Sri Chakra* in different *tirathas* before his purported visit to Sharda. *Sri Chakra* being taken from Sharda by Adi-Shankara and installed at various mutts in the South is not a fact.
- Lord Ram and Lord Krishna's name are associated with many places and landmarks, as devotion and to keep veneration of these *Avtars* alive, while on pilgrimage to Sharda. There is no evidence that either of them visited Kas'mira.

- Transition of names of three rivers of Sharda pilgrimage was in stages; to Kishanganga, Madhumati and Saraswati, not in one go and our own ancestors had a hand in their naming.
- Adi-Shankara's visit to Kas'mira and Sharda Temple remains unresolved; in fact there is no evidence of his visit to Kas'mira or Sharda. 8th and 9th Century's were blessed by Adi–Shankara, by his religious philosophy, *advaita*, and revival of Hinduism. In spite of lack of evidence of his visit stories have been woven out of devotion to his religious philosophy and his stature.
- Attribution of his authorship of *Panchastavi* is depriving the honours to that anonymus *Dharma Acharaya* (Religious Scholar), who had imbibed *Tantric Sadhana* of South, but definitely belonged to Kas'mira. Though there is similarity in technique, theology and philosophic contents of *Panchastavi* and *Saundarya Lahiri*, yet even attribution of the latter to Adi Shankaracharaya is contested.
- Goddess Sharda, identified to be Kas'mira *Vasini,* gave a well deserved designation for the identification of the valley; Sharda Desh. We did not have to go to far off places to trumpet our beliefs; the believers came to learn it from us.
- It is wondered as to why Kalhan has remained silent on one of the important facets of Kas'mira; Sharda. There are three reasons for it; first he basically concentrated on the valley portion and the Kings. Secondly, his father Champaka was a Kashmiri noble man, who held the office of *Dwarpal* or commander of the frontier defences during the reign of the ill fated King Harsha (1089-1101 AD) and he had developed cold feet towards the King. Thirdly, he has penned down facts. The myths and lores connected with the Goddess Sharda or his temple were not there during his time and as such he did not dwell in these in his chronicle. He definitely does not write about an institiution called as Sharda Peeth or University. He called Kas'mira as 'Land of Aryans'. There is no evidence of Sharda Peeth, first as a Pontiffs seat as Peeth, nor as a University. These are conjuctures only and one wonders why such a university would have been established outside Kas'mira, in an area which had most inhospitable terrain and weather. The premise of Sharda Temple is limited and there is no sign of a seminary, normally associated with a learning place. Over the centuries scholars, who possibly had not even visited Sharda Temple or areas around it, started imagning a place of learning with just a temple of Goddess Sharda and in their write ups called it Sharda Peeth (University).
- Last but not the least, it is the efforts of our ancestral scholars and their magnanimity to remain anonymous, being givers than seekers, which made me to write, boldly though, on the inferences which got obliterated with our giving credit to every one from outside.

10

Era Abberations in Kalhan's Rajatarangini

> "The wise man overcomes anger through mind control, lust through the renunciations of desire... Through conduct he should protect mind and speech. ...Through constant vigilance he should shed fear and through the service of the wise, he should overcome pride."
>
> –"*Brahma Purana* 235.40-42."

Rajatarangini – Style, Sources

From an early date ancient historical themes, whether in Bharatvarasha or in Kas'mira (Kashmir), were mainly framework for the display of subtle poetic art and rhetorics, which constituted the characteristic object of ancient *Kavyas* (Sanskrit Poetry). Almost all the historical *Kavyas* (*Caritas*) which have been found, deal with the exploits of the poets princely patrons or latter's immediate predecessors, contents and style depending on courtly patronage. Kalhan's Rajatarangini, for history of Kas'mira, represents a class of Sanskrit composition, *Kavya*, in form but with a scope and aim widely different from that of the *Caritas*. It offers a connected narrative of various Kings, dynasties, which ruled or presumed to have ruled Kas'mira, from earliest possible period down to his own time. The narrative begins with invoking of Hara (Shiva) in the form of *Ardhanarisvara,* representing Shiva's union with Parvati (Verse 1 and 2 Book (Taranga) 1), legends representing earliest popular traditions, history and beliefs of Aryan Saraswat Brahmins of Kas'mira, followed by narrative of Kings, in chronological order, taken from old records, manuscripts, treatises and details recorded with personal experience as living witnesses of his own time. Many events, details, anecdotes before composition of Rajatarangini would have definitely come from his relations, word of mouth and as Kalhan himself accepts from

(Translated); "Eleven works of former scholars containing the chronicles of Kings, I have inspected, as well as the opinions of the Sage *Nila* (Verse 14 Taranga 1)." In the same breath he mentions that oldest works containing royal chronicles had become fragmentary, including that of *Suvrata*, who had condensed them in a booklet form called '*Suvrata's Poem*' (Booklet). This booklet did not show dexterity and was troublesome reading by 'misplaced learning' (Verse 12 Taranga 1). *Suvrata* was a poet chronicler much before Kalhan's time, whose exact dates/era cannot be traced. It is doubtful that this booklet was available to Kalhan while writing Rajatarangini. Though accepting Ksemendra's; 'List of Kings' as work of a poet dismisses it; "not a single part in Ksemendra's 'List of Kings' (*Nrpavali*) free from mistakes" (Verse 13 Taranga 1). About his sources of information (Translated): "By looking at the inscriptions recording the temples and grants by former kings, at the laudatory inscriptions and at written works, the troubling arising from many errors has been overcome (Verse 15 Taranga 1)." In the next five verses (16 to 20) the sources of various Kings Chronology is attributed to Nilamat Puranam and other compositions for 'fifty two' rulers listed in the beginning of Rajatarangini. Actually this list names nineteen Kings and places another thirty five as 'lost Kings' in the "Chronological and Dynastic Tables of Kashmir Kings." Kalhan accepts having read *Pasupata Brahman,* Helaraja's 'List of Kings' (*Parthivavali*) of twelve thousand *Shloka's*, work of another poet Padamamihira, who had listed eight kings in his work, probably taken from Helaraja's work. Helaraja, a Kashmiri ascetic lived in 9th/10th Century AD and had written a commentary on the *Vakyapadiya*, of which fragments were available till later part of 19th Century AD in Kas'mira. Nothing much is known about scholar Padamamihira. Recovery of details of another five Kings from Ashoka, The Great, to the last on the first list (Abhimanyu) including Turuska Kings (Kushan Kings Huska, Juska and Kanishka) are attributed to another scholar, Chavillakara.

Rajatarangini contains over 7800 verses, in eight parts, of high poetic merit in Sanskrit; written during 1148-1150 AD, covering a period of 3050 years with dated accounts from AD 813 onwards with eighth part being exhaustive. Kalhan was possibly born in the end of 11th Century or beginning of 12th Century, his father was a Kashmiri noble man during the reign of King Harsha (1089-1101 AD). Rajatarangini has been updated from time to time, even under Muslim rule.

General Contents

Rajatarangini contains 8 Tarangas (Books) containing 7826 Verses and was started in the 24th year of Laukika Era (Sapatrishi Samvat). In medieval times century was not mentioned. Rajatarangini was composed in forty second century of the Laukika Era, thus the year in which writing started is 4224 Laukika Era (Sapatrishi Samvat), 1070 Saka Era (Saka Samvat; Saka

Samvat began in 78 AD); both corresponding to 1148-49 AD (Verse 52 Taranga 1). In verse 3404 Taranga 8, Kalhan, talks of 25th year of Laukika (4225 Laukika Era corresponding to 1149-50 AD), when Rajatarangini was completed. Rest of forty five verses in 8th Taranga are devoted to concluding remarks and synopsis; two Verses (3405 and 3406) as concluding remarks, followed by forty three verses as synopsis of the reigns. In the beginning of Rajatarangini he poetically insists (Translated); "Imbibe, therefore, straight with the folds of your ear shells this 'River of Kings' (Rajatarangini) which is rendered pleasant by under-currents of powerful sentiments (Verse 24 Taranga 1)." Rajatarangini is concluded thus (Translated); "Just as the Godavari river after flowing rapidly with its seven tumultuous mouths falls into the ocean to repose (There), thus verily this "River of Kings (Rajatarangini) after proceeding rapidly with its (first) seven sonorous waves (Taranga) falls into the ocean of the mighty race of the illustrious *Kantiraja* to find its end (there) (Verse 3449 Taranga 8)." Kantiraja was the ancestor of Kings Sussala (1112 –1120, 1122 - 1128 AD) and Jai Simha (1128 AD- 1155 AD). Apparently this verse is meant to refer to generalised account in the first seven Tarangas, followed by detailed account in the eighth Taranga.

Translated version of Rajatarangini by Sir Auriel Stein (1900 Print) in addition contains "Chronological and Dynastic Tables of Kalhan's Record of Kas'mira Kings", tabulated from the eras given in each Taranga (Book). In first three Tarangas and major portion of Taranga 4 of Rajatarangini, no chronological data has been given in the text and dates have been tabulated from the stated length of reigns, few general dates and figures in the Tarangas. Except for Taranga 1 wherein total aggregate length of reigns of initial fifty four Kings has been calculated, this Chronological and Dynastic Table gives Laukika Era (Sapatrishi Samvat) year/dates of accession. From later part of Taranga 4 dates of accession, political events or important events have been indicated with Laukika Era, with month and day.

Eras mentioned by Kalhan: Narration of reign of the Kings in Taranga 1 starts from Kaliyuga, also called Kali Samvat, and gives total duration of initial Kings mentioned in Taranga 1 to 2268 years in Kaliyuga. Verse 51 Taranga 1 mentions that (Translated); "when 653 years of Kaliyuga had passed away, the *Kurus* (*Kuravs*) and *Pandavas* lived on the earth." The year of starting Rajatarangini is in Laukika and Saka Era and Saka Samvat is repeated in Verse 56 (Translated); "When King *Yudishthira* ruled the earth, the *Munis* (the Great Bear – Sapatrishis) stood in the *Nakshatra Maghah*. The date of his reign was 2526 years (before) the Saka Era." Thus, three eras; Kali Samvat, Laukika Era (Sapatrishi Samvat) and Saka Era, have been used, though Laukika Era has been frequently quoted.

Laukika Era has been extensively used in the medieval age in Kas'mira together with Saka Samvat, in addition to Vikrami Samvat and continued till middle of 19th Century. While Saka Samvat fell off the radar of Kashmiris in the beginning of 20th Century (year 2012 AD being 1934 Saka Samvat), Vikrami Samvat (started in 56 BC, current year 2012 AD being 2069 Vikrami Samvat) was used till early fifties of 20th Century, before being replaced by Christian era. Laukika Era is still used in *Panchangs* and New Year (*Navreh*) starts from the first day of Laukika Era with *Thal Barun;* year 2012 AD being 5088 Sapatrishi Samvat. Vikrami Samvat had relevance in Kas'mira till it was official calendar of Jammu and Kashmir Government and the first day of the month called *Sankrath* related to *Sankrathi Vrat* (Fast). There was one important event of Vikrami Samvat; *Thal Barun* on the last day of the month of *Phalgun* and the first day of *Chaitra*, called *Sonth*, connoting the onset of spring. Kalhan, while quoting eras talks of *Brhatsamhita* (Verse 55 Taranga 1), another treatise on the Kashmiri calendar (More of it later).

Scope: Rajatarangini is a master piece by itself and authentic available history of the Kings of Kas'mira from ancient times to Kalhan's times i.e. 1150 AD. The style of writing, the lucid contents and the way an event has been poetically framed itself is unique. It has made a place for itself in the history of Kas'mira and Bharatvarasha and it is 'nearly blasphemous' to find errors or faults or aberrations in the book. Kalhan wanted the book to be (Translated); "Worthy of praise is that power of true poets, whatever it may be, which surpasses even the stream of nectar, in as much as by it their own bodies of glory as well as those of others obtain immortality-Verse 3 Taranga 1." Acceptance of the fact of later changes, that (Translated); "Men in later time should supplement the narrative of events in the works of those who died after composing each the history of those Kings whose contemporaries they were? Verse 9-10 Taranga 1." Availability of material to Kalhan for reference are; eleven works of scholars; Nilamat Puranam; Suvarata's *poem*, fragmentary though; Ksemendra's *Nrpavali*, opinion of Helaraja's *Parthivavali* (9th/10th Century), works of Padmamihira, Chavillakara and *Brhatsamhita* by Varaha Mihir. Some of the works are, however, dismissed as fragmentary, troublesome and not even a single part being free from mistakes (Verses 11 -13 Taranga 1). Mention of "inspection only" of work of eleven scholars (Verse 14 Taranga 1), gives an impression that their contents were not fully accepted as authentic or details contained therein not included by Kalhan. Details from Nilamat Puranam, works of Padmamihira and Chavillakara, even though included, connected contents have been framed differently; both in names as well as chronology. For example significant deviation can be observed on comparison of the contents of Verses 59 – 73 Taranga 1, dealing with first King of Kas'mira, with the contents of Nilamat Puranam (Verses 1- 10 Book 1 Nilamat Puranam), which are claimed as the base for composition thus; (Translated); "Gonanda and (his successors) have been taken from Nilamata. Verse 16 Taranga 1." Sir Auriel Stein in his translation of Rajatarangini has commented on the chronology of the Kings in his book "*Kalhana's Rajatarangini- A Chronicle of the Kings of Kasmir.*" Sir Stein based his comments on his own observation, analysis, plethora of books, reports, explanation, and interpretation by his Kashmiri scholar friends and various papers. Sir Stein comments on the Chronology of initial Kings viz 653 to 1919 Kali Samvat, thereafter thirty seven princes of first three dynasties reigning for 1784 years with high or low average reigns or 300 years allotted to King Ranaditya (Verse 470 Taranga 3). He also points out that the average dates of some of the known Kings like Ashoka, Kanishka and many others have been antedated ranging from 1000 years (Ashoka), Kanishka and other Kings (1100 years) to 1200 Years (Mihirkula (Mihir Kul) 550 AD). Even popular founder of Pravarpura (Srinagar), King Pravarsena II (6th Century AD), has been antedated by nearly 500 years in the chronology. Rajatarangini, however, narrows the gap in later Tarangas closer to Kalhan's era. These gaps, however, continue to exist till quoting of Laukika Era begins (Verses 703 and 7‑6 Taranga 4).

The aim is not to repeat variation already in public domain, but concentrate on other specific spheres, **not touched so far by any writer/scholar**. These aberrations are basis of certain fresh chronology, contradictions, which would have otherwise been known to Aryan Saraswat Brahmin Kalhan during his time. These aberrations are something like glow of light to Aryan Saraswat Brahmins of Kas'mira, which may give them somewhat correct era and chronology of the earliest Kings of Kas'mira, as scholars/writers, including Sir Stein have so far gone strictly by dates mentioned by Kalhan.

Origin of Various Eras/Calendars

Eras/Calendars: As a results of various surveys, carbon dating, archaeological finds, artefacts, common usage of the era in Bharatvarasha, Indus Valley excavations, excavations and survey results in Kas'mira, it has been proved that Sapatrishi Samvat is indigenous to Bharatvarasha, connected with pre Harappan civilisation in the Indian subcontinent (Bharatvarasha), tracing back to the Palaeolithic period; about 6000 BC ±. Apparently as the time elapsed, this period was taken as the base for Laukika Era (Sapatrishi Samvat). Arya Bhatta, an ancient Brahmin writer on Astronomy, born in Kusuma-Pura (Modern Patna; 550-476 BC- Dates somewhat disputed), author of *Aryabhattiya*, which is somewhat amendment to earlier work of Sage Maya (*Surya Siddhanta*), is the calculator of this era, which was widely accepted and used in Bharatvarasha and Kas'mira Earlier calendar in Bharatvarasha was with 60 cycles of 60 years each, 27 *Nakshatras* and twelve months. Notices by the Greek historians *Pliny* and *Arrian* suggest that, during the Mauryan Dynasty (322–185 BC), the calendar used in Bharatvarasha began in 6676 BC. It is very likely that this was earlier Saptarishi calendar, with a beginning of 6676 BC. Arya Bhatta's (550–476 BC) calculations and tradition places *Mahabharata* war to 3137 BC; 35 years before the transition of *Dvapar Yug* to Kaliyug and calculating start of Kali Samvat as 3102 BC. *Surya Siddhanta*, a document evolved earlier than *Aryabhattiya,* states that sun was 54 degrees away from vernal equinox when Kali Samvat started on a new moon day; Ist Day of *Chaitra Shukla Paksh* (Bright Half) corresponding to February 17/18, 3102 BC, at Ujjain. It is said that Kali Samvat could not begin as long as Lord Krishna was touching Earth with His holy feet and it was only after He left this world, it marked the end of *Dvapar Yug* and commencement of Kaliyug and Kali Samvat. There are some minor differences; 20 February 3102 BC or 18th February 3102 is also talked about as the day of commencement of Kali Samvat. From all confirmatory astronomical calculations Kali Samvat is believed to have begun when Krishna "died" at the age of 125 on Friday 17/18 Feburary 3102 BC. The commencement of Laukika Era or Sapatrishi Samvat has indirect connection with Kali Samvat. Sapatrishi's were in *Maghah Nakshatra*, 75 years prior to Kali Samvat and remained so for next 25 years after Kali Samvat had commenced. It is on Ist *Chaitra Shukla Paksh* (Bright Half) of 3076 BC Sapatrishis (Ursa Major) moved into *Poorva Nakshatra* BC and Laukika Era or Sapatrishi Samvat commenced.

The difference in what was being adopted before Arya Bhatta's calculation has connection with the present Laukika Era or Sapatrishi Samvat and a remarkable coincidence of 60 years cycle for 60 years totalling 3600 years. Earlier Sapatrishi Samvat was a repetitive i.e. 6676 BC less 3600 years coinciding with commencement of current Sapatrishi Samvat. Around 500 AD, another major review of the Indian calendar was 'attempted'. Varaha Mihir, a Kashmiri Aryan Saraswat Brahmin (505-587 AD; (some scholars state that he was born at Ujjain and some claim he belonged to Persia) and others used *Nakshatra* references and that Sapatrishis (Ursa Major) were indeed in *Maghah Nakshatra* at the time of the *Mahabharata* War. While Arya Bhatta declared the War to have occurred in 3137 BC, Varaha Mihir assigned it 2449 BC (653 Kali Samvat). This discrepancy arose from different assumptions regarding the *Nakshatras*; actually 27 as correctly calculated by Arya Bhatta and Varaha Mihir's assumption of 28 as against 27 *Nakshatras* based on *Nakshatras* as given in Atharv Veda, which was found to be incorrect. Only 27 *Nakshatras* fitted the well made astronomical calendar propounded in *Surya Sidhanta* and later in Arya Bhatta's work, *Arryabhattiya*. Commencement of Laukika Era or Sapatrishi Samvat is thus placed on *Chaitra Sudi* 1 (First day of Bright Half of *Chaitra;* also the New Year (*Navreh*) of Aryan Saraswat Brahmins of Kas'mira) of Kali Samvat 25 (expired) or the year 3076 BC. Current Laukika Era is 5086 (2012 AD).

One wonders as to why a new era was started immediately after Kali Samvat in the form of Laukika Era (Sapatrishi Samvat). One of the explanations was that on *Chaitra Sudi* 1 (First day of Bright Half of *Chaitra*) Sapatrishis moved from *Maghah Nakshatra* to *Poorva Nakshatra;* a phenomenon once in hundred years. One would ask why on move to *Poorva Nakshatra* only. While *Poorva Nakshatra* is considered auspicious, why not more auspicious *Nakshatras* or the first auspicious *Nakshatra* of the calendar i.e. *Ashwin*. Apart from wait for the next *Nakshatra*, start of a new era barely twenty five years after Kali Samvat is curious. It is evident from these facts that the new era became due, after the ancient calendar of 60 by 60 years cycle.

Aryan Saraswat Brahmins of Kas'mira for long have been associating commencement of Laukika Era with that of the entry of Aryan Saraswat Brahmins into Kas'mira. Laukika Calendar came into being in Bharatvarasha as a result of the revision of major astronomical calendars by Arya Bhatta's in 550-476 BC. With Kali Samvat having been established, 25 years gap surprisingly coincides with date of *Swargarohanam* (Entry into heaven) of Pandavas. It is also said that Sage Vyasa dictated the epic to Ganapati only after *Swargarohanam* of Pandavas. Thus possibly, to my mind, commencement of Laukika Era (Sapatrishi Samvat) can be attributed to the dates of *Swargarohanam* of Pandavas, which they would have done on an auspicious day. Pandavas left for their last journey on *Aswayuja* Bright (*Shukla Paksh*) 12th Day (*Dwadashi*) when Yudishthir was 128 Years old (3102 BC) and their *Swaragarhonam* is dated about 25 years later of Kali Samvat.

Laukika Era reckoning is to be found in all handbooks of Indian chronology. Two other prevalent Samvats also were in use in Kas'mira; Vikrami Samvat and *Sakabda* or Saka Samvat (Also called *Shalivahana* Saka), difference between the two being 135 years. Saka Samvat commenced in 78 AD and is presumed to be related to the coronation of famous Kushan King Kanishka. Present Christian calendar came into vogue in 7 AD, while in Bharatvarasha, since ancient times, lunar calendar was followed.

Relevant Acceptance of Kali, Laukika and Saka Samvats by Kalhan: As mentioned above, Taranga 1 of Rajatarangini starts quoting three eras (Samvats); Kaliyug (Kali Samvat), Laukika Era (Sapatrishi Samvat) and Saka Samvat (Also called *Shalivahana* Saka). Kalhan has rightly accepted beginning dates of these Samvats and these can be tabulated from his verses also; Kali Samvat to 3102 BC, Laukika Era to 3076 BC and Saka Samvat 79 AD. Certain other accepted facts connected with these eras, directly or indirectly are; acceptance that Great Bear (Sapatrishis) moving from one *Nakshatra* to another in hundred years; Yudishthira of Mahabharata fame ruled when Sapatrishis were in *Maghah Nakshatra*. However, there is doubt created in that *Mahabharata* War (Also called Bharata War) took place at the end of the *Dvapara Yug* (Verse 48-49 Taranga 1), indirectly meaning that it took place much later in Kaliyug.

Kalhan, from all accounts, was very well conversant with Sage Ved Vyasa's epic *Mahabharata*, as can be noted from this verse (Translated); "With tears in their eyes they devoted themselves to reciting hymns (*stotras*) such as *Stavrajas* in the *Mahabharata*..... Verse 106 Taranga 8." The epic is also mentioned in Verse 1728 Taranga 7. It has been endeavour and argument in Rajatarangini to prove Kali Samvat 653 as the starting point of Kas'mira Kings Chronology, corresponding with coronation of Yudishthira. Till the time of Kalhan, Kas'mira had renaissance of religious fervour from 5th Century onwards. It is also a fact that apart from Shaivism, Vedas, *Mahabharata*, Nilamat Puranam and scores of religious scriptures had been composed during this period. Contents of *Mahabharata*, its chronology, beginning of Kaliyug (Kali Samvat) after the war would have been in the common domain of the people of Kas'mira, more so known to scholars of the calibre of Billhana and Kalhan. It was also fully known that *Dvapar Yug* had finished with the death of Lord Krishna and Kali Samvat could not begin as long as Lord Sri Krishna was alive. It is surprising Kalhan would continue with the misconception of Lord Krishna being alive during Kali Samvat. It is also clear that Kalhan was conversant or having known contents of the work of Sage Maya (*Surya Sidhanta*) and Arya Bhatta's work, *Aryabhattiya*. Contents of Varaha Mihir's (505- 587 AD) *Brhatsmhita* have been erroneously accepted by Kalhan and with this indirectly that of *Arya-Siddhanta*, a lost work on astronomical computations based on the older *Surya Siddhanta,* which used midnight-day-reckoning, as opposed to sunrise in *Aryabhattiya* of Arya Bhatta. By the time of Kalhan, it had been amply proved by astronomically connected works, that Arya Bhatta's work over rode the later work of Varaha Mihir. Thus overall the documents available to Kalhan at the time of writing Rajatarangini were all indicators of the commencement of Kaliyug, 25 years prior to Laukika Era.

Aberration in Dates

Dates of *Mahabharata* War: Nowhere dates of *Mahabharata* War have been directly indicated in Rajatarangini, though they were available to scholars throughout Bharatvarasha and Kas'mira from around 500 BC onwards, when pioneering works on astronomy were available. It is mentioned in Rajatarangini that Bharata War (*Mahabharata*) did not take place at the end of *Dvapar Yug* (Verse 48-49 Taranga 1), indicating Kalhan's assertion that it took place in Kaliyug. Indirectly Kalhan places Bharata War to Kali Samvat 653 (Laukika Era 628); 7th Century of Kali Samvat, assuming that Yudishthir coronation (second time) occurred in 653 Kali Samvat, which actually happened, for the second time, at the end of *Mahabharata* War in *Dvapar Yug*. There were certain astronomically connected indicators of the Bharata War available to scholars during Kalhan's time. These are; Yudishthir birth roughly 15th August 3229 BC. Lord Krishna born on *Shravan* Dark

(*Krishna Paksh*) 8th (*Ashtami*), just after midnight in Taurus (*Mithun Lagana*) and was approximately 4 years younger to Yudishthir (August 3225 BC; Roughly 125 years before Kali Samvat). Yudishthir coronated for the first time when he was 46 years old (August 3183 BC). Yudishthir again coronated when he was 91 years 3 months and 10 days old (January 3136 BC). Apart from glossing over this information, *Nakshatra* of Sapatrishis in Kali Samvat 653 have been mixed up. Though commencement of Kali Samvat 25 years prior to Laukika Era in *Maghah Nakshatra* is accepted, *Nakshatra* used more than 6 Centuries later in Kali Samvat 653/623 Laukika Era remains the same i.e *Maghah*. In spite of overwhelming available opinion of Varaha Mihir's wrong calculation of eras, Kalhan relied on Varaha Mihir's dates of the Bharata War i.e. 2449 BC to around 653 Kali Samvat, corresponding to 628 Laukika Era. Bharata War (*Mahabharata*) took place approx 35 years plus prior to Kali Samvat, starting on 13/14th Day, Tuesday, when Yudishthir was 91 years old (December 3137 BC). Just the previous day, when opposing armies were rehearsing *Vyuhas*, Arjuna fell into gloom occasioning Lord Krishna's famous *Bhagvad Geeta* discourse (called *Geeta Jayanti* Day till this day). It may be argued that the present calculations, after nearly 1500 years after Varaha Mihir, have been possible due to advancement in astronomy etc. However, it is known fact that various astronomical calculations and calendars from Arya Bhatta's time were available from 500 BC onwards; Lagadha's *Vedanga Jyotisha* (1st Century BC), other astronomical works of Brhmagupta, Bhaskara I (disciple of Arya Bhatta), Bhaskara II, Varaha Mihir's *Brhatsamhita* (6th Century AD) and many more papers. **This single aberration resulted in complete distortion in the initial chronological history of Kings of Kas'mira.**

Kalhan's Assertion Sapatrishis (Munis) in Maghah Nakshatra in 2526 Saka Era (653 Kali Samvat Laukika Era 628).

In verse 56 Taranga 1 Varaha Mihir's *Brhatsamhita* (xii-3) is quoted and in previous verse "*Muni's* (Sapatrishis) moved from one *Nakshatra* to another in 100 years." Saka Samvat, 2526, quoted in the same verse, corresponds to 2449 BC. Kali Samvat Era and Laukika Era commencement is accepted in Rajatarangini; corresponding to 3102 BC and 3076 BC respectively. It is also a known fact, even at that time, Laukika Era started when Sapatrishis (Great Bear) moved from *Maghah Nakshatra* to *Poorva Nakshatra* in 3076 BC. As has been enumerated, earlier calendar in Bharatvarasha started in 6676 BC with 60 cycles of 60 years i.e a block of 3600 years making next block to start in 3076 BC. Thus, 25 Kali Samvat is the commencement of Laukika Era (Sapatrishi Samvat). Even if we assume that new calendar started on commencement of Kali Samvat, *Nakshatras* would start with *Ashwin Nakshatra* and as on Kali Samvat 653 (Laukika 628) Sapatrishis would be in seventh *Nakshatra* i.e. *Punarvasu*. Calculating reversely Sapatrishis at the time of Kali Samvat 653 and Laukika Era 628 were in *Maghah*, it would mean that Kali Samvat and Sapatrishi Samvat started when Sapatrishis were in *Rohini;* fourth in the sequence of *Nakshatras*. Evidently a fresh era could not have started in the middle of *Nakshatras*. Actually Sapatrishis were in *Anuradha Nakshatra* in 653 Kali Samvat (628 Laukika Era). **This miscalculation can be attributed to Kalhan's reluctance to accept more authentic astronomical works available from 400 BC onwards.** Even Bhaskara II, as late as 7th Century AD, had reinforced Arya Bhatta's assertions. Kalhan in this regard falls short of his own assertion of having taken note of inscriptions at temples, laudatory inscriptions and written works and the 'trouble arising from many errors had been overcome (Verse 16 Taranga 1)'.

Yudishthir's Coronation Dates by Kalhan: As is known Yudishthir was made crown prince when he was 31 years and five days old (Roughly 96 years 7 months pre Kali Samvat era corresponding to August 3198 BC). Yudishthir was coronated for the first time when he was 46 years old (August 3183 BC) (Also read above). Yudishthir's second time coronation took place sometime after the Bharata War (*Mahabharata*). The war was followed by twelve days mourning followed by *Pandavs* return to Hastinapur and thereafter coronation of Yudishthira on *Pausa* Full Moon Day (*Puranmashi*) (Roughly 35 pre Kali Samvat, 60 years Pre Laukika Era, corresponding to Jan 3136 BC). There were certain astronomically connected indicators available to scholars, including Kalhan, during his time. These are Yudishthir's birth dates (Roughly 15th August 3229 BC), first coronation, second coronation etc (Read above). As per Rajatarangini calculation Yudishthir took over as King 2526 years before Saka Era (Verse 56 Taranga 1), corresponding to 653 Kali Samvat, 628 Laukika Era, 2449 BC). This makes Yudishthir 780 years old, as per Kalhan, when he was coronated. The verse quoted is also silent as to whether this was Yudishthir's first or second coronation. If it pertains to first coronation, then as per *Mahabharata* Chronology, coronation took place in 81 Years Pre Kali Samvat, 106 Years Pre Laukika Era corresponding to August 3183 BC and Yudishthira being 699 Years old. Even by the *Mahabharata* Standards, this age is beyond comprehension as Yudishthira, as per the astronomical calculations/ chronology, was 128 years old when he coronated his grandson Parikshit at Hastinapur (Kali Samvat 1 Pre Laukika Era 24, corresponding to Jan/Feb 3101 BC). The date Yudishthir died is not known but their (*Pandav's*) *Swaraarohanam* (Death) may have been 25/26 years later (Roughly around Kali Samvat 25-26/ Laukika Era 1-2, corresponding to 3076 BC).

Mystery of Kali Samvat 653/2526 Pre Saka Samvat: Verse 82 Taranga 1 states; "When six hundred and fifty-three years of the Kaliyuga had passed away, the Kurus and Pandavas lived on the earth." The date of Yudishthir's coronation is given as 2526 before Saka Samvat (653 Kali

Samvat, 628 Laukika Era (Verse 56 Taranga 1)). Nowhere in eight Tarangas (Books) of Rajatarangini, directly or indirectly, the basis for quoting this Samvat (653 Kali Samvat) has been explained, which has been used as the beginning era of the chronology of Kings of Kas'mira. *Brhatsamhita* of Varaha Mihir is briefly referred to and apparently the dates of Bharata War (*Mahabharata*) have been taken as 2449 BC, as propagated by Varaha Mihir in 6th Century AD, which corresponds to Kali Samvat 653. Strangely 'only' this aspect of Varaha Mihir's composition has been taken. Sapatrishis moving from one *Nakshatra* to another in 100 years and commencement dates of Laukika era and Kali Samvat though have been taken from age old astronomical works of Arya Bhatta and others. **The result has been post dating of chronology in Rajatarangini by Kalhan by more than 653 years, starting with Gonanda I. This major aberration by Kalhan has been overlooked for all these centuries.**

Erroneous Dating of Gonanda I and Chronology

Gonanda I: Verse 16 Taranga 1 mentions that the details of four Kings of Kas'mira viz Gonanda I and his successors have been taken from Nilamat Puranam; a sacred composition dated around 600 AD. First 10 Verses of Nilamat Puranam mentions Gonanda and his successors, as an enquiry conversation between King Janmejaya (Great Grandson of Yudishthir) and Vaisampayana (Pupil of Sage Vyasa). Though characters from *Mahabharata* are quoted, like Madhava, Vasudeva etc., no names of Kings of Kas'mira except male child Gonanda are quoted. The query is about non participation of 'King of Kas'mira' in Bharata War (*Mahabharata*), assuming Kings name was Gonanda, Nilamat Puranam indicates this event of Pre Bharata War. It also talks of coronation of pregnant queen being coronated and Gonanda (II) being a child at the time of Bharata War and that is the reason his support was not asked for by either side. Damodara as King and son of King Gonanda (I) and father of Gonanda (II) and listed by Kalhan, is not talked about.

Immediately after mentioning coronation of Yudishthir, Kalhan talks of glory of 'King of Kas'mira (Verse 57 Taranga 1)' and gives the details of the event as enumerated in Nilamat Puranam but with different contents and characters (Verses 59 to 70 Taranga 1 and 3407-3409 Taranga 8)). These verses state that King Gonanda of Kas'mira had been invited by his relative Jarasamdha, King of Magadha, father-in-law of Kamsa (Krishna's maternal uncle), to help him in a war against Krishna (*Krsna*). Gonanda complied and was slain on the battle field by Balabhadara. Gonanda's son Damodara then ruled earth (Kas'mira) and later went to Gandhara, when he comes to know that *Vrsnis* (Yadavas) had been invited to attend *Suyamvara* on the banks of Indus (Sindhu). Damodara was killed by Krishna, but taking into consideration the high sanctity of 'Kas'mir', Krishna coronated his rival's pregnant widow 'Yasovati' (Verse 70) 'till her child is born and then takes over the throne'. The child takes the name of Gonanda after his grandfather. Kalhan in Verse 82 Taranga 1 too confirms that Gonanda II being a child, his support was not sought in Bharata War (*Mahabharata*).

Chronology: In Nilamat Puranam as well as Rajatarangini, these events are pre Bharata War, including Gonanda II being a child at the time of Bharata War. Assuming Gonanda II was roughly ten years old at the time of Bharata War (*Mahabharata*), Gonanda I being roughly around 60 years old when killed and his son Damodara around 30 years old on taking over. This would date Gonanda I going to Mathura around 12-13 years before Bharata War (47/48 years Pre Kali Samvat, 72/73 Years Pre Laukika Era and around 3149/50 BC). Assuming that Gonanda I had been King roughly for 30 years at the time of his death, Gonanda I's reign would start around 77/78 years Pre Kali Samvat (3179/3180 BC, 3258 Pre Saka) as against 2526 Saka Samvat (2449 BC) given by Kalhan; a difference of around 730 years, from quoted era of 653 Kali Samvat. The miscalculated dates from Gonanda I could be as under:

- Gonanda I killed and Damodar's Coronation roughly 48 Years pre Kali Samvat, 73 Years Pre Laukika Era (Roughly 3149 BC; 3227 Pre Saka Samvat). Yasovati also coronated around the same time. It can be assumed Damodar's death took place 2-3 years after his coronation.
- Gonanda II assumed to be around 10 years old at the time of Bharata War can be dated as coronated around as 6 years old in 40 years pre Kali Samvat, 65 Years pre Laukika Era (3142 BC and 3220 Pre Saka Samvat).
- Even if Rajatarangini reference taking 653 Kali Samvat as base, dates of King Gonanda I would be at least 42-43 years before the era mentioned (Around 611/610 Kali Samvat).
- Thus the Chronology of the Kings of Kas'mira in Rajatarangini should have started from 77/78 Years Pre Kali Samvat, 102/103 years Pre Laukika Era (Sapatrishi Samvat) (3179/3180 BC ; 3257/58 Pre Saka Samvat). Historical narrations by our scholars have so far been quoting 653 Kali Samvat of Kalhan in all references to the Kings of Kas'mira; out by nearly 730 years.

Bharata War (*Mahabharata*) Dates Mix Up: *Mahabharata* War lasted a fortnight plus but has been quoted differently in the verses. When Yudishthir's coronation is mentioned, it is assumed that it was Yudishthir's second coronation after the Bharata War. Gonanda I's rule is also placed around same time after Bharata War (Verses 56/57 Book 1). Rajatarangini goes along with the narration of 'Gonanda's help' to 'Damodar's coronation' followed by his killing, Yasovati's coronation and finally her son Gonanda II being a child at the time of Bharata War (*Mahabharata*). These are contradictory with the dates/timings and sequence of events connected with the King's of Kas'mira. Kalhan does not recognise the time elapse between the four rulers and brackets it at the same time and that too with the coronation of Yudishthir, which happens immediately after the war. Is there a mix up?

Lost Kings–King Ashoka and Kanishka: Kalhan quotes that fifty two rulers from Gonanda I up to Gonanda III have not been recorded. Nineteen names of Kings in the narration in Taranga 1 are given and thirty five Kings after Gonanda II placed in lost kings, whose record of names and deeds have perished (Verse 83 Taranga 1). Rajatarangini, counts Huska, Juska and Kanishka as one entity, actually making the total to fifty four Kings. As per narration in initial parts of Taranga 1, these fifty four Kings reign for a total of 1266 years, starting from Kali Samvat 653 (Laukika Era 628-2448 BC). From Gonanda III onwards the number of years of the rule of the Kings (Verse 191 Taranga 1) is given (The era details have been calculated backwards from the Laukika Era given in Verse 703 Taranga 4). With this calculation, Gonanda III's reign begins in Laukika Era 1894 (1182 BC, Pre Saka Samvat 1204). Taking revised calculated dates of Gonanda I (3179/3180 BC (77/78 Years Pre Kali Samvat, 102/103 years Pre Laukika), total years of reign of these Kings, up to Gonanda III, totals to around 2000 years as against 1266 years given by Kalhan. We also know for sure that King Ashoka (304-232 BC) ruled from 273–232 BC and taking the average rule of these fifty four Kings and working on Kalhan's dates, Ashoka's rule is placed fully thousand years before his real known date. Similarly Kanishka's reign is dated as 78-144 AD by some chroniclers, though the dates are debatable, and as per Rajatarangini calculation Kanishka's rule has chronological error of about eleven hundred antedated years. If we take the Kas'mira Kings chronology from 3179/3180 BC, as deduced, this antedated gap increases to seventeen hundred years plus in case of Ashoka and nearly eighteen hundred thirty years in case of Kanishka. Also as per reworked chronology, the reign of fifty four Kings spans nearly three thousand one hundred years up to Kanishka, at an average of fifty eight years plus per King, which is very high as compared to normal averages in the complete book. The difference between actual dates of rule of Ashoka and Kanishka is one hundred fifty four years, in which only two Kings have been shown (King Jaluka son (descendant) of Emperor Ashoka and King Damodara II) at an average of more than seventy years. This average too is rather very high. Damodara II's name akin to Damodara I appears to be from a different dynasty than those listed prior to him (Mauryan Dynasty), possibly this King could be from the same old Gonanda dynasty (restored). This could also indicate that after the rule of Kushans (Kanishka, Huska, and Juska) the same dynasty was restored in the form of King Abhimanyu I, a known name from *Mahabharata* (Son of Pandav's, killed during the Bharata War during

Chakravyuh). Even after Abhimanyu I, the Gonandiya Dynasty, whether it is the same as initial Gonanda Dynasty is difficult to assert and as per Kalhan's Rajatarangini rules Kas'mira till about 2861 Laukika Era (180 BC). It is known that dynasties, after coming to power again, named King's on the lines of earlier ones. It is also known that Ashoka and reign of his successors in the region continued till 185 BC, when last in the line of Maurya Dynasty, King Brhadrata, was killed.

The period after Mauryan Dynasty up to Kushan King Kanishka (Coronation 78 AD?) was known to be part of Indo–Greek Kingdom, which has not been listed. Even after Kanishka, the line of successors as listed in History of Bharatvarasha are Huviska, Vasudeva (Juska), Kanishka I and Vasishka; in that order. Except Huviska (Huska) and Juska, who have been identified from places named after them in Kas'mira. *Kanishkpura* named after Kanishka is *Kanispor*, a village between Vitasta and road from Baramulla (*Varhamulla*). The locals treat it as a *Tirath* and attribute its founding to King *Kanistharaja* (King Kanishka). *Husakpura* (*Ushkar*) in *Varahakshetra* (Baramulla) is named after Huviska. As far as Juska is concerned, founding of Jusakpura (*Zukur*) a large village North of Srinagar (6.5 kilometres from Hariparbat) is attributed to him. No connecting artefacts or coins of later Kushan Kings other than mentioned have been found in Kas'mira and it is impossible to clearly define whether any of the other Kushan rulers reigned over Kas'mira.

As per mythology Harandev, second son of Parikshit (Yudshithir's grandson) is termed as first Pandav King of Kas'mira, after Gonanda II, followed by another twenty three in the line. This may well fit into the Kalhan's assertion (Verse 51) that '653 years of the Kaliyuga had passed away when the 'Kurus and Pandav's' lived on the earth'. On a fair estimate names and deeds of **nearly fifty other Kings and not only thirty five Kings, totalling nearly eighty five Kings, has been lost**. These could well be distributed; more than thirty five Kings after Damodara II (including Harandev and twenty three of Pandav lineage), between Kings Surendra and Godhara (later belonging to another family indicating change in dynasty), in the list of Kings recorded by Helaraja, Chavillakara and finally Indo Greek rulers after Ashoka's Maurya Dynasty and before Kushan rule.

Reign and Era-Kings Abhimanyu to Baladitya and Thereafter: In the initial part of Taranaga I, after Kanishka, King Abhimanyu I is listed at the end of the list in the calculation of total of 1266 Years (Laukika Era 628-1894). Narrative is thereafter resumed with the Gonandiya Dynasty from Laukika Era 1894 to 2896, giving a total of twenty one Kings totalling 1002 years duration of their reign, averaging more than fifty years per King; from about 1182 BC to 180 BC (Verse 191 Taranga 1 onwards). Actually these dates should have been in AD era, since King listed earlier (Kanishka) was 'known' to have ruled in 78-144 AD. Taranga 2 lists six Kings for a total of 192 years; Laukika Era 2896 to 3088 corresponding to 180 BC- 12 AD. Again these dates are out of tune with certain known names of Kings and their actual dates of reign.

In Taranga 3, ten Kings are listed for five hundred and eighty nine years; averaging nearly sixty years per King (Laukika Era 3088 to 3677 Corresponding to 12–601 AD); abnormally high average and in one case unbelievable three hundred years (Ranaditya (Tunjana III)). It is only at the end of Taranga 4 (Verse 703) records of exact dates for the various reigns in Laukika Era (3889 Laukika corresponding to 813 /4 AD onwards) are given. By this time gap between actual and stated narrows down to approximately twenty five years. Dates up to Taranga 3 give an impression of overstated duration of reigns of Gonandiya Dynasty (Taranga 1) and 'Restored Gonandiya Dynasty' (Taranga 3). The names from Gonanda III, apart from being heavily antedated, also give an impression that some of the Kings may have ruled for very short period or they did not exist. However, historical evidences of some of the listed Kings exist like Nara (Destroyer of Vijayesvara (Vijbroor) and founder of Narapura), Hiranyaska (Founder of Hiranyapura), Mihirkula (Mihir Kul), Nara II, Gopaditya (Gopadiri *Agrahara* fame; present day Shankracharaya), Khinkhila-Narendraditya, Meghavahana, Hiranya-Toramana (Established with help of coins of his era), Matra Gupta, Pravarsena I and II (Pravarsena II founder of Pravarpura (Srinagar)), Vikramaditya - Harsa of Ujjain, Lakhana-Narendraditya (Established from silver coins with the inscriptions which bears the legend Raja Lakhana Udayaditya) and to a certain extent Baladitya. In Taranga 4 from King Durlabha Vardhana (Karkota Dynasty) onwards the details are closer to dates confirmed by other chronicles, coins or foreign notices, travelogues of Chinese and other travellers etc. However, even after giving the dates of Karkota Dynasty Kings, there is a difference of twenty five years (more about this in next paragraph).

Mystery of 25 Years Difference in Taranga 4: Up to King Abhimanyu I, generally whole era from Gonanda I is given in total number of years. It is only from Gonanda III (Verse 191 Taranga 1) till Verse 703 Taranga 4, total number of years of reign of each King are given. In this verse (703 Taranga 4) Laukika Era (3889) beginning of the reign to the end of King Ajitpada reign (Laukika Era 3926) is given. Taranga 4 starts with King Durlabha Vardhana of Karkota Dynasty and the calculated date of his accession is marginally antedated by twenty five years from the actual dates calculated from other sources, mostly Chinese, which were recorded much earlier than the composition dates of Rajatarangini and have been proved to be more authentic dates. During the time of Gonandiya Dynasty the first Chinese reference to Kas'mira was traced to a record dated 541 AD, based on the account of an 'Indian Envoy' who reached China during the early part of the reign of T'ang

Dynasty (541 AD). Ninety years later Huen Tsang (631 AD), Chinese Pilgrim, gives vivid account of various places including Pravarpura and the Kings of Kas'mira. We have also reference in Chinese Annals to Durlabha Vardhana, the founder of Karkota Dynasty, who as per Rajatarangini ruled from around 600/601 – 636 AD, antedated by about 30 years. Another Chinese notice of Kas'mira contained in the Chinese Annals of the above T'ang Dynasty, records embassy from Kas'mira King in China (in or shortly after 713 AD). Chinese pilgrim Ou-K'ng (759 AD) had also extensively covered Kas'mira, its surrounding areas and recorded details of Kas'mira. From the comparison of dated found in Chinese and other records, more closer to actual dates of Karkota Dynasty, Kings in this Taranga (4) are antedated by around twenty five years including Lalitaditya Muktapira. This aberration, which occurs in dates of reign closer to the date of composition of Rajatarangini, when author would have had access to recent past records of the Kings and can best be explained that Kalhan, during calculations, possibly mixed up the dates with Kali Samvat years, which is antedated by twenty five years to Laukika era. This is also confirmed by the fact that the book suddenly gives beginning year of reign of King Ajitpada in Laukika Era, followed by end era of his reign; again in Laukika Era.

Other Misinterpretations: Kalhan holds an iconic position, very learned and Rajatarangini being unique chronicle of 12th Century in *Kavya* style. He apparently had studied lot of material available at that time; *Ramayana*, *Mahabharata*, Nilamat Puranam, works of Helaraja, *Parthivavali* (List of Kings), Suvrata's composition, Ksemendra's *Nrpavali*, Billhan, works of Arya Bhatta, Bhaskara, Varaha Mihir and other astronomers and many more chronicles and scriptures. It is nearly impossible to find faults or mistakes in the work but to err is human. We do not know the personal circumstances under which Kalhan completed Rajatarangini; did he revise it, was he correct in not accepting the historic works of earlier times or were they really not up to standard. Nearly nine centuries later it is difficult to sit in judgement of his work but with plethora of material available over the centuries, more reliable and correct information can be formed of the eras, Kings and events. Kalhan had thoroughly read various scriptures and it is but natural that his work should have been free of any errors or somewhat ambiguous references. There are few in addition to what have been enumerated above as under:-

- **Wrong Reference to Kamsa:** In Verse 59 Taranga 1 while referring to call for help by Jarasamdha, father in law of Kamsa, of Mathura town of the enemy Kamsa instead of Krsna (Krishna). It is apparent that he did not get time to revise the chronicle.
- **Rule of Kurus (Kuravs) and Pandavas:** Verse 51 Taranga 1 refers to the rule of Kurus and Pandavas till about 653 Kali Samvat. Again Verse 44 Taranga 1 refers to Gonanda III (As per Kalhan's reckoning Gonanda

III Kali Year 1919 (1182 BC) but possibly 2 Century AD) to be "contemporaries of Kuru's and sons of Kunti." The way events, quotes, characters from *Mahabharata* have been quoted in the chronicle; there is no doubt about Kalhan's mastery over the epic. However, the verse and few more give an impression that Kurus (Kuravs) and Pandavs were two different dynasties from the beginning and both continued to rule Bharatvarasha after the Bharata War. As per the mythology and scriptures, origin of Kurus starts from Dushyant and Shankuntala, whose son is Bharata. King Hastina, who established Hastinapur, was son of King Bharata and Kuru was King Hastinas son and the dynasty was called Kurus (Kuravs). Later in the line three brothers Dhritarashtra, Pandu, and Vidura were born. Dhritarashtra was blind, Pandu "the pale one", called as such as he was pale at the time of birth and Vidura, reincarnation of Sage Vyasa thought to be of humble birth. Pandu was set on the throne as the King and this became the bone of contention and finally resulted in Bharata War (*Mahabharata*). From here the distinction of Kurus (Kuravs) and Pandus (Pandavs) starts. Sons of Dhritarashtra (Kuravs) fought in the Bharata War. Duryodhana had twenty nine sons of which few survived. Upon the death of all, Ashwathhama crowned Durmukha, youngest son of Duryodhana as next King and continued struggle. After the war the defeated Kuravs migrated to west and formed the *Kathi* tribe, now living in Kathiawar (Gujarat). Pandavs line after Yudishthir is carried on by his grandson Parikshit, who after sixty years rule coronated his twenty five year old son Janamejaya and died. Parikshit had another son, Harandev, and he is termed as the first Pandav King of Kas'mira, roughly 30 years after Gonanda II (Also read above). The date of Kuravs and Pandavs thus pegged to 653 Kali Samvat is ambiguous.

- **Reference to Jina – Buddha?** In Verse 102 King Ashoka is referred to; "embraced the doctrine of Jina, covered *Susalaketra* (Village of *Hukhlitr*) and *Vitastatra* (Vithvutur village near Verinag) with numerous Stupas" during the reign of Ashoka. The reference of referring by term Jina to Buddha is different as Kalhan refers to Buddha (Gautam Buddha (May 623–547 BC) in the book as *Mahasakya* (Verse 140-144 Taranga 1), Sakyasimha (Verse 172 Taranga 1) and at many other places. Kalhan used 'Buddha' term in Tarangas 1, 3, 4, 5, 6. 7 and 8 while referring to Gautam Buddha. Generally when reference is to Jina, it refers to abhorring of killing, which is also associated with Lord Mahavira (575 BC) and who used to be also called Jaina (Jina). Hopefully the words Jina referred have not been used out of context in the chronicle by Kalhan.
- 150 years to Buddha from the reign of Kushan Kings (Verse 172 Taranga 1). In this verse *Sakyasimha* (Buddha) is placed just 150 years

before Kushan Kings. In the table of chronology Ashoka is placed five rulers above Kushan Kings, which also comes to about 150 years. Actually Ashoka (304–232 BC) ruled from 273–232 BC, nearly 300 years before Kushan Kings (Kanishka, Huviska, Juska). Gautam Buddha (May 623–547 BC) antedated Ashoka by nearly three centuries, making Buddha 600 years before the Kushan Kings. One cannot find any answer to this aberration as mentioned in the verse.

- Rajatarangini closing in the middle of the reign of the King (Jai Simha; 1128 AD- 1155 AD) may surprise many scholars. Was it that Kalhan knew that he could not cope up, physically, with the task or is it that he had sensed his death in near future. The synopsis at the end of Taranga 8 is indicative of his desire to finish the assignment, when Jai Simha was still the king. It is improbable that he died at that stage, as he would not have completed the synopsis of the book at the end. No one can really tell but there is enough indication that much as he would have loved to include complete reign of Jai Simha, he possibly could not do so because of circumstances beyond his control.
- Yasomati is named as the widow of slain King Damodara and on his death pregnant Yasomati is coronated as the regent till her child is born and fit to rule Kas'mira (Gonanda II). The event is around *Mahabharata* War and revolves around Krishna (Krsna). Yasomati name is not found in Nilamat Puranam nor any other scripture or chronicle. The name has got similarity with the foster mother of Krishna (Krsna); Yasovati (Yasomati. Did this make Kalhan to select name of Yasovati (Yasomati) as the name of mother to be and queen for his Rajatarangini?

Last but not the least it is easier for me to sit in judgment of classic chronicle composed nearly nine centuries earlier by Kalhan, who is revered as an icon by Aryan Saraswat Brahmins of Kas'mira. I have, however, felt convinced that there are era aberrations in Kalhan's Rajatarangini, as I see and analysed them.

Index

T